The Top 40 Angels of the Millenium

Michael   All-around favorite, the chief angel of God, angel prince of Israel, Catholic Saint, and the dragon slayer in the Book of Revelation.

Raphael   Favorite angel of healing and science, with a reputation for friendliness garnered from the Book of Tobit and Paradise Lost.

Gabriel   Favorite angel of strength, he will sound the trumpet call to Judgment on the last day.

Djibril   Favorite Islamic angel who revealed the Holy Koran to the prophet Mohammed.

Harut and Marut (count as two)   Favorite fallen angels of Islam who succumb to the temptation to sin while visiting Earth.

Raziel   Favorite angel of magic, said to have given a book of spells to the first man, Adam.

Abraxas   Favorite angel of Cabala whose name forms the basis of the magic word, "abracadabra."

Metatron   Favorite angel of Jewish mysticism, transfigured from the Biblical patriarch, Enoch.

Sandalfon   Favorite angel of Jewish prayer and known as "the tall angel," he makes garlands for God out of prayers. He was transfigured from the prophet, Elijah.

Lucifer   Favorite fallen angel, known in hell as Satan.

Semyaza, or Semihaza   Favorite fallen "Watcher" who mated with mortal women.

Sanvi, Sansanvi, and Semangalaf (count as three)   Favorite angels of Jewish legend who provide magic protection against evil.

Sophia   Favorite Gnostic angel, the aeon of wisdom.

Victoricus   Favorite Irish angel, the guardian angel of St. Patrick.

Shepherd of Hermas   Favorite early Christian angel of hope of for repentant sinners.

The Sistine Madonna Cherubs (count as two)   Favorite painted angels by the Renaissance master Raphael.

Urizen   Favorite neo-Gnostic angel, one of "the four Zoas" of the visionary poet, William Blake.

Vohu Manah, "Good Mind"   Favorite of the Zorastrian Amesha Spentas, he imparts enlightenment to humanity.

Moroni   Favorite Mormon angel who revealed the Book of Mormon to Latter Day prophet Joseph Smith.

alpha
books

Angel of the Odd Favorite angel in charge of freak accidents from the short story by Edgar Allan Poe.

Captain Stormfield Favorite angel of home-spun good sense from Mark Twain's novel, *Captain Stormfield's Visit to Heaven*.

Aetherius Favorite theosophical angel, a cosmic master from the planet Venus.

Changó Favorite orisha of "the Religion," Santería, known for his fiery, passionate personality.

Clarence Oddbody Favorite classic movie angel from Frank Capra's *It's a Wonderful Life*, played by Henry Travers.

Jordan (Mr.) Favorite angel bureaucrat from the film *Here Comes Mr. Jordan* (1941), played by Claude Rains.

Dudley Favorite charming angel from the movie *The Bishop's Wife*, played by Cary Grant.

Smith, Jonathan Favorite angel of TV melodrama *Highway to Heaven*, played by Michael Landon.

Tess, Monica, and Andrew (count as three) Favorite angels of prime time righteousness from TV's *Touched by an Angel*, played by Della Reese, Roma Downey, and John Dye, respectively.

Enniss Favorite guardian angel of the nineties, from the angel books of Eileen Elias Freeman.

Abigrail Favorite New Age angel from the self-help book, *Ask Your Angels*, cowritten by Alma Daniel, Timothy Wyllie, and Andrew Ramer.

Tal Favorite pulp-fiction angel from Frank Peretti's novel, *This Present Darkness*.

Stedfast Favorite abortion-clinic angel from Roger Elwood's novel, *Stedfast: Guardian Angel*.

Seth Favorite new movie angel from *City of Angels*, played by Nicolas Cage.

Avengelyne Favorite comic book warrior angel who is doing time on Earth.

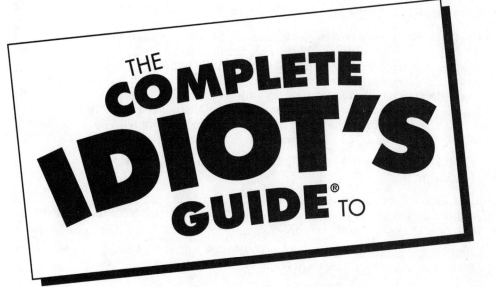

THE

COMPLETE IDIOT'S GUIDE® TO

Angels

by Jay Stevenson, Ph.D., M.A.

alpha books

A Division of Macmillan General Reference
A Simon & Schuster Macmillan Company
1633 Broadway, New York, NY 10019-6785

Macmillan Publishing books may be purchased for business or sales promotional use. For information please write: Special Markets Department, Macmillan Publishing USA, 1633 Broadway, New York, NY 10019.

International Standard Book Number: 0-02-862941-8
Library of Congress Catalog Card Number: 98-89591

01 00   8 7 6 5 4 3

Interpretation of the printing code: the rightmost number of the first series of numbers is the year of the book's printing; the rightmost number of the second series of numbers is the number of the book's printing. For example, a printing code of 99-1 shows that the first printing occurred in 1999.

Printed in the United States of America

Alpha Development Team

Publisher
Kathy Nebenhaus

Editorial Director
Gary M. Krebs

Managing Editor
Bob Shuman

Marketing Brand Manager
Felice Primeau

Editor
Jessica Faust

Development Editors
Phil Kitchel
Amy Zavatto

Production Team

Development Editor
Alana J. Morgan

Production Editor
Christina Van Camp

Copy Editor
Lynn Northrup

Cover Designer
Mike Freeland

Photo Editor
Richard H. Fox

Illustrator
Brian Mac Moyer

Designer
Scott Cook and Amy Adams of DesignLab

Indexers
Greg Pearson
Nadia Ibrahim
Lisa Stumpf

Layout/Proofreading
Angela Calvert
Julie Trippetti

Contents at a Glance

Contents

6 By the Book   71

Part 2: Jewish Angels   83

7 Old-Time Religion   85

Foreword

The good news is that angels are back. People aren't embarrassed to talk about them today. You're not considered crazy if you believe in them. Movies feature them, books describe them, and the media discusses them seriously without a trace of sarcasm or cynicism. To quote John Milton, "Millions of spiritual creatures walk the earth unseen, both when we sleep and when we wake"—and if you say you believe in angels, you're more likely to get a nod of agreement than a stare of disbelief.

The bad news is that there is so little available information about a subject that has so much history to it. For thousands of years, angels were as much a topic of conversation and theme of literature, the arts, and culture as of love or faith in God Himself. With the age of reason and science, there came a halt to a discussion of things that "can't be proven"—what couldn't be seen was dismissed as superstition. An almost universal belief was discarded in the dustbin of outdated ideas. The poor angels suddenly became politically incorrect. The early–20th century pronounced them inconceivable—impossible figments of the imagination with no claim to credibility or real existence.

Thankfully, the pendulum has swung back again—indeed, with a vengeance. Mysticism is no longer off-limits to the contemporary mind. There is new-found respect for ideas that bear the imprimatur of ages past, even as there is recognition of realities that transcend what can be perceived by the limited five senses. Maybe, just maybe, goes the more modern approach, what was accepted by the Bible and theologians, by the poets and artists, by the philosophers and the common man for centuries has a claim to validity even in our days.

So if there really are angels, what do they look like? What do they do for a living—or for a dying, for that matter? Are they forces for good who help us in difficult times without our even knowing that they are there? Or are some of them really responsible for those days when everything seems to go wrong, when we fall out of our bed in the morning and don't stop having "accidents" until we trip over our shoes when we want to go back to bed at night? And does Satan exist—so that when I feel "The devil made me do it" I'm really telling the truth?

We have to be grateful to Dr. Jay Stevenson, the author of this incredibly enlightening, entertaining, and inspirational book, *The Complete Idiot's Guide to Angels*, for providing us with an overview of a complex subject in such a readable and clear style. Whether you are a believer before you read this book or not, you'll definitely come away with far more profound awareness of what's involved and what's been taught, thought, and (perhaps) experienced throughout the ages. If, as the poet James Russell Lowell so beautifully put it, "All God's angels come to us disguised," you may even conclude—as I did—that this book isn't just good, it's a real angel.

Rabbi Benjamin Blech

Benjamin Blech is a nationally recognized rabbi, scholar, author, and lecturer. He serves as Professor of Talmud at Yeshiva University and has lectured around the world on topics dealing with religion and theology. He is the author of several major works on Judaism including The Complete Idiot's Guide to Jewish History and Culture.

Introduction

Whether or not you believe in angels, you gotta love 'em. Angels are everything people would like to be—transcendently beautiful, powerful, wise, kind, and, of course, equipped for flight! They operate beyond the earthly limitations faced by us mortals, and give us hints about what life might be like on the other side. Best of all, they show up on Earth with heavenly help just when we really need a hand, or a wing, or whatever.

These days, with a new millennium on the way, with fresh concerns about the fate of humanity, and fresh hope about the possibilities for a peaceful, harmonious planet, interest in angels is skyrocketing. Angel fans are all over, and they're flying their heavenly colors with unprecedented enthusiasm. Yet, despite all the excitement, most people know very little about our celestial feathered friends.

Of course, there are good reasons angels so often leave us in the dark. For one thing, they're mysterious by nature and tend not to like being examined and analyzed too closely—not that that keeps people from trying to figure them out! But the fact is, for good or bad, it's been impossible to pin them down and pick them apart. As a result, we don't know what makes them tick. After all, angels are just visitors to our little corner of reality, and any earthly tools we might use to probe them seem to dissolve just before we reach into their hearts.

But there's a better way to learn about angels than trying to pierce the veil of reality as we know it. If we set down our metaphysical forceps for a while, it's easy to see that the angel frontier stretches not only to heaven, but back into religious history and out into human cultures. By exploring these earthly frontiers, we can learn more about angels than they can tell us themselves. And it becomes clear they aren't just the flaky, fluffy, flying fad their detractors make them out to be.

The Complete Idiot's Guide to Angels is set up to help you see what there is to know about angels from an earthbound perspective. Whether you use it as a jumping-off point to higher realms is up to you.

This book is divided into six parts:

Part 1, "Angel Overview," provides background for getting a grasp on angels in general. This section talks about how angels appear, what they do, how people understand them, and how the idea of angels got started in the first place.

Part 2, "Jewish Angels," tells you about the oldest, richest, and most widely respected source of angel lore. This is the Hebrew Bible (otherwise known as the Old Testament) and related writings, the Apocrypha and Pseudepigrapha.

Part 3, "Christian Angels," acquaints you with angels in early Christianity. This section includes angels in the gospels, the Book of Revelation, the legends of Christian saints, and the radical set of beliefs known as gnosticism.

Part 4, "More Faiths, More Angels," shows what happens when angels fan out all over Europe and the Middle East during medieval times and into the Renaissance. They become part of the new religion of Islam, part of magical practices, part of philosophy, and favorite subjects of art and literature.

Part 5, "Angels in Mind (Angelology)," discusses the vital roles angels have played in some unusual but surprisingly successful religious sects. Starting with the visions of Swedenborg and Blake, the section goes on to discuss Mormonism, Theosophy, and "the Religion," otherwise known as Santería.

Part 6, "Angels in the Arts," talks about the strange places angels have come to occupy in today's world. The section treats the angels of New Age, eyewitness angel encounters, and angels in popular culture, including books and movies.

In addition, to help you get more out of skimming and flipping through this book, look for these boxes that encapsulate the wisdom of the angels:

Revelation

These boxes contain brief lessons and interesting facts that provide extra background or amusing trivia pertaining to everything angelic. After all, the first item in an angel's job description is to tell you what you didn't know already!

The Devil Makes You Do It

In these boxes you'll find warnings—what *not* to do if you know what's good for you! It also provides attitude adjustments for keeping on the same page with the angels.

Wing Tip

These boxes give you hints for how to keep your feet on the ground and your eyes on the sky as you deal with angels in your thoughts and actions.

Winged Words

Look in these boxes for brief definitions of terms and concepts that shed light on the heavenly hosts and their world.

Angel Artistry

Many of the illustrations used in this book are by the famous illustrators William Blake (1757–1827) and Gustave Dore (1832–1883). Blake was not only an artist, but an important English poet who frequently wrote about angelic beings and printed and illustrated his own works. He was generally considered a little eccentric in his own day, but has since come to be regarded as a brilliant artist and poet.

Dore enjoyed considerable popularity during his lifetime in his native France. He began as a cartoon journalist and worked his way up to doing illustrations for expensive editions of much of the world's greatest literature—including a good deal of literature about angels. You'll notice that Blake and Dore have very different styles.

A few of William Blake's angelic beings.

A gathering of some of Dore's angels.

Trademarks

All terms mentioned in this book that are known to be or are suspected of being trademarks or service marks have been appropriately capitalized. Alpha Books and Macmillan General Reference cannot attest to the accuracy of this information. Use of a term in this book should not be regarded as affecting the validity of any trademark or service mark.

Part 1
Angel Overview

It isn't easy taking a bird's-eye view of angels; they fly too high and shine too brightly. Even so, we can develop a composite portrait by comparing angel descriptions that have come down through the years. And whether they come down through the years or through the clouds, angels are always worth looking at.

The picture that emerges is glorious, scary, touching, even sexy, based on reports from virtually all over, from sacred scripture to the tabloids. Not that they're exactly posing for their picture, but the fleeting glimpses we have show them doing just about everything else. They don't just fly and sing; they also eat, sleep, talk, cry, shout, fight, fall down; almost all the things people do, only much better—or much worse.

There are so many elements to think about, from the physical image to the celestial hierarchy. Angels have been, and still are, a part of all faiths and cultures. In the following chapters, you'll learn the bare facts on angels, from the tips of their wings to their toes, from where they live to how to spot them in a crowd.

Vital Statistics

Despite proliferating reports of angel sightings in recent years, angels can be hard to spot and identify. Of course, there are certain tell-tale indicators. If you see what looks like a naked four-year-old blowing on a trumpet while flying in the sky with the wings of a bird and golden light streaming from its head, you're probably looking at an angel.

Sources disagree, however, as to whether this is what angels actually look like. In fact, sources disagree as to whether angels can be seen at all. And let's be honest, sources disagree as to whether angels actually exist. But the fact is, if everyone were in agreement all the time, we wouldn't have much use for angels anyway.

People have been reporting encounters with angels for over three thousand years now. Descriptions of what they've seen have changed considerably through the years. Appearances range from sweet to scary, from dazzling to invisible, and from fantastically outlandish to everyday and ordinary-looking. Thus, despite the growing number of sightings, angels remain mysterious creatures.

Glory Be!

Different people, of course, have different ideas about angels. People disagree about the nature of their existence, the purposes they serve, and the ways they behave. Most agree, however, that they are divine beings—entities with supernatural powers whose existence can't be explained in scientific terms. Also, angels tend to be benevolent (at any rate, they are supposed to be). An angel who isn't morally good is usually stigmatized as a fallen angel. Angels, then, are always good or bad. There's no such thing as a neutral angel.

The widely accepted notion that an angel can fall from heavenly grace shows that they aren't perfect, even if they manage to remain morally good. What's more, they aren't all-powerful. This means they aren't gods in their own right; their power derives from God Almighty. In fact, according to the most common view, angels work for God. An important aspect of this work is mediating between God and human beings. This is one reason people are excited about angel appearances: They show that God cares about us and has something he wants us to do or something we should know about.

When angels talk, people listen. That's been the case since Biblical times, as shown by Dore's illustration for the Book of Joshua.

Scoping the Angels

Angel spotting is a tricky proposition. Scientists who study bird migration often catch birds and tag them in order to keep track of them, but angel watchers haven't yet figured out a way to keep tabs on angels. The famous and important angels have names—there are enough of them to fill a small phone book. Unfortunately, though, the numbers aren't listed. These named angels are a drop in the bucket compared to the legions of unnamed celestial beings thought by many to flit back and forth between heaven and Earth. They seem to come and go according to no set rules or patterns.

Revelations

Since the late Middle Ages, many religious people have believed that angel appearances and other miracles happened only during ancient times in order to establish religion. According to this view, angels exist, but they have already served their purpose on Earth and no longer influence human lives. This widespread view, reinforced by the development of scientific thinking, hasn't stopped people from attesting to continued angel appearances. Thus, even among those who believe in angels, opinion remains divided over whether angels are a force in the world today.

There are two main aspects of angel identification, and each poses its own particular challenges. On the one hand, an angel encounter is often a personal thing and happens, if it happens at all, to different people in different ways. On the other hand, there are traditions that go way back in history that tell us about angels and their appearances. Accounts and images of these appearances have been handed down, modified, and added on from generation to generation. An angel appearance, then, can be understood as a one-of-a-kind event of indescribable significance and as an expression of a cultural tradition. Of course, personal angel encounters and traditional views of angels have influenced one another down through the years. In fact, each new account of an angel becomes part of an ongoing tradition of what angels are like. This tradition in turn influences future accounts of encounters with angels.

Friends in High Places

Not all reports of personal encounters involve actually seeing angels. People have claimed to sense angels as invisible presences, or to see, hear, or feel them at work in natural things such as wind, rain, fire, sun, clouds, and stars. Others have sensed angels at work inside them. Angels have appeared to some in dreams and visions.

Sometimes angels appear to some, but not to others who are in the same place. According to the Book of Numbers (a story from the Bible, chapter 22 verse 5 through chapter 24 verse 25), for example, an angel appeared to block the path of a magician named Balaam. Balaam was unable to see the angel for several minutes. His donkey, however, saw it right away, and stopped in his tracks. As you might imagine, Balaam had no clue about why the donkey wasn't moving. He beat the animal, trying to get it started again, before eventually seeing the angel too.

A personal encounter in which an angel actually appears is known as an *angelophany*. A person to whom an angel appears is an *angelophant*. Angelophanies are recorded in the Jewish and Christian scriptures, in the Koran, and in other religious texts written in ancient times and the Middle Ages. Since the rise of science during the late Renaissance, accounts of angelophanies have dropped off considerably.

In recent years, however, there has been a huge resurgence of angel sightings and angel experiences. Polls conducted in 1993 show that nearly a third of all Americans have at least sensed the presence of angels at some point in their lives. Clearly, something is going on. Perhaps people's sensitivity to angels is heightened as a result of the coming of a new millennium.

Winged Words

An **angelophany** is the appearance of an angel. The term derives from the Greek words *angelos,* meaning messenger, and *phainein,* meaning to show or to be manifest. Someone to whom an angel appears is an **angelophant.**

What's in Store?

Millennial expectations stem not simply from the fact that the year 2000 is nearly upon us. Many sense that we are going through a period of drastic social transformation which they believe will bring about important spiritual changes. Rising interest in angels results in part from a general feeling that something's got to give and, when it does, people want to be guided out of the wreckage of the old ways.

These social transformations include fundamental changes in sexual relationships, family relationships, business relationships, and intercultural relationships that can make it seem like we're faced with a completely different world from that of our parents and grandparents. These changes can seem both good and bad for various reasons, depending on your political views. Whatever the case, however, angels can help people feel they're headed in the right direction.

Wing Tip

Many expect cataclysmic changes to take place early in the coming millennium (thousand-year period). Don't go overboard with your preparations, though; similar expectations failed to materialize with the turn of the previous millennium.

Angel Attitudes

Most people these days who claim to have seen angels report that, however they appear, angels make them feel happy, strengthened, and loved. I met a woman recently who says that she met an angel who gave her a hug. Those people whose guardians angels show up to chew them out for their bad behavior generally aren't telling the world about it. Movies, however, are full of images of avenging angels, as well as supportive ones.

Similarly, angel encounters in sacred scripture are sometimes intimate and supportive and, on other occasions, terrifying and threatening. Scary angels are often dazzling and otherworldly, with awesome power. They have a way of making the people to whom they appeared feel insignificant. Often, these intimidating angels are on a special mission from God and they want to convey the importance of their message—hence their intensity. Messing with them is risky business.

This intensity is one of the reasons why angels have had special visual characteristics. Such attributes as wings, robes, or armor made out of flame and dazzling light indicate the power the angel possesses and elicit awe and obedience from those who see them. These features make ancient angels so scary that they would often have to reassure people before they could attend to business. Typically, the first words out of an angel's mouth would be "Fear not," or "Be not afraid."

Angels of recent times seem less inclined to throw their weight around—except in the movies. Perhaps this is because the contest between good and evil seems less like a mysterious cosmic battle than it once did, and more like an immediate personal and interpersonal challenge. As a result, most angels seem to have mellowed out. They've evidently become more concerned with helping people cope with their problems than with terrifying them into doing God's bidding.

Of course, not all ancient angel encounters were terrifying, and not all recent encounters have been warm and cozy, as you'll see in the upcoming chapters. In fact, many angel incidents reported in

The Devil Makes You Do It

Don't assume angels have nothing but love and goodness for all mankind. Angels sometimes use deadly force in accomplishing their purposes. To take an extreme case from the Bible, an angel wiped out 185,000 Assyrian soldiers who were preparing to make war against Jerusalem! This angel has been given many names throughout the ages, but most commonly we refer to him as the "Angel of Death"

Wing Tip

The apostle Paul's Epistle to the Hebrews in the New Testament offers some good advice: "Be not forgetful to entertain strangers, for thereby some have entertained angels unawares (13:2)." In other words, it's always a good idea to treat strangers with consideration and respect; especially if you consider that someone you're just meeting for the first time might turn out to be an angel.

ancient scripture and legend as well as in recent newsletters and popular paperbacks involve angels who look like ordinary human beings. In many cases, the angel-seers involved didn't even realize they were in the presence of angels until after the encounter had taken place. Only in retrospect—and for subtle, intangible reasons—have many angels been recognized as such.

High Fashion

Looking back, artists and storytellers have attributed special characteristics to angels that were originally described as ordinary-looking people. During the Middle Ages, it became common practice to paint these angels with wings and halos to set them apart from everybody else. These features made the angels easier to identify for those looking at the pictures.

Wings, halos, and shining robes don't necessarily represent the way the angels looked when they appeared to human beings, although this may sometimes be the intention of the artist. Instead, or additionally, they tell us something about the inward nature of the angels. They symbolize aspects of the angelic spirit.

Here are some of the most common traditional angel traits:

➤ *Wings.* They suggest a celestial nature and the ability to span large distances—particularly the distance between heaven and Earth. They can also serve a protective function. From taking someone under their wings to using their wings to beat off prospective evils, angels are equipped for any situation with these handy appendages.

➤ *Halo.* Also called a nimbus, it denotes glory, holiness, and wisdom. The circular shape also represents perfection and completeness. Saints are often represented with halos as well as angels.

➤ *Shining raiment.* White and diaphanous robes represent purity and spirituality. Luminescent or flaming robes represent wisdom and glory.

➤ *Armor.* Angels are often figured as soldiers in the battle between Good and Evil. Armor represents power and strength.

➤ *Musical instruments.* Music represents spiritual beauty, cosmic harmony, and the chief angelic activity of praising God.

➤ *The form of a baby or child.* A relatively late addition to the tradition of angel identification, this represents innocence and joy.

➤ *The human face.* The face is an easily overlooked but especially powerful symbol of angelic feeling. This can show love, compassion, anger, determination, hope, humility, reverence, and joy.

➤ *Stars.* Stars as angels represent cosmic order and multitude.

➤ *Sandals.* These denote antiquity, evoking the days before sneakers were invented!

An angel by William Blake epitomizes joy and innocence.

Revelations

Among the earliest angels were ancient Assyrian cherubim that had the bodies of lions or other animals, wings of a bird, and human heads. These angels were depicted in stone statues that stood at the thresholds of ancient temples to ward off evil. Since then, cherubim have often served the purpose of guarding doors and entryways. Cherubs first appear in the Bible at the entryway into the Garden of Eden after Adam and Eve have been banished from Paradise. It's their job to prevent the fallen couple from getting back in.

These conventional characteristics do not hold for all angels. The way an angel appears and the significance of the appearance depends on who describes it. Traditionally, angels have been represented by various kinds of people: prophets, philosophers, poets and storytellers, as well as priests, rabbis, or ministers. Although these roles are sometimes combined in particular people, they represent different ways of "seeing" angels.

Angels of Change

Prophetic accounts of angels tend to be startling. The prophet takes on the tough job of transforming society, often at the behest of an angel whose bizarre appearance calls for a dramatically new way of looking at things. With the help of an angelic vision, the prophet gets a glimpse of the future that provides clues for how people should behave in the present.

A powerful example of this kind of prophetic vision is the wheeled throne that appeared to the Hebrew prophet, Ezekiel. This was God's throne, and it was supported by wheels made of fire that had eyes in them and by cherubim with four wings and four heads—each head that of a different animal. Ezekiel's vision heralded a new way of life for the Jews who were faced with exile from Judah, their capital city, and forced to move to Babylon.

Other Hebrew prophets have also communicated striking angelic visions that have altered the course of the Jewish religion. The same can be said of Christian prophets, most notably John, author of Revelation, whose angelic vision in the Book of Revelation foretells the end of the world as we know it. Muhammad, the prophet and founder of Islam, also reported angelic visions that gave guidance to the faithful.

Since the founding of the big three religions of the West—Judaism, Christianity, and Islam—angelic prophecies have occurred infrequently and with diminished historical influence. An exceptional "latter-day" prophet is Joseph Smith, the American founder of Mormonism, whose angelic visions helped lay down a new set of religious guidelines. Still more recently, angel prophecy has merged with interest in extraterrestrial phenomena, including UFOs. Friends or foes, creatures from beyond portend big changes in the way we do things on Earth.

Prophets tend to see angels as astonishing and even terrifying creatures. Angels of prophecy may tell of death and destruction resulting from God's wrath. Angels may also foretell of hope and renewal, however, and these angels may be beautiful as well as fearsome.

The Devil Makes You Do It

Visionary prophecy tends to be a radical enterprise. You probably shouldn't try it yourself unless you're prepared to stir up trouble. Many prophets, including Mormonism's Joseph Smith, had to give up their lives for their visions.

The Wings of Poetry

Whereas the angels that appear in prophecy serve the purpose of transforming society, the angels that appear in poetry and legend help memorialize important events, account for suffering, and promote communal values. Stories of angels that help and protect the suffering provide moral lessons in the ideals that are worth suffering for. Such stories appear in ancient scripture and in legends of the Middle Ages. Many of these stories are figured in medieval paintings as well.

Legends of fallen angels and angelic battles in heaven mirror and explain the challenge of sorting out good and evil on Earth. This great Biblical theme has been taken up by the Italian poet Dante in the 14th century, and the English poets Milton in the 17th century and Blake in the late 18th and early 19th centuries. In telling us about the adventures of angels, these poets give us a broader, cosmic perspective on our earthly lives.

Artists and storytellers, together with painters and sculptors, have most strongly influenced conventional ideas of the appearances of angels. In turn, many artistic representations of angels have been influenced by prophetic accounts. Prophetic angelophanies have been popular subject matter for paintings and stories.

Winged Words

The **chain of being** is the medieval idea that everything in the universe is connected to everything else in a specified, hierarchical order. God is at the top of the chain, angels come next, then humans, then animals, plants, and then inanimate objects.

Lofty Speculations

Angels are also an important subject of philosophical speculation. In the eyes of the medieval philosophers, angels are an important link in the *chain of being* that connects all things in the universe. For these philosophers, it was impossible to understand the cosmos and the place of humanity within it without understanding the nature of angels.

Angel philosophers tend to be less concerned with how angels look than with how they act and what makes them tick. Even so, the notion that celestial beings can appear and speak to humans raises important philosophical questions. Some philosophers have suggested that angels are "shapeshifters," capable of adopting whatever appearance suits them at the time, depending on their mission and the needs of the person to whom they appear.

According to this view, an angel can appear as either male or female. Angels are usually represented as male in the Bible. In medieval and

Wing Tip

The heyday of angelology was the medieval period. A notable 18th-century angel philosopher is Emmanuel Swedenborg. For a 20th-century philosophical account of the nature of angels, see *The Angels and Us* by Mortimer Adler (Macmillan, 1982).

Renaissance paintings, however, they are usually female. The poet John Milton explains it this way:

> *Spirits when they please*
> *Can either sex assume, or both; so soft*
> *And uncompounded is their essence pure,*
> *Not tied or manacled with joint or limb,*
> *Not founded on the brittle strength of bones,*
> *Like cumbrous flesh, but in what shape they choose*
> *Dilated or condensed, bright or obscure,*
> *Can execute their aery purposes.*
>
> *Paradise Lost,* I (423–430)

Some think that angels are completely spiritual, but that they can assume a physical form in order to make themselves known to people who would otherwise lack the spiritual insight to see them. Still another view holds that angels don't actually appear to anyone, but appeal directly to our minds and feelings, prompting us to develop metaphorical descriptions and images to represent our experiences.

Philosophizing about angels has gone in and out of fashion at various times. The theosophy movement of the 19th century drew heavily on angels in accounting for the nature of reality. Speculation and theorizing about angels has become extremely popular in recent years, thanks to New Age spirituality.

Philosophers of the Middle Ages saw angels as a necessary aspect of the cosmos, as in Dante's Paradise Lost, *illustrated by Gustave Dore.*

Flying Leaps of Faith

Drawing on all three of these ways of seeing angels—prophetic, poetic, and philosophical—are priests, rabbis, and other spiritual advisors. These ministers are interested in angels largely from the standpoint of personal and communal spiritual growth and healing. Because an appreciation of angels can help people live their lives and fit into their communities, many spiritual advisors promote angel awareness.

Traditionally, the role of spiritual advisor has been filled by people authorized by established religion to instruct believers in the faith. More recently, all sorts of people, including teachers, psychologists, and gurus, are setting themselves up as authorities on spiritual matters, including angels. Religious and secular authorities vary on their attitudes toward angels. In fact, the religious significance of angels has been a hotly debated topic over the centuries.

Too Much of a Good Thing?

Angels have been a part of religious worship from the early days of *monotheism*, the belief in a single, all-powerful god. In monotheistic religions, angels function as intermediaries between God and humanity. Debates concern whether people should worship and pray to angels rather than God, Christ, saints, or prophets. A number of Christian authorities have expressed concern over the growing interest in angels among those who fall outside of mainstream Christianity. They worry that people will rely on angels as substitutes for God and Christ, and will be led astray by harmful cultic and spiritual beliefs and practices.

There have been moments in religious history when angels have been so popular that they have threatened to drown out the importance of other spiritual powers—in effect turning monotheism into *polytheism*, the belief in numerous gods. At such moments, religious authorities have taken steps to limit the role of angels in organized worship. In the year 343, for example, Christian Church authorities declared that the worship of angels was a form of idolatry known as *angelolatry*. Despite this declaration, angels have remained an accepted part of Christian belief. According to the Church, angels exist but should not be worshipped.

Many ministers have advocated the belief in—if not the worship of—angels as a form of spiritual guidance and support. The most famous to do so in recent years is evangelist Billy Graham. Graham believes angels do God's work by helping people on Earth.

Winged Words

Monotheism is the belief in a single, all-powerful god. The three big monotheistic religions are Judaism, Christianity, and Islam. All three of these religions stem from the ancient dualistic religion known as Zoroastrianism. Zoroastrians, like Jews, Christians, and Muslims, recognize angels as part of their spiritual cosmology. **Polytheism** is the belief in more than one god. **Angelolatry** is the worship of angels, declared idolatrous by the Christian Church in the year 343.

As this print by Blake shows, not everybody approves of angelic activity all the time.

Free Spirits

From time to time, people from outside established religious institutions have assumed the role of spiritual advisor. Such freelance priests have sometimes been persecuted and sometimes been accepted, or at least tolerated, by established religious authorities. In recent years, independent and loosely organized spiritual advisors have gained wide acceptance, thanks in part to the success of the New Age movement.

Many New Agers and other independent spiritual advisors recognize angels as important spiritual forces. Some believe that angels appear to people in times of need to provide help, but cannot be summoned. Others believe that techniques for increasing spiritual sensitivity can help people perceive and benefit from the power of angels. This belief has led to such practices as angel therapy and the consulting of angel oracles.

The New Age is not an organized movement, but consists of many different groups and individuals who hold various beliefs. Many of them reject labels such as

The Devil Makes You Do It

It's not always a good idea to tell others about your spiritual experiences. Many people become uncomfortable or suspicious when they hear about supernatural events in the lives of others.

"New Age," especially since the movement has been criticized on account of some of its more unusual beliefs and practices. Whether or not we call them New Agers, there are growing numbers of angel fans and angel watchers without strong religious affiliations who look to angels in order to derive spiritual benefits.

Angels seem to be appearing thick and fast to more and more people. Perhaps these appearances herald the coming millennium. Perhaps the time is finally coming of which it is written, *"your sons and daughters shall prophesy, your old men shall dream dreams, your young men shall see visions"* (Joel, 2:28). Then again, maybe wings are in this year because they look good with just about anything!

The Least You Need to Know

➤ Angel watchers claim angels make personal appearances, work through natural things, and appear in dreams and visions.

➤ Over 30 percent of Americans surveyed since 1993 have reported some kind of experience of angels.

➤ Angels have gradually developed traditional characteristics such as wings and halos over the centuries.

➤ Angels are recognized in different ways by prophets, poets, philosophers, and priests.

➤ Angel enthusiasm is on the rise, perhaps as a result of the coming millennium.

Job Descriptions

Many angels have long and impressive resumes. They've been on the job a long time and they've had to deal with just about every sort of problem imaginable. They keep the forces of evil at bay, make personal appearances to prophets and martyrs, protect the throne of God, guide souls of the dead to their final destination, and give directions and comfort to folks in trouble. Some say they even keep the natural world in gear, keeping the celestial warehouses supplied with thunder and hail, and making the sun shine, the wind blow, and the grass grow.

And, of course, there's the constant worshipping of God. Try chanting "Holy, holy, holy" for a while and see how long you can keep it up. The angels never stop. They work around the clock, running the whole show, and they never complain. It's a tough job, but someone's got to do it.

The Daily Grind—Angelicly Speaking

Other angels seem to have it pretty easy. They float around in the clouds singing and playing on harps all day, or they just kick back and contemplate the glories of creation. They ride the merry-go-round of the planets, or practice flight patterns through empyrean air space. They have no worries whatsoever, because they live in a state of perpetual bliss. Whenever it rains and they don't feel like getting their wings wet, they simply elevate above the clouds into eternal sunshine.

This might seem unfair to those of us here on Earth, but what do we know? Maybe the angels are trying out new management strategies that are replacing the traditional hierarchical divisions of labor. Maybe they are taking a cue from Marxist Catholics and are starting to practice liberation theology. Or maybe some angels just like working and some don't, so it's not a problem. In any case the lives of angels are characterized on the one hand by tireless, selfless service on behalf of others, and on the other hand, by eternal peace and happiness.

It's a tough job, but someone's gotta do it! This print by William Blake captures a rarely seen element of drudgery in angelic existence.

Angels Incorporated

Angel stories and movies of the 20th century sometimes humorously portray the world of angels as a bureaucracy resembling corporations or institutions on Earth. The angels have jobs to do, such as watching over human beings, but they are also watched over themselves and their performance is evaluated by "higher-ups" who expect results. They have to report to their superiors and take instructions from on high, just like people who work in offices. And angels have to do a good job, because getting fired is really hell.

> ### Revelations
>
> Fictitious accounts of angelic life that portray it in terms of human bureaucracy can be found in classic films, including *Here Comes Mr. Jordan* (1941), with Claude Rains as a suave angelic manager; and *It's a Wonderful Life* (1946), with Henry Travers as a bumbling angelic apprentice attempting to "earn his wings." A detailed portrayal of demonic bureaucracy is presented in the novel, *The Screwtape Letters* by C.S. Lewis.

Pecking Order

Actually, the notion that life for the angels in heaven is a version of organized society on Earth is an old one, going back at least as far the 1st century. The Bible identifies a number of groups of angels, such as cherubim and seraphim, but does not say how these groups are organized or state clearly what their separate functions are. Only later did the idea get started that angels worship God in heaven in the same way—according to similar schedules and supervised in a similar fashion—as people worship God on Earth. Inhabitants of the ancient monastery at Qumran, for example (where the Dead Sea Scrolls were discovered), evidently modeled their religions practices after rituals supposedly practiced by the angels.

Over the centuries, many schemes have been proposed for organizing groups of angels according to importance. Starting in the 6th century, these angelic pecking orders mirrored the chain of command in the Christian Church. In fact, the term *hierarchy*, used today to mean chain of command, originally meant "sacred rule," and was used to refer to the ranks of angels.

According to the hierarchies of the Middle Ages, the most important angels are those closest to God. The least important are those closest to human beings. God, of course, is at the top of the angel pyramid, corresponding to the pope at the top of the Church, followed by bishops, cardinals, etc., corresponding to the various groups of angels. Some names of angel groups, such as "Dominions," "Powers," "Authorities," and "Principalities," reflect the roles of leadership they were thought to fill. "Powers" and "Authorities" were words that were also used to describe leaders in the early Christian Church.

> ### Winged Words
>
> The term **hierarchy** originally meant "sacred rule" and was applied to the organization of angels as well as to the structure of the early Catholic Church in the west.

The angel hierarchy as it was recognized during the Middle Ages includes nine separate groups. Each group has different functions and attributes. Different traditions recognize different hierarchies, but the best-known is that set forward by the philosopher known as Pseudo-Dionysius, who organized the angels this way, from the top of the pyramid down:

➤ *Seraphim.* These are the angels closest to God. They continually sing God's praises. They are described in the Book of Isaiah as having six wings each.

➤ *Cherubim.* Representations of cherubim, or cherubs, range from bizarre winged animals, to chubby little winged children.

➤ *Thrones.* Based on the vision of Ezekiel, thrones are often said to take the form of fiery wheels covered with open eyes.

➤ *Dominions, or Dominations.* Often said to be the oldest angels, they have the job of supervising the angels below them (the ones above need no supervision).

➤ *Virtues, also known as Authorities.* These angels are the ones who work miracles on Earth and serve as guardian angels.

➤ *Powers.* If the Virtues are the "good cops" who take care of people, Powers are the "bad cops" who come down on evil. The main role is to keep demons, devils, and evil spirits at bay.

➤ *Principalities.* These angels protect cities and nations as well as the leaders of religious faiths on Earth.

➤ *Archangels.* These are messenger angels, delivering God's decrees to people on Earth.

➤ *Angels.* These are the buck privates of the heavenly army and work most closely with ordinary human beings.

The Devil Makes You Do It

Throughout the centuries, numerous conflicting views of angels have been set forth and interpreted in different ways. As a result, there is no single, definitive account of what kinds of angels there are and what they do and numerous conflicting ideas. For example, the angel Michael is sometimes said to be in charge of the Seraphim. Elsewhere he is the head Cherub. According to others, he is the leader of the Archangels.

The angelic hierarchy not only reflected the Church hierarchy, but also corresponded to the orbits or "spheres" of the stars and planets as they were understood by astronomers of the Middle Ages. Angel organization conformed to a strict medieval sense of the order of the cosmos. Back then, most people thought that the earth was at the center of a perfectly spherical universe.

According to medieval cosmology, the earth is surrounded by a series of concentric layers known as spheres through which the planets and stars orbit as the earth stands still. The final, largest, and most distant sphere is the abode of God. Philosophers believed the angels have the task of making sure the spheres revolve around the earth properly—making sure they move in accordance with their perfect geometrical design.

Keeping Things Humming

The geometrical proportions that regulate the movement of the spheres was thought to reflect the harmonies produced by harp strings of proportionate lengths. This idea gave rise to the concept of "music of the spheres." By moving in perfect geometrical proportions, it was thought that the spheres and the angels that controlled them make music, even though people on Earth cannot hear it.

The universe, then, is something like a big music box, playing continually as it turns. This music is not only the sound of the perfect motions of the cosmos; it is also the sound of angels praising God. The Bible suggests that angels have had the job of praising God with their music since the very first day when God created the earth. At this time, according to the Book of Job, "the morning stars sang together and the sons of God shouted aloud." In this passage, the morning stars and the sons of God are both generally taken to refer to angels.

Apparently, the angels have been singing without stopping ever since The Hebrew prophet, Isaiah, describes God's throne surrounded by seraphim who continually chant "Holy, holy, holy" (Isaiah, 6:3). Because of the angelic practice of praising God through song and music, the different groups in the angel hierarchy are known as *choirs*.

Winged Words

The **choirs** of angels are the nine groups of the angel hierarchy, from Seraphim to Cherubim down to Archangels and Angels.

Filling in the Middle

According to the medieval view of angels, only the lowest group, the angels themselves, have direct dealings with individual human beings. The rest have grander earthly or celestial functions. Angels at the top of the hierarchy don't concern themselves with earthly matters at all, but devote all of their attention to God. The higher-ups among the angels communicate heavenly knowledge to those below them.

Thus angels help bridge the enormous gap between the grandeur of God and the lowliness of ordinary mortals. God can seem too great, too distant, and too hard to understand for most people. Angels are smaller, more immediate, and can relate to human beings with more intimacy. There are enough of them so that they can pay attention to the little details of existence, including the minor but discouraging hardships of everyday life.

Of course, the precise nature of the mediating function of angels has been a subject of debate. Some scriptural passages mention God appearing to human beings as an angel, "the angel of the Lord." Authorities disagree as to whether this angel represents God or God's representative. Some scholars believe references to the angel of God in the Bible were inserted, not by the original authors, but by people who came later, to revise the idea that God appeared directly to human beings. To many the notion that God can simply appear to human beings seems hard to swallow, so references to God may have been replaced by "the angel of the Lord."

Special Delivery

Although angels serve numerous purposes, their main role is supplying a network of communication between God and humanity—heaven and Earth. The word "angel" is based on the Greek word *angelos*, meaning "messenger." This is the word used to translate the ancient Hebrew term *malakh*, used in the Hebrew Bible to refer to those celestial beings we have come to know as angels.

Wing Tip

If you want to get something nice in the mail, or if you want God to watch out for your mail carrier, try praying to the angel Gabriel, recognized by the Catholic Church as the patron saint of postal workers!

Big News

As heavenly messengers, angels have had a variety of messages to deliver to human beings. Sometimes the news has been bad, such as when angels have appeared to ancient prophets to report that God is fed up with humanity and about to destroy the world. Sometimes the angels bring good news, such as when they say that after the world is destroyed, everyone will be issued a brand new body and live forever. Angels are most commonly associated with the good news they bring.

Revelations

Most angel lore from ancient times was produced in a mishmash of different languages, including ancient Hebrew, Aramaic, ancient Greek, and Latin. Scriptures were written, translated, and re-translated, producing changes as well as continuities from culture to culture and text to text. Although Jesus spoke a Semitic language called Aramaic, the gospels were first written in a dialect of ancient Greek known as *koine*. Scholars haven't identified the "original" text of the gospels, but have continued working to this day to produce the most accurate version possible. This is difficult, however, because different scholars have different ideas about what the most "accurate" version would be!

In fact, the Christian word *gospel* means "good news" and refers to the message that Christ is coming. "Gospel," or "godspell," is an Old English translation of the Greek word *evangel*, which also means good news. In the religious sense, the evangel, or the gospel, is the story of Christ. According to Christians, this story was first told on Earth by the angel Gabriel, who visited the Virgin Mary and told her she would give birth to the son of God. It makes sense, then, that our words "angel" and "evangelism" both come from the same Greek word for "message."

Dore's interpretation of the Annunciation, in which the angel Gabriel appeared to the Virgin Mary to announce the coming of Christ.

Lots of Promise

To Christians, the gospel promise brought when Gabriel appeared to Mary was pretty important. Not long afterwards, another angel appeared to some shepherds on Christmas and told them Christ was born—in effect, the same gospel promise. Of course, everyone knows this already from watching Linus tell it to Charlie Brown in the yearly TV special, *A Charlie Brown Christmas*. This was only one of many such promises angels have brought people.

Angels brought similar messages to the Jewish patriarchs long before Christ was born. An angel appeared to Abraham and Sarah to tell them they would have a son named Isaac. Another appeared to Manoah and his wife to tell them their son Samson was on the way. Largely as a result of important religious messages like these, angels have become associated with the task of bringing good news, even in cases where the message doesn't become a part of religious scripture. Today, we sometimes think of angels as bringing ordinary good news to ordinary good people.

Angels are known for bringing people positive messages like "don't worry" and "cheer up." These messages can elevate your spirits, so to speak, simply by helping you feel that somehow your problems will be taken care of. In other words, the message brought by angels is not simply information, but accomplishes the purpose of helping people. In this way, the angels' primary function in religious scripture as messengers ties in with the popular folk belief in guardian angels. Angels not only give us directives from God, but they look out for and take care of us.

Of course, the idea of a guardian angel can cut both ways. They not only watch out for you and watch over you to keep you out of trouble, they watch you and report on you to God. This means, of course, that if you step out of line, God hears about it through your angel. That's what it says in the non-Biblical Apocalypse of Paul, at any rate.

The Devil Makes You Do It

Don't confuse the promptings of your guardian angel with your compulsive urge to drink, smoke, gamble, shop, or gossip about people. Helping you feel better during times of hardship is not the same as gratifying your irrational cravings!

Angel Extras

Guardian angels has become tremendously important to angel watchers of today. What has interested people most about angels in recent years is the idea that they appear to people who need them. In fact, this idea alone often seems to work as a source of comfort. It seems the mere thought of angels is often enough to make people feel happy and encouraged. This may explain why accounts of angels that have appeared to help people by providing comfort, wisdom, or assistance have become hugely popular.

Revelations

Biblical prophets not only receive prophecies from angels, but angels sometimes tell them how to behave during their prophetic visions and even tell them what the visions mean. Throughout the Book of Revelation, for example, the prophet John is coached by an angel who makes sure he sees the vision and understands it correctly. What's more, he rebukes John for trying to worship him.

Angels provide a subtle clue that Dante's Beatrice is important in Dore's illustration for the Divine Comedy.

It also explains one of the most common roles angels have played throughout their history: that of celestial window dressing and heavenly emphasis. Angels are part of the stock in trade of religious storytellers and painters. Whenever something miraculous or significant happens, they'll throw in an angel or two—or two thousand—to jazz things up a little.

Picture this scenario: A bunch of shepherds are sitting around at night watching their sheep, and one of them says, "I heard this virgin's gonna give birth to a guy who'll bring peace on Earth and goodwill to humanity." And the others say "That's nice. I'll take peace and goodwill over strife and hatred any time."

It's just not that special, is it? The show needs a little more excitement. So storytellers bring in the angels as exclamation marks. An angel makes a great emcee; more angels look great cheering in the audience; angelic stagehands make sure all the stars are in place; and, for those prophets who are always forgetting their lines, angels make great prompters.

Angels in Mind

Many people believe that the importance of angels is chiefly psychological. This doesn't mean that angels are simply figments of the imagination. Clearly, angels have a deep and long-standing cultural significance. Because angels have been important for so long to so many different people, some psychologists and others have argued that they represent aspects of the human subconscious. They say angels are ideas and representations of what cannot be known, symbolizing a *transcendent* reality—a reality that exists beyond the finite reality in which we exist.

Winged Words

Transcendence is existence above and beyond material reality. It sometimes refers as well to what is above and beyond the human capacity of understanding.

It is a short step from this idea to the metaphysical notion that the subconscious itself is linked to God and that angels play an important role in that link. Since the Middle Ages, angels have been described as "intelligences," able to understand the thoughts of God directly. Mary Baker Eddy, the founder of Christian Science, goes even further in saying that angels are the actual thoughts of God, perceived intuitively by people. Many believe that angels represent, convey, or even embody supernatural intuitions.

Seeing and Believing

The idea that angels are intuitions that come from God can obscure the fact that ideas about angels are passed along and adapted from one culture to the next. Ideas can be hard to trace, but it's clear that they tend to have traditional sources. Many ideas and stories about angels are based on older stories and ideas about gods and spirits from polytheistic religions (religions with many gods).

Changing beliefs about angels show that old religious ideas frequently get revised and incorporated into new religions. As people who believed in the Greek and Roman gods converted to Christianity, for example, they adapted many of their myths into Christian form. Often, angels provided adaptable figures who could fill the roles previously played by pagan gods. As a result, gods and other supernatural beings out of myth often were re-invented as angels. In the process, old myths acquired new meanings.

Guiding Lights

An example of this can be found in the idea of the guardian angel. Since the Middle Ages, many have believed that there is an angel who watches out for us, not only during our lives, but when we die. Traditionally, this is the angel Michael, perhaps the most important angel of the big three monotheistic religions—Judaism, Christianity, and Islam. According to legend, Michael guides the souls of the dead to heaven.

The idea that dead souls must be guided on their journey to a new life after death occurs in many ancient cultures, including Egyptian, Greek, and Roman. According to Greek myth, the souls of the dead are ferried to Hades across the river Styx by a ferryman named Charon. This and similar myths evidently formed the basis for the idea that Michael acts as a guide for souls to heaven.

Evolving Angels

Of course, angel traditions haven't simply crusted over from ancient times, but have continued to change. The ancient belief that Michael guided the souls of the dead received a new interpretation centuries later in America from African-American slaves. The idea lies behind the well-known African-American spiritual, "Michael, Row Your Boat Ashore." In this song, Michael rows a soul that has recently departed from its body across the River Jordan into the promised land.

In the Hebrew Bible, the promised land is the country promised the Jews by God. For the African-American slaves, the promised land represented both heaven, their destination after death, and escape from slavery in this life. Thus the angels in the song represent not only angels, but the guides who helped slaves escape to freedom. These were the "conductors" of the famous "underground railroad," the network through which many slaves escaped.

Wing Tip

Keep in mind that angel encounters are not always a unique experience from one person to another. Take a closer look at those stories with a wide perspective. There are some age old lessons that humanity has yet to learn!

Wing Tip

Want to give your newborn child a name with real clout? Try one of these angel names from the non-Biblical 3rd Book of Enoch: Radweriel, Sidriel, Satquiel, Barakiel, Sahakiel, Ruhiel, Zamiel, Kokabiel, Simsiel, Lailiel, or Aktariel.

Many African-American spirituals have this double meaning, referring to life in heaven and a life of freedom at the same time. Another famous example is "Swing Low, Sweet Chariot," in which a band of angels bring a chariot that will take the singer "home"—that is, to heaven or to freedom. This song is based on the story of Elijah in the Bible who, at the end of his life on Earth, doesn't die, but ascends directly into heaven on a chariot conducted by angels.

Angels continue to develop new meanings in different times and places. Actual people, children, for instance, are frequently described as "angels." People, especially volunteers, working in hospitals during times of crisis are often known as "angels of mercy." Financial backers of theatrical productions and other enterprises are also called angels. And, of course, Angel, Angelo, and Angela are popular names, as are angel names Michael, Gabriel, and Raphael.

Dealing with Death

Still other traditional and changing roles angels play include that of the "angel of death." According to traditions that go back to ancient times, the angel of death is responsible for taking the souls of those whose time has come to die. Sometimes this even involves killing people. Thus the angel of death is similar to the mythical figure of the Grim Reaper.

Sometimes the angel of death is portrayed as a minister who carries out divine punishment. There are many references in the Bible to angels who destroy sinful people, sometimes by the thousands. It is an angel who destroys the evil residents of Sodom and Gomorrah in the Book of Genesis, the first book of the Old Testament. The angel of death also visited the Egyptian captors of the Hebrews shortly before the exodus and destroyed all of their first-born children. In Revelation, the last book of the New Testament, an angel will wipe out a third of humanity during the final days before the last judgment.

In other stories, the angel of death is kind and caring, resembling a midwife who helps deliver the soul into its new life after death. In the Islamic tradition, for example, the angel Azrael gently coaxes the souls of believers from their bodies when their time has come. The souls of non-believers, in contrast, are wrenched violently from their bodies and thrown into hell.

Beware of Angels

Watching over people and guiding them to heaven is only one aspect of the role of guardian angels. Angels appear in scripture as guardians in a different sense, too. Instead of watching over people, they watch over sacred things and places in order to keep evil away. This is the role of the original cherubim in the Hebrew Bible. The cherubim are first mentioned in the book of Genesis when they are stationed in front of the Garden of Eden with a flaming sword to keep out Adam and Eve who have disobeyed God and fallen from grace.

The Devil Makes You Do It

Don't take angels at face value! Sometimes an angel is guarding you from something (and probably for a good reason) so tread lightly!

Later on, the Bible describes cherubim wrought in gold that are set into the ark of the covenant. The ark was perhaps Israel's most sacred symbol, said to be the throne of Yahweh, the God of the Hebrews. In it were contained the ten commandments according to which the Jews were to live as God's chosen people. Simply touching the ark or looking inside it without permission could result in painful oozing sores or even death. The golden cherubim were placed on the cover of the ark to symbolize angelic protection.

Revelations

The ark of the covenant really existed. According to the Bible, the Jews carried it with them into Canaan as they escaped from Egypt. King David later brought it to Jerusalem where King Solomon had a temple built for it around 957 B.C.E. It remained in the temple for years before disappearing. It was probably plundered by invading Babylonians led by Nebuchadnezzar by 586 B.C.E., after which its location and existence has remained unknown. The search for the ark by the fictional archeologist, Indiana Jones, is the subject of Steven Spielberg's hit adventure movie, *Raiders of the Lost Ark* (1981), starring Harrison Ford.

Angels, then, serve not only as guardians but as guards. They are soldiers too, doing battle with evil. Angel lore depicts many kinds of angel battles. They fight on Earth with demons and devils. Good angels fight evil angels in heaven. And angels do battle within people's minds and consciences. For centuries, fighting angels have symbolized the wrenching political and psychological conflicts people experience between good and evil. These holy wars are the subject of Chapter 5.

Odd Jobs

Clearly, angels are good to have in your corner when the going gets tough. They can turn things around for you just by providing a word of encouragement or by wiping your evil enemies off the face of the earth. On top of this power and charisma, they flock together by the billions and fan out to pay attention, when occasion requires, to any and every individual on Earth. Some even say that guardian angels exist for people's house pets!

Wouldn't it be great to have that kind of celestial work force helping you out all the time? Unfortunately, Angel Power Employment Services aren't in the yellow pages. Of course, the idea of angels doing menial labor seems incongruous to most people. Angelic activities are traditionally associated with the Sabbath, the day of rest.

Even so, many have indulged the fantasy of having angels to do their bidding. Some say that the angels did odd jobs—cooking and

Wing Tip

The traditional abbreviations, B.C. for "before Christ" and A.D. for "Anno domini" (Latin for "year of the Lord"), are obviously based on the coming of Christ. Since not everyone is Christian, it has become the more accepted practice to use the abbreviations, B.C.E. for "before common era," and C.E. for "common era."

The Devil Makes You Do It

Be sure and read the fine print on any contract you sign, especially if it sets forth an agreement with a party who claims to be an angel. In particular, watch out for the infamous "burn" clause, requiring you to relinquish your immortal soul. Sure, it seems unreasonable, but it may hold up in infernal court!

cleaning—for Adam and Eve in the Garden of Eden before the scandalous incident with the apple. Legends told about Christian saints include stories of angels who appear to lend a hand with work. One early Christian writer tells of angels building a stone tower that represents the Church.

During the Middle Ages, magicians believed they could summon and control angels by means of magic spells. These spells involved alchemy, astrology, numerology, and written symbols, including the manipulation of letters in the names of angels. Since angel magic runs counter to the teachings of mainstream religion, stories about these magicians tend to cast them in an evil, demonic light. The spirits they summoned were typically demons and devils, like Mephistopheles or Asmodeus, rather than angels of God.

The magicians themselves, however, did not necessarily think of their magic as evil. No doubt their spells had innocent spiritual and experimental purposes in addition to the mischievous ends commonly attributed to them. Who knows, maybe some of these sorcerers just needed a little help with the laundry or the gardening!

From a religious perspective, however, angelic activity is traditionally directed toward spiritual success in the next life, as opposed to practical success in this one. As an example, the Book of Tobit relates the story of the angel Raphael who, for services rendered (the usual guardian angel stuff—demon vanquishing, restoring sight to the blind, arranging a marriage made in heaven, etc.), was offered a pile of gold. Raphael wouldn't take it. "You can pay my employer directly," he said. "He handles the books. And by the way, he doesn't take Earth money."

The Least You Need to Know

➤ The angel hierarchies set forth in the Middle Ages reflect the organization of the early Christian Church.

➤ The word "angel" comes from the Greek word for "messenger." An important role angels play is delivering messages from heaven to Earth, including news of the coming of Christ.

➤ Angels mediate between humanity and God and between what can be known and what cannot be understood.

➤ The notion of the guardian angel has been adopted and altered many times from culture to culture.

➤ Fighting angels represent conflicts between human notions of good and evil.

Chapter 3

Angels at Home

In This Chapter

➤ Angels in heaven

➤ Where to go and what to see and do in heaven

➤ How to get there

➤ The side trip to Purgatory

➤ How to get ready for Judgment Day

A select handful of prophets and mystics claim to have made the trip to heaven to visit God and the angels. Elijah went in a fiery chariot. Muhammad went on the back of a winged horse. Enoch and others were carried there by angels. According to the gospel song, "All God's Children Got Shoes," heaven's a great place for street hiking.

By now, though, you'd think they'd have tour buses and give out maps of all the mansions of the most famous angels. You could see Michael's old world palace with its pearly gates and wing-shaped swimming pool; Gabriel's sprawling ranch-style spread with a sun-deck made of cedar wood from Lebanon and the tennis courts in the clouds; Uriel's chic adobe mansion with a fireplace in every room; Raphael's happy hunting grounds and fish farm. And the Angel Arms apartments where all of heaven's up-and-coming residents live.

There are many mansions in my father's house, said Jesus, so it may be that a tour of the angel's dwelling places could fill an eternity. It would take just about that long, anyway, to describe the visions of all those who have ever imagined what heaven is like. This chapter will tell you just some of the things to look for if you go. And you definitely want to check it out if you get a chance. It's off the high end of the scale of best places to visit. And who wouldn't want to live there?

Living the High Life

Of course, real estate in heaven is sky-high these days, what with all the great publicity it's gotten over the years. Even so, they say there will still be room for newcomers. There's the beautiful downtown area of New Jerusalem, and there are all the neighborhoods and suburbs expanding outward from town into infinity.

Revelations

Not all development plans work out. Perhaps the most famous heavenly building project ever to be abandoned was not actually intended for heaven, but was designed to rise up to it. This was the notorious tower of Babel, described in chapter 11 of the Book of Genesis. Planned for a site in Babylon, the project was intended as a monument to human ambition and cooperation. God didn't like the idea, however, and created confusion by introducing different languages. As a result, the builders couldn't understand one another and gave up.

They say you just take the Milky Way as far as it will go and you can't miss it. The trip is nicer with an angel along who can point out the sights on the way. Of course, you may have to be spiritually transformed and purified by the time you get there, but people in heaven say they don't miss their old sinful human flesh.

You can't go wrong in choosing a place in heaven to spend the hereafter. Here's a list of districts to choose from. Maybe there'll be a welcome mat with your name in lights on the front porch in one of these locales:

➤ *New Jerusalem.* Downtown heaven is the celestial version of the earthly city in Palestine. The Book of Revelation says the whole city will descend to Earth on the Day of Judgment. It has no walls, but four gates facing north, south, east, and west. The streets are paved with gold, and all the angels sweep them with their wings so they shine, just by walking in rhythm to the music they play.

➤ *The Seven Heavens.* From one to seven, they are Wilon, Raqia, Sehaqim, Zebul, Maon, Makon, and Arabot, as listed in the third Book of Enoch. Each heaven is a palace, one inside the other, with the throne of God in the center, the seventh heaven (hence, the saying "seventh heaven" as an expression of joy). This layout involves an unexplainable paradox, however, since the heavens are also concentric spheres with the seventh heaven as the outermost layer containing all the others. Each heaven has a gate guarded by angels to keep out the riff-raff— mystics from Earth who are not properly prepared to enter the supernal realms.

➤ *Paradise.* Heaven's garden district, it was once located on Earth but was transplanted in order to preserve the fruit on the tree of life. Paradise was originally a Persian concept based on the pleasure palaces of the sultans. According to the Muslims, heavenly paradise is inhabited by sexy angels known as houri.

➤ *The Promised Land.* Modeled after Canaan, the Biblical country between Egypt and Arabia that later became Palestine and Judea, this is the land of milk and honey promised to the Israelites. In an early American hymn, it is said to have "sweet fields," "rivers of delight," and "endless day."

➤ *Glory.* This is where everyone who has fought or suffered for God goes to spend the hereafter. Glory residents wear crowns made out of stars so everyone can see what they've been through on Earth.

➤ *The Pleroma.* The Gnostic section of heaven, situated far above everything else and inhabited by angelic beings known as aeons. The whole place is made of light and you have to be a spark of light yourself in order to live there.

➤ *Beulah Land.* Mentioned by the prophet Isaiah as a new name for Jerusalem, meaning "wedded land." Jerusalem will become Beulah when the city becomes wedded to God. According to some, this is the place where virtuous souls reside until Judgment Day.

➤ *The Fur-mament.* This is where all those cats and dogs end up that you buried out back, along with all those goldfish and turtles that you flushed down the toilet. The streets are paved with bones and catnip, and there are plenty of trees and fire hydrants.

The Devil Makes You Do It

Don't spend all your time in heaven with the houri in paradise. You'll miss out on all the other worthwhile sights and activities!

Wing Tip

If you come to heaven, don't forget your sunglasses! Not only are the streets paved with gold, the lights are dazzling.

The Big Send-Up

Originally, heaven, as it was pictured in the Bible, was not a place where the souls of the righteous went to stay. It was strictly the home of God and the angels. Only gradually did the house of God and the abode of the righteous become the same celestial place. The process involved the fusing of various ideas about paradise, the afterlife, and the big guy in the sky.

Heaven on Earth

One key idea behind the modern notion of heaven is the Promised Land. This did not start out as a place up in heaven, but as a place on Earth: the homeland God promised the Israelites as they made their famous exodus from Egypt. This was the land of Canaan, on the other side of the River Jordan, where the Israelites arrived after forty years of wandering (physically and spiritually) in the wilderness. Christians have re-interpreted this historical event as a metaphor for the process of life (wandering in the wilderness), death (crossing the River Jordan), and going to heaven (arriving in Canaan, the Promised Land).

Another idea that became incorporated into heaven is the ancient Persian concept of paradise. Originally, paradises were earthly pleasure gardens belonging to kings and sultans. The word was applied to the Garden of Eden by early Christians who translated the Bible into Greek. The concept is used to refer to heaven in the New Testament.

Revelations

Many Jews and Christians of the Middle Ages believed that paradise—the Garden of Eden—still existed on Earth and could be found and enjoyed through dauntless exploration. Some placed it in or around China. It is even identified on maps from the 9th to the 13th century. One map places it in China; another map locates it off the coast of India and shows it to be surrounded by a wall like a fort. According to legend, an Irish saint of the 6th century sailed successfully to the earthly paradise, where he encountered birds and animals that behaved as human Christians, keeping the fasts and feast days of the church!

Up Town

Still another earthly image that got projected into the clouds is the New Jerusalem. The original Jerusalem was, and still is, the holy city of the Jews. It later became holy to the Christians and special to the Muslims as well. The city was the site of much political and religious turmoil. It suffered invasion and subjugation by foreign powers such as Babylon and Rome. As a result, the Jews longed for a new holy city that would be free from foreign domination.

The Jews imagined a purified Jerusalem that would be wholly acceptable to God. The prophet Isaiah speaks of a Jerusalem that becomes "wedded" to God and renamed "Beulah." Later, the Christian prophet, John of the Apocalypse, imagined New Jerusalem as descending from heaven to Earth on Judgment Day, when the cosmic order would be fulfilled and transformed.

The prophet John sees New Jerusalem, as drawn by Gustave Dore.

God in Orbit

Yet another concept of heaven derives from ancient astronomy. People used to think that the earth was the center of the universe, and that the sun, stars, and planets revolved around it. Each of the known planets (five of them, not counting Earth, Pluto, Neptune, or Uranus) supposedly moved around the earth inside a big sphere. So did the sun. In addition, the stars all shared a single sphere.

The five planets, the sun, and the stars make up seven spheres that mark the boundaries of the seven heavens. The seven heavens were also conceived as palaces, one inside the other, so that the further in you go, the closer you get to the throne of God. The seven heavens are not traditionally thought of as the abode of human souls after death, but are reserved for God and the angels. Even so, legend has it that they can be visited in mystic fashion.

Sites for Sore Eyes

So what do you do when you get to heaven? You may want to take some time to get to know your heavenly hosts. They're real nice folks—good as gold, and they'd like nothing better than to hear about what you've been through on Earth.

If you start to feel nostalgic for the people and places you left behind, you can always look down on Earth and watch people who don't know you're looking. Would that be endlessly fascinating, or what? If you're lucky, you may even get a job reporting to God about people's evil deeds.

Not the voyeuristic type? Don't despair, there are plenty of other heavenly activities that are easy on the budget. In fact, since you can't take your money with you, everything's free. Here are some recommendations for things to see and do in heaven, prepared by the New Jerusalem Chamber of Commerce:

➤ *Visit the throne of God.* This is a big deal, of course, so there may be a long line, even before you get to the throng of angels. You'll want to check out the four-headed cherubim and the wheels made of fire covered with eyes.

➤ *Take a hike through the sweet fields.* The air is laden with the smell of spices—balm, myrrh, and spikenard. Go ahead and pick yourself a big bouquet of roses, you've got it coming. Contact the office of Celestial Parks Services to reserve one of the fields for a reunion of your loved ones.

➤ *Go to Pleroma Beach.* There's nothing like a dip in the Gnostic pool of light for a refreshing way to transcend time and space.

➤ *Go to Glory and march with the saints.* Toe-tapping music abounds as robed crown-wearers wend their way through piles of discarded armor.

➤ *Hang out in the Good Book Reading Room.* Here, at last, you can find out everything you've always wanted to know. Ask God or one of his angelic intelligences why the sky is blue, or why you had to go through life with that big mole on your nose.

➤ *Have dinner at Christ's.* Don't let the exclusive clientele of elect saints intimidate you. Christ himself provides top-notch service and the holy manna is out of this world.

➤ *After dinner, head for the Bosom of Abraham.* This rockin' spot is renowned in heaven and Earth for its ethereal blend of Judeo-Christian soul.

➤ *Or spend the evening in the paradisal pleasure gardens.* Popular with business conventions and caravans, this is the hot spot for a boys' night out. If you've been *real* good, an Arabian angel will fix you up with your own houri.

➤ *Head over yonder and rest in peace.* This activity is a timeless favorite. You can't beat it after a lifetime of earthly tribulation.

The Devil Makes You Do It

According to Islamic tradition, Azrael, the angel of death, keeps track of people's sins, so watch out for him. He is described as being 70,000 feet tall with 4,000 wings, four faces, and covered all over with eyes and mouths.

Wing Tip

Be sure and look for your name written in the Book of Life. If it's there, you'll know for sure that you've come to the right place.

One important frequently asked question is whether human beings become transformed into angels. Some say people become angels when they get to heaven. Others say no, we're different sorts of beings altogether. Some say the privilege of being an angel is reserved for virgins, martyrs, and saints. The rest of us will have to settle for eternal bliss without wings. Don't you just hate that?

Getting There Is Half the Fun

Most monotheists have reached a rough consensus about what it takes to get admitted beyond the blue as a permanent resident: Be good, love and fear God, and believe what God says. There is less unanimity, however, about how and when people go to heaven. Basically, there are several popular scenarios: (1) as soon as you're ready, (2) as soon as you're called, (3) at the end of time, and (4) when hell freezes over. It's almost universally agreed, upon, however, that regardless of when or how we get to heaven, we're going to need angels to show us the way and help us get there safely.

Getting a Head Start

Scenario 1 is the mystic's approach. This option is for people who don't let a little thing like still being alive prevent them from going to heaven. Mysticism is the spiritual equivalent of refusing to waste your sick leave from work on days when you're sick and won't enjoy them. Why wait till you're dead to go to heaven?

We have mystic visions to thank for much of what we know about heaven and the angels. Conversely, many mystics have angels to thank for the long lift up. Mystics who have reportedly been angelled up to heaven include the Jewish prophets, Elijah and Enoch; their followers, the Merkabah mystics; and Muhammad, the prophet of Islam and the Muslim mystics known as Sufis.

Not surprisingly, religious mainliners are a little uneasy about the idea of going to heaven before death. After all, who will the religious authorities have to instruct and discipline if their entire congregations are already up in heaven? While it's generally considered okay for a big-name prophet like Muhammad or Elijah to make the trip to the top without leaving the old body behind, mystics usually get accused of jumping the gun.

The Devil Makes You Do It

You might want to think twice about trying to hitch a ride with an angel. Most will not take unauthorized hitch-hikers.

Meeting Your Deadline

A more common view is that it's appropriate to wait until you die before going to heaven. Here again, angels perform an invaluable service in guiding the souls of the dead to heaven. Some believe this job falls to the angel who served as guardian angel to the soul during life. Others say that it is the archangel Michael who shows the way

Winged Words

Psychopomps are spirits (pagan gods or angels in monotheism), who conduct the souls of the dead to their abode in the afterlife.

to the newly departed soul. Still others say a whole swarm of angels take on the job, like Secret Service agents surrounding the president, or little kids surrounding Mickey Mouse. Whoever the angels, they are known as *psychopomps*, from the Greek word meaning "soul guide."

Guiding souls soon after death is only part of the job angels do for the deceased. In addition, they do battle with any evil spirits who stand between the soul and heaven. Again, Michael stands out as the most famous case study. He is said to have disputed with Satan over the soul of Moses.

Half-Way House

Even though the angels know the way, and know how to fend off devils and demons, it's still not a straight shot to paradise for most people. For many, a trip to Purgatory is in order. You go to Purgatory if you've sinned but have repented. Some have imagined this place as a monastery or prison-like environment, where you eat bread and water and wear a hair shirt and do a lot of praying and weeping. Your stay in Purgatory may be long or short, depending on how badly you have sinned, how repentant you are, which saints are praying for you, and how much indulgence money your loved ones have paid the priests to get you out.

Some say there is also a quick-fix purgatory. This is a river of fire that you must pass through in order to be purified of your sins. Passing through this river constitutes a second baptism. You'll be dipped in the flames by angels, of course. Hopefully they'll be waiting with a cool drink on the other side!

Revelations

There's a nifty interpretation of a passage from *Genesis* as a symbol of Purgatory. Way back when Adam and Eve got themselves booted out of Eden, God placed some cherubim and a flaming sword in front of the gate to keep them out. He did this because the Garden contained not only the Tree of Knowledge, whose fruit they had already eaten, but also the Tree of Life, whose fruit would make them immortal. God didn't want them to taste immortality yet, so he barred the entrance with his cherubic watchdogs and the flaming sword.

Going through Purgatory is like going past the cherubim, who purify you with the flaming sword. Once your sins have been singed and sliced out of you, you can get into heaven, or paradise, and eat the fruit of the Tree of Life. Then you can live forever as a purified immortal soul.

Last Call

Whereas many say that the right time to go to heaven is right after you die, others say that it's still too soon. Going to heaven on a first-come, first-serve basis is messy and disorganized, involving an inefficient use of angel-power. The alternative view is that everybody goes wherever they're going all at once.

Remains of the Day

The big move happens on Judgment Day when the angel Gabriel blows his horn to wake the dead. This is a Christian idea that was picked up by the Muslims. For Muslims, the wake-up trumpet blast comes from an angel called Israfel. The trumpet not only wakes up the dead, who will have been lying in their graves for however long, but also announces the second coming of Christ, and signals the angels to gather everyone together and start sorting them out. "Good souls move up, please; evil souls move down, thank you!"

This bizarre day of the living dead is known as the Resurrection. At this time, all the dead bodies of everyone who ever lived will come back to life, and will start wandering around in a daze until they are judged and angels tell them where to go. (Sound like a human resources nightmare? It shouldn't be any problem for the angels, who, by some estimates, outnumber all of humanity by a hundred to one.)

The Resurrection is a little piece of religious doctrine that has been a morbid poser to theologians for centuries. The problem is, how can a dead body come back to life if it has decomposed, been cremated, eaten by wild animals, and so on? The Bible is explicit about it: *Bodies* come back to life. Some believe we'll get new bodies and heaven will come down to Earth. Others say that our bodies will be protected by angels who will stand guard over our graves. (Talk about a boring job!)

Wing Tip

If you wake up in a daze on Judgment Day, look for celestial beings who *aren't* brandishing pitchforks. They'll be the ones who look like they *haven't* been rotting in their graves for centuries.

Wing Tip

If you want the scientific explanation for how the Resurrection is possible, check out "Reflections Touching the Resurrection," a treatise by noted 17th-century physicist, Robert Boyle. In short, the explanation is that God can do anything he wants to, even if it doesn't conform to the rules of physics as we know them.

Still others say we'll have to live with the bodies we've got in the condition they end up in. According to this view, part of the point of the experience is to confront our corporeal nature. We'll be naked as the day we were born and everyone who's ever lived will be there to see us.

No, it won't be a beauty contest. Instead, the only thing we'll have to show for ourselves will be our moral, spiritual characters. This will be clearly recognizable to everyone: God, the angels, and us. Stripped of our vanity and pretensions, we'll see the earth as the graveyard it's always been—and ourselves as corpses.

Hang Time

The end of the world may seem like a long time to wait before we get to go to heaven. Some say, however, that the time goes by really quickly when you're dead, so you hardly even notice. Others believe in a temporary celestial residence, such as paradise, for the souls of the virtuous. They can be happy there for a while, and then really happy after Judgment Day when they get their permanent reward.

The Devil Makes You Do It

It may take more than travel plans to get to heaven. As a well-known gospel song says, "Everybody talkin' 'bout heaven ain't goin' there."

Some say the angels are eagerly looking forward to Judgment Day. They sensed a deep loss when Adam and Eve fell from grace, and the loss will not be restored until the final day. At that time, cosmic harmony will be complete and their efforts and care on behalf of humanity will have paid off at last. The rest is all praising God for eternity.

A glimpse of heaven from one of Dore's illustrations for Dante's Divine Comedy.

Until then, the angels and mortals will just have to hold on. They'll be waiting for us to join them up in heaven—keeping New Jerusalem clean and shiny, watering the clouds, mowing the sweet fields, or just kicking back to do a little fishing in the rivers of delight.

The Least You Need to Know

➤ The Judeo-Christian concept of the afterlife in heaven stems from places on Earth: paradise, the Promised Land, and the city of Jerusalem.

➤ Many mystics believe it is possible to visit heaven and the angels in spirit without dying.

➤ Angels are thought to serve as judges and guides to heaven for souls of the dead, guardians against evil spirits, and attendants during purification of the soul.

➤ Angels are thought to guard the tombs of the dead until Judgment Day, when they will wake the dead and assemble them for judgment.

Prototypes

We can look at angel origins in two ways: first, in terms of their creation by God; and second, in terms of their creation, as divine ideas, by human beings. The first approach to the question is shrouded in mystery. If God used blueprints when he made angels, the plans have either been lost, or they're written in the stars where ordinary mortals can't read 'em.

The second approach is almost—but not quite—as mysterious. The idea of angels seems to have originated and developed in the middle of a complicated mix of ancient cultures. In fact, angels have played an important role in reconciling various religious beliefs. You might say that remembering angels has helped monotheistic religions keep in touch with their pagan roots without turning away from the idea of a single, all-powerful God. At the same time, angels, from the very beginning, have been a mono-theistic belief that pagans can relate to.

This is not to say that angels always worked as a way of smoothing over religious differences. Religious battles in the ancient world were frequent and fierce, and angels

Wing Tip

It often helps to be flexible about time when dealing with religious thinking. The Egyptian god Osirus is said to have created the gods who gave birth to him. With ideas like this, it's no wonder that the origins and seniority of divine beings are frequently disputed.

The question of angel origins is a real chicken-and-egg dilemma, as illustrated in this print by William Blake.

were often in the thick of them. But angels provided a way of making sense of the tribal conflicts of long ago. And, sometimes, they provided ways out of them, too.

Ancient Days

Celestial seniority says a lot about how important angels are. As with seniority in the workplace, the length of time an angel has been on the job ties in with power and prestige. Some theologians say that squabbles about seniority led to the war in heaven that resulted in Satan and his cohorts getting cast into the pits of hell. It's as if Satan was an ambitious senior vice president who forgot that God has seniority and caused trouble by demanding to be CEO. So he got demoted to the mail room where he plots revenge.

In the Beginning

The Biblical Book of Genesis, which tells the story of how God created the universe, doesn't mention the creation of angels. This omission has encouraged angel worshippers in the belief that angels, like God, are uncreated and eternal. This is an unorthodox view, however, since it elevates angels to the status of gods. If they've been around forever, their existence doesn't depend on the Almighty.

On the opposite extreme is the view expressed in the Talmud that God makes a host of angels every day out of fire to sing God's praises, and destroys them again at the end of the day. (The river of fire is supposedly formed from the sweat that comes off the bodies of the cherubim who carry God's throne.) This idea not only sees angels as created by God, but suggests their creation is not crucial to the existence of the rest of the world. It's as if God doesn't need angels, but is just showing off his power in making and destroying them.

Older and Wiser

A standard view of the origin of angels is set forward in the apocryphal Book of Jubilees. The account is similar to the creation story told in Genesis, except that it says God created angels on the first day, after creating the heavens and the earth, but before creating the firmament. Psalm 148 and Colossians 1:16 also mention God's creation of the angels together with the rest of the universe. An Islamic myth says God made humanity out of clay after he made the angels out of fire or gemstones.

The Book of Job suggests angels were either present before the rest of the universe was made or created near the beginning of the process. When Job questions God's seemingly unreasonable actions, God responds by saying, "where were you when I laid the Earth's foundations?…When the morning stars sang together and the sons of God shouted for joy?" (34:4–8). Here God is, in effect, pulling seniority on Job. God has been around a lot longer than Job, so he knows more about what's going on. The angels, referred to here as "sons of God," were there too.

The Devil Makes You Do It

Theology (the study of religious doctrines and matters of divinity) is an especially hard subject because it concerns areas which—according to theology itself—exceed the limits of human understanding.

Starring Roles

Philosophers of the Middle Ages considered the question of when and how the angels were created. Most agreed that they were created by God. Some suggested a new wrinkle, saying that God created the highest angels, who in turn created the next highest, and so on down the line. A related, and more popular, idea says that prior to the creation of any living species, God created an angel that was to be in charge of it. Some say that these angels are visible as stars in the sky.

In some versions of this guardian angel creation story, God creates the angels and asks them if they want to have material embodiments of themselves on Earth. If the angel gives the green light, the living, mortal thing gets created. If the angel says no, it's one less living thing to worry about. Some say God consulted with the angels about whether to create humans. They said no, but God went over their heads and made us anyway!

Revelations

One Jewish legend says that God creates the angels every morning and destroys them again at night. They are created out of a river of fire that is formed from the sweat of the four living creatures who support God's throne. Most Christian authorities, however, classify the four living creatures themselves as angels and regard angels as indestructible. This is why Satan and the other fallen angels were banished to hell rather than annihilated.

People since the Middle Ages have continued to speculate about angel origins. In the 18th century, the Swedish philosopher Emanuel Swedenborg wrote that angels evolved from the spirits of human beings. In the 20th century, at least one New Age angelologist says that angels may have evolved on distant planets.

Gods and Angels

Just as philosophers and theologians have different ideas about when angels were created, historians and archaeologists have different ideas about when human beings first started thinking about them. The answer to this question depends on whether you restrict your definition of "angel" to refer only to the heavenly beings of monotheistic religions (religions with just one god), or whether you go for the notion of pagan angels.

Follow the Leader

Many polytheistic (many-god) religions have divine beings and spirits that closely resemble angels in both appearance and function. Some of these go back a long way in history. The ancient Sumerian civilization left artifacts at the capital city of Ur that scholars have associated with angels. These include carved stone cylinder seals that date from about 4000 B.C.E.

Many of these cylinders depict a seated figure who represents a god and a standing figure who represents a mortal human. Next to the human is another standing figure who seems to be leading him or her to the god. Although these go-betweens have no wings, they evidently fill the role of angels, bridging the gap between God and humanity.

Another Sumerian artifact depicts what some have called the first angel. This is a stele, or stone panel, which represents a winged human form. This early angel has a jar out of which is spilling the water of life. A king, seated on Earth, holds out a cup to catch the water.

Winged figures appear on cylinder seals produced by various groups of the Middle East. The one pictured here is from Phoenicia and dates from 500–200 B.C.E.

King of the Hill

The Sumerians recognized hundreds of different gods, each of whom had a different role to play. The most important gods sometimes jostled with one another for supremacy. This jostling among the gods reflected earthly politics. As a group of human beings rose in social importance, the god special to them became more important too.

For example, the Sumerian sky god, Anu, enshrined at the city of Uruk, enjoyed supremacy over other gods for a while. Anu was eventually supplanted by Enlil, a sky god enshrined at the city of Nippur, when Nippur defeated Uruk in battle.

Of course, not all the gods were in competition with each other. Even so, there tends to be much less cooperation among heavenly beings in polytheistic religions than in monotheism, where everyone in heaven works together according to the will of a single god. This spirit of cooperation helps distinguish angels from their pagan predecessors.

Common Bonds

Despite this difference, angels share much in common with many pagan gods. Both celestial groups offer guidance and protection in affairs of national importance and in personal or household

Wing Tip

One of the advantages of monotheism is that it prevents squabbles over which of many gods is most important. One of the disadvantages is that it makes the will of God much harder to figure out. If good and bad things happen on the same day to a pagan, she can attribute the cause of these things to two different gods and try to appease the god who's causing trouble. If good and bad things happen to a monotheist, he can only guess at what God might be thinking.

matters. Both may serve as messengers to and from a higher being. Both may conduct human souls from the world of the living to the world of the dead. And both are sometimes thought to take charge of natural processes such as the changing of the seasons and the circling of the planets.

The Devil Makes You Do It

Beware of "cherubs" armed with bows and arrows. You may think they epitomize purity and innocence, but if they turn out to be cupids, they can make you fall madly in love with someone!

It's not surprising, then, that pagan deities sometimes exhibit a striking resemblance to the angels of monotheism, especially when these gods are portrayed with wings. The Assyrian sun god, Shamash, sometimes appears with wings to show his power to move through the sky. The Egyptian fertility goddess, Isis, is also frequently winged, in keeping with her role of nurturing and protecting.

The Greek goddess of victory, Nike (who gives her name to a famous brand of sports equipment) is also traditionally depicted with wings, to indicate her speed and strength. These gods and goddesses evidently influenced early Christian depictions of angels. The same may be true of the winged figure of the Greek god, Eros, also known by the Latin name, Cupid. Cupid's youthful appearance resembles that of the Christian cherub.

Revelations

Ritual practices honoring pagan gods called *mysteries* took place throughout the Mediterranean area from the 6th century B.C.E. These were often fertility or initiation rites intended to establish mystic connections between the participants and their gods. Most were performed by Greek cults, although the practice spread to pagan groups in Egypt and elsewhere. Scholars disagree about whether Jewish and Christian sects imported pagan-style mysteries into their religious rituals. Although direct evidence is inconclusive that Jews and Christians adopted pagan rites, it appears that some Jewish and Christian sects did practice pagan-style magic, casting spells by calling on pagan gods, together with angels.

Spreading Their Wings

There are a number of explanations for the similarities evident between pagan gods and monotheistic angels. One is that other cultures—Sumerian, Babylonian, Assyrian, Egyptian, and Greek—influenced Jewish and Christian conceptions of angels. The early

Semitic tribes that gave rise to Judaism traveled from place to place and came into contact with ideas from Sumer, Babylon, Assyria, and Egypt. They adopted many of these into their own lore and beliefs.

By the early days of Christianity, Greek and Roman ideas had spread all over the Mediterranean. Christians picked up on them as they developed their own religious beliefs. This kind of cultural transmission may account for similar stories, beliefs, and depictions in painting and sculpture.

Revelations

During the early days of Christianity, pagan ideas from Greece and Egypt were combined with Christian thinking in a body of early philosophical writings by unknown authors. During the Middle Ages, these writings were attributed to a mythical philosopher known as Hermes Trismegistus and came to be known as Hermetic philosophy. At that time, it was mistakenly believed that these writings were written in Egypt during the time of Moses (about 600 B.C.E.) and that their Christian references were prophetic of the coming of Christ. Medieval readers accounted for the appearance of Christian ideas in these texts by saying God had directly inspired Hermes Trismegistus with the knowledge of Christian truth.

Déjà Vu: Retelling Stories

There are many more parallels between monotheistic angels and pagan gods and spirits. The Jewish idea of the cherubim that stand guard over a sacred place derives from ancient Assyria, where winged sphinx-like statues stood at the thresholds of palaces to ward off evil.

Myths and stories of pagan gods were sometimes retold in Jewish or Christian contexts as angel stories. One example is the story that says the archangel Michael will weigh souls on the Day of Judgment in order to decide their fate for the rest of eternity. This stems from a myth about the Egyptian god Anubis, the jackal-headed guardian of the dead. Anubis weighed the hearts of the dead to decide their station in the afterlife, the heavier the heart, the better the score!

One of the best-known angel stories in the Old Testament is Genesis 18 and 19, which tells of angels who appear to Abraham and Sara, and later to Lot, in the guise of ordinary visitors. The human hosts provide respectful hospitality for their angelic visitors and are rewarded for their efforts. In contrast, the men of the city of Sodom try to rape the visitors. Is the distinction between good and evil behavior clear enough for you? As a result of their depravity, the entire city is destroyed.

This story closely resembles the myth of Baucis and Philemon, an elderly couple from the country of Phrygia. They were the only people who showed hospitality to the gods, Zeus and Hermes, who disguised themselves as mortals. As a result, Baucis and Philemon were saved while the rest of the town was destroyed.

Angels in the Melting Pot

Monotheistic religion, especially Christianity, continued to pick up on polytheistic ideas even after getting started. As Christianity spread to new parts of the world it didn't always totally replace existing beliefs. Often, local beliefs were incorporated into the new way of thinking, and vice versa, as angels assumed the functions of pagan gods. This sort of religious blending is called *syncretism*: the combining of separate belief systems into one.

One of the many roles of the Greek god, Apollo, is that of messenger. Apollo is also an oracular deity, with the power to foretell the future. Both of these functions involve duties performed by angels. In fact, some ancient writings from the early days of Christianity invoke the aid of Apollo together with angels in bringing communications from a higher god in order to foretell the future.

Winged Words

Syncretism is the merging of several different beliefs into a single religion. Many pagan gods have been turned into angels by becoming syncretized with Christianity.

Angelic figures often appear wherever different kinds of symbolism are fused together. This early 16th-century engraving by Albrecht Durer personifies Temperance, Fortune, and Nemesis, a figure from Greek mythology.

Us and Them

Syncretism has taken place between angels and several different pagan deities at once. Hecate, the Asia Minor goddess of the underworld, has been linked with the Egyptian goddess, Isis, and the Greek goddess, Artemis. An ancient "curse tablet"—a writing intended to cast a spell on an enemy—refers to this triple goddess as an angel and beseeches her help.

Syncretism is a prominent feature not only of ancient religious belief, but of the New Age movement as well. Many New Agers combine an interest in angels with non-monotheistic ideas, including witchcraft, paganism, and Far Eastern philosophy. Today, as in ancient times, syncretists have aroused the enmity of more orthodox believers.

Jewish scripture relates many stories of Jews who have adopted non-Jewish and syncretic beliefs and been severely punished by God as a result. To take just one example, a story in the Second Book of Maccabees, 12:32–45, tells of a battle between the Jews and their enemies, the Idumaeans. The Jews were victorious and only a few of their number were killed. When they went to bury those who had died in battle, they found that each of the dead soldiers wore a pagan amulet, associated with a non-Jewish idol. The story says that God arranged for these "soft-core" Jews to die as punishment for their forbidden beliefs.

There was a time, however, when elements of pagan worship were accepted features of the religious practices of the Israelites. One of the names the Israelites used for God is El, who was a chief god of the pagan Canaanites. El was matched with a female consort named Asherah, who was a fertility goddess.

Many Israelites, including King Solomon, worshipped Asherah, together with El. Starting in the 8th century B.C.E., however, the high god of the Israelites came to be identified as Yahweh. At this time, El became incorporated into Yahweh while Asherah was demonized, becoming the consort of the demon known as Baal.

Typecasting

Cultural transmission and syncretism doesn't account for all ideas about angels and angel-like beings. In fact, some see angels as *archetypal* figures, figures that appear in distinct, unrelated cultures that reflect shared unconscious creative tendencies present in all people.

These days many scholars reject the idea of archetypes, saying that shared cultural characteristics reflect common social and environmental circumstances rather than an essential, universally shared, human subconscious. Most agree, however, that

Winged Words

An **archetype**, according to psychologist Carl Jung who coined the term, is a manifestation of the shared aspects of the human subconscious. Archetypes provide an explanation for resemblances among separate cultures.

angels and angelic beings are common to many cultures both as a result of direct influence (as when a Christian artist uses the Greek goddess Nike as a model for an angel) and as independent ideas (as when a Native American sky spirit takes the form of a human being with wings).

Ain't that a Shaman

Among the spirit beings that resemble angels but come from independent traditions are the spirit emanations of shamanism. Shamanism is an aspect of many tribal religions from all over the world, but the term "shaman" comes from Siberia. A *shaman* is a tribal doctor and priest who heals the sick by appeasing the spirit world.

Many tribal cultures believe in souls that can exist independently of the body. The soul may leave the body, not only in death, but also during sleep or in traces. Often, when the soul leaves the body, it is thought to take the form of a bird or other winged creature.

Winged Words

A **shaman** is a Siberian word for a tribal practitioner of spiritual medicine. Shamans are found not only in Siberian tribes, but virtually all over the world.

Shamans sometimes venture into the spirit world by going into a trance, often with the aid of hallucinogenic drugs. In some cultures, shamans visit the spirits by going on actual journeys. In keeping with the spiritual nature of the journey, a shaman may put on a bird costume, including wings. In this guise, he is better prepared for spiritual encounters.

Wings Over the World

The concept of a spirit world that has an influence on physical existence seems to be nearly universal. The ancient Greeks referred to human souls as daemons. A person's daemon influenced his or her behavior and guided the individual through life. (The Roman word for daemon is "genius," and is popularly thought to be responsible for a person's intelligence.)

Wing Tip

The shamanistic dream journey has been revived in recent years as "astral travel." The idea is that everyone has an astral body that is separate from our physical selves. Supposedly, some people are able to go anywhere in their astral bodies, leaving their physical bodies behind!

Gradually, the word "daemon" acquired a negative connotation as it came into contact with other religions and was used increasingly to mean "evil spirit." Even so, daemons were sometimes regarded in a neutral or positive sense and associated with angels. The Jewish neo-Platonist philosopher, Philo, for example, says that angels and daemons are the same.

Whether through cultural transmission, syncretism, or as archetypes, angels serve as a kind of celestial glue connecting diverse religious ideas. Even though they are not always full-fledged servants of the one high God, the notion of winged spirits that help people and convey messages to a higher power clearly appeals to many cultures.

The Least You Need to Know

➤ The Book of Genesis doesn't mention the creation of angels, but the apocryphal Book of Jubilees says they were created on the first day.

➤ Drawings of winged creatures appear on Mesopotamian stone tablets starting around 4000 B.C.E.

➤ Sumerian, Assyrian, Egyptian, Persian, and Greek cultures all may have contributed to ancient conceptions of angels.

➤ Angels serve many of the same functions as pagan deities and the two were sometimes fused into one.

➤ Tribal cultures from all over the world recognize spiritual beings that influence the physical world.

The Flap Over Good and Evil

Understanding good and evil is a delicate business, requiring a grasp of the big picture. It can be hard to tell whether evil comes from you, from other people, or whether it's just part of the way things are. Stories and legends about good and evil angels have helped people get a broad perspective on this puzzle and sort out for themselves the fine, blurry, and wavy lines separating right and wrong.

The concept of fallen angels is crucial. They seem like perfect beings, worthy of love and trust, but they turn out to be absolute devils. Fallen angels show that evil can come from high places where you'd least expect it. And even though the difference between good and evil can be fairly subtle and sometimes hard to determine, it makes all the difference in the universe. Take one wrong step and it's a long way down.

Of course, angels aren't all that different from people. Good and evil angels dramatize the good and evil potential in us. When angels choose sides and fight with one another, versions of that fight are also going on between groups of humans and within individuals. After all, even though our personal battles may not seem important to those who aren't involved, it feels like they have cosmic significance.

Knowing Right and Wrong

There are many ideas about where evil comes from. Several of the most important explanations involve angels or angelic beings and their evil counterparts, fallen angels or demons. According to traditional Christian belief, evil angels were originally good, but fell from grace. Other religions have different scenarios.

Revelations

Evil angels help explain the existence of evil within religions that worship an all-powerful, benevolent God. The thinking goes that if fallen angels bring about evil, God doesn't directly create it. Portions of the Hebrew Bible, however, suggest God is responsible for evil as well as good. Here are two examples:

"I form the light and create darkness; I make peace and create evil; I the Lord do all these things."

—Isaiah 45:7

"Out of the mouth of the most high proceedeth not evil and good?"

—Lamentations 3:38

Two Sides of the Question

According to the Zoroastrian religion, good and evil angelic beings have been around from the beginning, even before the creation of the world. These opposed forces are pitted against each other in a continual struggle for supremacy. Zoroastrians believe the good angels will emerge victorious in a final battle. Human beings can help by aligning themselves firmly with the good side.

Although Zoroastrianism is often referred to as the first monotheistic religion (it is even older than Judaism, which it influenced), it differs from the big three monotheistic faiths in emphasizing a dualistic (two-fold) view of creation. The God of Zoroastrianism, Ahura Mazda, is not all-powerful—as in Judaism, Christianity, and Islam—but vies for control with the evil spirit, Angra Mainyu.

Dirty Work

In contrast, Yahweh, the God of the Jews, has control over all of creation. Even evil spirits must do his bidding. Not even Satan can act independently of God. In fact, Satan does not start off as a Prince of Darkness, but as an angel who does God's bidding whose specific role is to oppose or test evil tendencies in human beings. This angel is known as "the Satan"—not a name, but a position or title meaning "the adversary."

The Satan appears in the Book of Numbers as an angel who stands in the way of Balaam, a magician whose work opposed the will of God. Here the Satan prevents Balaam from doing evil. The Satan seems more mischievous in the Book of Job as an angel who ruins the happiness and prosperity of Job, one of God's most devoted human servants. But even here, the Satan obtains God's permission before doing his dirty work. The Book of Job stands as one of the most important works of all time on the subject of good and evil. It shows how difficult it can be to keep the two things separate.

Elsewhere in the Old Testament, the Satan prompts human beings to do evil. For example, in Chronicles, he incites the Jewish King David to take a census of all his people so he can tax them. This struck some Jews as a clear sign of satanic influence. Interestingly, in the second Book of Samuel, it is not the Satan, but Yahweh, or God, who puts David up to this dirty deed in order to punish the Jews for their sins!

Wing Tip

If bad things happen to you, don't automatically assume that it's the work of the devil. God may be testing you to see what kind of stuff you're made of!

The Mark of the Beast

The Jews of the Old Testament didn't generally associate the Satan with absolute evil. They did have other monsters and demons that represented everything that is bad in the universe. These include the beasts known as Behemoth, Leviathan, and Rahab. Scripture also identifies the serpent and the dragon as manifestations of evil.

These evil monsters may have their origins in an ancient Babylonian myth in which a god creates the universe by killing the monster known as Chaos and making the world out of its dead body. Several passages in the Hebrew Bible use monsters like Leviathan as metaphors for the enemies of the Jews such as the Babylonians or the Romans. Only later, during the rise of Christianity, did these ancient monsters become associated with the fallen angel known as Satan.

The Devil Makes You Do It

Be careful how you talk about Satan! Jewish legend holds that if a man tells his pregnant wife to go to the devil, Satan will have possession of the unborn child for life!

Similarly, the serpent in the Book of Genesis who tempts Eve to disobey God's commands is not originally referred to as Satan. Later interpretations of the story associate the serpent with the Prince of Darkness. In fact, evil spirits mentioned in the Bible and the Apocrypha tend to be associated with Satan by subsequent interpreters. That's one reason why Satan has so many names.

Vice Squad

See if you can pick these embodiments of evil out of the biblical lineup:

➤ *The Satan.* The adversary, originally an angel who did God's bidding in opposing misguided humans, but later the fallen angel Satan, the Prince of Darkness, chief of all the fallen angels and enemy of God and humanity.

➤ *The serpent.* Tempted the first woman, Eve, in the Garden of Eden to transgress God's commands and appears throughout the Bible as a manifestation of evil.

➤ *Leviathan, Behemoth, Rahab, the dragon.* Giant sea beasts originally associated with the evils of non-Jewish nations.

➤ *Beelzebub, Lord of the Flies, also known as Baal.* Originally a heathen god of the Canaanites who was later demonized by the Jews as the Prince of Devils.

➤ *Azazel.* The fallen angel in the Book of Enoch who taught men to make weapons and taught women to use cosmetics. He appears in the Old Testament Book of Leviticus as a desert spirit who receives scapegoats—goats ritually infected with the sins of the Jews.

➤ *Semyaza,* or *Semihaza.* Leader of the fallen angels in the Book of Enoch who mated with mortal women.

➤ *Iblis.* The chief of the fallen angels of Islam who rebelled out of envy of humankind.

Wing Tip

Notice that the same divine being may be good according to one religion and evil according to another. Many devils and fallen angels in the Bible are gods worshipped by the enemies of the Israelites. Take Baal for example.

Going Down

The widely known story of Satan's rebellion and fall from heaven is not the first of the fallen angel stories. An earlier legend tells of the birth of the Nephilim, a race of giants who wreak destruction on Earth. Part of their story appears in the Book of Enoch and the rest is told in the Book of Jubilees. Possibly because they represent unorthodox religious views, these books were excluded from the Hebrew Bible. A trace of the Nephelim story can be found in the Book of Genesis.

Mixed Marriages

The story of the Nephilim describes angels as the sons of heaven who lust after human females, have sex with them, and produce offspring. Their leader was the angel named Semyaza. He and his cohorts do nasty things like teach people to use weapons and make-up, both of which are biblical taboos. It was not generally approved of to kill or harm another, and make-up was seen as an inherent part of one of the seven deadly sins: Pride. The children of the mixed marriages between the angels and mortal women are the giants known as Nephilim. They eat everything they can get their hands on. After they eat all the food belonging to the ordinary humans, they start eating people.

Poet and printer William Blake tells of woes resulting from mixed love relationships between different orders of creation. This illustration shows the immortal Urizen shamefully in love with his female emanation, Ahania.

God was not pleased with Semyaza and the other angels who started all this trouble. Thus they fell from grace and became devils. God commanded the angel Gabriel to imprison them on Earth until the Day of Judgment. Meanwhile, the Nephilim continued to menace humanity until they were destroyed in the great flood. (This is the flood familiar from the story of Noah's Ark.)

Many Jews may have known the story of the Nephilim in ancient times. Although it is not recounted in the Bible, the Book of Genesis (6:2–5) alludes to it in explaining why God decided to destroy everyone on Earth except Noah and his family. Here the fallen angels are referred to as "the sons of God." Also, despite the disclosure that the Nephilim were destroyed in the flood, subsequent passages refer to their descendants, who are giants who survive the flood.

Revelations

The angels who have sex with human women in the Book of Enoch resemble legendary beings called succubi and incubi. During the Middle Ages, succubi were thought to be female spirits who had sex with human men while they slept. Incubi were male spirits who had sex with human women. Merlin the magician was said to be the offspring of a human male and a succubus. Although these stories came from European folk traditions unrelated to the Bible, it is likely that some regarded the succubi and incubi as fallen angels like those that fathered the Nephilim in the Book of Enoch.

Sibling Rivalry

An alternative account of the fallen angels holds that they fell from grace not out of lust, but envy of human beings. The apocryphal book, the Life of Adam and Eve, tells that when God created the first humans, he commanded the angels to bow down and submit to them. Satan refused, arguing that he was created first, therefore human beings ought to worship him. So God kicked Satan out of heaven.

Wing Tip

Myths about battles in heaven among angels or pagan gods serve the purpose of endowing human disagreements with cosmic significance. If you want to persuade people that your problems are really important, try telling them that good and evil angels are fighting about them!

Moslems have a similar idea about fallen angels. They tell of an angel named Iblis who refuses to worship the first human beings and incites a rebellion in heaven. Iblis, an Islamic version of Satan, is cast out of heaven along with his followers. Iblis later tempts human beings to disobey the commands of God. Some interpretations give this story an interesting twist by portraying Iblis not as especially evil, but as especially loyal to God. According to this view, Iblis loved God so much that he couldn't worship Adam.

The New Testament Book of Revelation says Satan is chained in the abyss amid a lake of fire for seducing the nations into evil ways. This book is an important source for the idea of a battle in heaven between good and evil angels. Christian interpretations have elaborated on this idea, saying that Satan led a rebellion in heaven against God and the good angels. The rebel angels were cast into hell.

Ups and Downs

The story of Satan's rebellion is widely known among Christians. It accounts for good and evil in the world as Christians have traditionally understood it, answering the tricky question of why God, who is all-powerful and good, permits evil to exist. The answer to the question is that God wants people to be good and worship of their own free will.

According to this view, God made angels as well as human beings with free will to choose between good and evil. He made humans this way so that they could participate in their own salvation, rather than simply be passively or automatically perfect. This way, people can learn, grow, and improve themselves during the course of their lives.

The fallen angels had free will too, but fell from grace permanently because of their pride and arrogance. Because they lost their free will, they became enslaved by their own vices. Thus, they are imprisoned not only in hell, but also within their own minds. People, of course, face the danger of becoming like the fallen angels, living their lives in hells of their own devising.

Pesky Little Devils

Tradition has it that Satan was known in heaven as Lucifer before he was kicked out for his monstrous arrogance and for inducing other angels to rebel. Some say he was even head of all the angels, superior even to Michael. One third of all the angels created by God joined with Satan to wage war in heaven against God and the loyal angels.

Satan and his crew were defeated and hurled out of heaven into the burning lake of hell where they are confined for eternity. From time to time, however, they are able to make forays up on Earth in order to tempt and deceive human beings. Thus Satan and the other devils pose a challenge to human beings on Earth.

This challenge is all part of God's plan for humankind. Those who meet the challenge and resist temptation successfully get to go to heaven; those who don't join the fallen angels in hell. This account of the fallen angels became a popular standard view, especially after it became the subject of the famous epic poem, *Paradise Lost*, written in 1667 by John Milton. Milton's fallen angels build their own city in hell, known as *Pandemonium*.

The Devil Makes You Do It

You know you're living in a hell of your own devising when the things you love most are great sources of conflict and unhappiness. In traditional religious terms, these things might be seen as sins of the flesh. In psychological terms, these things are obsessions and compulsions.

Winged Words

The word **pandemonium**, meaning chaotic uproar, was coined by poet John Milton as the name of the capital city in hell. The word is Latinized Greek for "place of all demons."

Satan tempting Christ with earthly power, by Gustave Dore.

The fall of the rebel angels, one of Dore's illustrations for Paradise Lost.

Milton really did his homework before writing *Paradise Lost*, which provides lots of background information on the fallen angels. Check out these excerpts from Milton's catalog of the lost from Book I, lines 392–482:

First Moloch, horrid king besmeared with blood
Of human sacrifice and parents' tears
Though for the noise of Drums and Timbrels loud
Their children's cries unheard, that passed through fire
To his grim idol.

(Children are sacrificed to Moloch and their parents can't hear their cries because the demonic ritual celebrations are too loud. Is that mean or what?)

Next Chemos, th' obscene dread of Moab's sons...
Peor, his other name, when he enticed
Israel in Sittim on their March from Nile
To do him wanton rites, which cost them woe.

(The Israelites lost faith in God during the exodus from Egypt and started worshipping Peor by doing kinky things.)

With these in troop
Came Astoreth, whom the Phoenicians called
Astarte, Queen of Heaven, with crescent horns
To whose bright image nightly by the moon
Sidonian virgins paid their vows and songs.

(Astarte's "horns" are the corners of the crescent moon.)

Thammuz came next behind
Whose annual wound in Lebannon allured
The Syrian damsels to lament his fate
In amorous ditties all a Summer's day.

(According to legend, Thammuz is god of a river that flows red with blood every summer.)

Next came one
Who mourned in earnest, when the captive ark
Maimed his brute image, head and hands lopped off
In his own temple...
Dagon his name, sea monster, upward man
And downward fish.

(Dagon fell over when the Ark of the Covenant—a receptacle commissioned by Yahweh to hold holy texts—was set beside his statue. When the statue hit the ground, it's head and hands broke off.)

After these appeared…
Osirus, Isis, Orus, and their train,
With monstrous shapes and sorceries abused
Fanatic Egypt and her priests to seek
Their wandering gods disguised in brutish forms
Rather than human.

(These Egyptian gods have human bodies and the heads of animals.)

Revelations

As you can see, Milton identifies pagan gods and goddesses as fallen angels. This practice goes back to the Old Testament, which demonized the gods of other (non-Jewish) religions in order to promote monotheism. This move presents everything about pagan religions in a bad light, suggesting that they are all about sex, violence, bestiality, and ignorant superstition. Of course, this highly critical view ignores the polytheistic roots of monotheism, many of which are evident in myths about angels—the good ones as well as the bad.

Milton's Pandemonium is just one suggestion for where the fallen angels reside. (In Milton's poem, a region known as Chaos separates hell and Pandemonium from Earth.) An alternative (and much older) view is that the fallen angels are imprisoned within the earth, or even somewhere on the surface of the earth. The Second Book of Enoch says that some of them suffer torment in the second heaven, not far from paradise. As Enoch (see Chapter 10) passes through, they ask him to pray to God for them. The same book says the Nephilim are imprisoned in the fifth heaven.

Souls on Sale

Although fallen angels have been imprisoned for their despicable crimes against God and humanity, many believe they have at least limited power and freedom, enabling them to cause trouble on Earth. Sources disagree in regard to Satan's power over humanity on Earth. Some say Satan and the fallen angels are stuck in hell where they have power only over the lost souls who are condemned to an afterlife of endless torment. Others say that devils walk the earth and interfere in the lives of mortal humans. Somewhere in the middle is the view that devils can appear on Earth only when summoned through black magic.

Many stories and legends tell of satanic temptations in which the devil comes into our world and attempts to win peoples' souls by doing them favors. A famous example is the legend of Faust, an astrologer who sells his soul for 24 years added on to his life, during which he will enjoy, power, knowledge, and wealth.

Faust the magician casting a magic spell in an etching by Rembrandt.

The legend is based on an actual astrologer and magician, Dr. Johann Faust, who became notorious in 16th-century Germany for seeking forbidden knowledge. His story became the subject of famous plays by Shakespeare's contemporary, Christopher Marlowe (1564–1593), and by the German Romantic poet, Johann Wolfgang Von Goethe (1749–1832). Satan's agent is the snide demon known as Mephistopheles, who provides Faust with all he desires, including the legendary beauty Helen of Troy as a mistress. Needless to say, Faust gets what's coming to him in the end.

A more recent tale of demonic temptation is Ira Levin's novel, *Rosemary's Baby*, made into a film directed by Roman Polanski in 1968. As in Faust, an ambitious man makes a bargain with Satan. Unlike the Faust legend, the man's soul isn't part of the deal. Instead, the devil gets to impregnate the man's wife, played by Mia Farrow. The child is to become the satanic messiah.

Wing Tip

Some people regard reckless types as evil or foolish. It may be more accurate, however, to think of them as trying to best the devil.

Rosemary's Baby doesn't spatter blood and guts all over the place like most horror movies, but it's still pretty scary, relying on suspense, rather than gore, to induce creepy feelings in the audience. The devil is played by ex-policeman and occultist Anton LaVey, who founded the Church of Satan in 1966 and wrote the occult bestseller, *The Satanic Bible* (1969).

The Devil's Countries

Satan and other supernatural forces of evil were frequently associated with a political and religious schism in the ancient world. Rival religious and philosophical viewpoints were held by Greek and Roman pagans, mainstream Jews, Jewish sects such as the Essenes of the Qumran settlement, Christians, and Christian offshoots including Gnostics. These groups often criticized rival groups by linking them to satanic activity.

Name-Calling

One way Jews and Christians put down pagan religions was to demonize their gods, regarding them as devils or fallen angels. Beelzebub is an early example of a pagan god who became a Jewish devil. Some early Christians regarded the gods of the Romans as devils. This helps to explain why Roman officials so harshly persecuted Christians during the spread of the new religion.

Radical Jewish and Christian sects also used Satan and other devils to criticize the Jewish and Christian mainstream. The New Testament Gospels represent Jesus as struggling simultaneously against the Jewish scribes and Pharisees and against Satan and other devils and demons. Satan tries to persuade Jesus to abandon his mission by offering him earthly authority such as that enjoyed by Jewish priests and Roman magistrates. The implication here is that such authority stems from satanic influence.

Winged Words

An **ethnarch** is the guardian angel of an entire country. In a recent book, theologian and literary critic Herald Bloom (see Appendix A) named the angel Metatron as the ethnarch of the United States.

Look Homeward Angel

Many Jews believed that each nation was watched over by its own national angel. Since Biblical times, such national angels are called *ethnarchs*. Legend says that God assigned the ethnarchs to each nation when people began speaking different languages after construction on the tower of Babel came to halt. (See Genesis 11:1–9 for the story of the Tower of Babel, an edifice designed to reach up to heaven.) Ethnarchs might be good or evil and could account for a nation's moral character.

The Book of Daniel names Michael, one of the good angels, as a prince in charge the nation of Israel. Some Jewish legends name evil angels as the ethnarchs of

Israel's enemies. The fallen angels Dubbiel, Sammael, and Rehab are sometimes referred to as the ethnarchs of Persia, Rome, and Egypt, respectively. The fact that evil angels guided these nations explained why they were enemies to the nation of Israel.

Inner Demons

Just as, according to legend, nations could be influenced by evil angels, so too could people. Usually, however, your guardian angel is considered to be a good angel, who exerts a subtle but positive influence on your life. Conversely, evil influence is usually attributed to demonic possession. Demons who possess human beings don't waste their time tossing banana peels in their paths. Instead, they crawl right inside people's bodies and make them sick or control them like puppets without their knowledge.

Their Own Worst Enemies

According to another time-honored tradition, good and evil spirits have like and equal influence. The early Christian writer known as Origen popularized the idea that an angel and a devil influence each of us. This notion has been trotted out in TV shows and cartoons of the 20th century to dramatize struggles between good and evil in such characters as Spanky of *The Little Rascals*, Fred Flintstone, Homer Simpson, and Sylvester the Cat.

Revelations

A medieval concept of inner struggle is called "psychomachia," from the Greek for "soul battle." Psychomachia was represented in allegorical writings depicting personified abstractions such as Temperance and Gluttony dressed up as knights jousting with one another. Psychomachia between one's personal angel and devil remains a popular idea, especially in cartoons that show a tiny devil with a pitchfork attacking a tiny angel, often shown with a halo and harp. Both the angel and devil are aspects of the personality of someone who is torn between a good and evil course of action.

A related idea is Jerome's notion that if you sin, you drive away your guardian angel. A contrasting view is set forward by Ambrose, who says that righteous people don't have guardian angels, since they have no need of them. (Jerome, Ambrose, and Origen are among the writers known as "fathers of the church," who were influential in establishing church doctrine in the first millennium C.E.)

Happy Landing

Fallen angels tend to stand for evil, as opposed to the uncorrupted, perfectly good angels. Not all angel sources see things in these stark dualist terms, however. According to one legend, there was a group of angels who chose to remain neutral during the war in heaven, refusing to fight for either side. A version of this story says that the neutral angels took up residence on Earth and became human beings.

Another account of angels who choose to become human takes place in Wim Wenders' film of 1987, *Wings of Desire*. This movie stars Peter Falk as an angel who steps down from heaven to become human. He does this in order to enjoy earthly pleasures unavailable in heaven, such as coffee and cigarettes!

Finally, there is a widely recognized (but rarely acknowledged) tradition of Earth-bound, flightless angels who are only superficially connected with God. These are minor—even piddling—spirits who preside over exasperating events like the stubbing of toes and unexpectedly high credit-card bills. These angels are commonly invoked in such situations as witnesses of human annoyance.

Here's a list of some of the better-known angels of irritation. How many have you called upon lately?

➤ *Jumpin' Jehosephat.* Named for an Israelite king from the Bible whose most memorable deed was not changing his silly name, J.J. incites people to do unexplainable things that tick other people off.

➤ *Jiminy Cricket.* Also known to Scandinavian Americans as Yumpin' Yiminy, he is the patron of flummoxation and dad-blastedness. His lovely crooning voice is legendary, thanks to the years he spent as the guardian insect of the fabled liar, Pinnochio.

Wing Tip

One of the Ten Commandments says, "Thou shalt not take the Lord's name in vain" (that is, "don't swear"). But the Bible doesn't say not to use words that sound like swearing, such as "consarn it," "dad-blame it," "heck," etc., so go ahead and vent your frustration, gosh darn it!

➤ *Cheese and Crackers.* These twin apparitions preside over human mistakes and ineptitude.

➤ *Gee Whiz.* The patron of juvenile disappointment, invoked at bedtime, bathtime, and whenever the TV is turned off. He intercedes on behalf of those who whine to him in the name of his father, Gosh Golly.

➤ *Jeez Louise.* The older sister of Gee Whiz, she is the angel in charge of getting yelled at for not taking out the trash.

➤ *Holy Moly.* Born in a chariot drawn by Holy Cow, Moly is the angel of astonishment responsible for humiliating upsets in sporting events.

➤ *Mergatroid.* Invoked only when bewilderment and disgust fuse into a near mystical experience, this angel is the fabled son of Holy Moly and a monkey's uncle.

➤ *Shish Kabob.* This angel of dumbfoundation often appears in mixed company at the last possible second!

The Least You Need to Know

➤ In Zoroastrianism, evil angels can operate independently of good ones.

➤ In the Hebrew Bible, the Satan is the adversary who must do God's bidding.

➤ Many different demons and monsters from the Bible have since been lumped together as manifestations of Satan.

➤ Different sources attribute the fall of evil angels to lust and pride.

➤ Religious groups have a history of characterizing rival religions as demonic.

By the Book

Angels don't always play by the rules—at least not the rules invented by human beings. This makes them especially hard to pin down. At the same time, since it's an angel's job to span the gap between heaven and Earth, you can't really penalize them for flying out of bounds. Wherever they may be, you get the feeling they're supposed to be there, whether it's at the right hand of God or out in left field.

In fact, angels have a tendency to cause problems for religious authorities who have the job of deciding which ideas, beliefs, and practices should be adopted by their religion and which should be left out. In arguments and controversies between orthodox faith and revolutionary, radical beliefs, angels have a way of getting caught in the middle. They play an important role in religious thinking, but sometimes they threaten to become too important, at the expense of other powerful figures such as God, Jesus Christ, and human authorities.

Conflict and uncertainty about the importance of angels has played a part in attempts to codify religious thinking for thousands of years. These conflicts are reflected in the history of religious scriptures, and have helped determine which texts get accepted as Holy Writ and which texts get relegated to theological footnotes. Look at the religious writings that talk about angels, and you'll see that the angels rise and fall with the status of the scriptures.

Wing Tip

When you're on vacation or a business trip and you don't have any good reading material with you, try the top drawer of the dresser or night stand in your hotel room. Chances are you'll find a Bible, compliments of the Gideon Bible Society. You don't have to be a Christian believer to enjoy the great stories inside!

It Is Written

Angels play an important role in the beliefs of the big three monotheistic religions—Judaism, Christianity, and Islam—as divine beings that are subordinate to God. Angels are just one of many things these religions have in common. Another important shared trait is that all three are firmly based on scripture. They are "religions of the book," or "religions of the word"—the word of God, that is.

Most of what we know about angels in the ancient world comes from holy scripture and similar writings written thousands of years ago. This knowledge has been collected and reinterpreted in different ways by different people ever since. This chapter talks about the various books and kinds of writings that are the sources of angel lore in Western monotheism—especially sacred scripture, but also religious writings that didn't make it into Holy Writ.

A print by William Blake illustrates word processing as it may have been done back in the early days of Christianity.

Stop the Presses

God may have written the holy scriptures of religion, but it is the angels who are editors, publicists, marketing reps, and typesetters. Sometimes they even serve as holy ghost writers! Prophets and apostles help out too, of course, and the rest is religious history.

Religions of the word have writings that are set apart from other writings, thought to be the revealed word of God. Often, there are stories about how these writings got from God's word into book form. Moses received stone tablets with the Torah written on them during a famous conference with God on Mount Sinai. Many prophets received scrolls from angels. Often these symbolize inspiration, as when a scroll appears to Ezekiel and an angel tells him to eat it!

The Koran, the sacred book of the Muslims, was written in heaven where it remains as an inviolable testimony of God's word. It was dictated verbatim by the angel Dibril to the prophet Muhammad. According to the story, Muhammad was reluctant to assume the role of prophet. Dibril coerced him by smothering him with the book!

Joseph Smith founded the Protestant sect of Mormonism in the early 19th century. The angel Moroni, who is the resurrected soul of a historian living in the 5th century, visited Smith. During his life, Moroni and his father, Mormon, engraved the Book of Mormon onto golden plates. As an angel in America, Moroni showed the plates to Joseph Smith, who translated them into English with the help of special "specular stones," prepared by God.

Words on Words

Many ancient religions have a body of sacred writings that constitute the foundational ideas and beliefs of the religion. In addition, there may be commentaries that explain and supplement the original texts that get added on over the centuries. This is especially true of Judaism, the oldest of the major religions in the West.

There are many layers of Jewish religious writings, and they all include beliefs and stories about angels. The most important of these is the Hebrew Bible, known to Christians as the "Old Testament." This collection of sacred texts includes writings that go back to about 1000 B.C.E. Many of these writings are based on oral traditions that go back much further.

The Bible is actually a huge collection of texts by many different authors writing across a long stretch of history—from 1,000 B.C.E. to 100 C.E. At various times, these texts have been collected in batches and edited according to the practices and beliefs of the

The Devil Makes You Do It

Even though the Book of Mormon is supposed to have been revealed by the angel Moroni, Mormonism takes its name from Moroni's father, Mormon. Thus, it is not appropriate to refer to the religion as Moronism, as suggested by a character in Tony Kushner's play, *Angels in America*!

many religious communities that have drawn inspiration from them. Although the main work of putting the Bible together was accomplished long ago, the process of interpreting it still goes on as theologians (religious scholars, or God-ologists) translate, clarify, and adapt the meanings that have been handed down in written form.

Reading List

Through the process of elaborating on scripture, additional religious writings have been produced. Some of these are commentaries, interpretations, and guides for applying Biblical lore. Others are stories and legends that flesh out the often sketchy background of Biblical people and events. These are the most important writings in the history of Judaism, including scripture, commentary, and legendary background:

➤ *The Hebrew Bible.* Known to Christians as the "Old Testament," this is the collection of sacred scriptures recognized by the Jews, who do not accept Christian scriptures (the "New Testament").

➤ *The Torah.* Named from a term meaning "the law" or "the teaching," this consists of the first five books of the Hebrew Bible. It is also known as the Pentateuch, which means "five scrolls."

➤ *The Apocrypha and Pseudepigrapha.* Named for terms meaning "outside writings" and "falsely attributed writings," these religious texts, written from 200 B.C.E. to 100 C.E., were excluded from the official Bible by rabbinical decree.

➤ *The Dead Sea Scrolls.* Discovered in 1947, the scrolls include copies of known writings including the oldest known copies of many texts from the Bible, as well as newly discovered works resembling the Apocrypha and Pseudepigrapha.

➤ *The Talmud.* Written from 200 to 500 C.E., the Talmud consists of commentary on the Bible as well as sermons and religious lore known as Midrash.

➤ *The Zohar.* Written during the 13th century, the Zohar is the most important of the medieval Jewish writings. This is a book of magic and mysticism central to the tradition known as Cabala.

These books are the main sources of Jewish religious thought, belief, and lore, and include a gold mine of ideas and stories about angels. In addition, folk tales, legends, and philosophical and literary works augment the tradition of Jewish angel writings.

An Old Story

The Jewish Bible, which Christians call the "Old Testament," includes the Torah, which means "the teaching" or "the law." According to tradition, the Torah is the word of God, received by Moses on Mt. Sinai, inscribed on stone tablets. Many believe it was brought to Moses by angels. (Curiously, it is Christians who are especially fond of saying that the law was brought by angels, since this suggests Jewish law is not "God-given." Christians, therefore, are safe in not following it!) Because the law or

Torah consists of the first five books of the Bible, it is often referred to as the Pentateuch, which means "five scrolls."

Revelations

Since the Bible was written, Jews have avoided writing the full name of God. Not writing God's name symbolizes the belief that God is unknowable. Instead, only the consonants in the name are written, which correspond to the letters YHWH or JHVH. These letters in Hebrew are known as the *tetragrammaton* (from the Latin words, "four letters"). Christians have traditionally translated these letters as the name, "Jehovah." Theologians today recognize "Yahweh" as a more accurate translation.

The Torah represents a covenant between the Jews and their God, Yahweh. It contains God's commandments according to which they are to live as God's chosen people. God, in turn, promises them a homeland. The Hebrew Bible includes this covenant, as well as prophecies, poems, sayings, and stories of mythic and historical struggles of the Jews and their ancestors, beginning with the first human beings, Adam and Eve, and extending down through the legendary kings, David and Solomon.

These kings established the Jewish temple in Jerusalem, which was destroyed by invading Babylonians around 587 B.C.E. At this time, most of the Jews were exiled from Jerusalem. The destruction of their temple, together with their exile, may have prompted scribes, rabbis, and other Jews to preserve, copy, and organize the texts that later came to be known as the Hebrew Bible.

Revelations

The five books that make up the Torah are traditionally attributed to Moses, although theologians identify several authors, known as J, the Yahwist (or Jahwist); E, the Elohist; P, the Priestly author; D, the author of the Book of Deuteronomy; and R, the redactor (to redact is to edit or revise). A best-selling translation of *The Book of J* by poet David Rosenberg created a stir in 1990 by presenting much of the Hebrew Bible not as austere and solemn, but as playfully and humorously written. In an introduction to this translation, literary critic Harold Bloom suggested that J was a woman from the Jewish upper class.

Almost Holy

The Jews continued to produce religious writings during subsequent years. Many of these newer works are collected in books known as the Apocrypha and the Pseudepigrapha. Apocrypha means "secret, or outside, writings," so called because they were excluded from the collection of sacred scriptures that became part of the Bible. The Pseudepigraphic writings were also left out of the Bible. The name means "false attribution" and refers to the common practice of falsely claiming a particular text was written by a famous Biblical figure.

The Devil Makes You Do It

If you're a writer who dreams of having your work incorporated into holy scripture, don't hold your breath. Even if you claim your work was written by a Biblical prophet or patriarch like the "pseudepigraphic" writers did, it's unlikely to become Holy Writ!

Wing Tip

Keep in mind that what counts as part of the Bible for some religions doesn't count for others. The Jews rejected a number of Biblical texts that were preserved only in Greek but not in Hebrew, including the books of Tobit, Judith, Baruch, and 1 and 2 Maccabees. The Roman Catholics and the Eastern Orthodox Churches accepted these books as part of the Bible. Centuries later, the Protestants rejected these books.

Banned Books

In part, the Pseudepigrapha was excluded from the official Hebrew Bible because it is filled with stories about angels. Many of these stories contain prophecies that angels will transform the world. Such prophecies are known as apocalypses and often predict dire punishments in store for evil-doers.

Typically, angels are the ministers of divine justice in apocalyptic writing, playing the role of God's hit-men. Many apocalypses were written during a time when the Romans occupied Jerusalem and they foretold destruction to the Romans and their gods. This made them dangerous writings with the potential to stir up bad feelings and bring down official punishment.

In political terms, we might say that the early rabbis considered the books of the Apocrypha and the Pseudepigrapha too radical to be considered official religious scripture. Mainstream Jews were trying to exist peacefully under Roman rule and didn't want to make big religious waves and risk being punished by the government. In addition to this political motivation, there were theological reasons for leaving these books out of the Bible.

Although many Jewish authorities recognize the existence of angels, the faith holds that God is all-powerful and unrivaled in heaven. The early rabbis felt that the apocryphal and pseudepigraphic writings gave too much reverence to angels and not enough to God. By denying these books sacred status, they helped to standardize the Jewish faith along clear monotheistic lines. The angel stories in these non-Biblical texts were not lost, but they were afforded less religious importance than accounts in the Bible.

Scrolling by the Sea

The Apocrypha and Pseudepigrapha were not the only Jewish religious writings that got left out of the Hebrew Bible. In 1947, new writings were discovered, stored in clay jars in caves on the Eastern edge of the Dead Sea that were once inhabited by an ancient religious community now known as Qumran. These are the famous Dead Sea Scrolls. A shepherd in search of a wayward sheep discovered the first of these.

Many of the Dead Sea Scrolls include radical religious visions that resemble those found in the Apocrypha and Pseudepigrapha. The Qumran community was a Jewish sect that withdrew from the rest of society to practice religion in its own way. They believed that God would favor them and make them leaders of the Temple in Jerusalem (see Chapter 8 for more about the Temple). In addition to prophetic writings and the rules of the Qumran community, the scrolls also contain the earliest known copies of many Biblical texts. The scrolls date from approximately 100 B.C.E. to 70 C.E.

Study Guide

The Qumran community was only one of a number of Jewish groups struggling for survival in and around Jerusalem under Roman occupation. The Romans destroyed the Temple in Jerusalem a second time in 70 C.E. (the first time was around 587 B.C.E., when Babylon invaded Jerusalem). Deprived of their temple, Jewish rabbis turned to books as the best way of preserving their religion.

The early Jewish tradition of scriptural study eventually gave rise to the Talmud, written from 200–500 C.E. This large work, whose name means "instruction," explains and interprets the Bible and provides sermons and guidelines for life and worship as a Jew. Many Jews of today continue to regard the Talmud as a source of the most authoritative interpretations of scripture.

Wing Tip

Notice that the books of both the Old and New Testament have been organized into chapters and verses for easier reference. Jewish scholars divvied up the Hebrew Bible in the 9th century and Christian scholars did the same for the New Testament in the 13th century. Chapters and verses are the same in every Bible, no matter which version or translation.

Second Opinions

The Hebrew Bible is a foundation not only of Judaism but Christianity as well. Christians have adopted this book, calling it the "Old Testament," and have supplemented it with the New Testament, which tells the story of the coming of Christ and the formation of the early Christian Church.

The Good Book 2

The New Testament includes the four Gospels, which were written and compiled during the 1st century C.E. from thirty to fifty years after the death of Jesus. The

Winged Words

The **Messiah** is the King of the Jews whose coming is predicted in Biblical prophecy. The word means "anointed one" and refers to the ancient practice of pouring oint-ment on the heads of kings. Devout Jews still expect the Messiah to come and usher in the Kingdom of Heaven on Earth. Christians, of course, regard Jesus Christ as the Messiah.

Winged Words

The **apostles** are followers of Jesus. The term is often used to refer specifically to twelve disciples appointed by him to convey his teachings. Like "angel," "apostle" comes from a Greek word meaning "messenger."

Gospels tell Jesus' story and lay the groundwork for the way Christians have interpreted the Hebrew Bible ever since. Christians see Jesus Christ as the *Messiah* foretold in Jewish prophecy. In fulfilling the ancient prophecies, Jesus both draws on and modifies Jewish teachings in ways that Jews do not accept.

Also included in the New Testament are accounts of the *apostles*, the followers of Jesus, and their efforts to spread the message of Christianity, as well as the letters of the apostle Paul, written to the early churches providing advice on how to live as Christian communities. Like the early Jewish rabbis, Paul was concerned about the prolif-eration of angel worship that seemed to be obscuring the importance of God. He cautioned against angel worship since, in his view, the angels had outlived their impor-tance as go-betweens for God and humanity now that Christ had come to fill that role.

Buried in Books

Paul strongly influenced the authorities in the early Church as they decided which writings to include among the collection of sacred Christian texts. Just as the rabbis left many of the more radical religious texts out of the Hebrew Bible, the Church fathers decided to exclude Christian religious writings that did not reflect Christian theology as they accepted it. As a result, there are apocry-phal Christian as well as Jewish texts. These include gospels, such as the Gospel of Thomas and the Gospel of Truth, as well as accounts of acts of apostles.

Like the Dead Sea Scrolls, many of the apocryphal Chris-tian writings have been discovered in the 20th century. In 1945, an Arab farmer in Egypt discovered a jar contain-ing 13 leather-bound papyrus books buried near a big rock. These were the first of a large collection of 52 texts that became known as the Nag Hammadi library.

The books found at Nag Hammadi were written by an unorthodox group of early Christians known as Gnostics. They include many unorthodox beliefs about Jesus Christ and Christianity. For example, some deny that Jesus rose from the dead or was born to a virgin mother. They also include a distinct approach to angels. Some Gnostic teachings even attribute the creation of the world to angels, rather than God.

Many Gnostic beliefs were considered heretical and challenged the views of the early Christian Church. For this reason, Gnostic Christians evidently conducted many of their religious practices in secret. This may explain why the Gnostic writings at Nag Hammadi remained unknown for so long. While other early Christian writings were copied and spread throughout the ancient world, the Gnostic writings literally went underground.

Revelations

Paul, the apostle and saint, is one of the most important figures in Christianity. He was originally known as Saul of Tarsus, a fierce persecutor of Christians, but he converted to Christianity and changed his name to Paul after being temporarily struck blind on his way to Damascus. He became an important Christian missionary and many of his letters to early churches (some of which caution against the worship of angels) are part of the Bible. He was beheaded in Rome for his belief, whereupon, according to legend, milk instead of blood flowed from his veins.

Last Words

Despite the tendency to restrict the presence of radical religious visions in holy scripture, the New Testament concludes with the Book of Revelation, which foretells the destruction of the world as we know it. This prophecy, written by John of the Apocalypse, is chock-full of angels.

Angels appear to John and warn him of what is to come and tell him to spread the message. A war will take place in heaven in which angel armies do battle with one another. More angels, known as the four horsemen of the apocalypse, will bring about the end on Earth. They will spread famine, disease, and death throughout the world. Finally, when it's all over, righteous human beings will get new bodies and share eternal life with the angels.

The Devil Makes You Do It

The prophecies in the Book of Revelation figure prominently into the 1988 film, *The Seventh Sign*, a thriller starring Demi Moore and Jürgen Prochnow. The intriguing premise is that in the 20th century, Demi's unborn child will bring about the apocalypse foretold in the Bible.

Just as Jewish theologians continued to write commentaries and supplements to the Bible following the destruction of the Temple in Jerusalem, early Christian scholars did the same with the writings of the New Testament. Though these commentaries were not collected into a single book like the Talmud, many have been recognized as authoritative interpretations of Christian doctrine, including belief as applied to angels. They include the writings of Ignatius (50–107), Tatian (110–180), Irenaeus, (150–202), Origen (185–254), Augustine (354–430), and Thomas Aquinas (1225–1274).

The earlier commentators are known as the Church fathers. They exerted an influence on which writings became accepted as Christian scripture. Each "father" had a different set of preferences, but a consensus was ultimately formed based largely on how closely connected the author was thought to be to Christ.

Biblical Bloopers

According to the Christian Church, the Bible is the revealed word of God—God's message to humanity conveyed by means of divinely inspired writings. The word, however, doesn't always get through as God intended it. Over the years there have been some ungodly gaffs that have crept into various editions of the Bible. You'll want to think twice about heeding some of these Biblical boo-boos:

➤ *"Wicked" Bible.* Printed in London in 1632, it leaves out the word "not" from the seventh commandment, to read "Thou shalt commit adultery"!

➤ *"Rebecca's Camels" Bible.* Edition of 1823 that says in Genesis 24:61, "Rebecca arose, and her camels." The verse should read "…and her damsels"!

➤ *"Bug" Bible.* This Bible, printed in 1535, translates Psalm 91, which usually reads "Thou shalt not need to be afraid of any terror by night" to read "Thou shalt not need to be afraid of any bugs by night"!

➤ *"Placemakers" Bible.* This Bible of 1562 contains the uplifting sentiment from the Gospel of Matthew: "Blessed are the placemakers." The word should be "peacemakers"!

➤ *"Wife-hater's" Bible.* This 1810 edition has Jesus tell his followers that no one who does not hate "even his own wife" can be his disciple. The text should read "life"!

➤ *"Breeches" Bible.* Another name for the important Geneva Bible, first published in 1560. Here the translation of Genesis 3:7 says of Adam and Eve, "The eyes of them both were opened…and they sewed fig leaves together and made themselves breeches." The text should read "britches"!

➤ *"Discharge" Bible.* In this 1806 edition, the apostle Paul writes to Timothy, "I discharge thee before God and his angels…that thou observe these things." The verse should read "charge."

➤ *"Murderer's" Bible.* Instead of "murmurers" in Jude 16, this Bible of 1801 reads, "These are murderers, complainers, walking after their own lusts."

➤ *"Ears to Ear" Bible.* In this 1810 edition, Matthew proclaims "He who hath ears to ear, let him hear"! You guessed it, the text should have read "ears to hear"!

➤ *"Treacle" Bible.* This 1568 translation inserts the word for a popular English sweet in place of the word usually translated as "balm," to read "Is there no treacle in Gilead?"

➤ *"Printer's" Bible.* This Bible of 1702 contains a printer's error that turns out to be a self-fulfilling prophecy: King David complains that "Printers have persecuted me without cause." The line should read "princes"!

Revelations

One printer's mistake that proved to be of Biblical proportions did not involve the text of the Bible, but the illustrations that went with it. The infamous "Leda" Bible of 1572 includes woodcuts originally made for Ovid's *Metamorphosis*, a Latin book of Greek mythology. Among them are many inappropriate depictions of pagan myths, including a depiction of the god Zeus having sex with Leda in the form of a swan. The kinky prints caused an outrage!

Allah in the Family

Like Judaism and Christianity, the third major Western monotheistic religion, Islam, has its sacred scriptures, known as the Koran. According to Islamic tradition, the prophet Muhammad recited the Koran over a period of 23 years, beginning in 610 C.E. Muslims hold that an exact copy of the Koran exists in heaven.

The Koran contains the teachings of a new monotheistic religion that supplanted the older polytheistic beliefs of the Arabs. According to Muslims, the God of Islam, known as Allah, is the same God worshipped by Jews and Christians. In fact, the Koran mentions and accepts many of the Biblical prophecies and teachings. In the eyes of Muslims, Jesus is the great prophet of the Christians, much

Wing Tip

If you're interested in prophets and want to learn about how they lived and worked, try studying Muhammad. He's the only prophet of a major religion whose life is well known from historical sources. The others tend to be shrouded in mystery.

The Devil Makes You Do It

Be careful what you say about the infamous "satanic verses" of the Koran. Author Salmon Rushdie was condemned and received death threats from Muslims who were offended by what they felt was the disrespectful attitude of Rushdie's novel, *The Satanic Verses.*

as Muhammad is the prophet of Islam. This is not to say that the Muslims regard Jesus as equal in importance to their prophet; only that they accept many Jewish and Christian teachings.

According to tradition, Muhammad was prompted to recite by the angel Gabriel, who not only appeared to him, but also enveloped him in a suffocating embrace until he agreed to recite. The name Koran, in fact, means "recitation." Muhammad and his followers had many other encounters with angels. Some of these are mentioned in the Koran. Still others are described in the Hadith, or the Traditions of the Prophet, which supplies background and commentary on Muhammad and the Koran. The Koran and the literary tradition that has grown up around it have made important contributions to the angel lore of the world.

The Least You Need to Know

➤ Jews, Catholics, and Protestants accept different texts as part of sacred scripture.

➤ Many apocryphal religious writings emphasize the role of angels.

➤ The Talmud is a Jewish book of commentary on the Bible.

➤ The Dead Sea Scrolls and the Nag Hammadi library were both discovered in the 1940s.

➤ According to Muslim tradition, Muhammad originally recited the Koran at the behest of the angel Gabriel.

Part 2
Jewish Angels

The first full-fledged angel watchers date back from the time of the old Jewish patri-archs. They didn't learn angel-watching in a vacuum, though; they picked up ideas from other Mediterranean and Middle Eastern cultures. Some of the angels they saw were virtually no different from people. Others were completely unlike anything on Earth. Eventually they really perfected their angel-watching techniques, so by the time of later prophets, the Jews were seeing angels almost everywhere.

The Jewish patriarchs helped develop the concept of the angel hierarchy as we see it today. They are in many ways the first ones to put together what angels do and why they do it. It would be hard (if not downright impossible) to truly understand the mysteries of the angels and their actions without the help of these early observations.

Chapter 7

Old-Time Religion

In This Chapter

➤ Angels and the Biblical patriarchs

➤ The angel of the Lord

➤ Sarah and Hagar

➤ Abraham and Isaac

➤ Jacob's ladder and his wresting match

➤ Manna from heaven

The first books of the Bible—the five Books of Moses—show God and the angels taking a close, personal interest in the well-being of a man named Abraham and his descendants. These people were shepherds who lived a nomadic life following their flocks around through the desert. Even the wealthiest of them lived in tents.

The celestial beings appear to these shepherds to provide guidance and support, pose challenges, or just drop by for lunch. Whatever the occasion, however, they always have one thing foremost in their minds. Their plan was to turn a little tribe of shepherds into a great, powerful, God-fearing nation.

The many personal angel encounters in the Books of Moses all point toward the destiny of the descendants of Abraham, who came to be called the Israelites. They would go forth and multiply, and eventually get a homeland for themselves. To reach this goal, it would take a lot of trust in God and help from the angels.

Funny, You Don't Look Angelish

Angels go by many names in the Hebrew Bible. Typically, the Hebrew word *malakh*, or "messenger," identifies an angel. It's generally clear from the stories they appear in that these messengers aren't just from the local courier service. As God's messengers, they run special, and sometimes mysterious, errands.

In addition to the angels called malakh, the Bible makes several references to *cherubim*, special watch-dog angels set to protect holy places. These are such bizarre creatures that there's no confusing them with ordinary people or animals. The prophet Isaiah describes another kind of outlandish angel called *seraphim*. Again, these are marvels of earthshaking significance.

Only two angels in the Hebrew Bible are referred to by name. These are Michael and Gabriel, who appear in the Book of Daniel. There they are referred to simply as "men," but they are described as having a supernatural appearance. Sometimes the Bible refers to angels as children of God. This can be confusing, because the Bible sometimes refers to the Jewish people as children of God, too.

What can be even more confusing is the fact that a number of stories in the Bible refer to angels as "men," even though they are not really just people in any ordinary sense. In several places, it is obvious that these "men" are visitors to Earth from heaven. In other places, though, it's hard to tell that they aren't just human beings themselves as they interact directly and personally with people.

The Devil Makes You Do It

Watch out for gratuitous angels! In addition to the many angel appearances mentioned in the Bible, artists and interpreters have had a tendency to add more. Usually angels appear in the Old Testament for a specific and important reason and exert a powerful influence on those to whom they appear. Often, however, paintings and drawings of Biblical scenes depict angels by the dozens as part of the scenery.

Right Neighborly

Chapters 18 and 19 of Genesis tell of some "men" who appear to Abraham and Sarah. Two of these men turn out to be angels. A third is the Lord himself! Yet they seem to be ordinary human beings. Fortunately for them, Abraham and Sarah treat God and the angels with great kindness and respect, providing them with food and a place to rest from their travels.

Abraham and Sarah spend time with God and the angels as if they were ordinary visitors passing through on their way somewhere. There seems to be nothing unusual about them as they take off their sandals and eat their lunch underneath a tree. Then, as if he was making small talk, "the Lord" says, "I'll come back about this time next year, and Sarah will have a son."

Dore's depiction of Abraham's angelic visitors.

Now, having children was tremendously important to most people in ancient times. This was especially true of sons, since they enabled the family name to be carried on.

Children, though, were something of a sore subject with Sarah. She had tried unsuccessfully to have kids ever since she married Abraham. In fact, she was so determined to give Abraham a child that she told him to sleep with Hagar, her Egyptian slave girl. As a result, Abraham got the son he wanted but, as you might imagine, it made Sarah's blood boil to think of it.

By the time God and the angels paid their visit, Sarah was too old to have children. In fact, she was ninety. Abraham, at ninety-nine, was no spring chicken either. So, when God said she would have a son, she laughed—possibly a bitter laugh. But God said he was serious, and asked, "Is anything impossible for the Lord?" Then Sarah lied and said "I didn't laugh," and God said, "Oh, yes you did." Incidentally, the child was named Isaac, which means "laughter."

This story shows how cozy and casual angel encounters in the Old Testament could be. You'd

Wing Tip

Keep in mind that people wrote the Bible from a deeply patriarchal culture that regarded the transmission of the father's name through his bloodlines as a matter of paramount importance. This patriarchal priority is reflected in the traditional conception of God as "God the Father." Feminist theologians of this century have been working to change the view of God as male in order to promote femaleness as equally divine.

think it was a meeting with Sarah's gynecologist! Yet even though it wasn't characterized by the visionary pyrotechnics that go along with some of the more dramatic angel appearances in the Bible, the meeting meant a lot to Sarah and Abraham. It meant a lot for the history of the Jews, too, since the son Sarah was about to conceive was their ancestor, Isaac, who became the father of Jacob, whose name was changed to Israel, the namesake of the Jewish people.

Playing Favorites

Many of the angel stories in the early books of the Bible tell of angels who appear to Abraham and his descendants to offer support, comfort, and encouragement. Or else they appear to put them to a test. In either case, God and the angels have a clear, particular concern for the group who became known as the people of Israel. God is even referred to in family terms as "the God of Abraham." Abraham, Isaac, Jacob, and Jacob's sons are known collectively as the Biblical *patriarchs*. A patriarch is a ruling father. Paternal authority in the Bible tends to enforce rules aimed at maintaining the physical, spiritual, and cultural purity of the Jews. In short, patriarchal rules say not to worship strange gods, eat strange foods, or sleep with strange women.

The God of Abraham and his angels repeatedly promise to make a nation out of Abraham's line and to make them possessors of a homeland. As you might expect, this gives the people of Israel a big advantage over other people competing for territory in the Near East. At the same time, it also involves a special responsibility on their part to do what God wants.

Winged Words

A **patriarch** is a father who is the ruler of clan. The term is used specifically to refer to Abraham, Isaac, Jacob, and Jacob's sons, who were absolute rulers of their families. This was before Israel recognized priests or kings, so the patriarchs filled these roles.

If Looks Could Kill

Even though Abraham and his descendants have a remarkably intimate connection with God and the angels, they feel fear and awe in their presence. They evidently believed that anyone who looked upon God would die instantly. This helps explain the terror they often felt on encountering angels.

The Devil Makes You Do It

You might want to think twice about going out in search of angels. The Bible suggests that looking at an angel can cause death!

Angels, after all, represent God, so seeing an angel is not so different from seeing the Almighty himself. After Hagar met with an angel, she said she was amazed that she had seen God and still remained alive. Similarly, after wrestling with an angel, Jacob gave the place where he wrestled the name of Peniel, which means "the face of God," because he felt he had seen God and lived.

Covering for God

The Hebrew Bible in several places mentions "the angel of the Lord," who is often hard to distinguish from God. In some stories, it seems that the angel of the Lord *is* the Lord. For example, when God appears to Moses in the form of a burning bush in Exodus 3:1–10, he is first referred to as the "angel of the Lord." Shortly afterward, it is God who is said to speak from the burning bush, saying "I am the God of your forefathers."

In this story, the "angel of the Lord" seems to be an appearance of God. In other stories too, the angel of the Lord may be God appearing as an angel. Or the angel of the Lord may be a distinct celestial being who is God's special representative on Earth. In fact, scholars disagree on this point, and offer various accounts of what this angel is.

Word Up

Some Christian theologians have said that the angel of the Lord who appears in the Old Testament is actually Christ, prior to becoming incarnated on Earth as Jesus. Thus, the angel of the Lord may be equated with "the *logos*," the word that was present with God from before the beginning of the universe. Many object to this view since it finds newer, Christian meanings in ancient Hebrew scriptures that were written by people who never heard of Jesus Christ or the logos.

Revelations

Christians have a long tradition of reading the Hebrew Bible, or "Old Testament," as an anticipation of the coming of Jesus Christ. They have identified many pre-Christian Christlike figures, called "types of Christ," including Moses, Isaac, and Samson. Christians see the stories of these figures not only as accounts of Jewish history, but as metaphors for the story of Jesus. They say that similarities between Jesus and these older figures show that God had Jesus in mind from the beginning. Differences, on the other hand, show that Old Testament teachings need to be completed, fulfilled, and illuminated by Jesus. In fact, this traditional way of reading the Old Testament goes back to Jesus himself, who calls himself "the bread of life," in comparison with the manna eaten by the Israelites in the wilderness.

A more down-to-earth explanation for the confusing presence of the angel of the Lord is that it represents an editorial decision on the part of ancient scribes and scholars who were uncomfortable with the idea of God simply appearing directly to human beings. It may be that these scholars went through whatever scriptures that were available to them and substituted "angel of the Lord" for "God" in places where God appears.

The Bible is inconsistent in that it refers sometimes to the angel of the Lord and other times to the Lord himself, possibly because the editors missed a number of places. This may be why the celestial being that appears to Moses in the burning bush is called both the angel of the Lord and God himself. Then again, it may simply be that the ancient Jews were comfortable thinking of the angel of the Lord both as God and as God's representative.

Family Secrets

The first angel mentioned in the Bible to appear in a helpful role is "the angel of the Lord." This angel appears to Sarah's slave girl, Hagar, who gave birth to Abraham's first son, Ishmael. Even though it was Sarah's idea for Abraham to sleep with Hagar, she became terribly jealous and mistreated Hagar. Hagar got fed up and ran away into the wilderness.

The angel of the Lord appeared in order to talk things over and persuade Hagar to return to Sarah and put up with Sarah's abuse. She would be rewarded for her patience with a son who would found an entire nation. In fact, the Muslims regard Hagar's son Ishmael as their ancestor. Just as Sarah and Abraham's son Isaac founded the nation of Israel, Hagar and Abraham's son Ishmael founded the nation that later became known as Islam.

Revelations

According to Islamic tradition, Ishmael and Abraham went to Mecca where they built a shrine to God, known as the Kabah. (This shrine was built independently of the religious developments of the Israelites by pagan Meccans, long before the rise of Islam.) Many centuries later, the Islamic people looked to Ishmael as the first Muslim, who practiced Islam long before its prophet, Muhammad, spread the faith to the rest of the Arab world. Thus Muslims see their religion as being older than Judaism, even though it did not become established until the 7th century C.E. The Kabah is a large black stone that Muslims on pilgrimage to Mecca touch or kiss to show their devotion. Some scientists believe it is an asteroid that fell to Earth in ancient times.

An angel helped Hagar once again, this time when Sarah drove her and Ishmael away out of jealousy. Again, the setting for the appearance was the wilderness. Hagar and her child Ishmael had no more water left, and Hagar had given up in despair, turning away so as not to have to see her son die of thirst. Just then, an angel appeared and reassured Hagar that God was with her son and pointed out a well with water for them to drink.

Angels seem to like breaking the news to women that they are, or are about to become, pregnant. The angel of the Lord appeared to the wife of Manoah to say that she would have a son who would deliver the people of Israel from the power of the Philistines. This was the mighty Samson. In the New Testament, an angel appeared to the Virgin Mary to say Jesus was on the way. This angel came to be known as the Angel of the Annunciation.

Something to Offer

The angel of the Lord reappears in one of the most famous—and strange—stories of the Hebrew Bible, the story of Abraham and Isaac. As in the episode of Moses and the burning bush, "God" and "the angel of the Lord" appear interchangeably. God appears to Abraham and tells him to make a sacrifice of his son, Isaac. He tells him when, where, and how, but he doesn't say why.

No Father-Son Picnic

Abraham, despite his love for Isaac, doesn't ask any questions, but carries out the instructions. Suspense builds as Abraham and Isaac make the journey to the land of Moriah and gather wood for the sacrificial fire. The trip takes three days, which must have been murder, considering what had to have been going through Abraham's mind. Can you imagine trying to make small talk under those circumstances?

"Dad, can we stop off for some root-beer floats on the way home?"—"We'll see, son."

"Is God a nice guy? Did he say he likes us? Will he let me be a prophet when I grow up?"—"We'll see, son."

"Are we there yet?"—"Don't be so impatient."

Wing Tip

The 19th-century Danish philosopher, Soren Kierkegaard, discusses the story of Abraham and Issac in his famous work, *Fear and Trembling*. The story exemplifies Kierkegaard's belief that, even though we can't understand God, we must take a leap of faith and believe in him anyway. The story also supplies inspiration for the Bob Dylan song, "Highway 51."

The Devil Makes You Do It

You should probably think twice about killing someone, even if you think it's God telling you to do it. Keep in mind, you're not a Biblical patriarch, so you don't have the authority Abraham had to do crazy things. Also, during Abraham's time, the commandment "Thou shalt not kill" hadn't been handed down yet. These days, killing is a definite no-no.

"Can I light the fire for the sacrifice? I'll be real careful not to burn myself."—"Not this time, son."

"Dad, I think we should sacrifice a goat instead of a sheep. I hate the sound of a sacrificial sheep bleating. Don't you?"—"Sheep, goat, what's the difference?"

"What's the matter, Dad, swallow some sand or something?"

"Are we there yet?"

Fit to Be Tied

Finally, father and son arrive at their destination and prepare the altar. Abraham ties Isaac up and puts him on top of the firewood on the altar. By this time, you'd think Isaac would have got the idea that something funny was going on. But the story doesn't say.

The reader is left to imagine Isaac's confusion and later, fear, as Abraham ties him up. Some interpreters believe Isaac figured out what was going on, but didn't resist. Instead, he obeyed the word of God without question just as Abraham was doing. Also left to the imagination is Abraham's anguish as he obeys God's commands. All we are told is that he "stretched forth his hand and took the knife to slay his son…"

But just in time—you guessed it—the angel of the Lord, alias God, says no. (Commentators since the story was written have said that the intervening angel was Michael, who is known for his fondness for human beings.) God was only testing Abraham on his faith and obedience—and old Abe got an A+.

Just Kidding!

The Talmud says the whole thing was Satan's idea. He persuaded God to put Abraham to the test. Then he tried to persuade Abraham to refuse God's command. Then he tried to get Isaac to rebel. Like Job who came later, Abraham and Isaac refused to turn their backs on God, even though they didn't understand why he was putting them through hell.

At some point, Abraham turned around and saw a ram that had gotten its horns tangled in a thicket. He took the hint and sacrificed the ram instead of the kid. Then came the good news. The angel announced that he would multiply Abraham's descendants until they matched the number of stars in the sky and grains of sand on the beach. "And in thy seed [offspring] shall all the nations of the earth be blessed; because thou hast heard my voice."

Again, we can only imagine what took place after the sacrifice:

"Dad, you weren't really gonna go through with that, were, you?"

"Heck no, I was just keeping up appearances so God would multiply our descendants like sand on the beach."

"That's what I thought. Good thinkin', Dad."

> **Revelations**
>
> The Bible doesn't say how Abraham and Isaac got along in the immediate aftermath of the sacrifice. In fact, rabbinical scholars have noted that Isaac is not mentioned again where the Bible tells of Abraham's return from the mountain. Some have interpreted this to suggest that Isaac didn't return home with Abraham, preferring to keep away from his father. This would certainly make sense under the circumstances!

Up the Ladder

God and the angels were not shy about showing support for Abraham and his descendants. One of their most spectacular displays was made for Isaac's son, Jacob. Jacob had left home and had gone off in search of his uncle Laban's place where he was to find a wife. On the way he stopped for the night and dreamed he saw a ladder rising out of the ground and stretching all the way up to heaven.

Jacob's ladder, by Gustave Dore.

Wing Tip

If you want to learn the names of all Jacob's sons in order, check out the Webber-Rice musical, *Joseph and the Amazing Technicolor Dreamcoat*, which recounts the adventures of Jacob's son Joseph and includes a tongue-twisting song naming the whole clan.

Going up and down the ladder were "the angels of God." At the top of the ladder, looking down from heaven, was God himself, who said that the land where Jacob lay would someday belong to his descendants, who would be as "the dust of the earth" or, in other words, numerous.

The Man at the top of the ladder didn't lie. As it happened, Jacob went on to marry his uncle's two daughters, who proceeded to hold a contest to see which of them could have the most sons. They each got their slave girls in on the action, too, as surrogate mothers. When the dust had settled, Jacob found himself with a dozen sons. Legend has it that each son founded one of the twelve tribes of Israel.

Stellar Match-Up

While staying with his uncle Laban, Jacob not only got lots of children but also became wealthy, with big herds of sheep, goats, oxen, asses, and camels. After twenty years of hard work, he decided it was time to return to his homeland with his herds and his family. On his way he had one of the most memorable of all Biblical angel encounters.

Jacob learned that his brother Esau was coming to meet him and was worried because there had been bad blood between the two in the past. Esau had threatened to kill Jacob for tricking their father Isaac into bestowing on Jacob his blessing, putting him in charge of his brothers. Jacob was afraid Esau and his men would kill him and his entire family. He sent his family and his herds up ahead and remained behind with his worries as night fell.

At that point an angel appeared. You might think the angel would have said, "Don't worry Jacob, everything's going to be okay. God and I are watching out for you." But no. The angel didn't say anything. Instead, for reasons we can only guess at, the two started wrestling.

Surprisingly, Jacob held his own against his angelic opponent, despite the fact that the angel hit Jacob so hard in the thigh that he dislocated his hip. Jacob held out until morning when the angel finally said, "Let me go." Jacob said he wouldn't let go unless the angel blessed him, which he did. He gave Jacob the new name of Israel, which means "God strove."

The story goes to show that even if God likes you, it doesn't necessarily mean things are going to be easy. God sometimes likes to watch people struggle. The story also shows that imaginary problems are often much worse than the real thing. It turned out Esau had no intention of hurting Jacob or his family.

Jacob wrestles with the angel, by Gustave Dore.

More Heavenly Help

Things were not easy for the Israelites. Abraham's descendants became enslaved in Egypt where they lived in bondage for many years before making their escape led by Moses and, at times, by pillars of fire and clouds representing the angel of the Lord. The Bible says that the angel led the people. In addition, tradition has given angels credit for other kinds of assistance.

Written in Stone

Many theologians have suggested that when Moses went off by himself up Mt. Sinai to receive the ten commandments, the angels wrote them down on stone tablets. These commandments were the laws God's chosen people were to live by. In writing out the commandments, the angels bridged a yawning gap between divine and human law, putting everyone on the same page.

Sadly for them, not all the Israelites stuck to the commandments. They abandoned God and made an idol in the form of a golden calf. As a result, despite their divine guidance, Moses and his people spent decades wandering in the wilderness unable

Wing Tip

Keep in mind that people in ancient times took a pragmatic attitude toward religious belief. If your god didn't work for you, it probably meant that it was time to get a new god who did. This helps explain some of the religious flip-flopping of the Israelites.

to find the land that God had promised them. During this time, the Israelites faced many hardships, including hunger. At one point, they would have starved, were it not for some timely angelic assistance.

Angel Food

As you may remember, Abraham provided a meal for some angels who were tired and hungry from their travels. When the Israelites were lost in the wilderness, the angels took the opportunity to return the favor. At least, that's how many theologians explain the sudden appearance of the edible stuff the Bible calls "manna."

Manna is a sweet, bread-like food that appeared magically on the ground, like morning dew, to feed the Israelites. Some say that the manna actually refers to a liquid substance secreted at night by a kind of tree called a tamarisk. This substance drops to the ground and hardens by morning. Others, including the author of Psalm 78, say that it is the bread of angels.

Revelations

Jewish legend says a good deal about manna that you won't find in the Bible. For example, manna is said to be ground by angels in a mill in the third heaven (see Chapter 3). Humans who eat it become as strong as angels and don't need to evacuate! You don't have to cook it, and it tastes like anything you happen to be hungry for, except to the heathen, to whom it tastes bitter. Even though it appears on the ground, it's always clean because the ground has first been swept by the wind and rinsed by rain. What's more, the manna is encased in frozen dew. Lawsuits could supposedly be decided according to where the manna appeared every morning. It is also said to melt into rivers that the pious will drink from in the next life.

The idea that angels need to eat is one more indication of just how similar, according to the Bible, they can be to human beings. They can be very different too, especially those that appear in prophecy. These weird prophetic angel visions are the subject of the following chapter.

The Least You Need to Know

➤ God and the angels promised to make Abraham and his descendants a great nation.

➤ The Muslims trace their ancestry to Ishmael, Abraham's son by Hagar, an Egyptian slave girl.

➤ The angel of the Lord may be a manifestation of God.

➤ God tested Abraham by asking him to sacrifice his own son. Luckily Abraham passed the test with flying colors, and his son was spared!

➤ Jacob was given the name "Israel" after wrestling with an angel.

➤ Manna is the food of the angels, eaten by the Israelites in the wilderness.

Big Visions

As you might imagine, receiving a prophetic message from God and figuring out what to do with it can be daunting and confusing—it's every bit as difficult as installing a new software program into your computer. Perhaps you've had this experience of trying to figure out a long set of perplexing instructions that seem to come from a totally different level of reality.

Chances are you needed to talk with the software company's support staff to make sure you understood the instructions—someone who knows what's going on who could answer your questions. Do the lightning flashes and the earthquake mean something is wrong? How can I keep the whole system from crashing? Should I make an icon for this application?

The same is true with prophets and their visions. They don't always know what the visions mean and what to do with them, so it's important for them to be able to get clarification and reassurance from somebody who really understands. That's why it's good to have angels around. They're like the support staff for God Incorporated.

Voice of the Nation

As the nation of Israel grew, human encounters with God and the angels were often less intimate than they were in the time of Abraham. God and the angels began appearing to individuals not just with personal messages, but with instructions for the entire nation. On the one hand, this development made angelic encounters even more fearsome and awe-inspiring. On the other hand, it meant that you didn't have to be a tribal ancestor for God to speak to you. You could be a prophet instead.

Dore's rendition of the prophet Ezekiel.

Gradually, the family-style rule of the patriarchs gave way and the Israelites came to be governed by judges, priests, and kings. Political pressures grew along with the nation, followed by turmoil from both within the nation and outside of it. As society and social problems became more complex, the word of God had to reach more people to take effect.

During these turbulent years, the voices of the prophets became a powerful and galvanizing influence. Israel's prophets came from all walks of life. Some were priests, some were insiders at the king's court, and some lived on the fringes of society. Yet all were deeply concerned about the threats they perceived to the nation of Israel.

Light Show

As we saw with the patriarchs, angels tended to arrive during times of crisis in the lives of those to whom they appeared. Often they spoke directly to the situation of the individual involved. This was not always so with the prophetic angels. Often, the reader is told little or nothing about the situation of the individual prophet. That is not what is important. What matters is the nation of Israel; the prophet is simply there to communicate God's will to the people.

Prophetic activity in the ancient holy land spanned the centuries from the time of the patriarchs to the early days of Christianity. Over the years, the prophets made many predictions. All of these tended to be variations on a single important message to the community: Shape up or face the consequences! Typically, these messages were accompanied by special effects such as thunder, lightning, fire, earthquakes, and, of course, angels.

Wing Tip

Some religions recognize only one prophet. For Muslims, Muhammad is "the Prophet." For Mormons, "the Prophet" is Joseph Smith. Most Christians and Jews, however, recognize numerous prophets. The Book of Joel foretells of a time when everyone in Israel will prophesy.

Revelations

Because Judaism and Christianity are based on two different interpretations of religious history, the two religions have a different view of what counts as prophecy in sacred scripture. Jews recognize the earlier prophets, whose writings are contained in Joshua, Judges, Samuel 1 and 2, and Kings 1 and 2, and the latter prophets, including Isaiah, Jeremiah, Ezekiel, and the twelve minor prophets from Hosea to Malachi. Christians recognize only the latter prophets as books of prophecy, to which they add the Book of Daniel.

Many prophecies took the form of mystic visions, seen in sleep or while awake. Angels played an important role in many of these. Some visionary angels played symbolic functions, representing particular manifestations of heavenly power, or pointing toward the prophetic destiny of people on Earth.

A prophetic vision of Zechariah, by Dore.

Other angels of prophecy served interpretive functions, explaining to the prophet (and his readers) the meanings of his bizarre visions. In this way, they filled the traditional angelic role of mediating between God and humanity. Together with interpreting, angels of prophecy helped sustain the prophet through the heady experience of the prophetic vision. After all, it's not easy standing face to face with God and his angels.

When angels appear in prophecy, they typically form part of what is known as the prophet's call. This is the vision that first shows that the prophet has special insight into the will of God and the fate of nations. In the prophet's call, God or the angels summon the prophet and give him his prophetic mission. Two of the great visionary angel encounters of all time occur in the calls of Isaiah and Ezekiel. They are visually bizarre, yet richly symbolic.

Prophecy is serious business, but that doesn't make it humorless. Prophets often presented their warnings as spoofs of legal hearings, official decrees, and funeral speeches for the dead. The joke is that God is the lawyer or official, and Israel's morality is the defendant or the dead person. Prophets sometimes drew attention to themselves by doing outrageous things like tearing up their clothes in public. They might be compared to performance artists of today.

Calling All Prophets

Isaiah heard his prophet's call in the year 742 B.C.E., the year of the death of Judah's King Uzziah, who had a long and seemingly prosperous reign. The wealthy were flourishing, but the poor were struggling amid unchecked social injustice. Other prophets, Amos and Hosea, had already started to spread the message that a day of reckoning was on the way. It was at this time that Isaiah went to the Temple in Jerusalem. Here, Isaiah reports that he saw God seated on a throne. According to tradition, the throne of God was positioned above the Ark of the Covenant contained within the Temple. Isaiah says the skirts of God's robe filled the Temple. God then appeared enormous in size, towering high above the Temple floor.

God was attended by an unspecified number of *seraphim* that flew around through the Temple. Each one had three pairs of wings. With one pair they covered their faces, possibly to protect themselves from the dazzling presence of God. With another pair they covered their feet. This indicates their modesty and respect for God.

As they flew, they chanted, "Holy, holy, holy is the Lord of Hosts; the whole Earth is full of his glory." Jewish scholars refer to this song as the Trisagion, a song of creation. Visionary cherubim in the Christian Book of Revelation picked up the words "Holy holy holy." Centuries later, in 1826 C.E., these words formed the opening lines of one of the most popular Christian hymns ever written in English.

Although this song has made generations of Christians happy to be in church, it filled Isaiah with terror. The sound shook the foundations of the Temple as smoke billowed forth from the altar. "Woe is me!" he cried. "I am lost, for I am a man of unclean lips and I dwell among a people of unclean lips; yet with these eyes I have seen the Lord of Hosts."

Winged Words

The word **seraphim** means "fiery ones" and is derived from the word for "serpent." Although Isaiah is the only Old Testament source to use the term, the Book of Numbers 21:6 speaks of poisonous (or fiery) serpents sent by God to punish the Israelites. This passage is sometimes taken to be the first mention of the seraphim.

Hot Lips

By "unclean lips" Isaiah did not mean that he and his people needed to wipe their mouths after eating. He meant that he and his people spoke profane speech that could not hope to do justice to the transcendent glory of God. Isaiah was afraid God would kill him in order to prevent him from telling of his vision in imperfect, "unclean" words.

Fortunately, one of the seraphs saw the problem and came up with the solution. He picked up a glowing coal from the altar in a pair of tongs and flew to Isaiah, touching him on the mouth with the hot coal. In this way, Isaiah's lips were spiritually and symbolically purified, enabling him to speak of God without profanity. "See," said the seraph, "this has touched your lips. Your iniquity has been removed and your sin is wiped away."

The seraph was not simply doing Isaiah a favor, but preparing him to receive God's words so that he could communicate them to the people. God's pronouncement did not contain good news. Just as Isaiah's lips had to be purified, so too was the entire nation in need of purification for the people's sins. God threatened to cause the cities to fall, the land to go to ruin, and the country to become desolate. Israel and Judah were in big trouble. Only through desolation could peace and righteousness be restored.

Bad News

In fact, Isaiah's prophecy came to pass. At least, that's one way of looking at the decline of Israelite sovereignty that followed, leading to the eventual destruction of Jerusalem. Just eight years later, in 734 B.C.E., most of Israel was annexed by the Assyrians. In 722, the northern capital of Samaria fell to Assyrian rule.

Revelations

Various Jewish prophets tell of a Mashiah ("Messiah" in English), or anointed one, a king who will vanquish the enemies of Israel. Some prophets suggest this will be a climatic event in the history of the world; others suggest a less grand scenario. Isaiah advised the Jewish king, Ahaz, not to make deals with the invading Assyrians but to rely on God to work things out. He then prophesied that a child named Immanuel, which means "God is with us," would be born as a sign of the coming destruction of Assyria. Christians have seized upon this prophecy as a foretelling of the coming of Christ. Many of the writings attributed to Isaiah were set to music by George Frederick Handel and included in his famous oratorio, *The Messiah* (1749), widely performed in church every Christmas season.

So the Israelites became vassals of Assyria. Things got even worse before they got better. In 587, the Babylonians invaded Jerusalem and destroyed the city, including the Temple that meant so much to the Israelites. The Ark of the Covenant was lost. Many, especially those of the upper classes, were exiled from their capital.

Troubled Waters

At the start of this period of exile, about 150 years after Isaiah received his call to prophesy, the exiled priest, Ezekiel, stood on the shore of the River Kebar in Chaldaea in southern Babylonia. A popular song of today, "By the Waters of Babylon," tells of the heartbreak felt by the exiles as they remembered their homeland. But while his fellow exiles wept, Ezekiel was called to prophesy. Ezekiel's call involved a vision that was even stranger and more heavily laden with symbolism than that of Isaiah.

Wing Tip

Next time you're exiled from your homeland, think about using the change in venue as an opportunity to have a profound religious, artistic, or intellectual experience that will change you forever.

A Rare Breed

Ezekiel saw a storm approaching. The storm symbolizes the coming wrath of God, but the storm clouds also carried the angels and God as they appeared in Ezekiel's vision. In the clouds were flashes of fire and bright light, and inside the fire in the sky were "four living creatures" with four faces and four wings each. Each had the face of a man, the face of a lion, the face of an eagle, and the face of an ox. These creatures have been subsequently identified as cherubim.

They had straight legs with hooves like a calf's that glittered like bronze. They didn't turn or flap their wings, but moved through the sky without moving their bodies, powered by spirit. One pair of wings were spread and the other folded across their bodies. Under the wings were human hands. Fire and lightning flashed back and forth among the creatures as they landed in front of Ezekiel.

Revelations

Ezekiel lived during an important time of transition for Judaism. With the destruction of the Temple in Jerusalem in 587 B.C.E., religious focus shifted from the temple and the sacrifices that were performed there to the idea of community and the study of the law. These two aspects of Judaism—law and community—have remained central to Jewish life throughout the centuries as large numbers of Jews have continued to live in exile through the ages.

Hot Wheels

Then Ezekiel noticed wheels on the ground next to the cherubim. These shone like topaz and the rims were covered with eyes. Inside each wheel was a smaller wheel, and together they could move in any of four directions without being steered. The wheels moved together with the cherubim, powered by their spirit. These wheels have been identified by later interpreters as the class of angels commonly called thrones, although sometimes they are called wheels instead.

The Devil Makes You Do It

Watch out for fiery chariots in the sky driven by angels from outer space! Some New Age interpreters of Ezekiel's vision say that he saw a UFO. The extraterrestrials on board have been credited with teaching human beings agriculture. Perhaps they returned to outer space. If not, they may be living in the undersea city of Atlantis!

These wheels and the winged cherubim resemble the Ark of the Covenant, which was covered with gold cherubim and, before being stored in the (now destroyed) Temple in Jerusalem, was sometimes wheeled around in a cart or wagon. The ark in the Temple, as you may remember, was exactly where Isaiah had his vision of God surrounded by the seraphim.

While Ezekiel's vision resembles the Ark of the Covenant, it exhibits some important differences too. The eyes on the wheels and the four faces on the cherubim, and the ability of the whole shebang to move in any direction, suggest the omnipresence of the throne of God which, before Ezekiel's time, was located specifically in the Temple at Jerusalem. Now that the Temple had been destroyed, the Jews needed to know that God still cared about them and could find them, even in exile in Babylonia. Ezekiel's vision symbolizes the power of God to see and move everywhere.

Hard to Swallow

Above the wheels and the cherubim, Ezekiel saw the image of God—the likeness of a human being glowing like fire, seated on a throne made out of sapphire. This was too much for the priest to cope with, and he fell on his face. A voice then told him to stand up as a spirit moved into his body and lifted him to his feet.

Standing before God with the spirit inside him, he received instructions to denounce Israel for rebelling against God. This was a typical assignment for a prophet. God's next demand, however, was pretty weird. Ezekiel was told to open his mouth and eat what God gave him.

God held out a scroll and unrolled it. On it was written words of woe and lamentation. God said, "Eat this scroll; then go and speak to the Israelites." Ezekiel was not exactly in a position to question God's orders. So he did what he was told and had a snack of sacred scripture. It turned out to taste as sweet as honey.

Familiar Faces

Ezekiel's vision, like Isaiah's, showed that he was qualified to communicate the word of God to the Israelites. The angels in both visions helped prepare the prophets to receive God's messages. These famous visions have inspired other religious and artistic visions of angels in the centuries to come.

Six-winged seraphim based on Isaiah's vision became a staple of religious art, found in Byzantine paintings and on Puritan gravestones. From Ezekiel's vision stems the interesting tradition of representing angels with eyes on their wings. The archangel Michael is often pictured with wings plumed with peacock's feathers, since the marks on peacock plumage resemble eyes.

Wing Tip

The tradition of representing Michael with peacock-plumed wings may stem partly from the Greek myth of Argus, a giant with eyes all over his body. When Argus was killed, the goddess Hera saved his eyes and stuck them on the tail feathers of her favorite bird, the peacock.

Driving Themselves Crazy

Many different traditions have drawn on Ezekiel's symbolism, steering the chariot-throne in new directions. One unusual tradition is the esoteric Jewish doctrine known as Merkabah mysticism. "Merkabah" means "chariot" and refers to God's chariot as depicted by Ezekiel.

Merkabah mysticism consists of teachings and practices that were kept highly secret. The basic idea seems to be that, by going through the proper rituals—including study, fasting, singing mystic hymns, and going into a trance—it is possible to ascend to the throne of God without actually having to die first. This mystic journey was considered perilous and involved passing through seven gates guarded by angels.

If you were not properly prepared for the journey, you could die or go crazy. The special hymns were supposedly those sung by the cherubim as they carried God's throne. Legend has it these same hymns were sung by the cows that pulled the Ark of the Covenant around from place to place.

Reading Between the Lions

An angel in Isaiah's vision purified him with a hot coal. A spirit entered Ezekiel's body and lifted him up to face God. These are significant acts of support, compensating for human weakness in the presence of the Almighty. Equally significant, though not as dramatic, is the act of interpreting prophetic visions of rams, lions, scrolls, and other mysterious apparitions. The prophets known as Daniel and Zechariah get angelic help in figuring out what their visions mean.

Revelations

The prophets of monotheism have their pagan counterparts, known as sibyls. Sibyls are women with a special connection to the oracle of Apollo and foretell the future by interpreting cryptic oracular messages. The first sibyl was named (what else?) Sibyl, and she was a wrinkled old woman who went into ecstatic trances, setting the precedent for this form of pagan prophecy. According to legend, the gods granted Sibyl a long life but forgot to give her eternal youth to go along with it.

Many sibylline oracular writings still exist. Most of these, like the apocalypses of the Judaic tradition, have a strong gloom-and-doom flavor. Some sibylline oracles incorporate Jewish and Christian beliefs, showing the influence of these religions on paganism. Renaissance painters often paired sibyls with prophets. Michaelangelo's great Sistine Chapel painting, for example, includes five Old Testament prophets standing opposite five sibyls.

Beastly Behavior

You need to be an angel in order to interpret the bizarre symbolism in the Book of Daniel. Daniel sees four beasts come out of the ocean. The first is a lion with eagle's wings—but it gets its wings clipped off and has to stand on two feet. The fourth beast has iron teeth and bronze claws and eats everything in its path.

It also has ten horns, but three of the horns fall out to make room for a new, smaller horn. This new horn has eyes and a mouth on it and speaks arrogantly about how great it is—you probably know the kind! The beast was killed and burnt, but that didn't stop the horn, which continued to wage war with the holy saints.

Daniel's interpreter is the angel Gabriel. This is the first of only two angels (the other is Michael) mentioned by name in the entire Hebrew Bible. Gabriel explains that the beasts represent kingdoms. The talking horn with eyes represents a powerful king who would take control of the earth. This king would be defeated in battle by the archangel Michael.

Despite these relatively minor roles in the Bible, Michael and Gabriel have become huge in angel legend that developed since Daniel's time. Michael is the angel *par excellence* of monotheism in general, often thought to be the chief of angels. His name means "who is as God." The Book of Revelation says that he will slay the dragon, Satan. As a result, he is often represented clad in armor and holding a sword.

Legend credits Michael with many noble deeds, from writing one of the psalms to restraining Abraham when he was about to sacrifice his son Isaac to God (see Chapter 7). He is said to have scales for weighing the souls of the dead, whom he conducts to heaven. He is even said to have acted as an attorney in defense of the nation of Israel when it was accused by the fallen angel Samael. He is the ethnarch, or prince, of the Nation of Israel, as well as a Catholic saint.

Gabriel is said to have appeared to the Virgin Mary, and to Joan of Arc. As Djibril, the Islamic equivalent of Gabriel, he (or she, since some say Gabriel is female) appeared to the prophet Muhammad and taught him the words of the entire Koran. The Talmud says Gabriel is the only angel who can speak every language, and that he helped the boy Moses before he became leader of the Israelites. Some say it was Gabriel who wrestled with Jacob in the desert. Gabriel is assigned the job of blowing the trumpet that will wake the dead on the Day of Judgment.

The Devil Makes You Do It

Don't get confused about which angels are mentioned in the Bible and which aren't. Gabriel and Michael are mentioned in the Hebrew Bible (Old Testament). Raphael is mentioned in the Apocrypha, accepted as part of the Bible by Catholics, but not by Jews or Protestants. Ariel is mentioned in the Book of Isaiah, but as another name for the city of Jerusalem, not as an angel. Ariel appears as an angel only outside the Bible.

Stay of Execution

Together with his prophetic visions, the Book of Daniel relates other, more personal, angel encounters. An angel appeared to save Daniel's friends, Shadrach, Meshach, and Abednego, who were condemned to be burnt in a furnace by the Babylonian king, Nebuchadnezzar. Nebuchadnezzar had made an idol out of gold and commanded everyone to worship it. When the three friends refused, they were tied up and thrown into the fire.

The furnace was so hot that the heat killed the men who tied up and threw the convicts into the flames. Yet, as Nebuchadnezzar peered into the furnace, he saw the three standing in the flames unhurt. And they were not alone. With them was a fourth figure, an angel, who kept them from harm.

Daniel reports that a similar incident happened to him when he disobeyed an edict forbidding people to pray to anyone other than King Darius of Persia. Daniel deliberately let himself be seen praying to God. As a result, he was arrested and thrown into a pit of hungry lions.

But God sent an angel who kept the lions at bay throughout the night. In the morning, Daniel was let out of the pit and his accusers were thrown in, together with their wives and children. The lions didn't even wait till they fell to the bottom of the pit before eating them.

Minor Miracles

The prophet Zechariah, like Daniel, tells of an angelic interpreter who helps him make sense of his visions. Among these many strange sights was a stone with seven eyes, a scroll that flies through the land sweeping away thieves and perjurers, and a barrel with an evil woman inside that is sealed and whisked away by two female angels with wings. In short, the stone with eyes means that God sees what's going on; the business with the scroll and the barrel mean that evil will be punished.

Revelations

Zechariah prophesies the fate of Wickedness, whom he personifies as a woman who has been trapped inside a barrel that has been sealed with a plug made of lead. The barrel is being carried away by two women who have wings "like a stork's." These flying women are not identified as angels, but they certainly appear to be angelic. The trapped woman, Wickedness, is to be carried away to a house that is being prepared for her in Shinar, a place in Babylon, the country from which many Jews had recently been returning from exile. Thus, instead of the Jews being exiled to Babylon, it is now Wickedness who is to be banished there.

Zechariah is important to angel buffs because of his angelic visions. In his own right, however, he is considered one of the twelve so-called "minor prophets." Christians place less importance on Zechariah than on Daniel, Ezekiel, and Isaiah, in part because his prophecies are more difficult to interpret as premonitions of Christ. In contrast, the Jews recognize Elijah as the most important prophet.

Straight to the Top

Elijah did not exactly have any big angelic visions of his own, though he did important things like go head to head with the priests of Baal to show them their god was unreliable. But he became an angel himself when, after a distinguished career of prophecy, he ascended straight into heaven in a flaming chariot in a whirlwind, body and all, without going through the usual preliminary step of dying.

Many legends have been told about Elijah since his appearance in the Biblical books of Kings 1 and Chronicles 1, where his story is told. Jews believe that Elijah will return to Earth to announce the coming of the Mashiah, or "Messiah" as he is known in English. Traditionally, at Jewish Passover seders, an empty chair is provided for Elijah in case he shows up!

Dore's rendition of Elijah ascending to heaven in a fiery chariot. Elijah is shown waving to his friend and successor, Elisha.

In the meantime, he resides in heaven as the angel Sandalphon, where he serves as guardian angel to newborn children. According to legend, he decides whether they'll be boys or girls before they are born. He is also said to appear to devout scholars in order to explain hidden meanings in the Torah.

The Least You Need to Know

➤ Prophetic angel encounters tend to be impersonal, but concern matters of national importance.

➤ Angels appear in the calls to prophesy of Isaiah and Ezekiel to establish their worthiness to communicate the word of God.

➤ The angels in Ezekiel have subsequently been identified as belonging to the groups known as cherubim and thrones.

➤ Angels appear in Daniel and Zechariah to interpret these prophets' symbolic visions.

➤ The prophet Elijah was taken to heaven in a chariot by a whirlwind where he became the angel, Sandalphon.

Chapter 9

Syndicates and Spin-Offs

In This Chapter

➤ The Apocrypha and Pseudepigrapha

➤ Angels as match-makers

➤ Tobias, Sarah, and Raphael

➤ Aseneth, Joseph, and the chief angel

As everyone knows, the Bible was a big hit. The word of God was one of the hottest books going and everyone wanted to read it. It wasn't long before it went into syndication—well, sort of. It was translated from the original Hebrew, first into Greek and later into Latin. In this way it reached wider and wider audiences, just like your favorite TV shows that appear as reruns on local networks!

But even these syndicated features weren't enough to satisfy the growing demand for Biblical stories. So, they started coming out with spin-offs. These spin-offs added accounts of Biblical figures that weren't originally included in the Bible, often popularizing them to make them more appealing to a wider audience: the further adventures of Adam and Eve; more about Moses when he was a kid; what the prophet Enoch saw when he went to heaven—that sort of thing. These stories provided background in the lives of everyone's favorite Biblical characters. Some of them also make good love stories.

Angels, of course, figure prominently in the list of people's favorite Biblical characters and, sure enough, the syndications and spin-offs are full of angel tales. Some show that, in addition to their usual work, angels act as go-betweens for people in love. Many of these stories are not widely known today, since they didn't become part of sacred scripture. Angel enthusiasts, though, regard this almost-Biblical literature as a veritable treasure-trove of angel lore.

Following the Script

During the 1st and 2nd centuries, the rabbis and the early church fathers looked back over the mountains of religious scripture that had been produced over the centuries and faced a tough question: Which of these writings represented the word of God, and which represented merely the fruits of feverish human imagination?

Of course, the various religious honchos had differing opinions on the subject. Some had personal favorites that others didn't appreciate. Some wanted to emphasize ideas that not everyone agreed with. Eventually, however, the mainstream authorities from each religion reached a consensus on which books to include in the Bible.

Lost in Translation

For years, religious scriptures were written and translated in several languages, especially Hebrew, Aramaic, and Greek. Eventually, during the 3rd century C.E., a bunch of Greek scholars got organized and translated the entire Bible from Hebrew into a Greek version known as the *Septuagint,* from the Greek word for "seventy." According to legend, 70 or 72 Jewish sages did the work over the course of 72 days. Supposedly each sage prepared a separate translation, but when they compared their efforts, each translation was exactly the same as all the others, word for word. This miracle showed God approved of the project.

Winged Words

The **Septuagint** is the Greek version of the Hebrew Bible, including other sacred scriptures. These other sacred scriptures are not included in the Jewish **canon**, which is the body of writings that a particular group of people officially accept as part of the Bible.

Miracles aside, the Septuagint effectively re-released the Bible for the Greek-speaking world. The translators did their job so thoroughly that the Septuagint includes writings for which the original Hebrew versions—if they ever existed—have been lost. These works without a Hebrew version are not accepted as part of the Bible by the Jews. They are left out of the Jewish *canon*—the collection of works considered sacred.

Canon Fodder

The Christians, however, accepted the Septuagint writings that the Jews rejected. These books are known as the Apocrypha. (The term can be confusing, however, since it is also used in a more general sense to mean any religious work that is not in anyone's Bible, or simply any kind of writing that is of secondary importance.) The official Apocrypha is sort of like a syndicated show for which the original producers gave up the rights!

Revelations

The Apocrypha includes writings that were originally in Hebrew, but were retained only in Greek translations. This applies not only to whole works, but to fragments as well. For example, the apocryphal writings called Susanna and Bel and the Snake were evidently originally parts of the Biblical Book of Daniel. In fact, they don't make a whole lot of sense unless they are read together with Daniel. Even so, because the Hebrew versions of these fragments are lost, they are left out of the Hebrew Bible and printed separately.

That's how the matter rested until the Protestant Church split off from the Catholic Church. The Protestants decided they wanted their Bible to be more like that of the Jews, so they left the Apocrypha out of their canon. It's still part of the Catholic Bible, though, and is also accepted by the Eastern Orthodox Church.

All Things to All People

The official Apocrypha includes 15 books. The most important of these as far as angel watchers are concerned is the Book of Tobit, since it tells the story of Tobias and the angel Raphael. This has become one of the all-time favorite angel tales, perhaps partly because Raphael does more than simply appear in time of need, but sticks around, pulling strings to make sure that everything works out okay.

Many angel appearances are highly significant but brief. Angels come and point out a new direction, then fly away into the sunset. Some say that it is the nature of angels to undertake only one mission on Earth at a time, providing a concentrated focus for their celestial power. This rule doesn't apply to Raphael's mission in the Book of Tobit. In this story, the angel helps solve several problems at once.

Getting an Eyeful

The tale is set in the Assyrian city of Nineveh in the 8th century B.C.E., although it was probably written about 500 years later. It concerns a man named Tobit, who has problems. He is a pious Jew trying to get by in Assyrian exile. Although he is lucky enough to get a job working for the king, he falls into disfavor when he buries the dead bodies

Wing Tip

Angels resemble birds in many respects, but the resemblance is merely superficial. Angels would never have made Tobit go blind the way the sparrows did!

of Jews who were the king's enemies. (For Tobit, burial is a basic way of showing respect to the dead. Obviously, the king was being spiteful in not wanting to see the bodies buried.)

As if that wasn't bad enough, he falls asleep at the foot of a wall in which sparrows were nesting, and some sparrow droppings land right in his eyes! The story doesn't say what the sparrows had been eating, but it must have been something nasty, because the droppings cause Tobit to go blind. From that point on, Tobit's wife Anna has to support him and his adolescent son, Tobias.

Suicide Hot Line

This was hard for Tobit to take, given the patriarchal values he was brought up with, so he raised a fuss and accused Anna of stealing when she came home with a kid (baby goat) that an employer had given her. Anna let him know he was being a jerk, and he felt pretty bad—useless and all washed up. So he prayed to God to take his miserable life.

Talk about coincidences. At the exact same moment, a young woman named Sarah, who lived in Ecbatana in Media, was praying the exact same prayer: "Please God, just kill me now and save me from this misery." Sarah had her problems, too. She had been married seven times and was still a virgin. As you can imagine, this was tough for her, but it was even tougher for her seven husbands: They were all killed on their wedding day by a demon named Asmodaeus. (It seems Asmodaeus had the hots for Sarah, so he wouldn't let anyone else go near her.)

So that's the situation. Here's how Raphael stepped in to fix both Sarah's and Tobit's problems at the same time.

Revelations

Raphael's name means "God heals," and, as tradition has it, he has a way with physical as well as spiritual ailments. Some say he healed Abraham after he was circumcised. (A delicate case if ever there was one!) Legend also credits Raphael with fixing Jacob's hip after it was dislocated in a wrestling match with an unidentified angel (see Chapter 7). What's more, tradition says Raphael has a good bedside manner. He's supposed to be an especially friendly angel, willing to hobnob with human beings just for the heck of it. He becomes buddies with Adam, the first man, in Milton's epic, *Paradise Lost*. The two chew the fat about such topics as astronomy, food, and even sex. (Raphael says angels get it on in a spiritual kind of way!)

Tobit decided that before he died he wanted to provide his son Tobias with a wife and a nest egg to get started with. Back in the days when he was employed by the king, he had stashed some extra money at the house of a relative in Ecbatana. So he sent Tobias to Ecbatana to get the money and, while he was there, find himself a wife.

Fortunately for all concerned, a young man who said his name was Azarias showed up and agreed to be Tobias's guide on the long journey from Nineveh to Ecbatana. Little did anyone suspect that Azarias was none other than the archangel Raphael.

Gone Fishing

So Tobias and Raphael set off on their journey, accompanied by the dog. (Nice touch on the story-teller's part, don't you think? In a later syndication known as the *Vulgate* version, the Latin translation of the Bible made late in the 4th century, the dog wags his tail at the end of the story.)

Winged Words

The **Vulgate** is a Latin translation of the Bible used by the Catholic Church. The work was done late in the 4th century and attributed to Saint Jerome.

On the way, Tobias, Raphael, and the dog stopped by the River Tigris where Tobias dipped his feet in the water. Suddenly, a huge fish leapt out of the water, attempting to take a bite out of Tobias' foot. Fortunately, among his many other accomplishments, Raphael could clean fish, and told Tobias how to do it, telling him to save the heart, liver, and gall bladder. You just never know when fish innards may come in handy!

Dore's depiction of Tobias and Raphael.

Well, it doesn't get any better than this: a boy, his dog, his angel, and a successful fishing trip—just like something out of a Norman Rockwell painting. Well, Rockwell may not have painted the scene, but this was a popular subject among painters of the Renaissance. In contrast, painters have been much less interested in the rest of the story.

Happy Ending

Speaking of the rest of the story, when they get to Ecbatana, Raphael sets Tobias up with Sarah (who's really good-looking and has a rich dad). He tells Tobias to burn the fish's heart and liver in the bridal chamber so the smell would keep the demon, Asmodaeus, away. In fact, Asmodaeus thought the smell was so foul that he flew all the way to Upper Egypt. Raphael went after him and tied him up.

Wing Tip

It usually pays to look for broader meaning behind Biblical stories. Tobit, for example, can be interpreted to represent all Jews. His blindness represents a crisis in faith. The fish gall bladder represents the Torah, the teaching that can help people "see" again.

Fortunately, the smell didn't seem to bother the newlyweds at all. After a week-long party in Ecbatana, they returned to Nineveh with Raphael and Tobit's money. Best of all, they still had the fish gall bladder! Raphael told Tobias to smear the gall bladder over Tobit's eyes, which he did. Tobit's blindness was healed and everyone was happy. Tobit and Tobias were so pleased they offered Raphael half of the money they brought back from Ecbatana.

It was then that Raphael revealed his true identity: "I am Raphael, one of the seven angels who stand in attendance on the Lord and enter his glorious presence." Raphael told them he conveyed their prayers to God, but the whole scheme was God's idea, so they should thank God—which they did, a lot; and, if what some say is true, the dog wagged its tail. This is a sure sign of a happy ending!

What's in a Name?

There is a great deal of religious writing that was done between about 200 B.C.E. and 500 C.E. that didn't make it into the Jewish or the Christian Bible. Many of these works are collected in the Pseudepigrapha. This title means "falsely attributed writings," and refers to the fact that they are supposedly—but not actually—written by famous Biblical figures. A bunch of complete unknowns wrote them and *said* Moses, Solomon, or Adam and Eve wrote them!

Brand-New Episodes

There are different ways to look at this practice of saying a work is by someone who didn't really write it. From one perspective, it's a lot like forgery. If you wrote a story, people would sit up and take notice if you could persuade them it was by Ernest Hemingway or Mark Twain, even if the story were pretty lame in its own right.

Even so, the writers who wrote the Pseudepigrapha were not simply lying and trying to fool people. Instead, they were trying to make connections between Biblical figures of long ago and situations of their own day. Pseudepigraphic writing was a way of showing that the old tradition was still relevant.

Pseudepigraphic writing was also a way of filling in the gaps and fleshing out the bare bones of many of the old Bible stories. Bible stories frequently mention a person or an event in passing without providing details or background. This makes people want to know more, so they tell legends that provide the missing information. Just as popular TV shows often have spin-offs, the Pseudepigrapha tells spin-offs of Bible stories.

The Devil Makes You Do It

While they stem from Biblical stories, the Pseudepigrapha includes writings that draw on some far-out theological influences, including paganism, Gnosticism, magic, and mysticism.

You Can See Forever

The Pseudepigrapha tells about dozens and dozens of Biblical figures, adding more about their lives and personalities. This is true not only of the human figures, but of the angels, too. A great deal of esoteric angel lore stems from the Pseudepigrapha, much of which is visionary and apocalyptic, and consequently describes how the angels get ready to do battle and how they throng around the throne of God.

By far the fullest treatment of the angels is contained in the pseudepigraphic Books of Enoch, which have so much on angels that they deserve the next chapter all to themselves. These books are cosmic, describing how angels make the stars shine and the wind blow, and how they live in alabaster palaces out in the seven heavens. The Enoch books also talk about the amazing things that can happen when angels leave heaven to visit people on Earth, and when people leave Earth to go visit God and the angels.

Change of Heart

In addition to prophetic visions and apocalypses, the Pseudepigrapha contains plain old angel stories about how angels come and help people from the Bible. One of the most beautiful of these angel appearances takes place in the story of Joseph and Aseneth. This highly symbolic tale is a good story in its own right, telling how a pagan princess named Aseneth converts to Judaism in order to marry a Jew. It also provides interesting background for the Biblical story of Joseph, the son of Jacob, and his adventures in Egypt.

Revelations

Joseph was the eleventh of the twelve sons of Jacob. According to the Book of Genesis, Jacob liked Joseph best because he was born during Jacob's old age. In addition, he was the first son born to Jacob's favorite wife, Rachel. Genesis tells the story of how Joseph's brothers became jealous and sold him as a slave in Egypt. Joseph overcame his bondage, however, and rose to be a prominent government official under the Egyptian pharaoh. Eventually, he was reunited with his father and brothers. Aseneth isn't mentioned in the Biblical story.

Wedding Bell Blues

Aseneth is the beautiful daughter of Pentephres, chief priest of the Egyptian pharaoh. She is so beautiful that everyone wants to marry her, including the pharaoh's son. She is proud, however, and refuses all her suitors. Instead of getting married, she stays holed up in her father's palace worshipping her pagan idols.

One day Joseph, who, as you may know from the Bible, has been put in charge of Egypt's food supply, tells Pentephres he will stop by for a visit. Pentephres tells his daughter Aseneth that he wants her to marry Joseph. True to form, Aseneth refuses and locks herself in her room with her idols.

When Joseph arrives, she looks out her window to see him enter the palace, whereupon she is instantly smitten with love. (It's one of those all-over things, with wobbly knees, dry mouth, and a fever.) She suddenly realizes she'll die if she doesn't get to marry Joseph.

Wing Tip

Evangelists these days are saying that faith in God can "cure" homosexuality. On the other hand, maybe homosexuality can "cure" evangelism!

Different Strokes

Now Joseph, as you may know from the Bible, had had run-ins with pagan women before, and in his book they spell trouble. In particular, the wife of a man named Potiphar tried to seduce him. When she failed, she accused Joseph of trying to seduce her! So Joseph said to Pentephres, "Don't even think about setting me up with Aseneth." Pentephres replied, "Actually, she doesn't like men," and Joseph said, "Oh, that's cool, I don't have any problem with that."

Joseph did have a problem with Aseneth's idol worship, though, and made her feel bad with the things he said about pagan rituals, namely that she ate the "bread of strangulation" and drank from "the cup of insidiousness," and anointed herself with "the ointment of destruction." Aseneth took it personally and started to cry, which made Joseph feel bad—not that he thought he was wrong, but he felt bad for her. So he said a prayer asking God to let her eat the bread of life and drink from the cup of blessing.

Ash and Ye Shall Receive

Well, it seems things had got off on the wrong foot, but Aseneth was ready to change her whole attitude. She renounced her bread of strangulation and her cup of insidiousness and smashed all her idols and fed the sacrificial idol-food to the dogs (not nice pets, but the mean ones out back). Then she put on a black tunic—it was probably made out of sackcloth—and rolled around in the fireplace—which had lots of ashes in it. (People back then used sackcloth and ashes to show how sorry or unhappy they were.)

Aseneth wept and fasted and rolled in the ashes for seven days, on account of how bad she felt about her cup of insidiousness, etc. Finally she prayed to God (the real one, not one of the idols). The prayer goes on and on for five pages, so you can see how sincere she was. At last, her prayer was answered by no less than the chief of angels himself. (Most people think this is Michael, but he refuses to tell Aseneth his name, saying it's too holy to be spoken on Earth.)

Switching Brands

Aseneth had a feeling the angel was no ordinary visitor. This may have been because he had a face like lightning, eyes like sunshine, hair like fire, and hands and feet like iron that's glowing in flames, with sparks shooting off from them. What's more, he said what angels almost always say when they appear to ordinary mortals: "Be not afraid."

The angel told Aseneth that God had given her the go-ahead to marry Joseph. Better still, her name was written in the book of life up in heaven, right on the very first page. The angel says he wrote it there himself, and it would never be erased. From that day forward, she would eat the bread of life, drink from the cup of immortality, and anoint herself with the ointment of incorruptibility. Try getting that from your Avon lady!

The Devil Makes You Do It

Unfortunately, allegorical symbolism such as that found in the story of Joseph and Aseneth has largely dropped out of fashion, so comparatively few writers use it. It tends to sound kind of corny to people these days.

Honey, I'm Home!

As you may have guessed, all the bread, cups, and ointment in this story symbolize holiness, but the symbolism doesn't stop there. The angel tells Aseneth she will become a City of Refuge, and the many people (not just Jews, but other nations, too) who have faith in God will be sheltered under her wings. And the angel's sister, whose name is Repentance, will be her guardian.

Then the angel tells Aseneth to bring her a honeycomb, which is a symbolic honeycomb. Even though it's symbolic, it tastes and smells really good, like a real one. Aseneth and the angel both have some, and after the angel breaks off some of it to eat, it grows back the way it was. The honey was made by the bees of beatitude from the roses of life that grow in paradise. It's what the angels eat, and people who eat it will never die.

Revelations

The story of Joseph and Aseneth, with its sensual symbolism, provides some unorthodox answers to frequently asked questions about angels. Do angels eat? Many would say no. Another traditional view is that they eat manna. In this tale they eat honey from paradise, despite the fact that the Book of Genesis suggests God created paradise for unfallen human beings, not for angels. Do angels have sex? Again, many would say no. The chief angel stresses that his sister, Repentance, is a virgin; perhaps this means that not all angels are. Gender is still another undecided question about angels. Some say angels can appear as either men or women. Many say they are androgynous. Here there is a clear distinction between the male chief angel and his female sister.

This next part is really trippy: The angel makes a scratch in the honeycomb with his finger in the shape of a cross and it gushes out blood instead of honey. Then bees start to fly out of the cells of the comb—thousands and thousands of them. They are snow white with purple wings and they wear scarlet capes and golden crowns and they swarm all over Aseneth.

The bees made another honeycomb in Aseneth's mouth, and then they ate it. You'd think this would make them happy, but some of the bees were cantankerous and wanted to sting Aseneth. That's where they went wrong! The cantankerous bees dropped dead in their flight patterns just for thinking about sticking their stingers in the symbolic City of Refuge!

The other bees had the right idea. They finished the honey and flew off to heaven. No hard feelings, though, for the dead bees. The angel revived them and made them fly off to the courtyard outside to live in the fruit trees there. You might say they were demoted from being symbolic bees of beatitude to ordinary bees.

Then, the finale: The angel zapped the honeycomb with his right hand and it burst into flames and was completely burned away, leaving only a pleasant smell throughout the room. As smoke from the honeycomb wafted up to the heavens, the angel departed. He probably had that departing cowboy swagger that says "My work here is done."

Aseneth looked out the window and saw him riding eastward up to heaven in a chariot drawn by four horses. From that time forward Aseneth and Joseph felt pretty much the same way about things. They had a splendiferous wedding and later fended off an evil plot laid by the pharaoh's jealous son, who was just like another cantankerous bee.

Veils by Paul

The story of Joseph and Aseneth would make a great made-for-TV vehicle for one of those really-good-looking but not-too-talented actresses they like to showcase. For one thing, the whole story is so symbolic the acting wouldn't need to be believable. "I renounce you, pagan idols, yet woe is me, for I am unworthy to worship the true God!" I mean, who cares if she really feels the part? The important thing is she gets to appear in at least four different sexy outfits.

Wardrobe!

They'd probably show a flashback of Aseneth rejecting suitors wearing something really elegant and expensive. Then when she meets Joseph, she'd wear something simple, but definitely low cut. In fact, the story mentions that Joseph touches her cleavage when he's fending her off near the beginning. Then there's the sackcloth, which would, of course, be strategically torn in just the right places. (The rending of clothes signifies remorse.)

When the angel appears, he tells her to wash up and put on a brand-new outfit, namely, a new linen robe with a girdle of virginity, which she does. Ten minutes later, even before the business with the honeycomb and the bees, the angel tells Aseneth she can marry Joseph and should change into her wedding dress. When the angel departs and she changes for the wedding, she is "transformed to heavenly beauty." Evidently, they were every bit as into women's clothes back in ancient times as they are these days!

The Devil Makes You Do It

If an angel appears to you, don't expect it to give you advice regarding your wardrobe. Clothes have lost much of the ritual significance they had back in Aseneth's time.

Lifting the Veil

In fact (and here's what all this wardrobe stuff has to do with angels), people in Biblical times ascribed a theological significance to women's clothes. The point isn't just that Aseneth looks stunning in her new linen robe belted with a girdle of virginity, but that the outfit says something about her purity. This purity applies not just to her sexuality, but to her spirituality, too.

Religious people during Biblical times argued about what women should wear on religious occasions. One notable debate concerns the question of whether women should wear veils when they worship God. The Christian apostle Paul makes a famous—and confusing—argument in 11:2–16 of 1 Corinthians that women should wear veils on account of the angels.

The apostle Paul, by Albrecht Durer.

Theologians and Biblical scholars have had a good old time trying to figure out what Paul means. Do veils show respect for the angels? Do veils protect women from angels? In any case, the gist of Paul's reasoning seems to be that women are subordinate to men and should demonstrate their submission by wearing veils.

It's possible that the author of Joseph and Aseneth would have been among those who disagreed with Paul, because, when Aseneth changes into her new linen outfit with the girdle of virginity, she also has a new linen veil. When he sees her in the veil, the angel says, "Take off the veil; you're a chaste virgin and your head is like that of a man."

These different attitudes toward women wearing veils when angels are around was evidently at the bottom of a complicated theological debate involving a variety of religious ideas, possibly including Judaism, Greek paganism, Christianity, and early Gnosticism. Jews generally wore veils, pagans generally didn't, Christians did sometimes, and Gnostics did God knows what! The debate takes on added importance, of course, because the angels are watching!

This ancient debate has generated a recent debate among Biblical scholars of today. One interesting (and controversial) view is that the removing of women's veils symbolizes a Gnostic return to the *androgynous* state of humanity that existed before God separated the bodies of Adam and Eve from one another. According to this Gnostic view, God didn't first create man and then woman. Instead, he created an androgynous human and split it in half to make the two sexes. This splitting, and not Eve's eating of the apple, marked the fall of humanity. You can read more about gnosticism in Chapter 14.

Winged Words

If you are **androgynous**, you have female and male characteristics at the same time. Androgyny was an important aspect of Gnostic belief, since many Gnostics associated the separation of the two sexes with the fall of humanity.

The Least You Need to Know

➤ The Apocrypha is recognized as Holy Writ by the Catholic and Eastern Orthodox Churches, but not by Jews or Protestants.

➤ The Book of Tobit provides the fullest Biblical account of the angel Raphael.

➤ The Pseudepigrapha is a collection of writings falsely attributed to famous figures from the Bible.

➤ In the story of Joseph and Aseneth, the chief of the angels appears to consecrate Aseneth's conversion prior to her marriage to Joseph.

Enoch Is Too Much

Hold on to your hats, junior birdmen! You're about to read about the cosmic, angel-crammed adventures of human and celestial beings who have stepped over the edge. These are extreme encounters in which angels and people face—and move beyond—their essential differences to challenge the rules of God-made reality and get to the heart of the most burning questions ever asked on Earth or in Heaven.

How high can you fly if you're a flesh-and-blood human being—as the seven heavens fill your head with spinning stars and the cherubic hymns echo through your chest—before you begin to think that Forever is your middle name, written in flames by the hand of God across the corridors of light? And how are you going to explain what's making you late for dinner?

How low can you go if you're a celestial spirit, created to extol the Almighty with your eternal, radiant purity, before the vileness of your despicable depravity makes you writhe in ceaseless torment like a snake in the fires of hell? And what is it about Earth girls anyway?

All this and more is revealed in the almost-Biblical Books of Enoch, where angels and earthlings step across the great divide that lies between mortal existence and timeless eternity.

Seventh Heaven

The Books of Enoch, contained in the Pseudepigrapha, are among the most angel-ridden of any group of writings anywhere. They claim to relate the first-hand experiences of the ancient man known as Enoch who, as legend has it, traveled as a living human being through the seven heavens to the throne of God.

The Devil Makes You Do It

The Bible may not be entirely trustworthy concerning the ancients, who, according to the Book of Genesis, lived to be hundreds of years old. Before geology, scholars tried to determine the age of the earth by calculating backwards with the help of the ages given in the Bible for the ancients. For this technique to yield results that are even slightly accurate, the ancients would have to have been not hundreds but *millions* of years old. Apparently, the Bible underestimated the length of the lives of Adam, Enoch, and the others!

A Big Lift

Enoch is mentioned in the Book of Genesis as one of the descendants of Adam leading down to Noah. ("And So On begat So Forth, and So Forth begat What's His Name...") He is the father of Methuselah who is the oldest human being mentioned in the Bible. Methuselah dies at the age of 969. (And we think *our* social security system is in trouble!) Genesis adds a curious detail about Enoch, however, that makes him stand out from the others. Enoch "walked with God" and "was seen no more, because God had taken him away."

What this meant at the time it was written is anybody's guess, but it has come to be interpreted as saying that Enoch was so virtuous that God took him up into heaven before he died. (The same thing happened to the prophet, Elijah, as described in the Second Book of Kings.) Naturally, everyone was curious to know more about Enoch. Fortunately, a whole slew of would-be Biblical writers came up with stories that were later collected into the four Books of Enoch. Not all the Enoch stories agree with one another in every detail, but cosmic angelic encounters are common in all of them.

Enoch and Elijah in paradise eating fruit from the tree of life, from a book of charms from the Middle Ages in Syria.

Devilish Angels

The first book tells the story of the Watchers, the angels mentioned in Genesis who lusted after human females and fathered a race of giants known as the Nephilim. These angels are called Watchers in Enoch, but the Bible refers to them as "sons of God." They became fallen angels for their crime and are sometimes associated with pagan gods.

Revelations

Legend says the Watchers are especially tall angels. It makes sense, then, that they gave rise to a race of giants, the Nephilim. One reason for the great size of the angels is the way their height is calculated: The Hebrew letters of each angel's name correspond to a numerical figure that is multiplied by a distance of several miles. Some angels are of such a height, it would take years to travel the length of their bodies!

Enoch fleshes out this story considerably. The Watchers and the Holy Ones are the highest of all the angelic groups, and not all of them succumbed to the temptation of lust. The angel Semyaza leads the lustful angels. He is joined by Azazel, who taught human beings the arts of war, cosmetics, and jewelry. Many believe the world would be a much better place without these things as they were seen as tools of the sins of pride.

The angel Amasras taught humans horticulture and magic spells. (These spells later became associated with the esoteric tradition of the Middle Ages known as the Cabala.

Wing Tip

Notice that the sinful behavior of the Watchers constitutes an economic, as well as a moral, disturbance to the community. The story may serve as an imaginative warning against the abuse of power on the part of earthly rulers, which can have disastrous social and economic repercussions.

In addition, black magic is said to be learned from the scattered leaves left behind from the Tree of Knowledge in paradise). Barakiyal, Kokarerel, Tamiel, and Asderel taught humans astrology.

All this knowledge only led to trouble for the human race. Before the Watchers came along, everybody was naturally sweet and innocent. Afterwards, they started killing each other and acting seductive with their make-up and casting evil spells on one another.

Corrupting humankind was bad enough, but their offspring, the giant Nephilim, did even worse things. For starters, they ate everybody out of house and home. Then when the food was all gone, they went after people in order to eat them. This is the sort of abomination in the sight of God that can result when you use your celestial power to seduce innocent Earth women.

William Blake's depiction of an angel in chains—not from the Book of Enoch, but from his poem America; a Prophecy.

God punished the Watchers for their sinful behavior, calling upon the righteous angels to carry out his decrees. Raphael bound Azazel hand and foot and threw him in a hole in the desert and covered the hole with big, sharp rocks. Michael was sent to bind Semyaza and the rest underground for 70 generations. Meanwhile, the Nephilim were condemned to do battle among them until they killed each other off.

Who's Sorry Now?

The Watchers were understandably unhappy about their punishment, and asked Enoch to intercede for them. He was just the guy to do it, because he was going on a tour of the entire cosmos and was about to come face to face with God. In fact, according to the story, God chose Enoch to function as a witness to future generations.

God thought that when people noticed the Watchers writhing in torment, they might say, "God sure is mean; why doesn't he show some mercy once in a while?" So God wanted to keep Enoch around so he could say, "Actually, those Watchers are totally evil and are guilty of serious defilement. They're only getting what they richly deserve—I oughta know, I was there when they did it."

The Devil Makes You Do It

If you find yourself in the holy presence, you probably don't want to look God in the face, especially without sunglasses. Also, you should definitely resist the urge to tan your bare buns in God's radiant glory. This could have disastrous consequences far worse than sunburn!

Even though he was God's chief witness, Enoch took pity on the Watchers and prayed to God on their behalf. He did this in a vision in which he ascends into heaven to the throne of God. Beneath the throne are fiery Cherubim and on the throne is God himself, whose glory is so great that not even the angels can look at his face. God then told Enoch that the Watchers will face the consequences of their sin, and that's that.

On the Rise

Enoch continues his journey, making a tour of the entire cosmos. He sees the alabaster palace of heaven, the storehouses of the four winds, and the pillars of fire that hold up the earth. He also meets the seven holy angels and lists their names and functions as follows:

➤ *Uriel*—Angel of eternity

➤ *Raphael*—Angel of the spirits of humankind

➤ *Raguel*—Angel of vengeance

➤ *Michael*—Angel of obedience and benevolence

➤ *Saraqael*—Angel in charge of sinners

➤ *Gabriel*—Angel of the Garden of Eden

➤ *Remiel*—Angel of those who rise

This is only one of several lists of angels contained in the books of Enoch. It's worth noting that these lists don't always agree with other sources (or even with other accounts in the books themselves!). For example, in one place the *Galgallim* and *Ophanim* are treated as separate classes of angels. These are the angels shaped like wheels, made of fire with eyes in them. Elsewhere in the Enoch Books they are both part of the same class.

Enoch is borne by angels through the seven heavens and eventually to the throne of God, who tells him the secrets of the universe and human destiny. When Enoch returns to Earth, he tells his descendants to worship God. Enoch later tells of the flood that will come and wipe out the fallen angels together with the humans they taught to sin.

God will mysteriously transform the flood waters so that they will seem like fire to the fallen angels. Fortunately for the future of humanity, Enoch's grandson, Noah, would save people and the other living things. Finally, Enoch is carried away by angels to reside with God forever.

Winged Words

The **Galgallim** and **Ophanim** are angels in the shape of wheels made out of fire with eyes in them. They stem from Ezekiel's vision of the chariot-throne of God and correspond to the group known as Thrones in the hierarchy proposed by Pseudo-Dionysius.

Blazing the Trail

The high point of Enoch's cosmic tour is passing through the seven heavens to the throne of God. This feat inspired others to attempt to replicate it. Rabbi Ishmael, who ascends through the seven heavens much like Enoch, in fact, supposedly writes the third Book of Enoch.

Wing Tip

If you try to achieve a state of trance by singing hymns with your head tucked between your knees as the Merkabah mystics are said to have done, you might want to make sure you're alone. Otherwise, someone is likely to call an ambulance!

Merky Doings

Rabbi Ishmael was not the only one to emulate Enoch. The idea of rising through the seven heavens to the throne of God forms the foundation for a whole set of esoteric practices and teachings known as Merkabah mysticism. *Merkabah* is the Hebrew word for "chariot," and refers to the chariot-throne of God that appeared in a vision to the prophet Ezekiel.

Little is known about this esoteric system, since it was usually taught only to selected initiates. The idea is that through proper preparations, including fasting, prayer, and other rituals and disciplines, it is possible to go into a trance and experience a vision of the throne of God. Aspiring mystics evidently induced trances in part by singing hymns with their heads tucked between their knees!

According to legend, four rabbis of yore made this mystic journey to heaven. They were scholars from Palestine who lived during the 2nd century. One was killed, one went insane, another renounced the Jewish faith, and the fourth went in peace. The assent to God was clearly perilous, and not for everyone.

Name Dropping

According to some, it helps to know the names of the angels in charge of each of the seven heavens in order to make it through safely. You'll want to know the names of the princes and the seven heavens in case you ever get a chance to make the trip yourself:

➤ *Sidriel*—rules Wilon, the first heaven

➤ *Baraqiel*—rules Raqia, the second heaven

➤ *Baradiel*—rules Sehaqim, the third heaven

➤ *Sahaqiel*—rules Zebul, the fourth heaven

➤ *Satqiel*—rules Maon, the fifth heaven

➤ *Gabriel*—rules Makon, the sixth heaven

➤ *Michael*—rules Arabot, the seventh heaven

Enoch imagines the seven heavens as palaces, one inside the other, with the throne of God inside the palace of the seventh heaven. Each palace has a gate that is guarded by angels. Each palace also has a name and is ruled by a different angel prince. Each prince is attended by 496,000 myriads of angels (that's literally 4,960,000,000 angels!). Talk about security!

Revelations

The idea of seven heavens ties in with ancient and medieval astronomy, according to which the earth, at the center of the universe, was surrounded by seven spheres. These spheres are layers, kind of like the layers of an onion, one inside the other. The spheres slide around and around, and each one of the planets slide around inside them as they rotate the earth. This is only one conception of the layout of heaven. According to other views, there are nine heavens. One account even says there are 955 heavens!

Going Over Their Heads

Ordinarily, human beings don't get to go to heaven and meet God without dying first. Enoch did something that had never been done before—something pretty special. At least, human beings tend to think it was special. The angels felt differently about it though, especially since Enoch didn't remain human, but was transformed into an angel. The other angels objected to this act of God, but what the Almighty says goes.

At least, this is the story according to the third Book of Enoch. Enoch was not simply given the standard-issue harp and halo and told take his place in the choir with the rest of the angelic host. He became the greatest angel ever, taking over (from Michael) as the chief angel. He sat in judgment over heaven and Earth with myriad angels doing his bidding.

According to the story, Enoch's body slowly turned into flames as he became transformed from a human being to an angel. As an angel, he changed his name to Metatron (who is the patron angel of the United States). No one is really sure what this name means, but it sounds pretty important! And he is. Sometimes Metatron is even referred to as the "lesser Yahweh."

Throne for a Loop

Does this blow your monotheistic mind? You're not alone. When a Rabbi named Aher replicated Enoch's feat and ascended into heaven without dying first, he encountered Metatron, "the lesser Yahweh," seated on a throne and thought there must be two Gods. The idea of a second God was too much for him to take and he left Judaism.

According to one legend, the angels surrounding God's throne never sit. Not only are they not supposed to, they're not even able to. For one thing, they don't have thrones, and for another, they don't even have backs! Instead, they have faces that look forward in four directions so they can see God wherever he is. This is why Rabbi Aher was so astonished to find Metatron seated on a throne in heaven that he left Judaism. After this meeting with Rabbi Aher, God punished Metatron for sitting by sending the angel Anapiel, who struck Metatron with 60 lashes of fire and made him depart from his throne.

To make matters even more confusing, according to one Jewish tradition, there are actually two Metatrons. Their names are spelled slightly differently—one has an extra Hebrew letter in his name. God created one Metatron with the rest of the angels before the creation of the world. The other Metatron was born as Enoch, but later was transformed into an angel.

The Devil Makes You Do It

Many people turn from their religions because they fail to live up to their prior expectations. It's probably best not to form any rigid ideas about what God is like and what he (or she) will do for you if you want to stay happy in your faith.

Created or transformed, Metatron is an angel to be reckoned with. His height is the distance you can cover on a 25,000-day journey. (Calculations of angels' heights were sometimes made by assigning number values to the letters of their names, adding up these letters, and multiplying them by 1,000. It's sure easier than using a measuring rod!) His body is made of fire, and sparks fly from his fingertips. Metatron also has 70 additional names, including Laplapiron and Gabgabib. God, too, has 70 names. With that many names, it's almost possible to pray to God by accident!

Revelations

The names of angels and of God evidently had magic and mystic significance to many of the faithful in ancient times. The letters of some names were assigned numbers with numerological significance. Some believed that out of these letters God formed the world. Scholars believe that some angel names may stem from the practice of speaking in tongues. This involves an ecstatic experience in which a person is filled with the holy spirit and speaks spontaneously in the language of the angels. The Book of Acts of the Apostles mentions an incident in which a roomful of Christians were caught up in the holy spirit and began speaking in tongues. Several onlookers thought everyone was drunk!

Give 'Em El

Some, but not all, angels get their names through the ecstatic practice of speaking in tongues (the ecstatic gibberish-language of the angels). Many are named in a common-sense fashion after the functions they perform. The Books of Enoch provide a long list of them.

These angels and their names are associated with various natural functions. Baradiel is in charge of hail, Salgiel is in charge of snow, Lailiel is in charge of night. Their names seem to be formed by adding "el" to the end of a word. The name Baraqiel, for example, is formed by adding "el" to the end of the word for "lightning." Voilà, we have an angel in charge of lightning!

El, or *Eloha*, is one of the Hebrew words for God. The angels are sometimes known as *elohim*, which is the plural of Eloha. Elohim is also used in other ways. It can refer to pagan gods, to spirits, or even

Winged Words

Elohim is used in several ways. The plural form of eloha, a word for God, it can refer to angels, to pagan gods, to spirits, or simply to God himself.

as another term for God, even though it takes the grammatical form of a plural word. As a suffix added on at the end of an angel's name, "el" can suggest that they are god-like, or that God acts through the angels in certain ways. The name Raphael, for example, is translated as "God heals."

Flopping Their Wings

One of the fascinating things about the Books of Enoch is the fact that a human being is chosen to become the chief of all the angels. This is especially important because angels are often represented as being extremely status-conscious. They all know exactly where they stand in relation to one another, to God, and to other creatures.

The Books of Enoch dramatize this situation in a number of ways. For one, they provide a long list of angels in order of their celestial importance, and say what they do when they run into an angel that is ranked above them: If they're on horseback, they dismount (getting off their high horses, so to speak). Then they doff their golden crowns from their radiant heads and fall prostrate. (The account doesn't say what they fall on up there in heaven, but prostrate they fall nonetheless.)

Thus the angels who guard the gate of the palace of the second heaven fall prostrate in the presence of the angels who guard the gate of the palace of the third heaven, who fall prostrate when the see the guardians of the fourth heaven, and so on. From a modern-day earthly perspective this might seem like a lot of unnecessary wear and tear on the old angel knee joints, but there's a perfectly good reason for all this prostration.

It's not simply a matter of discipline, or making sure everyone knows their place. Instead, the idea seems to be that angels are truly awestruck in the glorious presence of angels more exalted than they are. Imagine an encounter with an angelic being who makes you tingle all over and makes your knees weak and your hair stand on end—like Cindy Crawford or Brad Pitt, only even more resplendent. This angel is so magnificent you don't know what to say. You're not worthy even to look at such a glorious being.

Wing Tip

If you meet with a glorious angel and feel the urge to prostrate yourself, go for it. Chances are the angel appeared to you for a reason and will lift you up and set you on your feet—or higher. Many prophets report having this experience.

There's no use trying to be cool or casual about it. Even if you were able to speak coherently, you wouldn't want to cheapen the moment by stammering "Love your halo" or "Great wings, are they water-repellent?" The sensible thing to do is not even pretend to be on anything like the same majestic level as your heavenly superior. The best you can hope for is not to be totally despised for being the lowly worm God made you. Clearly, etiquette, as well as your wobbly knees, demand that you grovel.

Okay, so now imagine that radiant, celestial creature running into someone who seems as far above them as they are above you. They feel the same cosmic sense of unworthiness you felt in their presence. Now imagine *that* superior celestial being in the presence of a still more magnificent angel. See how pathetic human beings are? See how ultra-magnificent God is, who's way at the top of all these belly-flopping angels?

Doing the Rite Thing

The Books of Enoch are pretty far out in their own right as a collection of angel lore. As stories and legends, they evidently provided entertainment and religious instruction, especially for those with deep feelings for angels. There is evidence, however, that the Enoch Books provided more than just inspirational reading to some religious communities.

The esoteric practice of Merkabah provides some of this evidence, suggesting that the Enoch Books were involved in mysterious cultic practices. Additional evidence comes from the dramatic discovery of the Dead Sea Scrolls. The scrolls make up an entire library belonging to a monastic community who lived in caves in Qumran near the Dead Sea. The monks of Qumran may have been members of a Jewish sect known as the Essenes, a group that strongly opposed the mainstream policy of compromising with Jerusalem's Roman rulers.

Prominent among the collection of scrolls are accounts of the fall of the Watchers and the ascent of Enoch. Numerous copies of the First Book of Enoch were discovered at Qumran. Enoch-related stories are also found in several copies of the Book of Jubilees numbered among the Dead Sea Scrolls. Because of the prominence of these books in the Qumran collection, some scholars think angels held a special place in the thinking and ritual of the community.

A further indication of the importance of angels at Qumran is a collection of psalms found among the scrolls known as the Angelic Liturgy. A *liturgy* is a plan for organized group worship, so the angelic liturgy is the system of worship practiced by the angels. The Angelic Liturgy psalms include specific descriptions of how angels worship God, and suggest that human beings are to worship God in the same way.

We don't have a clear picture of what life and religion were like in the Dead Sea community. In fact, there has been an unusual amount of bickering and disagreement among scholars about the significance of the scrolls. (The squabbles have stemmed in part from delays in publication of the scrolls and limited access to unpublished material.) As a result, we can only guess at how the people of Qumran made angels a part of their lives and belief system.

Winged Words

A **liturgy** is a plan for group worship. The term is usually used in the context of Christian worship services, but also applies to worship practiced by angels, as in the group of psalms called the Angelic Liturgy.

The Least You Need to Know

➤ The pseudepigraphal Books of Enoch tell of humans ascending to heaven to learn angelic wisdom and angels descending to Earth to have sex with humans.

➤ The story of the Watchers and the Nephilim provides background for the Biblical story of the flood.

➤ Enoch was raised bodily into heaven and transformed into the angel Metatron and placed above all other angels.

➤ The Books of Enoch may be tied to mystic attempts to behold the throne of God in trances and visions.

➤ Several copies of the First Book of Enoch were found among the Dead Sea Scrolls, providing evidence of a keen interest in angels among the monks of Qumran.

Chapter 11

Angel Magic

In This Chapter

➤ Angels in the occult philosophy of the Middle Ages

➤ The Cabala and the sefirot

➤ Lilith's escape from paradise

➤ Angel names and the Hebrew alphabet

➤ The Zohar and the Book of Raziel

Everyone knows that angels heed the word of God Almighty, but not many know about the sorcerers of the Middle Ages who played God in order to get the angels to do their bidding. These were magicians and occult philosophers, schooled in esoteric wisdom hidden from ordinary mortals. Some say their teachers were the angels themselves.

They say their power stems from the word of God that existed before the world was created. This word and its power can still be found in secret combinations of the letters of the Hebrew alphabet. It was by means of these letters that God created the world, and by learning their secrets, magicians of the Middle Ages believed they could figure out how he did it.

The letters could be used in secret combinations to spell the 72 names of God and the names of countless angels. These mystic names revealed correspondences between divine and earthly reality and, it was hoped, would put the divine and human worlds in sync with one another. In addition, they made great love charms and headache remedies!

Waiting for the End of the World

Much of the infectious energy behind Judaism and Christianity during the first millennium of the common era had to do with the belief that the end of the world was on the way. The scriptures said the Messiah would come—or come again—at any time, transforming the cosmic order by sorting out good and evil once and for all. The decades passed, however, and still no Day of Judgment. Gradually, as the dust of expectation settled, many believers found themselves all dressed up for the apocalypse with no place to go.

As a result, there developed a tendency to turn inward—stemming from the mystic traditions of Jewish Merkabah, Christian Gnosticism, and Islamic Sufism—and a tendency to turn to worldly things—stemming from Greek natural philosophy and an old-fashioned desire to be prosperous. Until further notice, in other words, the plan for many was to develop personal spiritual powers and use them in practical ways. One formula for the use of divine knowledge for spiritual and practical ends took shape in the Jewish occult belief system of the Middle Ages known as Cabala.

Revelations

Much Jewish thinking, including Cabala, responds to the problem of exile. Jews have always regarded themselves as a nation, even though they have gone through much of their history without a homeland. In Biblical times, Palestine was taken over a number of times by foreign powers. During the Middle Ages and the Renaissance, Jews were often persecuted or even forced to leave the countries where they lived. Jews were kicked out of England in the 12th century and kicked out of Spain late in the 15th century. Anti-Semitic Christians say this ongoing exile is God's way of punishing them for rejecting Christ. In contrast, many Jews say this problem shows that they are atoning for the sins of the entire human race. In general, the Jews have tried to compensate for exile by maintaining a strong religious tradition through scriptural study, commentary, and interpretation. The Cabala fits into this practice of making ongoing use of an already rich Biblical tradition.

Keeping the Secret

Cabala (or Kabbalah) means "received tradition." Supposedly this tradition was passed on by word of mouth down through the centuries and kept out of books in order to keep it secret. Cabalist tradition stems in large part from Jewish *midrash*, commentaries and interpretations of the Bible that are passed down from generation to generation.

The Cabalist beans eventually got spilled in book form in the 13th century in Spain and France. The most important Cabalist book is the Zohar, but many other Cabalist writings exist as well. They all draw on the long history of Jewish Biblical interpretation, on Jewish folk beliefs, and on theological and philosophical ideas from all over.

Bringing It All Together

The Cabala says the world emanated from God in the form of ten levels or aspects called *sefirot*. Each sefirot is an aspect of God and also an aspect of the original and eternal human being known as Adam Kadmon. Adam Kadmon is the unfallen Adam who bears the likeness of the angels.

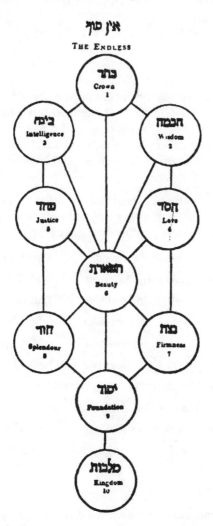

The ten sefirot of Cabala.

Winged Words

Midrash is the tradition of Jewish Biblical commentary and interpretation passed down from generation to generation. The **sefirot** are the ten levels of reality which, according to Cabalism, emanate from God.

Cabalists say that before Adam fell from grace by disobeying God's command, he was of enormous size and radiance, like the angels. As a result of his sin, however, he was diminished in stature and glory. The ten levels of Cabalist reality, figured as an arrangement of the ten Sefirot, represent this glorious original human being.

In addition, the sefirot are said to make up four different worlds, but they all work together in influencing and organizing human existence. Alternatively, they are conceived of as parts of God's body. In addition, each of the ten sefirot is personified by a different angel and associated with its own class of angels.

Power Stations

Knowledge of the sefirot was thought to impart spiritual power. Cabalists believe that God exists beyond human comprehension, but created the world in order to bless human beings with at least limited knowledge of his power. The world is a reflection of his power that emanated from him in the form of thought, words, light, and finally, material reality. The Cabala shows how these various levels that emanated from God fit together and lead back to divine knowledge.

The Devil Makes You Do It

Although Cabala is seen as a Jewish tradition, don't be fooled into assuming that Cabalist belief and practice were limited to the Jews. During the Middle Ages it was taken up by non-Jewish philosophers and magicians as well.

These are the names of the ten sefirot that emanated from God. Each sefirot corresponds to an angel as well as to a different group of angelic beings:

➤ Kether, "the Crown," Metatron, Living Creatures

➤ Chokmah, "Wisdom," Ratziel, Wheels

➤ Binah, "Understanding," Tzaphkiel, Thrones

➤ Chesed, "Mercy," Tzadkiel, Shining Ones

➤ Gevurah, "Power," Khamael, Seraphim

➤ Tiphareth, "Beauty," Raphael, Kings

➤ Netzach, "Victory," Haniel, Gods

➤ Hod, "Glory," Michael, Sons of God

➤ Yesod, "Foundation," Gabriel, Cherubim

➤ Shekinah, "Kingdom," Sandalphon, Fiery Souls

Coming Out of Their Shells

The sefirot provide a way of understanding good and evil. Cabalists look at the sefirot as ten jars, or vessels, filled with light that has emanated from God. As legend has it, the light was too strong for the jars, and so they broke. The result is that the light is streaming everywhere, and there are a lot of pieces of the broken jars lying around.

These broken bits, or "shells," are the abode of demons. They also have trapped sparks of the divine light that once circulated among the sefirot. It's the job of human beings to get these sparks back into circulation again by doing good deeds.

Another way of understanding the sefirot is as ten pieces of fruit hanging from the Tree of Life. The fruit have husks which prevent people from eating them and which are bad to eat in themselves. Like the shells of the broken jars, the husks have trapped sparks of divine energy. The shells are also called *sitra achra*, an Aramaic phrase meaning "the other side." This is the abyss ruled by the fallen angel Samael and his consort, Lilith.

Adam's Ex

Lilith, according to Cabalist legend, was created to be Adam's wife before Eve came along. When Lilith found out she was supposed to be subordinate to Adam, she said, "I'm outta here!" and left paradise. They say she uttered one of the magical names of God, which enabled her to fly away. Adam complained to God, who dispatched three angels named Sanvi, Sansanvi, and Semangalaf to bring her back.

Revelations

Lilith is said to be the mother of a whole class of demons known as "lilin." Some say these demons became "succubi," female spirits who have sex with mortal men in their sleep. Succubi can have demonic offspring as a result of their trysts with mortals and are sometimes said to exchange these children for human children. Thus, if your child turns out to be a little hellion, he or she may actually be a "changeling"—one child substituted for another!

On the Case

The angels caught up to Lilith on the other side of the Red Sea. She was holed up among some rocks, and they fanned out to surround her. Sanvi had this bullhorn, or megaphone, known as a *shofar*, and he used it to communicate with the fugitive. He said, "All right, darlin', we know you're in there. How's about bein' a good girl and coming back home with us?"

Lilith didn't feel like being a good girl. "Stick it up your sphincter, ya flyin' pig!" she yelled.

"Come on now, hon, we don't want any trouble. You come on back to paradise and make yourself a nice fruit salad. You'll feel a whole lot better. Won't that be nice?"

Winged Words

A **shofar** is a trumpet made of a ram's horn traditionally sounded as a call to repentance. They say the shofar will sound to announce the coming of the Messiah.

Wing Tip

If you want to become invisible, try uttering the words of Genesis 19:11 in Hebrew: "And they smote the men that were at the door of the house with blindness, both small and great." This passage, referring to the angels in Lot's house as they strike the Sodomites blind, was used as a magic spell for invisibility by Cabalist magicians!

Immortal Enemies

Meanwhile Sansanvi snuck around the other side of the rocks and got the drop on Lilith, putting her in a winglock so she couldn't scratch out any of his numerous eyes. Semangalaf rushed in sideways and laid down the law. "What the hell you doin' runnin' around the desert all by yourself? I've got half a mind to lock you up and throw away the keys to the abyss!"

Lilith managed to cough out a defiant response, despite Sansanvi's chokehold: "You can't touch me, flyboy. I read the midrash on free will!" The three angels looked at one another in exasperation. Lilith was right. Everyone is free to choose between good and evil. Lilith had chosen evil and there was nothing they could do about it.

"Now you listen here, devil doll," said Semangalaf. "I don't ever want to find out that you've been hanging around decent, God-fearin' people, you hear me? If you ever so much as come near a house that has my name written on the wall, I'll zap you so hard, you'll think you're going through the hot flashes!"

So Lilith went off on her own and eventually became a demon, hooking up with the fallen angel, Samael. The two caused a lot of trouble, both together and separately. In particular, Lilith is known for causing impurity and doing strange things to little babies. To protect a newborn baby from Lilith, the names of Sanvi, Sansanvi, and Semangalaf can be written in Hebrew on the door or on an amulet hung on the wall.

Amulet with a charm for warding off Lilith, containing the names of Sanvi, Sansanvi, and Semangalaf.

Magic Spelling

One Jewish tradition holds that angels understand only Hebrew, so it is useless to try to contact them—either through prayers or magic spells—in a vernacular language such as the Aramaic spoken by many Jews. (Only Gabriel is supposed to know all human languages.) Frequently, however, magic spells were written in Aramaic so people could remember them, but then recited in Hebrew.

Hebrew was special as the traditional language of the Jews. It was thought to contain and reflect the ordering power of God, who created the world by speaking. (This is yet another way to understand the emanation of the sefirot. Their power is produced and maintained through the divine word.) Even the letters of the Hebrew alphabet—or "aleph-bet," since the first Hebrew letter is called "aleph"—were thought to have magical powers.

The Devil Makes You Do It

In the Middle Ages, the power of magic was difficult to disprove. If a magic spell failed, the fault was not necessarily thought to be in the spell itself, but in the magician attempting it.

A Spelling Bee in Heaven

Legend has it that before God created the world, he thought about it for a while. As he was thinking, he scratched his head, and nudged his crown a little bit to one side. His

145

crown was a radiant circle of light, with all the letters of the Hebrew aleph-bet written on it in fiery letters. The letters could feel the wheels in God's mind turning and knew something big was about to happen, so they shook themselves off the crown and formed a ring around the throne.

As yet there was no order to the letters, but one by one they appeared before the Almighty. Each requested that it be given the privilege of initiating creation, and each pleaded its case by listing all the beautiful, powerful, and virtuous words that began with them—kind of like the letters on *Sesame Street*. God nodded his head patiently throughout each letter's speech, but rejected each one in turn on the grounds of the bad things that they also represented.

Finally, the letter "bet" (or "b" in English) requested to be first in creation, pointing out that it is the first letter in the word "barach," which means "blessed," as in the often repeated phrase, "Blessed be He who created the world." God rubbed his chin and decided that the word "barach" had a nice ring to it, so he chose "bet" to start the creation ball rolling. As a result, the Hebrew name for the first book of the Bible (Genesis in Greek) begins with bet: "Bereshith," which means "In the beginning."

Wing Tip

Want to perform Cabalist magic but too busy to learn Hebrew? Try learning just the names for the letters of the Hebrew alphabet. One story tells of an illiterate man whose prayers were always answered. Others wanted to know why his appeals to God were so successful, so they asked him how he prayed. He said he simply recited the alphabet and let God put the letters together into words as he saw fit!

Lucky Charms

Hebrew letters not only make up words, they stand for numbers as well. In fact, for those Jews who weren't familiar with Roman or Arabic numbers, there was no other numerical system separate from the aleph-bet. This gives you some idea of the power of Hebrew letters. They are the basis for math as well as language. Names could be transnumerated into numbers and numbers could be transliterated into names to reveal all kinds of secret magical correspondences.

Often, the power of angels and the power of their names written in Hebrew were considered essentially the same thing. Angel names could be written on amulets or doorposts as protection against all kinds of misfortunes, as in the case of Sanvi, Sansanvi, and Semangalaf, which protect against Lilith. These magical names did the work of the angels themselves.

Angels, in other words, figure into Cabalist thinking not only as celestial human figures but also as spiritual power and energy. Although there are many stories associated with Cabalistic tradition in which angels act as embodied celestial beings, Cabalists also saw angels as abstract concepts that could be used to channel the flow of divine power. Angels govern the interactions of the ten sefirot in an abstract, spiritual way. You could even say angels *are* these cosmic interactions.

The abstract power of angels doesn't mean, however, that angels don't also appear in Cabalistic stories as embodied celestial beings. In fact, many Cabalistic angel stories help explain Cabalistic magic in down-to-earth terms. They help people see the more secret and abstract meaning of the Cabala.

What's Your Handle?

Cabalists believed that angels governed people and things of the natural world. Angels, in turn, are ruled by God, who directs them by speaking their names. Magicians who know the names of angels and are able to recite them in the proper way were supposedly able to harness the power of the angels. In fact, the most famous magic word, "abracadabra," is a Cabalist variation of the name of a Gnostic angel named Abraxas.

Revelations

The angel Abraxas (sometimes called Abrasax) shows a significant point of contact between Cabala, a Jewish tradition, and gnosticism, which is Christian in origin. As a Gnostic angel, or aeon, Abraxas is said to be the source of 365 emanations. The number 365 also corresponds to the numerical value ascribed to Abraxas's name. This name was thought to be especially powerful among Cabalists, who used it in spells and talismans.

Earth Angel

Many stories connect the power of angels with their names. For example, they say that angels are immaterial and invisible, so when they want to appear to human beings, they have to make artificial bodies. They do this by taking dirt that has never been plowed and molding it into human shape. They infuse themselves into the form, and you'd think they were ordinary mortals.

This may seem like a difficult trick to pull off, especially if you're not an angel yourself, but they say that Cabalist magicians have managed to replicate this feat. The magician shapes the body out of dirt, dances around it, and recites the proper angel names. Then he writes a magic name on a parchment, which he rolls up and places under the tongue of the body.

Finally, he writes the tetragrammaton, the letter of the name of God, on the forehead of the body. What lump of dirt could resist power like this? The body comes to life and has to do the magician's bidding! Eat your heart out, Dr. Frankenstein!

Winged Words

The word **golem** is Hebrew for "unformed." A golem is an artificial human being made of earth by a magician, either for experimental purposes or for use as a servant.

The creature produced in this manner is called a *golem*, which means "unformed." They say that whatever angelic attributes golems possess, unfortunately intelligence isn't one of them. Tell them to do the dishes and they'll start with the ones that are already clean. Tell them to take out the trash and they'll dump it out on your front porch.

Perhaps for this reason, the Cabalist magicians never went into mass production with their golems. The word "golem," though, still gets used as a put-down. Go to Eastern Europe and bump into an elderly Jewish lady without looking where you're going and see if one of the things she calls you isn't "golem"!

Raziel Dazzle

Some Cabalists say that angel magic is as old as Adam. It seems Adam was feeling depressed about having just been kicked out of paradise. He was worried that he wouldn't be able to cope with all the problems that would undoubtedly come his way

Winged Words

A diet of worms is *not* what they make you eat for switching from Catholic to Protestant. **Worms** is the name of a town in Germany where Martin Luther, the founder of Protestantism, was named a heretic. A **Diet** is a legislative assembly of the Catholic Church. The Diet of Worms, then, was the group that said Luther had gone too far.

as a fallen individual. So he prayed to God for help for three days straight until the Lord took pity on him and sent down the angel Raziel with an angelic gift.

The gift was the Book of Raziel, containing magic words, symbols, spells, and more angel names than you can shake a stick at. Raziel told Adam the book would help him fend off all those woes and cares he'd been cursed with. Sure enough, with the help of the Book of Raziel, Adam and his descendants lived to be hundreds of years old!

Unfortunately, the book got misplaced one day. It may be that Noah forgot to bring it with him on the Ark, so it got soaked. Anyway, some of it was remembered and passed down, until what was left of Raziel's teachings turned up in the hands of a rabbi named Eliazar who came from a town in Germany called Worms. Thanks to Eliazar, the Book of Raziel became an important source for angel magic.

Use Only as Directed

As you might imagine, not everyone thought magic was a good idea. To some it seemed superstitious and posed a distraction from the real point of religion, whatever that may be. Even magicians acknowledged that their art was dangerous. Most said they were not in the business for their own sake, but for the sake of others who were threatened by evil. Cabalists generally saw their magic as white magic ("good" magic), even though others sometimes accused them of demon-worship.

Lost Art

Sometimes Cabalist magicians with good intentions became subverted by demons. Take, for example, the story of Joseph alla Reina, an especially ambitious magician who meddled with the dread Samael, evil prince of fallen angels. Joseph wanted to summon Samael in order to make him repent his evil ways.

The magician plied his Cabalist arts and succeeded in summoning the dark power. Samael turned the tables, however, and persuaded Joseph to turn from God. By the way, Cabalists believe in reincarnation. Sinners may be reincarnated as animals or stones as punishment. If the animals were sacrificed or the stones were broken, the crime could be forgiven.

Joseph came back as a black dog. The dog was later immolated by a fellow Cabalist who did a lot of that sort of thing—smashing stones and stabbing frogs and chickens to expiate the crimes of those who had done wrong in previous lives. His story was told as a warning to those who might practice Cabalist magic incautiously.

Wing Tip

Notice that Cabalism supplies a new rational for sacrifice. Traditionally, an animal is sacrificed as a gift to a divine power. Cabalist sacrifice is done to punish and expiate the sins of the soul who is trapped in the animal's body.

Revelations

The Bible forbids sorcery, even though Jewish Biblical figures sometimes engaged in sorcery contests with non-Jewish magicians. Moses' brother Aaron, for example, is pitted against Pharaoh's sorcerers. Aaron throws down his staff and it turns into a serpent. Then Pharaoh's sorcerers throw down their staffs and they turn into serpents too. Aaron emerges the better magician when his serpent swallows up all the others! Some Jews say Abraham learned sorcery in Egypt, but gave it up after receiving the blessing of the angels. Some also say that Jesus learned sorcery in Egypt too. Unlike Abraham, however, he never gave it up until it was too late. When Jewish magicians contacted his spirit in hell, he admitted that he should have remained a Jew!

In the Cards

However dangerous it may be, Cabala has had an enduring appeal among those into the occult arts. It continues to be popular as part of New Age thinking. During the Middle Ages and the Renaissance, philosophers and magicians—both Jewish and Christian—drew on Cabalist knowledge, often combining it with other arts, including astrology and alchemy. In addition, some have found connections between Cabala and the fortune-telling cards known as the tarot.

Cabala enjoyed a resurgence of interest in the 19th century as a result of the work of the Theosophical Society founded by Helena Blavatsky. Blavatsky contended that Cabala originated in the East 50,000 years before the time of Moses. She even claimed that she had writings documenting this eastern Cabalist tradition that, unfortunately, were lost.

Before the Beginning

Notice that many occult and religious traditions identify their own origins far back in antiquity. In other words, those who claim to have divine knowledge seem to go around saying, "My book's older than your book." Evidently, many seem to believe that the older and more original an idea is, the truer and more powerful it is. Here's a list of examples in which new traditions try to travel back in time in order to claim dibs on spiritual power:

➤ The Book of Raziel was written by writers of the 12th or 13th century who claimed it was given to Adam by an angel.

➤ Cabalists say the Hebrew aleph-bet existed before God created the world.

➤ Gnostics say they come from a world of light that existed before this world was created.

➤ The Egyptian God, Osirus, is said to have created the world, including his own parents.

➤ Jesus said, "Before Abraham was born, I am" (John 8:58), suggesting that he existed as an aspect of God, who identified himself as "I am" to Moses in Exodus 3:14.

➤ Muslims trace their religion back to Ishmael, the son of Abraham, even though the prophet, Muhammad, did not reveal their scripture until the 6th century C.E.

➤ Fortune-tellers who use tarot cards say the art originated in ancient Egypt, despite the fact that the practice got started during the Renaissance.

The Devil Makes You Do It

These days, the practice of claiming to have been the first to come up with an old idea is less and less convincing. Too many people have read their history books to be taken in. Instead, the trend is to claim your idea is totally new!

➤ Helena Blavatsky, the founder of the Theosophical Society, claimed to be familiar with a lost tradition of eastern Cabala that began thousands of years before Moses.

The Least You Need to Know

➤ Cabala is a magical and spiritual tradition based on mysticism, folk belief, and Jewish Biblical interpretation.

➤ The sefirot are emanations from God that make up reality.

➤ Sanvi, Sansanvi, and Semangalaf are angels who protect mortals from the demon Lilith, who was Adam's first wife.

➤ The letters of the Hebrew alphabet are thought to have magic powers. They were instrumental in God's creation of the world and were used in angel magic.

➤ Angel spells contained in the Book of Raziel were given to Adam by an angel to help him cope with being thrown out of paradise.

Part 3
Christian Angels

The coming of Christ put a whole new spin on things, not only for Christians, but for the angels, too. With a new big-man in heaven, Angels Incorporated gets completely restructured in keeping with the ideas of the new leadership. People want new beliefs, and God wants to give 'em to them. This means angels have to do some serious readjusting.

The following chapters will show you how the advent of Christianity shook up prior beliefs about everything celestial, from God to Christ, and of course, the angels themselves. The role of angels was redefined by the introduction of Christ, who became seen as the closest you could get to God. Did the angels mind this demotion? There are differing views on this subject, and you'll get to see all sides of the issue in these chapters.

Getting the Word Out

According to Christian theology, the coming of Christ changed everything for human-kind. Now everyone has a savior who will redeem them by atoning for their sins. By putting faith in Christ, we can all have eternal life with God and the angels in heaven.

This is a pretty basic idea and most people who are familiar with Christianity know this already. What is less widely known is the idea that the coming of Christ also changes everything for the angels. Suddenly they're not the next best thing to God anymore. What's more, they no longer have the exclusive responsibility of mediating between God and humanity. Christ, after all, is both God and human, so he can bridge the God-gap better than our fine-feathered friends ever could.

In general, the angels and their fans seem to be good sports about the new situation. The standard view is that we're all on the same team, so what difference does it make who scores the winning run, as long as the job gets done? Jesus is the go-to guy in the clutch, and if the angels don't like playing second string and warming the bench, they can ask to be sent down.

Grand Finale

As it usually does, the Bible provides only a bare-bones account of what happened when word got out that Christ was coming. The angel Gabriel appeared to Zechariah and Elizabeth, the future parents of John the Baptist, to let them know they'd better start knitting booties. A little later, Gabriel appeared to the Virgin Mary with a similar message that Jesus would soon be on the way.

Revelations

The Christian Gospels aren't the only sacred scriptures to report the appearance of Gabriel to Mary. The Koran includes a version of the story in which Mary hears the news that she will give birth to Jesus and, within the hour, becomes pregnant and gives birth. Gabriel is there through the whole episode and helps her assuage her birth pangs by telling her how to get figs from a withered tree. In an apocryphal version of the story from the 2nd century, the unborn Christ appears to Mary in the form of the angel Gabriel, and enters Mary in the form of the Word. According to this account, Mary was not afraid as she was in other versions, but laughed, evidently finding the visitation a pleasurable experience!

Just to make sure Mary's husband Joseph didn't jump to any false conclusions about how his virgin bride happened to get pregnant, another angel appeared in a dream to fill him in. Finally, on the night of Jesus' birth, *lo*, the angel of the Lord appeared to some shepherds who were tending their sheep. The angel let them know their savior was born, so they could start rejoicing.

Winged Words

No, "**lo**" is not the name of the angel of the Lord. It's a Middle English interjection that means something like "hold on to your socks!"

Then, to really make the shepherds flip their lids, a whole host of angels appeared singing, "Glory to God in the highest, peace on Earth, good will to humanity." This is one of the most famous of all the angelic appearances, relived every year at Christmas in song, story, and greeting card. According to many, however, this would be the angels' last earthly hurrah until the second coming of Christ at the end of the world. With Christ taking center stage, it was time for the angels to fade away into the wings.

Saying It with Flowers

Subsequent interpretations have fleshed out these episodes and put various spins on them. Gabriel's appearance to Mary has become known as *the Annunciation*. He is depicted in paintings carrying a lily along with his message to indicate Mary's purity. There's even a variety of lilies named after the event called a madonna lily, or annunciation lily.

Although Gabriel is the only angel mentioned by name involved in spreading the word about Christ, the traditional view is that all the angels participated. Most think that, despite getting overshadowed, the angels were thrilled by the coming of Christ—as well as amazed by the news. This shows what good sports angels are—real team players. They often appear on Christmas cards, filled with giddy enthusiasm about Christ for the sake of humanity.

In keeping with medieval angelology that organizes angels into hierarchical groups, the early Church fathers say that the angels closest to God knew first about the coming of Christ. They told the angels below them, who passed the word down the line until it finally got to the shepherds watching their flocks. Knowing about Jesus was a privilege, and all the angels were excited about the savior. Stories and painting show angels swarming to the stable in Bethlehem where Jesus was born, celebrating and proclaiming the good news.

Winged Words

The Annunciation is the appearance of the angel Gabriel to Mary when he told her she would give birth to Christ. This is not to be confused with the other angel-related Christian event, the Ascension, which is the rising of the resurrected Christ into heaven. This, in turn, should not be confused with the non-Biblical legend of the Assumption, in which Mary ascends into heaven, or with the Transfiguration, in which Jesus appeared to shine like an angel.

Dore's Annunciation.

National Interests

The same Christian tradition that has the entire angelic universe throwing their weight behind Jesus Christ also says, in effect, that the angels failed in their job on Earth of guiding humanity. As the early Church fathers saw it, it was the angels' job to keep people in line. They were doing this pretty well for the nation of Israel, but the so-called heathen nations were getting into all kinds of trouble, committing idolatry, tyranny, and such things as uncleanness and abomination.

This idea, stemming from the Book of Daniel, says that each nation has an angel, known as an ethnarch, assigned to it, as its own national guardian angel. The ethnarchs have the job of restraining the evil tendencies of the nations of the world, in effect to make the world safe for God's chosen people, the Jews. Unfortunately, they weren't doing so well. In fact, as mentioned in Chapter 5, the Jews regarded many of the ethnarchs as fallen angels!

Christian theologians explain that ethnarchs of non-Christian, non-Jewish nations correspond to guardian angels of non-Christian, non-Jewish individuals. These guardian angels aren't evil. In fact, the idea is they want their charges to become Christian, but their wings are tied. There's only so much you can do for a nation or individual that doesn't believe in you. Try convincing someone who doesn't think you exist that they're wrong. It isn't easy!

New Kid in Town

Fortunately for the nations, Jesus Christ took up their case and turned things around. Not only would Christ help keep the nations from causing trouble for the Jews (well...that's the theory, anyway), he would also enable those nations to become God's chosen people themselves, just by accepting Christ as their savior. So, thanks to Christ, the nations got on the right track. The ethnarchs were all smiles about this.

Wing Tip

Be a good sport when things change. Should someone younger take over your work, realize that now you might be able to swing a coaching or consulting job. The angels made a similar adjustment with the coming of Christ.

Some see this as a turnaround from the way it was when God made the first human beings. The angels sensed that Adam and Eve spelled trouble, and couldn't understand why God was so pleased with them. The angels were a little jealous, of course, and they feared human recklessness and our uncanny power to rock the cosmic boat. Christians say the coming of Christ—also known as the second Adam—came as a big relief to the angels.

Some say that after Christ came, the ethnarchs became Christian missionaries, appearing to gentile saints in various regions of the world and prompting them to spread Christianity and found churches and monasteries. This scenario explains the founding of the first Christian monastery in Egypt. An angel is said to have appeared to the monastery's founder, Pachomius. As another example, Victoricus is an angel who appeared to Saint Patrick on numerous occasions to encourage his efforts to spread Christianity in Ireland.

Revelations

The Gospels say that the angel of the Lord appeared to some shepherds to tell them about the birth of Christ. Some Christians read this story symbolically, saying the shepherds represent the ethnarchs, or guardian angels, of the various nations. The angel of the Lord, in other words, was not just telling a bunch of real shepherds about Christ, but was telling the "shepherds" of the whole world. The comparison suggests that, just as the shepherds are filled with amazement in the Bible, so were the angels amazed when they learned about Jesus Christ. What will God think up next?

Another way of understanding the angels' response to Christ is through the old bridegroom metaphor. Christ is like a bridegroom, and everybody's waiting eagerly for him to show up. This is not just because weddings are a lot of fun, but because Christ is connected to a really good family. His dad is a big name in the holiness business, so the marriage will mark the end of the story of religious struggle and suffering and let everyone live happily ever after.

The bride is the church—the only virgin pure and holy enough to be married to the Prince of Peace. Human beings—Christians, at any rate—count as friends of the bride. Angels, on the other hand, are friends of the groom. It's their job to throw him a party and make jokes about how they'd just as soon be crucified as get married. Of course they're really happy for him, even though they know that things will never be the same.

The Devil Makes You Do It

You can run into problems if you go too far with the metaphor of the Church as the bride of Christ. As the English Renaissance poet John Donne jokes, the more men who fall in love with Christ's "bride," the happier Christ becomes!

Rise and Shine

Christian theologians have taken the few passages from the Bible that talk about angels in connection with the coming of Christ and woven them together into a fully developed scenario in order to show how God, humanity, Christ, and the angels all relate to one another. While the Bible is sketchy about the Annunciation, it is even more vague about the role of angels in the resurrection of Christ and his ascension (known as *the*

Ascension) into heaven. The Gospels suggest that angels were on hand, but they don't make clear how they were affected by the death and spiritual rebirth of the Christian savior. As a result, later writers have had to fill in the blanks.

The Devil Makes You Do It

Watch out for angels who have a chip on their shoulder about having to play second harp to Christ. According to some, notably epic poet John Milton, author of *Paradise Lost* (1667), Satan led the angelic revolt in heaven when God told the angels to worship his son. In Milton's poem, this happens even before God created the world.

A Grave Situation

The Gospel of John says that Mary Magdalene saw two angels dressed in white sitting in Jesus' tomb. Then she turned around, and there was Jesus, alive again. The Book of Acts mentions "two men in white," perhaps the same angels, who showed up on the scene as Jesus was finally lifted up into heaven. These men/angels said that Jesus would return again. The Book of Matthew says that an angel rolled away the stone covering Jesus' tomb to let him out. This is pretty much all that the Bible says directly about the role of angels in the Ascension of Christ.

As you can probably guess, subsequent interpreters see angels flocking around Christ on his way to heaven like pigeons after bread crumbs. Christ is said to have risen up through the realms of the angels right to the throne of God, thereby taking a superior position. Christians support this idea by pointing to psalms in the Old Testament that talk about God on his throne.

Dore's angel in the tomb.

Reserved Seating

A number of psalms take the form of enthronement hymns. These are poems sung by the ancient Jews as part of religious festivals. The throne of God was an important concept associated with the Ark of the Covenant. The Jews saw the throne as being both close by, and universal, showing that God ruled over the whole earth and that he was particularly interested in the Israelites.

One such enthronement hymn is Psalm 47, which says, "God is seated on his holy throne. The princes and the nations assemble...The mighty ones of Earth belong to God, and he is raised above them all." Christians interpret this psalm, which was written at least 500 years before the birth of Jesus, as predicting the time when Christ would rise to take his place on God's throne with the angels of the nations gathered around him. According to this interpretation, the angels take a back seat to Christ.

Been There, Done That

Some say that, in rising above the angels, Christ symbolically lifted humanity above the angels too. This is a pretty grand claim, but it shows how big a difference Christians think Christ makes in the world. He turns things around in heaven and on Earth, so that nothing is the same any more.

One implication of this view is that people should stop looking to angels for help with their problems, but should turn to Jesus. As the Son of God, not only is Jesus Christ above the angels, he is more in tune with human problems, since he spent time as a human being himself. He found out the hard way the kinds of difficulties people are up against.

Christians aren't the only ones who have tried to keep angels down. Many Jewish authorities have suggested that human beings are more important than angels are. The Talmud says that the angels waited on Adam and Eve in the garden of Eden, preparing their food and serving them.

Just as Christian authorities downplay angels in order to promote appreciation for Christ, Jewish rabbis have done the same to foster awareness of God. Their point is that each individual can have a close, immediate relationship with God. This view sees angels not as go-betweens between God and humanity, but simply as demonstrations of God's glory whose job is to worship him.

Wing Tip

Remember, you can't please everyone—even if you're an angel.

Open Season on Angels

Many mainstream Christians are interested in promoting Christ and downplaying the angels because they regard angel worship as a threat to their theology. Although angels are undeniably a part of the Christian tradition, they don't play an important part in bringing about human salvation. This is why mainstream Christians sometimes complain that angel-worshippers are missing the point.

A Paul Over Angels

One of the first mainstream Christians to complain about the spread of angel worship was Saint Paul. The apostle Paul was one of the most important authorities of the early Church. His letters to various Christian communities are included as part of the New Testament.

Revelations

Although angel lovers may not hold him in high regard, the apostle Paul is one of Christianity's biggest heroes. He started out as a member of the Jewish sect, the Pharisees. Back then he persecuted early Christians under the name of Saul. The Book of Acts reports that one day while traveling to Damascus, Paul heard the voice of Christ saying "Why are you persecuting me?" He was then struck blind. Three days later his sight was restored and he converted to Christianity. After that he worked energetically to spread the new faith. He died as a martyr in Rome, as he was executed for being a Christian.

Paul wrote a letter to the community living in Colossae, a Roman province in Asia, warning them against angel worship and other practices that Paul saw as detractions from Christianity. This letter actually characterizes Christ as the victor in a battle with the angels who has taken them captive and leads them in triumph. This surprising depiction associates angels with Jewish law (some say the law was given to Moses by angels), which Christ has replaced with the new Christian order.

Paul is credited with other letters containing anti-angel propaganda. In his letter to the Corinthians, he says that human Christians will some day sit in judgment over the angels. A letter to Hebrew Christians attributed to Paul asserts that Christ is superior to the angels.

High on Angels

As Christianity first began to spread, many people started mixing Christian ideas with other sorts of religious beliefs. Angels provided an easy way of bringing Christian, Jewish, and pagan beliefs together, since pagan gods could be turned into angels. These angels were sometimes worshipped and invoked as magical powers.

What's more, people wrote stories and philosophical discussions about angels and attributed them to famous prophets and other figures from the Old Testament, in effect writing their own religious scriptures. Often these texts blended elements of Christianity, Judaism, paganism, and secular philosophy. Because it was often associated with practices and beliefs of fringe elements, the Christian mainstream quickly perceived angel worship as a threat, and this is why they emphasized the superiority of Christ.

The Devil Makes You Do It

It's much easier to condemn the beliefs of others than it is to be right yourself.

Spin Cycle

The disagreement between mainstream Christians and angel worshippers of the 1st and 2nd centuries B.C.E. has been revived in recent years. During the 1990s, evangelical Christians and mainstream Catholics have made complaints about New Age angel watchers that closely resemble the complaint made by Saint Paul about angel worship among the Colossians. Today's conservative Christians, like the apostle Paul, say that all the excitement about angels is taking away from the significance of Christ.

These Christians point out that Jesus is not like the other prophets who took instructions from angels. They say the angels didn't tell Jesus what to do because, as the son of God, he is more important than they are and even knows better than they do what's going on. Instead, the angels serve as Christ's ministers, much as they serve as ministers of God.

This argument seems to depend on differences, not in what the angels do for Jesus, but in the way they do it. Angels appear and supply Jesus with food after he fasted in the wilderness and withstood the temptations of Satan. An angel also provided food for the prophet Elijah. Since the Bible doesn't say in either case that they ordered from a menu or left a tip, it's a judgment call whether the angels involved were less important than Jesus, but more important than Elijah.

Go Transfigure

Not all Christians, however, are opposed to angel watching. In fact, some see Christ himself as an angel. There are a number of places in the New Testament that represent Jesus as an angelic figure. The Gospels of Matthew and Mark report an episode in which Jesus was transfigured on a mountaintop in the presence of some of his followers.

Suddenly, Jesus' face began to shine like the sun and his clothes became white as white light. This description of the transfigured Christ resembles descriptions of angels, who have been said to appear with shining faces and fiery raiment. As so often happens in the presence of angels, the people with Jesus at the Transfiguration were afraid.

Dore's Transfiguration.

During the Transfiguration, Moses and Elijah briefly appeared. (The prophet Elijah may be said to have undergone a transfiguration himself, when he ascended to heaven without dying and became the angel Sandalphon.) God himself appeared too, in a cloud, and announced that Jesus was his beloved son.

Revelations

The Transfiguration showed James and John, the companions of Jesus, that he was the Messiah. On the way down the mountain after the Transfiguration, the disciples asked Jesus if Elijah was coming again to herald the Messiah as the Jews believed. Jesus responded that Elijah had already come, but no one recognized him. The disciples realized that Jesus was referring to John the Baptist, the herald of Christ, as Elijah.

The point of the Transfiguration story is to show that Jesus is the Messiah, but it seems significant that the story does this by ascribing to Jesus angelic features. Another reason for seeing Christ as an angel is his association with the *logos*, the Word that was with God from the beginning of time. Christians say Jesus Christ is the Word made flesh, the logos incarnated as the human Son of God.

Some Christians also say that before the Word became incarnated as Jesus Christ, it was the venerable angel of the Lord, who represents God in the Old Testament. According to this view, Christ is the Word, God, a human being, and an angel. In fact, some say that, just as Christ became human when he came to Earth to be with ordinary mortals, he became an angel as he was rising through heaven to the throne of God.

Tough Choices

Despite Christian efforts to downplay angels after the coming of Christ, angels don't disappear from the scene. An angel shows up in the Book of Acts, appearing to help the apostles after the Ascension of Christ. When Peter and John are thrown into prison, the angel sets them free. Clearly, not all Christians believed the angels had outlived their usefulness.

An even more striking indication of the importance of angels in Christianity is the fact that Jesus himself evidently had his own guardian angel. In general, the Bible represents Jesus as amazingly sure of himself and confident in his role as the Son of God and the Messiah foretold by ancient prophecy. Even so, he was evidently not too God-like to benefit from angelic assistance.

Power Outlets

Luke says an angel appeared to Jesus in the Garden of Gethsemane and gave Jesus the strength he needed to go through with his impending crucifixion. This is an often ignored angel appearance, but it shows a very human side of Jesus, who finds comfort the same way as anyone else lucky enough to be visited by their guardian angel.

This doesn't prove that angels are more important than human beings, or that Jesus is less important than angels are. Instead, it suggests that the question of who is more important isn't the important thing. The nice thing about angels is that they do their jobs, which include praising God and watching out for people, regardless of where they belong in the celestial pecking order.

Winged Words

The Christian concept of **logos**, the Word, combines two ideas. Logos, to the ancient Greeks, was the natural process of the universe, which could be understood philosophically. Ancient Jews understood the Word of God as the means by which he created the world. The Gospel of John draws on both these senses of logos in saying that Christ is the Word made flesh.

Wing Tip

If you want to exercise your free will in regard to a particular problem and no angels appear to help you, it's a good idea to read up on whatever it is you're dealing with. This will help you make informed choices rather than impulsive decisions.

Although angels occasionally issue divine commands, they often appear as consultants, rather than bosses. (The Talmud says even God consults with the angels. For example, he asked them their opinion on whether he should make humankind. They said no, but God went ahead with the plan anyway!) This means that the people to whom they appear often get to exercise their own discretion in choosing what to do. In fact, you could make the case that angels are all about free will.

The Will and the Way

In his epic poem *Paradise Lost*, Milton says that the angels who worship God do so freely and that God wouldn't want it any other way. After all, it's not exactly worship if it's something you *have* to do. The angels who didn't want to worship God (and his son, the pre-incarnated Christ) could go to hell.

Similarly, Adam and Eve are given a choice about whether to obey God's command not to eat the fruit of the tree of knowledge. The angels try to help them make the right choice, but nobody—not even God—prevents them from choosing for themselves. Of course, after they commit the big original sin, they face the consequences of their choice, but facing up to decisions is what helps people learn to make better choices.

The Agony in the Garden, by Albrecht Durer.

To get back to Jesus in the Garden of Gethsemane, it's interesting that he didn't want to have to decide. He prayed, "Father, if thou be willing, remove this cup from me; nevertheless, not by my will, but thine, be done" (22:42). He didn't want to go through with the crucifixion (heck, who would?) but he wanted God to let him off the hook—maybe by providing a ram in the bushes for the sacrifice, like he did for Abraham and Isaac.

Then the angel appeared. The Bible just says the angel "strengthened" Jesus, but doesn't say how. Maybe the angel said, "It's your call, big guy. You can still back out if that's what you've gotta do, but we're all counting on you and we know you're up to it." Who knows, if it wasn't for the angel in Gethsemane, we'd all be celebrating Mithras-mass every December.

The Devil Makes You Do It

Don't let the hope of divine assistance distract you from the fact that the problems you have to deal with are earthly predicaments. Angels may give good advice, but so do many people.

The Least You Need to Know

➤ Selected angels were involved in the birth of Christ and in his ascension to heaven. Christian tradition says that those not directly involved were enthusiastic spectators.

➤ Many passages from the New Testament, and many mainstream Christians, suggest that Christ has rendered the angels obsolete.

➤ One of the first and most notable Christians to denounce angel worship is the apostle Paul.

➤ Jesus occasionally appears as an angelic figure in the New Testament.

➤ The Gospel of Luke suggests that Jesus was visited by a guardian angel in Gethsemane.

Chapter 13

The End Is Near

In This Chapter

➤ Angels and the apocalypse

➤ Cosmic politics

➤ Striking back at the empire

➤ The Book of Revelation

➤ Today's judgment days

You may have seen them out on the street carrying signs that say "The End is Near." They're the doomsayers who know how to read the writing on the wall and foretell the downfall of the human race. Should you worry? Maybe, but keep in mind, people have been saying "the end is near" for well over two thousand years now.

The trend was started back in Biblical times by a new breed of prophet who wasn't content with just preaching reform to his own group, but wanted to shake everybody up. The best way to do that was to go for the whole ball of wax—planet Earth and all the people on it. The idea is that when the evil world as we know it has been annihilated, God can start all over and build a new world, putting the good people in charge this time.

But the real problem runs much deeper than the world as we know it. According to the prophets of doom, our problems on Earth result from tumultuous upheavals in heaven and hell. Hideous beasts have been let loose and the angels are mustering their forces to stop them.

Bad Day at Work

Prophets of doom have inside information that the end is on its way. They rely on visions, oracles, angel visitations, and natural wonders, as well as fishy political doings, to tell them what they know about the fate of humanity. Taken together, these things point to the cataclysmic event known as the *apocalypse*.

Winged Words

The word **apocalypse** comes from the Greek word for "revelation." Thus it does not originally refer to the end of the world per se, but to divine visions in general. The term has come to refer to any event that transforms the world as we know it and any prophetic writing that says how this event is going to happen. The most famous apocalyptic text is the Apocalypse of John, better known as the Book of Revelation.

Evil Empire

Apocalyptic tradition stems from the time-honored practice of Jewish prophecy, but is also influenced by ancient Babylonian soothsaying. In fact, the Babylonians encouraged the Jews to make the transition from ordinary prophecy to apocalypse in more ways than one. Not only did they set an example with their highly symbolic magical thinking, but they also supplied motivation by dominating the Jews politically and militarily.

To the Jews, the foreign apple was rotten to the core. Babylonian rule made Jewish prophets want the end of the world to come, so that God would punish the Babylonians once and for all. Being subject to a foreign power brought out the apocalypse bug in Israel's prophets. Daniel, Isaiah, and Zechariah all talk about the end of the world in their prophecies. They portray foreign kingdoms as beasts that will face destruction by God and his angels.

Cosmic Causes

Many Jewish apocalyptic writings never made it into the Bible, most notably the First Book of Enoch, one of the first apocalyptic works to be written. These writings probably got left out of the Bible because they were falsely attributed to famous figures that didn't really write them. There's a Christian apocalypse, for example, attributed to the Virgin Mary. Another reason these writings were kept out of the Bible may have been because they are so full of angels that it made mainstream religious authorities uncomfortable.

Apocalyptic writings tend to be stuffed full of angels in order to explain how and why the world is going to come to an end. One reason the world is supposedly coming to an end is that there is so much evil on Earth that God has to destroy it. The evil is here because supernatural evil powers—the devil, the beast, fallen angels, and so on—have taken control of this world. What's more, they're trying to take control of heaven.

Cosmic battle in Dore's illustration for the Book of Revelation.

Apocalyptic writing, in other words, tends to ascribe cosmic significance to earthly political problems, and proposes drastic cosmic solutions for those problems. Typically, the earthly political problem involves persecution and domination by a foreign power. The cosmic significance is that the foreign power is an agent of Satan. The drastic cosmic solution is that God and his angels will put the forces of Satan to rout by waging war in heaven. In the process, evil people on Earth will get theirs too, while the righteous will be vindicated and reap their eternal reward in the new world.

Come Again?

Apocalyptic writing envisions all of human history as a proving ground for good and evil leading up to the final battle. So far, in other words, we've just been choosing up sides. Once God and humanity have sorted out whose side we're on, then we reach the beginning of the end. Plagues, prodigies, and portents show disruptions occurring in the natural world, the social order, and in heaven.

The Devil Makes You Do It

Apocalyptic thinking may have worked for the ancient prophets, but you probably don't want to try it yourself. People will think you're crazy and a troublemaker. On the other hand, it seems to have helped some people in New York City get their own cable access show!

Apocalyptic thinking has made a big mark on Judaism and Christianity. It lies behind the concept of the Messiah, the savior who comes on the last day to save the righteous from destruction. Both religions have traditionally stressed the importance of being ready for this event. No one wants to be caught goofing off when the Messiah arrives.

John Says We're Outta Here

Christians caught the apocalypse bug while suffering under Roman rule just as the Jews had it years before under Babylon. For John of the Apocalypse, the author of the Book of Revelation, "the beast" is one of the Roman emperors, who persecutes Christians, forcing them to worship him as a God or face punishment. Revelation also hearkens back to Jewish apocalyptic writings by describing the downfall of "the whore of Babylon." John uses Babylon as a metaphor for Rome, suggesting that Rome persecutes Christians just as Babylon persecuted the Jews.

Revelations

John of the Apocalypse wrote Revelation from Patmos, an island in the Aegean Sea used as a penal colony by the Roman Empire. It's likely that John was imprisoned because of his activities as a Christian missionary/agitator. His work can by read as a long, elaborate curse on the Roman Empire. Perhaps to avoid getting into even more trouble than he was already in, he refers to the emperor by using a numerical code to indicate the letters of his name to those who knew the code. That number is "the number of the beast," 666. Scholars are uncertain which emperor he's referring to. The leading candidates are Domitian (81–96 C.E.), who was notorious for instituting a policy of emperor-worship, and Nero Caesar (54–68 C.E.). It has also been suggested that John believed Nero was reincarnated as Domitian.

A Crash of Symbols

The whore of Babylon and the beast are just two of many familiar symbols from the Book of Revelation's symbolic grab bag. You may already be familiar with others. The spectacle includes the four horsemen of the apocalypse, the seven seals, the hill of Armageddon, the seven bowls of God's wrath, the seven trumpet blasts of the seven angels. The sun turns pitch black; the moon turns blood red; the sea is smooth as glass. Christ appears as a warrior on a white horse with his robe dipped in blood. You definitely get the feeling something big is going to happen.

Dore's pale rider, Death, one of the four horsemen of the apocalypse.

And of course, there are angels everywhere; "*myriads* and myriads" of them. (That's a lot.) Thousands of good angels battle evil angels. More angels cheer them on. Other angels perform ritual, symbolic acts. Still others explain what's happening. Angels direct traffic, dictate the action, change the scenery, and slaughter a third of the human race. Angels are even imagined as the audience, reading the account in the form of a letter. Revelation is of the angels, by the angels, and for the angels.

Winged Words

Technically, a **myriad** is ten thousand, but it comes from the Greek word for "uncountable." Angels are often visualized by the myriad, as in the Book of Revelation.

Closing Credits

The Book of Revelation is a cinematic spectacle, and every scene is a show-stopper. Best of all, it has an angelic cast of thousands. Scroll through the credits (listed in order of appearance) while they sing the Hallelujah Chorus:

➤ An angel tells John the contents of the revelation.

➤ Christ appears, shining like an angel, holding seven stars in his hand. The stars represent the angels of seven churches. The Book of Revelation is a letter addressed to these angels.

➤ "Four living creatures" worship at the throne of God. These are modeled after the cherubim and seraphim of Ezekiel and Isaiah. They have six wings and various animal faces and are covered with eyes, inside and out. I guess this is so they can see inside their own bodies!

➤ A "mighty angel" asks who is worthy to break the seven seals that contain the fate of the world. (The answer is the lamb of God, who has been scarred as a result of being sacrificed, and is equipped with seven eyes.)

➤ Myriads and myriads of angels surround the throne.

➤ The four horsemen of the apocalypse are sometimes considered angels. The first, on a white horse, is usually said to be Christ (but evangelist Billy Graham equates him with the powers of deception). The next, on a red horse, represents war; the black horse is famine, and the pale horse is death.

➤ Four angels at the four corners of the world control the four winds.

➤ An angel bears the seal of the living God to mark the foreheads of his faithful servants in order to preserve them from the coming destruction.

➤ When the lamb of God breaks the seventh seal, the seven angels of the presence are given seven trumpets with which to herald further catastrophe. (The angels of the presence are the ones that get to remain closest to God.)

➤ The fifth trumpet blast causes a star to fall, which unlocks the key to the abyss, releasing millions of locusts with stingers like scorpions. They also have the appearance of armored horses, golden crowns, human faces, long hair, and the teeth of lions. Their king is Apollyon, the angel of the abyss.

➤ The sixth trumpet blast releases four angels that have been tied up near the River Euphrates. They kill a third of humanity with 200 million squadrons of horsemen.

➤ A "mighty angel" wrapped in a cloud and with the rainbow around his head brings a scroll that is eaten by Saint John.

➤ The archangel Michael leads the angels of heaven in battle with the dragon and his angels. The dragon (Satan) and his angels are thrown down.

➤ Three angels appear, flying in mid air. The first proclaims the eternal gospel to the nations; the second announces the fall of Babylon; the third warns that those who worship the beast will drink the wine of God's wrath.

➤ Angels appear with sickles to gather in the grape harvest for God's wine. When the grapes are crushed in the wine press they ooze out blood.

➤ The "living creatures" (cherubim) hand out seven bowls full of the wrath of God to seven angels, who pour them onto the world as seven plagues.

Revelations

A popular gimmick among apocalyptic prophets is to say that the prophecy was written long ago and was sealed up until "just now," when it is revealed to humanity for the first time. In the Book of Daniel, for example, an angel tells the prophet to "seal up" his book until the time is near. John alludes to this convention in Revelation when the seven seals are opened, revealing the fate of the world. Later, however, he reverses the same convention in regard to his own writing. The angel who brings John his revelation tells him *not* to seal it up, because the prophecies are about to be fulfilled in the immediate future.

Out with the Old

Fortunately for what's left of the world, Christ and the good angels win the battle and "New Jerusalem" (sort of a pre-fab heavenly city) descends from heaven where the righteous may dwell with God. John said Christ would rule on Earth for a period of 1,000 years, otherwise called the *millennium*. Christians who await the 1,000-year rule of Christ are called *millenarians*.

Apocalyptic millenary thinking is affecting the way people look forward to the year 2000. The change to a new millennium gets people thinking about the millennium of Christ, or at least about the possibility of cataclysmic events. One cataclysm that may be in the offing is known in computer lingo as Y2K (year 2,000), the time when the two-digit year codes on many computers will register "00." Alarmists worry that the resulting computer-generated confusion will lead to catastrophes such as missile systems getting accidentally launched and the Federal Reserve accidentally giving all its money away to China.

Winged Words

A **millennium** is a 1,000-year period. *The* millennium is the 1,000-year period during which Christ will supposedly rule the earth. **Millenarians** are groups that believe the millennium is imminent.

Clearly the Book of Revelation has had a lasting effect on Western thinking, fueling a deep-down paranoia about what's in store. It's worth noticing, though, that John predicted the apocalypse was coming soon and his prophecies were not realized. Roman rule and persecution of Christians continued until the emperor Constantine converted to Christianity early in the 4th century. Constantine, incidentally, was persuaded that Christ helped him win an important military battle in which his troops were outnumbered.

Apocalypse Now

Despite the fact that, so far, the dire prophecies of the ancient seers have not been fulfilled, strains of apocalyptic thinking persist in our day. Some, but not all, of these strains are religiously oriented. Starting in this century, however, doomsday has become an increasingly secular fear.

The Devil Makes You Do It

One recent idea to facilitate credit purchasing suggests tattooing a bar code on all consumers so that just scanning the tattoo can access their accounts. Doomsayers have interpreted this proposal in apocalyptic terms, saying that it would represent the mark of the beast. Revelation says the beast "caused everyone...to be branded with a mark on his right hand or forehead, and no one was allowed to buy or sell unless he bore the beast's mark, either name or number." Maybe we'd better stick with plastic!

Wing Tip

Think of the ancient prophetic promise of "New Heavens and New Earth" as an early version of the New Age concept of a paradigm shift, in which people are becoming aware of newly evolved psychic powers that will transform existence for the better.

The Beast Is Back

It can easily seem that the forces running our lives—government, business, the media, and technology—are so corrupt and inhuman that they've become part of some diabolical plot. (Want proof? The portrait of George Washington on the dollar bill can be folded so as to look like a mushroom-shaped cloud! And even now, you're reading Chapter 13!) Paranoid worries like this can give rise to unreasonable hopes of a cosmic solution. Such hopes and fears have led to some bizarre and tragic situations.

Not long ago, a house full of people were found dead in the western United States. They had evidently killed themselves by taking poison while expecting an angelic visitation from outer space. They believed a UFO would come and take them away.

Back in the 1970s, the Jonestown massacre took the lives of an entire community of followers of a charismatic cult leader. Cult members drank from vats of Kool-Aid laced with deadly poison. Not all who died did so voluntarily, but those who took their own lives evidently thought something better was waiting for them after death.

Fortunately, such mini-apocalypses occur infrequently, but the feelings that gave rise to them—the sense that life as we know it is deeply unjust and the hope for some kind of cosmic escape hatch—are things many people can relate to.

New Ends in View

Mainstream religion these days tends not to put a lot of emphasis on apocalyptic thinking. Although Jewish belief includes the coming of the Messiah, and many Christians expect the second coming of Christ, few would argue that these events would inflict horrible deaths on growing numbers of evil people in the world. In fact, while the traditional view of apocalypse may still hold among some—that growing evil in the world is hastening the end—the opposite view may be at least equally strong—that transformation will take place as things get better, not worse.

The famous evangelist Billy Graham says assuredly that God would not permit the destruction of the human race. Of course, not everyone shares his optimism, especially since mass destruction seems completely possible through natural or technological means, rather than through acts of God. These days, the more likely the apocalypse becomes, the less God seems to be responsible.

Accidents Happen

Ever since the start of the cold war between the United States and the Soviet Union, nuclear holocaust has seemed like a very real possibility. This possibility seems less likely now that the cold war has ended, but nuclear weapons are still around, and they're as destructive as ever. As a result, we no longer associate doomsday with the blast of an angel's trumpet, but with the blast of an atomic bomb.

To many, the environment is facing serious threats from factors related to technology and overpopulation. Some fear that, as holes in the ozone layer grow, the ecology of the planet will be thrown off-kilter. Weather patterns are shifting; the polar ice caps are melting and the sea is rising, as are incidents of skin cancer and air pollution levels. Some fear that government and industry are not acting quickly or forcefully enough, looking to short-term profits rather than long-term solutions.

Asteroids have been in the news lately as possible causes of humanity's downfall. Many paleontologists believe that asteroids collided with Earth millions of years ago and wiped out the dinosaurs. If so, it stands to reason that the same fate could befall the human race—especially since they seem to cross Earth's orbit at fairly regular intervals.

Wing Tip

Impress your friends with these famous last-day words from "The Hollow Men" by the dour Modernist poet, T.S. Eliot: "This is the way the world ends/Not with a bang, but a whimper."

The Devil Makes You Do It

Don't let the coming apocalypse distract from brushing, flossing, and practicing good hygiene. You'll want to look and feel your best when Judgment Day comes.

We Can Always Just Rewind

Whenever the end may come, the most significant fact to keep in mind about doomsday is that, for better or worse, it isn't here yet. In fact, there's probably time to rent and watch another video. Here's a list of apocalypse flicks, taking various perspectives on the grand finale:

➤ *Apocalypse Now* (1979). Loosely based on Joseph Conrad's short novel, *Heart of Darkness*, this war movie set in Vietnam stars Marlon Brando as a wacko who copes with the war by inventing his own ideas about good and evil.

➤ *Dr. Strangelove, or How I Learned to Stop Worrying and Love the Bomb* (1964). Peter Sellers starring in multiple roles steals the show in this off-beat cult classic cold war spoof that culminates with exploding A-bombs.

➤ *Cocoon* (1985). Pods from the sea turn out to be angelic aliens in Ron Howard's morality tale. Human selfishness gums up the works, but the gang at the retirement community get to go to outer-space paradise in the sequel.

➤ *Terminator 2—Judgment Day* (1991). It's only a bad dream, but the opening sequence includes one of the most graphic depictions of a nuclear holocaust on film. Arnold Schwarzenegger plays a cybernetic guardian angel with an assault rifle.

➤ *The Seventh Seal* (1957). The black plague threatens to bring the apocalypse in Ingmar Bergman's masterpiece set in the Middle Ages. A famous scene shows the hero playing chess with the angel of death.

➤ *The Seventh Sign* (1988). Demi Moore finds chapter 23 of the Book of Revelation (the one in the Bible only has 22), gives birth, and averts the apocalypse as a good and an evil angel look on.

➤ *Prophecy* (1996). Directed by Gregory Widen, and starring Christopher Walken and Eric Stoltz, a cop trained as a priest gets caught up in the second war between angels.

The Least You Need to Know

➤ The shift from ancient prophecy to apocalypse has been spurred in part by the domination of foreign powers.

➤ Apocalyptic thinking conceives of worldly political problems in terms of cosmic war between good and evil angels.

➤ Apocalyptic thinking lies behind much Jewish and Christian theology.

➤ The Book of Revelation may constitute a symbolic protest against the command of the Roman emperor that he be worshipped.

➤ Apocalyptic thinking today reacts to global threats posed by nuclear weapons, environmental imbalance, and asteroids from space.

Chapter 14

School of Hard Gnosis

In This Chapter

➤ Angels in Gnosticism

➤ The pleroma and the aeons

➤ Sophia and Ialdabaoth

➤ The female Christ

➤ The archons and Noria

New religions have a tendency to reinterpret the ideas of other religions in such a way as to make the old ideas seem woefully inadequate. The Jews take the old pagan gods and turn them into lifeless idols, fallen angels, and evil ethnarchs; the Christians take the idea of Jewish law and say it was only a stop-gap measure while the world awaited the coming of Christ.

It's not that the old ideas are completely wrong, it's just that they're misleading and incomplete. They're missing the real point. The new religion fixes this problem by providing a bigger picture. To use the modern-day language of business management, the teachers of new religions "think outside the box."

Of course, the monotheistic God is, by definition, outside the box already. Or is he? Could there be a monotheistic religion that says the idea of God and his angels are really misleading notions that paint an incomplete picture of what is really a higher truth? You bet your sweet biblios there is. It's called Gnosticism, and it puts God and the angels inside a whole new ball game.

Deep Secrets

Gnosticism is the name referring to a diverse group of sects, usually Christian, which proliferated in the first few centuries following the death of Christ. It comes from the Greek word, *gnosis*, meaning "knowledge." Mainstream Christians of the times generally regarded the Gnostics as *heretics*, since they claimed to be Christians, but held beliefs that Christian authorities thought were outrageous. The Gnostics were so severely criticized for their offbeat religious ideas that they generally kept underground, keeping their religion secret among small groups of insiders.

Back in Circulation

Because the Gnostics were secretive—and because their ideas were condemned by the mainstream—their views have remained only partially understood for centuries. Until recently, the only information on Gnosticism came from Church authorities that complained about how bad it was. In 1945, however, a whole library of Gnostic writings written in the 4th century were discovered in Egypt at a site known as Nag Hammadi.

Winged Words

Heretics are Christians who hold beliefs that are condemned by the established Church. The Gnostic Christians were generally considered heretics during the early days of Christianity.

The Nag Hammadi Library contains dozens of Gnostic works. These have been translated and published only recently and, as you can imagine, scholars are thrilled to have these previously unknown documents to wrap their brains around. The ideas they contain include astonishing interpretations of Christian and Jewish teachings that, in effect, turn traditional monotheism around and stand it on its head.

Which Way Is Up?

The Gnostic writings reinterpret the roles of many of the most important figures in the Bible: God, Christ, Adam and Eve, the serpent in the Garden of Eden, and, oh yes, angels. In fact, Gnostics see the world itself in a completely different light from other Christians. According to the Gnostics, God made a big mistake when he created the world. He's only fooling himself and those who believe that he is Almighty, all-knowing, and merciful.

Need to think about that? The situation, as the Gnostics saw it, is a lot like the problem faced by the hero, played by Arnold Schwarzenegger, in the sci-fi movie *Total Recall* (1990). He's forgotten his true identity and thinks his mind is telling him what is actually going on, but the truth is, his memory has been almost completely erased by an evil power who wants him to *think* he's living in reality, whereas actually, the whole thing is a setup.

God and the world really exist, but they stand in the way of what's important—the divine spiritual realm that lies beyond God as most Christians understand him.

According to the Gnostics, getting in touch with real spirituality means getting past the fear of God. His power and authority, they say, is all in people's minds.

Revelations

Some scholars see Gnosticism not only as a particular tradition, but as a characteristic way of thinking that challenges orthodox beliefs and changes the way good and bad usually get sorted out. This broader conception of Gnosticism includes mystics who set themselves against conventional religious belief.

Wise Guys

Here's a typical Gnostic reversal of a traditional idea: There's an old religious saying that says, "The beginning of wisdom is the fear of God." The usual meaning of this saying is that it's wise to fear God, because he's so powerful and you should worry about the risks of doing wrong and making God mad at you. Gnostics reinterpret this saying to mean that it's God who becomes afraid when people start getting wise to him. This gives you an idea of how Gnostics interpret things.

Gnostic writings reinterpret the Bible and Christian ideas along these lines, to portray God as selfish and human life as a struggle to overcome the delusory influences of the world that God created. To take another example, Gnostics point to the Biblical passage in which God says "I am a jealous God; thou shalt have no other gods before me." In its original context, this statement is God's warning to the Israelites not to worship pagan gods or idols, but to remain loyal to the faith of their ancestors.

Gnostics reinterpret this statement to produce an entirely different meaning. They claim that Yahweh, the Jewish God, would not have said this if, in fact, there were no other god. There is another god and he's more spiritual than Yahweh is. This is why he's jealous. The Gnostics say God's jealousy is the whole reason he created the world in the first place—to compensate for his feelings of inadequacy!

Wing Tip

Christianity involves serious changes from Jewish ideas. One big change is the notion that Jewish law is replaced by Christian mercy with the coming of Christ. But consider Gnosticism as going even further in this direction than mainstream Christianity. Not only is Jewish law being replaced, but the Jewish God is being replaced too. Also, just as mainstream Christians regard Jewish law as in need of correction through mercy, Gnostics regard God and the world as in need of correction through wisdom.

181

A Clearer Vision

Gnostics believe they can see past the appearances of life to spiritual reality. They see the material world as a kind of sick display put on by God, who just wants attention and power. God wants people to think he's the only God there is, and, according to some Gnostics, he even believes this himself. In contrast, say the Gnostics, there's a higher divine realm of light and angelic beings that most people aren't aware of. God, his angels, and the world they created only stand in the way of human efforts to see this more perfect truth.

Gnostics see the Jewish and Christian God as an angel named Ialdabaoth, or Samael, which means "blind god." He's also called Saklas, which means "fool." He's not the omnipotent ruler he claims to be, but only a *demiurge*, an inferior deity who creates the material world.

A famous demiurge, William Blake's Urizen, preparing to create the world.

This God is blind or, in other words, in denial about the realm of light that existed before he made the world, but this divine realm, known as the *pleroma*, which means "fullness," was there long before. In his arrogance, Ialdabaoth the demiurge claimed that no other gods existed and demanded that those he created worship him alone.

Of course, most of the monotheistic world takes the blind God at his word and worships him alone. Only a few special individuals, namely those who are Gnostics, are able to see through his pretensions. They will make the journey through God's delusive world back to the pleroma where they came from—despite the obstacles posed by Samael and the other angels, who want to prevent them from getting there.

Mistakes Were Made

Here's how, according to the Gnostics, we got into this mess in the first place. To begin with, there's the true, absolute, eternal, and unknowable God. From this eternal God issued an emanation, known as *Ennoia*, which is the Greek word for "thought." Ennoia is also the first aeon, a kind of angel. Ennoia is female and God is male, and together they reproduce and give birth to numerous additional aeons. Different sources list different numbers of aeons, commonly 15 male and female pairs, but sometimes 365 of them.

Together, the aeons make up the pleroma, the divine light. Their names suggest they're the kind of celestial beings you wouldn't mind sharing your pool of light with. They include Foresight, Divinity, Goodness, Kingdom, Insight, and Wisdom. So far, so good. Some accounts also include Christ among the aeons, but we'll get back to him later.

Wisdom, or *Sophia*, as she is known in Greek, is the last of the aeons to be born. True to the name of Wisdom, Sophia is a troublemaker. Some say she had a serious crush on her father, even though celestial incest was probably a no-no even back then.

Winged Words

A **demiurge** is a minor deity who creates the world. The Gnostics are not the first to attribute the creation of the world to a demiurge. The idea was set forward centuries earlier in the philosophy of Plato. The **pleroma** is the divine realm of light recognized by Gnostic Christians as existing above and beyond the reality created by God. Gnostics see themselves as sparks that have been separated from this light and hope to be reunited with it once more after the death of their bodies.

Wing Tip

The distinction between sexuality and spirituality is sometimes a blurry one, especially when one is used as a metaphor for the other, as happens frequently in religious writing.

A Difficult Birth

Actually, this isn't necessarily as kinky as it sounds. It means that Sophia wanted to *know* the Father without actually being able to. (He is, by definition unknowable, so Sophia, or Wisdom, would naturally feel frustrated about him.) The Gnostics talk about this knowledge in sexual terms. Sophia wanted to know—have sex with—the Father but couldn't.

So she decided to try to be like her father and give rise to an emanation of herself to conceive a child. The result was that she ended up getting herself pregnant without a father. This was kind of embarrassing for Sophia, so, when her time came, she took a trip outside the pleroma to have the baby in private.

Sadly, Sophia's offspring didn't have the same radiant glow about him that everything in the pleroma had. According to some accounts, the baby was stillborn, and became the lump of matter out of which Ialdabaoth made the world. (Ialdabaoth, you remember, is the Gnostic name for God, or Yahweh.)

Others say the offspring was Ialdabaoth himself. They say he was born with a lion's head, indicating there was something mean and strange about him right from the start. In any case, Ialdabaoth was the first of many evil creator-angels called archons. They have power over material creation and want to keep it that way.

The archons are also referred to as "powers" or "authorities." They are, in effect, the angelic police of the material world. They want to be worshipped by human beings, despite the fact that it is humanity, and not the archons, who have sparks of the divine pleroma inside them. Thus the archons are corrupt and abuse their authority.

The Devil Makes You Do It

Don't write off Gnosticism as an outdated religious group. Gnostic Churches exist today. Gnosticism has also had a pronounced influence on the work of poet and printer William Blake (many of whose works are reprinted in this book), psychologist Carl Jung, and writers Jack Kerouac and Philip K. Dick.

Shooting Off Sparks

Ialdabaoth wasn't as luminous and spiritual as all the aeons back in the pleroma were, but he had some of the pleroma's divine spark. Unfortunately, he didn't know what to do with it and so he isolated himself from everyone back home. This meant that there was less of the divine stuff up in the pleroma where it belonged. Sophia felt bad about this and devised a plan to fool Ialdabaoth and get it back.

While Ialdabaoth was off sulking by the depths of eternity, Sophia looked down out of the pleroma so he could see her reflection in the waters. The sight made Ialdabaoth want his mom to come and be with him, but he knew she wouldn't leave the pleroma just for him, with his ugly lion's head. So he made a model of a celestial being out of clay, hoping it would lure Sophia down to him. This is the Gnostic version of the story in the Book of Genesis in which God makes humankind out of clay.

After he had formed the body, he breathed life into it, but in doing so, the divine spark that came from the pleroma was transfused into the clay, resulting in the first human being. Sophia's plan had worked perfectly. Now all she had to do was get the divine spark that was breathed into humanity back to the pleroma.

As it turns out, according to the Gnostics, only certain human beings would inherit this divine spark. These were the Gnostics themselves. Everybody else is just so much dead wood. Unlike mainstream Christianity, then, Gnosticism isn't a universal religion in the sense of offering itself to the whole world.

Homeward Bound

So there you have it—the world according to Gnosticism is a cosmic mess. But there's another problem: The sparks from the pleroma that become people don't necessarily realize who they are or where they're from. They start to worship Ialdabaoth as the supreme God, Yahweh. To fill them in on what the real deal is, the eternal Father sends down Christ, who takes human form and teaches special communities of Christians the Gnostic secrets that will enable them to return to the pleroma after death.

Wake-Up Call

See why Christian authorities labeled the Gnostics as heretics? The Gnostics believe the God worshipped by other Christians is pretty much a lot of hot air. According to the Gnostics, Christ comes not to fulfill God's plan, but to help people escape from God's universe.

In effect, Christ has to wake people up in order to remind them of their truly divine origins. His crucifixion does not constitute the ultimate sacrifice that brings atonement with God as it does for mainstream Christians. Instead, it shows how useless and unimportant the material world created by Ialdabaoth is. It marks the escape of Christ from the body of Jesus back to the pleroma. In fact, some Gnostics believed that Christ bailed out of the body of Jesus even before the crucifixion!

Wing Tip

It helps to be flexible in your thinking about the distinction between male and female beings in Gnosticism. Some Gnostics recognize an androgynous (male and female) being who serves as an immortal counterpart of humanity on Earth. What's more, many aeons have male and female aspects that are often interchangeable. Some Gnostics even believe Christ was an embodiment of the aeon, Sophia.

Eat the Apple

Although the Gnostics regarded Christ as a teacher sent to point the way to the pleroma, he was not the first. Gnostic legend also recognizes the first woman, Eve, as a heroine of humankind, together with the serpent in the Garden of Eden, who persuaded her to disobey the commands of Yahweh (Ialdabaoth) by eating fruit from the Tree of Knowledge. Eating the fruit helped Eve see what was going on, and she let Adam, her husband, in on the secret.

Revelations

A number of feminist scholars have become keenly interested in Gnosticism because of the radical attitude toward gender roles revealed in many Gnostic writings. Female figures often play important roles as teachers and creators. In addition, androgyny is often presented as an ideal state. Scholars disagree over the extent to which Gnosticism constitutes early expressions of feminism.

This view of Eve as heroine contrasts with the traditional interpretation of Genesis that Eve is to blame for all human misery. According to this standard view, Eve was weak and foolish to allow herself to be seduced by the serpent into disobeying God by eating the fruit of the Tree of Knowledge. As a result, it's her fault that we grow old and die and have to work for a living.

Getting Past Our Differences

Some Gnostics saw the fall in a different way entirely. Instead of creating the first man and then creating the first woman, the idea is that God created an androgyne—a man-woman—who was a single, complete being. Later, God, or Ialdabaoth, divided the androgyne into two beings, a man and a woman. This was when all the trouble started—on Earth, anyway.

According to some Gnostics, a similar painful separation took place in heaven when Sophia was separated from Ialdabaoth. Thus, the division of man and woman re-enacts the previous loss of sparky stuff from the pleroma. They say, however, that a cosmic, immortal androgyne exists in heaven. Returning to the pleroma involves merging with this androgyne and becoming sexually whole again.

Gnostics are divided about whether sexual wholeness can be achieved on Earth. Some said that it can be restored simply by having sex. Others said it's better not to have sex in order to save your fiery spark for the pleroma. Releasing it on Earth would just waste it! As you can imagine, this led to serious discrepancies in the ways different Gnostic sects practiced their religion. These discrepancies are evident in different versions of Gnostic myths that have been preserved in the old books.

The Devil Makes You Do It

Don't read ancient Gnostic writings simply for their religious justifications of kinky sexuality. There's more to them than that!

Parental Discretion Advised

In some Gnostic myths, it is Eve's daughter, Noria, who is humanity's first Gnostic teacher. Noria is a beautiful virgin who arouses the attention of the archons, the angelic powers who rule the world. They lust after her and attempt to seduce her, saying (untruthfully) that her mother, Eve, came to them (had sex with them) before Noria was born. Now, said the archons, it was Noria's turn.

There are two different versions of the story of Noria: One's rated PG-13 and the other is unrated—strictly late-night viewing. According to the racier version, Noria deliberately seduces the archons, who have sex with her. In doing so, they give up their celestial sparks, which leaves their bodies along with their seminal fluid. As a result, there's less of the sparky stuff for the archons and more for humanity, who will bring it back up to the pleroma with them after they die.

Revelations

According to some accounts, certain radical Gnostic sects went in for some pretty outrageous behavior, including sexual orgies and snake worship. Sexual orgies included rituals involving the sacramental eating of sexual and menstrual emissions. The idea was to preserve the spiritual light contained in the emissions. Other Gnostic groups rationalized licentious sexual behavior by saying that the flesh and the spirit had nothing to do with each other and that the spirit achieved salvation through knowledge rather than proper behavior. As a result, it's okay to indulge in any sort of horse-play you feel like! While some Gnostic groups practiced sexual freedom, others preached abstinence, saying that sex causes the divine light to leave the body.

In the tamer version of the story, Noria refuses to be seduced by the archons and yells for help. Her cries summon the aeon named Eleleth, or "Understanding," from the pleroma, who rescues her and helps her alert others to the evil doings of the archons. In either version, the important thing, say the Gnostics, is to realize the archons don't have any real power over true divinity, which lies with selected human beings.

Looking Death in the Face

This is important if your divine spark is going to make a successful journey back to the pleroma where it belongs after you die. The archons will be waiting for you at each of the seven spheres surrounding the earth, and you have to confront them and get past them. The Gnostics say you can do this by uttering words of defiance similar to those uttered by Noria when the archons tried to violate her.

The seven archons standing guard over the seven spheres are associated with the planets and signs of the zodiac. As this list shows, they're a bunch of tough and ugly customers:

Wing Tip

It's a long trip all the way back to the pleroma, but fortunately your divine spark doesn't have to make the whole journey all at once. According to Gnostic legend, your spark can camp out along the way in the sun and the moon.

➤ *Ialdabaoth*—The chief archon and demiurge who created the world. He has the head of a lion, and for that reason is also called Ariel, "lion of God."

➤ *Iao*—A serpent-faced archon with seven heads.

➤ *Sabaoth*—An archon with a face made of flame.

➤ *Adoneus*—A dragon-faced archon.

➤ *Eloeus*—An archon with the face of an ass (a donkey, that is!).

➤ *Oreus*—An ape-faced archon.

➤ *Astaphaeus*—An archon with the face of a hyena.

Off the Hook

Gnosticism turned the God-made universe upside down, making it seem like a cruel, cosmic hoax. Evidently, it didn't exactly have a calming effect on the early Christian Church, either. In fact, noted religious scholar Elaine Pagels says that Gnostic beliefs provided a rationale for Gnostic Christians to defy Church authorities.

Pagels says the cosmic view of Gnosticism is modeled on their view of the organization of the Church. The archons—the domineering angels who stand guard over material reality—correspond to the priests and bishops of the Church, who try to dictate the terms of Christian worship. Just as Gnosticism teaches that it's okay to go over the heads of the angels, Gnostics also went over the heads of Church authorities. In fact, the word "archon" means "ruler" or "authority." These are words that could be applied to Church officials as well as to angels.

It may seem surprising to learn that the Early Church (begun during the first three centuries of the Millennium) exerted a domineering influence on some of its sects. After all, these were the times when Christians in general were being persecuted by the officials of the Roman Empire. You'd think Christians would want to band together in a unified show of resistance rather than squabble about whether Christ was sent by Yahweh or emanated from the pleroma.

According to Pagels, views of Christ made an important real-world difference as far as the Gnostics were concerned. The mainstream authorities taught that Christ was crucified and resurrected as an incarnated being. He really suffered, really died, and really came back to life. Consequently, it's important for all Christians to be prepared to suffer and die, too. Many Christian martyrs did just that, losing their lives through public torture and execution merely for acknowledging their Christian beliefs.

Many Gnostics, in contrast, believed that Christ's crucifixion was not theologically important. His soul, or divine spark, was freed from his body when he died, but his death did not say anything special about his soul or divine status. To these Gnostics, it was not necessary to be willing to die in order to uphold your beliefs. It was okay to lie to save your life by publicly denying your Christianity or by accepting the emperor as a god.

This is just one more reason why Gnosticism must have really irked mainstream Christians. Not only did they put God in a box and turn him upside down, but they seemed to sneak their way out of having to face the most severe test of Christian belief. Obviously, the mainstream won out in the long run. While the Gnostics went underground, the Christians martyrs caused a sensation that attracted thousands of new converts.

Even so, the Gnostics have been praised at various times throughout the centuries as brilliant visionaries. Their religious views supply critical commentary on mainstream belief that often seems like profound psychological insight. Gnosticism, like many psychologists of the 20th century, suggests that the reason people believe in God is to compensate for feelings of isolation and inadequacy.

Wing Tip

These days, you don't have to be a martyr in order to be a good Christian. Just explain to yourself that Christ's sacrifice did the trick, so there's no need for you to die too.

The Devil Makes You Do It

It may seem logical that people believe in God in order to compensate for feelings of isolation and inadequacy. Then again, it may seem logical that people do just about anything to compensate for feelings of isolation and inadequacy.

The Least You Need to Know

➤ The Gnostics reduce the Christian God to an arrogant, blind demiurge.

➤ The pleroma is the Gnostic realm of eternal spirit that stands in contrast to the created material world.

➤ Aeons are angelic figures that inhabit the pleroma. Archons are evil angels that rule the material world.

➤ Sophia, or "Wisdom," gave rise to Ialdabaoth, the creator, when she ventured outside the pleroma.

➤ Gnostics believe they possess a divine spark that will journey back to the pleroma when they die.

Martyrs, Sinners, Saints, and Angels

There are two outs in the bottom of the ninth with the Devils leading the Angels 8 to 7 in game 6 of the year 254 C.E. World Series. The rivalry has been intense and crowds have turned out in huge numbers to see what many believe could be the Final Battle. A holy hush falls over the stadium as Mickey Martyr stands in at bat and faces the Devils' closer.

This Devil is a hot young prospect called up from the Roman Empire, a wicked spitter (pitcher) with unbelievable power and a nasty fork-ball. He's got an unearthly .666 ERA (earned run average), but no saves, thanks to his wild tendencies. Mickey knows that if he can just get on base, he'll bring the winning run to the plate—the real power of the Angels' lineup. This would give the home team a good shot at the ultimate victory and all the glory that goes with it. And hey, ya gotta believe!

One and two is the count. It's the wind-up (weirdly serpentine and intended to be distracting, but Mickey keeps his eye on the ball, just like they taught him in Little League). True to the pitcher's wild reputation, a high hard one comes straight at Mickey's head! Mickey has a split second to think about what to do next—and then he'll have an eternity to live with his decision.

The rational thing would be to duck out of the way, but Mickey knows this is just what the Devils want. He'd be left shaken and off-balance—all set up for the next wicked pitch. But if he keeps his head up, he'll get nailed! The pain would be torture! It would surely put him out of the game for good. But Mickey doesn't think about that. He thinks about getting started on that long trip to home and the sweetness of victory when it's all over...and he takes one for the team!

Winged Words

You probably already know that a **legend** is a popular story that gets told from generation to generation. The word originally meant the story of the life of a saint. Typically, these stories are filled with angels, miracles, and martyrdoms.

A Tough Act to Follow

Of course, the first martyrs weren't really baseball players. In fact, the first martyrs weren't even Christians, since the Jews before them were no strangers to persecution and recognized the sacrifice of one's life for one's faith as a holy act. It was during the early days of Christianity, however, that martyrdom really came into its own. It should come as no surprise that, according to *legend* (the lives of saints, that is) early Christian martyrs had many encounters with angels.

Dore's Martyrdom of Saint Stephen.

Who was the first Christian martyr? Asking *that* question is a little like asking who was buried in Grant's tomb. Obviously, the answers are Jesus H. and Ulysses S., respectively. Technically, though, Jesus isn't considered a "Christian," since Christians are followers of Christ. Anyway, Jesus inspired many to follow his example and give up their lives in order to promote Christian salvation. The first Christian martyr aside from Jesus is Saint Stephen. Stephen, like many of the martyrs, was and still is honored as a Christian saint.

Feeling Their Pain

Some early accounts say martyrs not only became saints, but angels. The transformation came not after death, but before, during torture. As angels, the martyrs could endure their torments more easily than as human beings. Interestingly, the Gnostics have a similar view of Jesus and the crucifixion. They say that Christ left the body of Jesus before getting crucified. As a result, the damage done to the body did no harm whatsoever. Instead, it represented the symbolic defeat of the material world.

Comforting as this thought may be, it was not a generally accepted belief. Instead, accounts of martyrs' deaths stress their humanity and emphasize the intensity of their suffering, attributing their fortitude to their spiritual strength rather than to a miraculous transformation. Legend says, however, that angels often provided strength and comfort to martyrs to help them face their torments and death.

Often, as disappointing as this may seem, angels provide only verbal encouragement. Polycarp is just one martyred saint who is told to "play the man" by an angel. This may mean he should act brave, but it could also mean he should act like Christ. Part of the grisly point of martyrdom is that the martyr is so fixed on God and heaven that earthly concerns don't make any difference—not even physical agony. As a result, there's generally no attempt made by the martyr, the angel, or the storyteller, to diminish or avoid the martyr's suffering.

Wing Tip

Before you decide to become a martyr, you might want to see what you can do for your cause without suffering and dying for it first.

Why Suffer?

Christians risked torture and execution by the Roman Empire simply for owning up to their Christianity. Suspected Christians were given a chance to avoid punishment by showing their support for state religion. They could burn incense or say a prayer to the genius of the emperor. Those who refused to perform acts of pagan piety could face horrific consequences.

Revelations

Christianity in itself was considered a crime by the Roman Empire. Christians were often made scapegoats (Nero blamed them for setting fire to Rome) and vilified in various ways. In fact, they were widely thought to practice incest and cannibalism. Some scholars think the suspicion of cannibalism stems from the Eucharist—the ritual eating of "the blood and body of Christ"! Of course, not all Roman officials were equally zealous about persecuting Christians. Even so, martyring Christians was part of the paganomics practiced by the Roman Empire. Local officials could make extra money by providing Christian prisoners who could be publicly executed. They were less expensive than professional gladiators!

Christians were sometimes tortured and killed as public spectacles. They could be thrown into the arena to hungry lions and other wild animals, flayed with whips, or incinerated. Despite this gruesome fate, many Christians willingly went public with their religion and defied the religion of the empire, regarding a martyr's death as a glorious achievement.

Martyrs were said to receive crowns in the next world after death, which they wore to show God's recognition of their trials on Earth. Some legends say the martyrs are crowned by the angels. Martyrs were praised by the earthly Church too, since their sufferings were thought to help spread Christianity. They were regarded as affirmations of Christian belief who inspired others to adopt and maintain the faith.

Attention Getting

The word "martyr" comes from the Greek word for "witness." This suggests that martyrs were supposed to have direct insight into the truth of Christianity. After all, you'd need to be pretty sure God loved Christians in order to give up your life for the Christian cause. This willingness no doubt impressed others and made them take Christianity seriously.

It's kind of weird, but while martyrdom served as a visceral source of excitement for pagan spectators, it served as a profound source of inspiration for Christians. Christians tried to transform the cheap thrills these public executions were intended to provide into religious awe. Rather than a crude display of the enemies of the state being shredded to bits, martyrdom became a mysterious affirmation of a higher reality.

It was the willingness on the part of Christians to be tortured and killed that made the difference. They *wanted* to make a spectacle of themselves in order to demonstrate the insignificance of earthly matters in relation to heaven, to win the martyr's crown, and to gain new converts for their faith. The whole Roman system of persecution through public torture and execution provided zealous Christians with just the exposure they were looking for.

Roman officials sometimes regarded martyrs as sick, suicidal show-offs, even though their deaths were staged by the government as public entertainment. You have to ask, though, if martyrdom was a sickness, whether it was the extraordinary religious fervor of the Christians or the circus-like punishments imposed on them that was responsible. Actually, both of these things worked together to fuel the fires of martyrdom in the early days of Christianity.

While their deaths were spectacular to begin with, stories of the martyrs are especially impressive, emphasizing their courage and serenity in the face of brutality. The stories are made even more impressive as a result of the miracles they describe, which take place during torture or death. Many of these miracles do not serve to protect the martyr from torture so much as to draw attention to the martyr's holiness. The pagans tried to incinerate Saint Polycarp, for example, but the fire had no effect, so they stabbed him instead. His blood gushed out in a huge torrent that put out the fire!

Wing Tip

Thinking about how a martyr could decide to undergo death and torture for the sake of religion may help you to understand God by forcing you to re-evaluate your personal philosophy (but beware—it may make you go crazy!).

Angels were often said to be present at the deaths of martyrs. Their presence is another way of drawing attention to the event. This extra attention attracted more new converts to Christianity. Accounts of martyrdoms sometimes say that spectators saw angels and converted. Of course, angel appearances generally indicate holiness, whether a martyr is involved or not. Sometimes when a saint dies, those present hear angels singing, or see the angels guiding the saint's soul to heaven.

Job Sharing

According to many early Christians and present-day Catholics, saints in heaven have a special role of praying to God on behalf of living people. Thus the role of the saint dovetails to some extent with the role of angels. In fact, The Catholic Church recognizes the three angels mentioned in the Bible—Michael, Gabriel, and Raphael—as saints as well as angels.

Saints are publicly revered and have often been thought to work miracles on Earth. Personal effects, and even bodily remains, of saints have been preserved as relics and thought to have spiritual powers. As with angels, however, the Church does not officially endorse the worship of saints, despite the fact that many saint cults have sprung up from time to time. One example of a "saint cult" would be in reference to the number of groups who directly worship Mary, but you could also consider Santeria a saint cult, although from a different region.

Angels with a Sudarium, by Albrecht Durer. A Sudarium is a cloth with the image of the face of Christ on it. Legend says that Saint Veronica wiped the face of Christ with a cloth on his way to Calvary and the cloth retained the image.

Revelations

Saints and angels have a great deal in common. Just as some pagan gods were incorporated into Judaism as angels (especially in ancient times long before the rise of Christianity), other gods were incorporated into Christianity as saints (especially as a result of Christian missionary activity in pagan countries). In fact, the African and West Indian religion known as Santeria recognizes angelic figures known as orishas who are both African gods and Christian saints.

Single-Minded Saint

One noted martyr and saint from the early days of Christianity is Agnes, who died under torture in Rome in the year 305. In stories told about her, her persecution as a Christian by the Roman Empire ties in with the temptation to sin under pressure from worldly influences. She was threatened with death by fire, both as a real punishment for being a Christian and as a symbol for the hardships of chastity, which involve "burning" desires.

According to her legend, Agnes had no trouble facing real or symbolic flames, thanks to her spiritual love for Christ. First she passed up a wealthy husband and later she gave up her life—both for her religion. In return, she won converts for God and some powerful angelic support.

Chaste and Chased

Because she was devoted to God and the holy life, Agnes turned down an offer of marriage from the son of one of the wealthiest men in Rome. The father of the rejected groom was so irate and spiteful about it that he pulled strings in order to have Agnes sent to a brothel. This would be a bad thing for anyone, but it was especially bad for Agnes, because virginity was a religious thing with her.

Fortunately for Agnes, an angel came to protect her. Not only did the angel keep customers away from her, but he filled the whole bordello with a heavenly light, which spoiled the ambience, exposed the customers, and made the prostitutes' make-up jobs look funny and unattractive. In short, having a righteous angel of God hanging around the cat-house was bad for business.

Easy Pray

As fate, luck, or some mysterious design would have it, one of the customers who came to see Agnes was the rich man's son whose proposal of marriage she had turned down. Evidently he couldn't take no for an answer. Anyway, it's safe to say his sex drive and his moral compass were both pointed in the wrong direction.

When he tried to approach Agnes, however, the angel struck him blind. In some versions of the story, he became deathly ill and died shortly after. The father soon found out about it and was pretty upset, but he learned his lesson. He realized that there was something special about Agnes, and he also saw that what he and his son had tried to do was pretty slimy. So he asked Agnes to pray for him and his son.

As a future saint, praying for sinners was right up Agnes' alley. Her prayers were so effective that the son was brought back to life. We don't know whether the son had an out-of-body experience and saw a distant light that got him in touch with his spiritual energy, but he was suitably impressed; so much so that he and his father converted to Christianity. Agnes was later put to death as a Christian.

Wing Tip

Don't forget to celebrate the feast day of Saint Agnes on January 21! And if you're a young virgin and you want to see a vision of your future husband, try fasting and praying the night before (St. Agnes Eve). If the old superstition holds true, your future mate will appear in your dreams.

Perpetua's Motion

Agnes is an important martyr and saint in part because of her virginity. Another famous martyr is Perpetua, who came from a well-to-do family and was put to death in Carthage. Unlike Agnes, Perpetua was a mother. She had recently given birth at the time of her public execution and moved spectators to pity on account of the milk that was dripping from her breasts as she faced torture. She is famous not just for this reason, but because she kept a diary that records her story. This diary is particularly remarkable because it includes accounts of her dreams.

On Top of the World

One dream serves as a premonition of her upcoming martyrdom and ascent into heaven. She is about to climb a tall ladder up into the sky. Above her is her teacher and Christian mentor, Saturus (as it turned out, Saturus was martyred along with Perpetua). To the sides of the ladder are spears and knives and other weapons that threaten to cut anyone who climbs the ladder on the way up. Underneath the ladder is a dragon.

Saturus calls down to her to watch out for the dragon, but she doesn't need to worry, since the dragon stuck its head out in front of the rungs of the ladder and let her step on it. The dragon represents the martyrdom that Perpetua faced, and it also helps her make it to heaven. She makes it to the top of the ladder and finds a man dressed as a shepherd milking a sheep. The man gives her some of the sheep curds he has milked, which Perpetua eats. The place is filled with people who say "Amen" as she wakes up from this dream of a ladder and a dragon with a sweet taste in her mouth.

Meeting the Man

Saturus, Perpetua's teacher, has a dream that is also recorded as part of Perpetua's story. Saturus dreams he and Perpetua have already been martyred and are flown up to heaven by angels who manage to carry them without touching them. They head toward a light and eventually set foot in a garden where they are welcomed by more angels. They also see people they knew who had previously been martyred.

Then they are escorted further into the garden and hear the sound of "holy, holy, holy" and they see God himself sitting on his throne, but it's kind of a low-key thing. They aren't dazzled and they don't fall on their faces. Instead, God, who is a fairly young-looking guy except for his snow-white hair, gets up and gives them a kiss. Then some elders who are there with God get up and kiss them too.

Saturus says, "Way to go, Perpetua, we made it." Then they are approached by some officials of the Church

The Devil Makes You Do It

When you get to heaven, leave your irritation with your earthly co-workers at the pearly gates before entering. No one will want to hear about it!

who had been involved in bureaucratic squabbles on Earth. The officials fall down at Saturus' feet and ask for his advice. Saturus helps them up as an angel says, "Tell them to stop bickering about unimportant stuff like Church bureaucracy." So the officials feel ashamed. Then Saturus notices how good it smells in heaven and he wakes up.

Both of these dreams should be seen as premonitions or visions in which each individual learns that they will become a martyr for their beliefs.

Nobody's Perfect

Of course, not all Christians ended up getting put to death for their beliefs. In general, though, Christians were expected to make personal sacrifices. They were supposed to give to charity and avoid the seven deadly sins: pride, anger, envy, sloth, lust, gluttony, and greed. Many Christians were so severe, they believed that if you sinned after being baptized, you could no longer get into heaven.

It's true that there were fewer TV commercials back then to tempt everyone into abandoning themselves to worldly pleasures, but even so, the "no sinning" rule made Christianity a pretty tough row to hoe. In fact, some Christians took a good hard look at themselves and had to admit they couldn't do it. One of these was a Roman Christian named Hermas, who lived in the 2nd century.

Revelations

The concept of sin provided a way of understanding psychological disorders and abnormal behavior back in the days before clinical psychology was invented. Sin was not only bad, it also made you suffer, much as a disease does. Repentance emerged as a popular cure for this disease.

Second Chance

Hermas wasn't a martyr or a saint, just a regular guy with a job and a family. Who knows, he probably liked to relax with a few bowls of wine after work. He knew that if God expected him to be holy and pure his whole life, he was in big trouble. Fortunately for Hermas, an angel appeared to him in a vision and told him he still had a chance to be saved. At least, that's what's written in the allegorical vision known as *The Shepherd of Hermas*, which Hermas wrote to show others how to get back in God's good graces after slipping up.

Hermas's story became extremely popular among early Christians. Undoubtedly his readers were encouraged to think that angels could appear and give help to ordinary people as well as to saints and martyrs. While most Church people were calling for spotless perfection and ideal religious purity, Hermas's story says that God is willing to cut people a little slack.

Wing Tip

If you need to make a public confession of a sin, lust can be a pretty safe choice. Jimmy Carter made this confession while president and it made nowhere near the bad impression the hostage crisis made on the American public! On the other hand, if you're going to try to keep your sin secret, lust can trip you up, since it's something lots of people want to find out about!

Hermas wasn't an evil person, but he was a sinner. It seems he was helping a lady up out of a pool where she had been swimming and—brace yourself—he lusted after her. This was his sin. In fact, the lady herself appeared to Hermas in a vision years later and told him so. She said in so many words, "I'm very flattered that you lusted after me, but you shouldn't have done it, being a Christian and all."

Hermas was pretty worried by this, since he thought God might be playing by the "one strike and you're out" rule. According to further visionary developments, however, this turned out not to be the case. Hermas still had one more chance, provided he quit sinning and give himself over to his guardian angel.

Owning Up

The angel appeared to Hermas in the form of a shepherd—he had a goatskin and a big sheep-crook and the whole get-up. (Jesus Christ is often thought of as the original "good shepherd," like in Perpetua's dream, but Hermas's good shepherd is an angel.) Hermas's job was to be the sheep and allow himself to be led by his shepherd, who was called the angel of Repentance.

The angel of Repentance came to help Hermas get back on track with Christianity. Hermas could get away with his one sin, just so long as he felt really bad about it, which he did. He did a lot of fasting and praying and called himself an ignorant fool when he didn't understand the symbolic visions the angel revealed to him.

Rocks on the Water

The angel of Repentance wasn't the only angelic influence in Hermas's visionary experience. According to the good shepherd-angel, everyone has two other angels with them during the course of their lives, the angel of Righteousness and the angel of Wickedness. The appearance of these two in *The Shepherd of Hermas* herald the beginning of a long, popular tradition. When we sin, it's because we listened to the bad angel, and when we do good, it's because we followed the good one's advice. The shepherd angel says all we have to do is decide not to listen to the bad angel.

Easy for him to say! Some peoples' angel of Wickedness can be pretty darned persuasive. In contrast, angels of Righteousness seem to have this strange, symbolic way of communicating. At least that's the way the good angels come across in Hermas's story. For example, right at the beginning of the story, he sees six good angels. These angels might have said to Hermas, "Hey, Hermas, remember to go to church; you'll feel better and God will like you again." But no, this would be too easy.

The Devil Makes You Do It

Blaming your bad actions on your angel of Wickedness may work in Sunday school, but it probably won't stand up in court.

Instead, the six angels get a myriad of helpers to bring them thousands of stones of all shapes and sizes. They take the stones and start building a tower—right on the surface of a body of water. Obviously the angels are pretty miraculous, since they can make stones float; even so, they're really particular about which stones they use to build the tower. Lots of the stones get thrown away—some near the tower and others further off.

Not surprisingly, Hermas wants an explanation for this sudden appearance of a tower in the middle of the water. Suddenly there's this lady who's explaining the vision to him (the shepherd angel shows up later) and she's like, "Well, duh! Think much?"—only she's warm and benevolent and not all snotty about it. Anyway, she explains that the tower represents the Church and the water it's built on represents baptism, the point being that Christianity depends on people getting baptized. The stones represent people, and some of them are good for Christianity and fit into the Church and others are like rolling stones, with no place in the order of things. The lady advised Hermas to try to fit in, or else he'd be left out in the cold when the Church was finished.

Efforts Bearing Fruit

The incident figures into the main point of the whole story, which is, even if you sin, you can repent and can still get into heaven. The stones that don't fit into the tower right away can perhaps be used later. They may get reshaped at some point, especially if they haven't rolled too far from the building. The lady tells Hermas he is like one of the stones that's near the tower that may still fit in someday.

Later on, Hermas has another angelic vision that makes a similar point. The archangel Michael appears with a pruning hook under a big willow tree. He's cutting branches off the tree and giving them to people who are gathered around the tree. There's a big crowd, so Michael has to lop off lots of branches. Even so, the tree remains as big and bushy as it was to begin with.

After everyone has been given a branch, Michael says he wants them all back again. So everyone turns in their branches. Some of the branches have withered up, and some got moldy, and some were eaten by bugs. Others were only partly withered, or moldy, or bug-eaten. Still others were green, pretty much like they were to begin with. Some were even leafier than they were to begin with, and a few were really leafy and even had fruits growing on them.

Michael rejoiced over the people whose branches had fruit on them. They were given crowns and got to go into the tower. Michael also rejoiced over those whose branches were at least, or almost, as green as they were at first, even though they didn't get crowns. Still, they got to go into the building too. Then Michael went away while everyone else with unhealthy branches had to stay outside.

Get the idea? The tree represents the Word of God, and the state of the branch you have reflects the kind of person you are. So, if your branch dies, the word isn't getting through to you. The people with fruit on their branches not only got the message but spread the word along. These were the martyrs. Those with extra-leafy branches had also undergone hardships for Christianity, but didn't give up their lives. Those whose branches were just the same as when they started were just plain old ordinary good folks. The rest were a bunch of sinners with varying degrees of sinfulness.

Wing Tip

You can think of Christian morality as being kind of like one of those virtual pets that you're supposed to take care of. Some peoples' morals die in the shell, others make it to the chick stage, and only so many survive to become virtual chickens. In other words, a certain percentage of people are going to say, "To heck with it, I don't have the time."

Revelations

The Shepherd of Hermas is an important early Christian work about the angel of Repentance, also called the angel of Penance. This angel is mentioned by other early Jewish and Christian writers as well. The Apocryphal Book of Henoch names this angel Phanuel. Origen and Clement of Alexandria also discuss this angel, saying his role is to encourage sinners to repent and to keep away devils who might tempt or accuse the repentant soul.

Sticking to the Church

All these varying degrees of sin and virtue suggest the "one strike and you're out" rule isn't really fair. This is especially true when the angel of Repentance is on your case. In fact, the story goes on: Even though Michael went away, it wasn't all over for the all those folks holding the short end of their religion sticks.

The angel of Repentance told everyone to put their sticks into the ground. Then he watered the sticks and left them there for a few days. (Get it? When the angel of Repentance waters your stick, it means you're sorry for the bad things you did.) Sure enough, when everyone took their sticks out of the ground, lots of people had healthy, green branches again. They had repented their sins and got to go into the building. (The vision doesn't say what happened to all the hopeless cases. Maybe they got turned over to the angel of Incorrigibility!)

The Least You Need to Know

➤ Many Christian martyrs died willingly for their faith.

➤ Saint Agnes was sent to a brothel where she was protected by an angel.

➤ Perpetua and Saturus had angelic dreams that prefigured their martyrdom and ascent to heaven.

➤ *The Shepherd of Hermas* tells how the angel of Repentance can give sinners a second chance.

American Dreams

Leave it to American know-how to come up with an entirely new spin on some of the most widely accepted and settled religious ideas—and to rewrite the history of the world in the process! All it takes is a little imagination and perseverance, and a lot of help from an angel. That's how the Church of Jesus Christ of Latter-day Saints, commonly known as Mormonism, got started.

The Mormon angel appeared, rewrote Christian religious history, and disappeared, taking all the hard evidence of his story with him. He left behind only a handful of eyewitnesses and a transcribed, translated copy of what is supposed to be ancient long-lost religious scripture. This was enough, however, to start a powerful, new, and controversial religion that, to this day, has missionaries working all over the world.

And Mormonism is just one of several American-made sects that adopt a radically different view of Christ, human salvation, and the angels. There's also Christian Science and Jehovah's Witnesses. All these groups have successfully resisted outside pressure to break down in the melting pot and remain great American originals.

Saints Alive!

Mormonism was founded by Joseph Smith, a pioneer leader who migrated west across America during the early decades of the 19th century. The religion is based on the Book of Mormon, a remarkable book of scriptures with a remarkable history. Smith claims he translated the book from ancient writings engraved on gold plates with the help of an angel.

Golden Oldies

Joseph Smith reports that he was lying in bed on the night of September 21, 1823, when an angel appeared to him in the shape of a man. He had resplendent white robes and a face like lightning. What's more, he was floating several feet above the floor. It turns out that the angel was once a man named Moroni, the son of Mormon, a descendant of Nephi, the son of Lehi, who was descended from the Biblical patriarch, Jacob. (Aside from Jacob, none of these figures are mentioned in the Bible.)

Revelations

Mormons tend to be avid genealogists, not only because they trace their religious beliefs and religious history back to the Biblical patriarchs, but also because they believe the unrighteous dead can be redeemed through the efforts of the living. Going along with this is the idea that the ancestors of the Mormons can be "sealed" into the Church of Latter-day Saints—can join Mormonism, that is, even from beyond the grave! For this reason, the Mormon Church keeps careful genealogical records. As a result, genealogists from all over the world consult Mormon records.

Moroni told Smith about the Book of Mormon. He said the book was written on gold plates that were buried under a rock in the side of a hill in upstate New York. The book contains the history of the descendants of Nephi, who sailed in ancient times from the Middle East to what is now known as America, but which was known to Nephi and his people as "the land of promise."

Repeat Performances

Moroni gave Smith instructions to go to the hillside in New York and dig up the plates. He even revealed to him in a vision exactly where the plates were located. Smith's job was to translate the plates into English and share the book with his people. (Mormons say the plates were originally written in a language called "reformed Egyptian.") After delivering his message, a conduit opened in the room through which the angel Moroni ascended back into heaven.

As you may imagine, Joseph Smith was filled with wonder. He lay in bed thinking about what he had seen. He had no need to run through the experience again in his mind, however, because shortly afterward that same night, Moroni appeared again and delivered the very same message a second time, and then disappeared as before.

You might think that seeing the same celestial vision twice in a night would be enough, but no; Moroni appeared a third time that night with the same set of instructions. The only difference was that this time Moroni added a warning. He strongly cautioned Joseph against selling the plates, or using them for any selfish purpose. The idea was to glorify God and spread his word, not to set up his own archeology exhibit or antiques dealership.

Soon after this third appearance was over, morning came and it was time for Joseph to get up and go to work. At work he found he wasn't feeling quite himself, so he started back for home. On his way he fainted. While he was in his swoon, Moroni appeared to him yet again with the same message. You get the feeling Moroni is a thorough messenger!

Seeing Is Believing

So, as the story goes, when Joseph recovered from his swoon, he went to the place Moroni told him about and found the rock under which the gold plates were buried. Buried along with the plates was an ancient breastpiece with two stones attached. These stones were none other than the *Urim and Thummim* mentioned in the Bible, together with the breastpiece that goes along with them. They symbolize the judgment of God and were used in divination.

The original Urim and Thummim served as fortune-telling tools. Lots could be cast that would result either in Urim or in Thummim to decide questions of guilt or to plan a course of action. Joseph Smith would use the Urim and Thummim as specular stones or "seeing stones." Looking through them at the gold plates would enable him to translate the ancient Hebrew into English!

The Devil Makes You Do It

Better not convert to Mormonism if you can't get by without cigarettes, alcohol, or caffeine. These things are strictly forbidden.

Winged Words

The **Urim** and **Thummim** are ancient symbols of the judgment of God and were used to divine God's will. Joseph Smith used them as "seeing stones." He said he was able to look through them and see the writings on the plates of Nephi translated from "reformed Egyptian" into English.

Plates du Jour

When he tried to remove the plates from the hillside, however, he found he couldn't. At that point, the angel Moroni returned again and told him the time had not yet come for him to translate the plates. It would be four years to the day when he could begin. In the meantime, he was to return every year on the same day to demonstrate his willingness.

Wing Tip

If you want to be a modern-day prophet like Joseph Smith, you may need witnesses who can attest to your miraculous experiences. The Book of Mormon begins with the testimony of three witnesses who say that the angel Moroni appeared to them and showed them the gold plates. Their statement is followed by the testimony of eight additional witnesses who say Joseph Smith showed them the plates and the engraving on them, which "has the appearance of ancient work, and curious workmanship."

Finally, the day came for Smith to begin his work on the plates. He says that while he had them in his possession, "multitudes were on the alert" to try to steal them. Smith guarded them carefully, however, and was able to complete the work. When he was finished, Moroni returned and took the plates back with him to heaven, much to the disappointment of archaeologists everywhere who would have loved to see such a unique piece of ancient handiwork! Smith's translation was first printed in 1830 and became sacred scripture for the Mormons.

A statue of the angel Moroni still stands on top of the Mormon Temple in Salt Lake City, Utah, and appears on the cover of many editions of the Book of Mormon. The figure has flowing robes and is blowing a trumpet (sorry flying-angel fans, no wings). It remains a symbol of the many unique characteristics of the Mormon religion, since it is, in effect, the angel who brought them.

Another Mormon tradition is the annual Hill Cumorah Pageant, a recreation of the story of Joseph Smith which takes place in Palmyra, New York. It draws thousands of Mormons and other spectators every year.

Ancient History

That's the story of how the Latter-day Saints got hold of the Book of Mormon. The book, as I mentioned, is all about the descendants of Nephi and his brother, Laman, starting during the life of Nephi's father, Lehi, in about 600 B.C.E. and ending in America, "the land of promise," around 400 C.E. At that time, around the start of the 5th century, the gold plates of Nephi were sealed up, until the Lord saw fit to have Joseph Smith translate them.

Hearken Unto the Word

The events recounted in the book fit in with a startling interpretation of history. The descendants of Nephi and Laman turn out to be the people we know as Native

Americans! According to this Mormon view of history, Christ himself appears to the Nephites some 30 years after his death in order to assure them of the truth of divine covenants that were wrongfully removed from the original Bible. These covenants, of course, are contained in the Book of Mormon as translated by Joseph Smith!

Revelations

The Mormons were not the first to associate Native Americans with the "ten lost tribes of Israel." According to the Bible (Second Book of Kings), these tribes were taken into captivity by the Assyrians and they haven't been heard from since. In fact, many groups of people, including Native Americans, have been nominated as possible descendants of one or more of the ten lost tribes, including certain Hindus in India, Japanese Shinto priests, Jews from the Crimean Peninsula in Russia, people in South America, Mexico, China, Burma, Australian aboriginals, and even people from Denmark. (The word "Danish" supposedly indicates descent from the tribe of Dan!)

The Book of Mormon is written in a very Biblical style—the way you would want to sound if you were trying to talk like they do in the King James Version of the Bible, using words like "wherefore" and "unto" and "and it came to pass" and "smite." (Mark Twain joked, after reading the Book of Mormon, that if you took out all the and-it-came-to-passes, there wouldn't be enough left to come to pass!) In fact, however, the Book of Mormon goes over a lot of territory that's covered in the Bible, only from the perspective of Nephi and his descendants. It frequently refers to events in Genesis and Exodus and rehashes a lot of the Book of Isaiah.

The book also explains why and how the gold plates were written—mainly to replace the portions of the Bible that were supposedly removed. All this is woven into the story of the Nephites. And it's not a bad story at that! If it weren't holy scripture, the Book of Mormon would have made a great historical romance. Best of all, in the course of the action, as you might expect, it describes many angelic visitations.

Family Feud

For example, early in the book (lo! a wonder!), Lehi, the father of Nephi, sees a pillar of fire. Then, in a vision, he ascends unto heaven and beholds God on his throne surrounded by his ministering angels. One of the angels descends from heaven and gives him a book full of prophetic portents.

Wing Tip

If you want to pick up a little Bible-speak to impress your friends or intimidate your enemies, try studying the Book of Mormon. It's generally easier to follow than the Bible, so it's easier to imitate.

The book says that Jerusalem would be destroyed (which it was) and that Christ would come (which he did). But even though we know Lehi's book turns out to be right, Lehi's neighbors mocked him when he warned them of what was in store. So God told Lehi to get out of Jerusalem with his four sons and live in tents in the wilderness.

Lehi's two oldest sons, Laman and Lemuel, aren't all that happy about moving to the wilderness, especially since they left all their gold and silver and precious possessions back in Jerusalem. What's more, they're none too convinced by Lehi's visions. Lehi's third son Nephi, however, is on the same prophetic page as his father, and exhorteth his brethren to hearken unto the Lord.

Brass Behavior

Nephi starts to shine above his brothers after God tells Lehi to send his sons back to Jerusalem to pick up some brass plates (not to be confused with the gold plates, which come later). Laman and Lemuel complain, but Nephi talks them into going. The plates are in the possession of a rich man named Laban and the brothers cast lots to see which of them will try to get them from him.

The lot falls to Laman. When Laman tells Laban why he has come, Laban calls Laman a thief and chases him away. Laman is all for giving up after that, but Nephi persuades him to go along with plan B: to get their gold and silver and precious possessions and offer to buy the plates.

The Devil Makes You Do It

Divine and paternal favoritism is frequently a source of family feuding in scripture. Famous sibling rivalries from the Bible include Cain and Abel, Jacob and Esau, Joseph and his brothers, and, from the New Testament, Mary and Martha. In all these cases, signs of divine and paternal recognition of a particular person sparked the resentment of that person's siblings.

When the brothers return with their money, Laban takes it from them without giving them the plates. Then he has his servants chase them away. Laman and Lemuel are really miffed about this. So much so, in fact, that they take unto themselves rods of iron with which to smite young Nephi. Fortunately for Nephi, however, the angel of the Lord intervenes.

The angel tells them to smite not their younger brother. Not only that, he says that Nephi has been chosen by God to rule over them because of their iniquities. He also commands them all to go back to Jerusalem and get the plates. Laban and Lemuel obey, but afterwards, from time to time, they fall out of line and have to be reminded that they have seen the angel of the Lord and that God likes Nephi best.

And it came to pass that Nephi was walking around outside of Laban's house where he came across Laban himself sprawled out on the ground, sleeping off a three-martini business lunch. Laban had his sword with him, so Nephi drew it out wherefore to smite Laban. And smite Laban he did, insofar as his head no longer attached unto his shoulders! So the brethren made off with the plates, which reveal the important news that Lehi is descended from the noted Biblical patriarch Joseph.

Last-Ditch Effort

So Nephi turns out to be an important figure in Mormon scripture. He and his descendants generally represent the "good guys" in the Book of Mormon, whereas Laman and his descendants are the troublemakers. There are exceptions to this rule, however, as Nephites occasionally turn from God and Lamanites occasionally turn to God. When this happens, though, the bad Nephites go over to join the Lamanites and the good Lamanites go over to join the Nephites.

Wing Tip

Why not name your son after a Mormon patriarch? In addition to Nephi and Laman, other interesting names include: Abish, Ablom, Agosh, Aha, Aminadab, Amnihu, Antiomno, Ezrom, Gazelem, Gimgimno, Helorum, Jeberechiah, Kishkumen, Liahona, Madmenah, Mathoni, Michmash, Migron, Ogath, Omni, Pagag, Rameumptom, Ripliancum, Sebus, Seezoram, Shemlon, Shiblom, Shimnilon, Tubaloth, Zarahemla, Zeniff, Zenoch, Zeram.

Unfortunately for the Nephites, the Lamanites finally smite them once and for all. Fortunately for the Mormons, though, the last of the Nephites, Mormon and Moroni, manage to hide the gold plates where Joseph Smith would later find them. As a result, the Mormons could tell the world how important Nephi was. Nephi was so important that the angel of the Lord appeared to him and revealed a long sequence of prophetic visions. These included many future events, some of which would take place in America, "the land of promise."

Know It All

Among the visions the angel of the Lord revealed to Nephi is a vision of the original coming of Christ. Nephi sees the infant Jesus with Mary. Later, he sees Jesus teaching and being worshipped by his followers. Then he sees him nailed to the cross and, finally, rising to heaven. The angel explains to Nephi that Jesus is the son of God.

Later, the angel grants Nephi a vision of "the land of promise." (The Nephites and the Lamanites will have sailed there in order to escape persecution in Jerusalem.) He sees Christ descending from heaven to appear to the Nephites and to bring them his gospel. The angel explains that this gospel will include precious truths that became lost from the Bible, which God wants to restore to humanity through the Nephites!

Then Nephi gets a vision of the gentile kingdoms of Renaissance Europe, and sees Columbus sailing across the Atlantic to the new world. Soon afterwards, he sees many more gentiles making the voyage. The angel explains that by this time, the Lamanites

Wing Tip

If you want to prophesy accurately, predict things that have already taken place and say the prophecy was written beforehand!

have taken over and have drifted away from God and become slack in their religion. In his wrath, God has the gentiles smite the Lamanites, all but completely destroying them. (In other words, the Europeans nearly annihilate the Native Americans.)

The gentiles in "the land of promise" turn out to be righteous, or God-fearing. To reward them, God lets them win the Revolutionary War. He also provides them with the important truths that were left out of the Bible. Near the end of his vision, Nephi learns from the angel about a gentile (Joseph Smith) who will reveal these truths to his people.

Still Ticking

Although the Nephites are finally smitten by the Lamanites, the seed of Nephi does not disappear entirely. ("Seed" is Bible-talk for offspring.) For one thing, the righteous among them go to heaven to be with Christ when they die—all but three of the righteous, that is. It was granted to three of the Nephites to stay alive on Earth until Judgment Day. This arrangement was worked out when Christ descended amid a throng of angels to consecrate the apostles and priests of the Nephites around the year 45 C.E.

It seems that Christ has special feelings for the Nephites, not only because they are so righteous, but because they are going to restore important divine covenants that supposedly disappeared from the Bible. So he personally sanctifies the Nephite apostles and priests. What's more, he grants them what they desire most from God. For most of them, this is to go to heaven and be with Christ. Three of them, however, decide to remain on Earth forever, sort of like the main characters in the movie and TV show, *Highlander*.

Revelations

The concept of restoration is crucial to the Mormon understanding of Biblical history. They see the history of the people of God as a sequence of fallings off and renewals. After a period of spiritual iniquity, a new prophet emerges to give people a renewed sense of what God wants. These new "dispensations," as they are called, are linked by a continuous priesthood that stretches all the way back to Adam. In fact, the hierarchical structure of the Mormon Church is modeled on this conception of Old Testament priesthood. This structure, together with the idea that the original Bible has things missing from it, and the idea that prophecy is an activity that should continue during modern times, all help set Mormonism apart from mainstream Christianity.

The Book of Mormon doesn't say who these three are—God said that their names should not be written. It was prophesied, however, that they would live among the Jews and not be known to them, and that they would live among the gentiles, and not be known to them either. They would remain on Earth as angels, ministering unto the righteous.

Only Skin Deep

The Book of Mormon concludes with accounts of Mormon and his son, Moroni, who inscribe the history of the Nephites on the gold plates and bury them in a hillside in what later became New York state around the start of the 5th century. They bury the plates to hide them from their enemies, the Lamanites. Because the descendants of Nephi's older brother Laman failed to maintain faith in God, says the Book of Mormon, they were "cursed" by God, who gave them the dark skin and the low-tech lifestyle associated with Native Americans!

The sad fact is, religion isn't always a pretty thing. In spite of the beautiful and uplifting ideas it contains, it often exhibits an exclusivist "holier than thou" attitude toward others. An example is the Book of Mormon's racist take on the Lamanites, who supply the Mormon account for the presence of Native Americans in the New World.

The book says that, because the Lamanites turned from God, "the Lord God did cause a skin of blackness to come upon them." (People reading are supposed to see this as a bad thing.) What's more, "they did become an idle people, full of mischief and subtlety, and did seek in the wilderness for beasts of prey." (Here we're supposed to think farming is more "civilized" than hunting.)

Even so, if you can get past the racism, it's a good story. Mormon and Moroni do their utmost to preserve the Word of God as they have received it but, because they finally lose out in their battle against the Lamanites, they are forced to seal up their records until, as is prophesied, the world becomes ready to learn of them fourteen hundred years in the future. This is when Moroni appears as an angel to Joseph Smith.

The Devil Makes You Do It

Many white Europeans used religion as a justification for the conquest of America. One early report from the New World said that the Indians "worshipped the devil out of fear."

Revelations

Traditionally, the racist innuendoes in the Book of Mormon have aroused far less furor than the now-outdated Mormon practice of polygamy (having multiple spouses, usually wives). Actually, the Book of Mormon suggests polygamy is a sin. Nevertheless, it came into practice among the Mormons some years after the book came out, thanks largely to further prophetic revelations on the part of Joseph Smith, who had several wives himself. The Supreme Court outlawed polygamy in 1879, although some Mormons continued the practice long afterwards.

Angels with Body

Moroni is one of a very few angels to appear on Earth who started out in life as a human being. He's in good company. Jewish tradition recognizes a couple of important humans-turned-angels too. One is Metatron, who started out as the Biblical patriarch Enoch, before ascending bodily into heaven without dying, where he was transformed into a top-ranking angel. Another is Sandalphon, who started out as the prophet Elijah, before he, too, was taken up into heaven as a human being and transmuted into the famous angel.

Moroni differs from these angels, since he does not ascend into heaven as a living body, but as a disembodied soul. According to Latter-day doctrine, however, Moroni appeared to Joseph Smith as an embodied being. In fact, Mormonism is unusual among modern religions in recognizing re-embodied angels—angels that were once human beings who became disembodied souls, but later acquired bodies again in order to appear on Earth.

These angels' embodiment helps maintain the human continuity of Mormon priesthood. Even though it comes from God, it is also passed along directly from priest to priest, when you consider that Moroni is actually a priest who appeared as an angel. In addition to embodied angels, Mormons recognize others, the disembodied angels. These are angels who were never human beings, but existed with God before humanity was created. Unembodied spirits may be either divine or infernal (having rejected God and joined with Satan).

Mormonism is the first but not the only major American-made religious sect with its own understanding of angels. Two others worth mentioning are the Christian Scientists and the Jehovah's Witnesses. Like Mormonism, these groups claim to be Christian, even though many of their ideas are rejected by the Christian mainstream.

All in Your Mind

Christian Science was founded by Mary Baker Eddy in 1866. Eddy describes God as an infinite mind. Human beings evolved from the infinite mind and are reflections of it. We're not completely separate from it, since God is all in all. Since God is all in all, you might think he is in gross things like tile grout and moldy cheese. Not the case, say the Christian Scientists. Material appearances are unreal. Matter doesn't exist!

This includes the human body—it doesn't exist any more than tile grout does. This helps explain why Christian Scientists are best known for recommending the healing power of prayer over medical treatment for illness. If we have no bodies, there's nothing to heal! In fact, according to Christian Science, evil doesn't exist either. It's simply an unreal belief that we can reject.

Christ exists, but he didn't come to atone for human sin—he came to reveal the truth that sin is an illusion. The Church of Christ Scientist exists as a community of truth and love. Angels exist as the thoughts of God that reach human beings.

The Devil Makes You Do It

Christian Scientists who choose to see the illnesses of their children as unreal beliefs may also be faced with the additional unreal beliefs of lawsuits and prison sentences for child neglect!

Immortal Act

Whereas Christian Science says that God and humanity are similar, Jehovah's Witnesses say they are different. Even Jesus Christ is inferior to God, according to Jehovah's Witnesses. In fact, they say that before Jesus came to Earth in the form of the son of Mary, he existed in heaven as the angel Michael. As an angel, he was not guaranteed an immortal existence, but had to earn immortality by sacrificing himself on the cross as a human being.

Angels, according to Jehovah's Witnesses, can die. They say evil angels like Satan will die. As creatures of God, angels are subject to the laws of the created universe. As a result, some say that they need to eat food to stay alive.

Wing Tip

If you want to learn more about Jehovah's Witnesses, you may be able to do so without exerting yourself. They often go door to door giving out literature about their views and practices.

> ### The Least You Need to Know
>
> ➤ Mormonism was founded by Joseph Smith, who claimed he was visited by the angel Moroni in 1823.
>
> ➤ Smith claims to have translated the Book of Mormon from ancient gold plates with the help of specular stones called the Urim and Thummim.
>
> ➤ According to the Book of Mormon, Christ appeared and spread the gospel to the people we know as Native Americans.
>
> ➤ Mormons recognize re-embodied and unembodied angels.
>
> ➤ Like the Mormons, Christian Scientists and Jehovah's Witnesses understand Christ, salvation, and angels in ways that differ radically from mainstream Christianity.

Part 4
More Faiths, More Angels

Of course, the Judeo-Christian tradition isn't the only source of angel lore. There are also the Middle Eastern religions, Zoroastrianism, and Islam. As you'll see, the spicy Middle Eastern flavor really makes a difference. Then, moving further south, we come to the angels of Africa and Latin America, who shatter all the Biblical stereotypes.

In this part of the book, we'll discuss angels and their connection to Zoroastrianism, Islam, and Santería. Although each faith is unique unto itself, all of them are linked by the winged beings that we are all fascinated by. It doesn't matter what they look like or what language they speak—angels are everywhere.

The Mark of Zoroaster

While the angels of Yahweh were doing their level best to help the Israelites realize their destiny, their angelic cousins in Persia (modern-day Iran) were rallying around their high God, Ahura Mazda, and his prophet, Zoroaster, in order to keep the universe pure and demon-free. Just like Judaism, Zoroaster's religious world is filled with celestial intermediaries who span the gap between the world's creator and ordinary mortals. This is just one feature the ancient religion known as Zoroastrianism has in common with the religion of the Jews.

In fact, some say that Zoroastrianism and Judaism exerted a mutual influence on one another during their formative years. If so, the sharing of ideas—and of angels—took place despite the fact that both the Persians of old and the ancient Israelites tended to see outside influences as evil. This shows how hard it is to keep angels under wraps.

While Zoroastrianism has intriguing affinities with Judaism—the religion of Palestine to the west—it also has a lot in common with Hinduism—the religion of India to the east. Celestial spirits are shared characteristics in both cases. In other words, Zoroastrian angels seem to have a wing in each hemisphere, occupying shared air space between distinct ancient regions.

Turning a Prophet

Traditional accounts of Zoroaster, or Zarathustra as he is also known, say he lived about 1000 years B.C.E., but most scholars these days place him closer to 600 B.C.E. According to the sacred book of Zoroastrianism called the Avesta, the Persian prophet was singled out by Ahura Mazda to spread his holy teachings, now preserved in the form of the *Gathas*. These are hymns attributed to Zoroaster, 17 of which are still in existence.

The *Gathas* form part of the Avesta, which also contains guidelines for worship and ritual as well as prayers and other hymns. The thrust of the religion is devotion to goodness and avoidance of evil—but this isn't as obvious as it sounds. Zoroastrians see good and evil as having nearly equal sway over the world. This makes it especially important for devout people to add their weight to the side of good.

Balance of Power

An important innovation in Zoroaster's teaching is his claim that it applied to everyone, not just his own tribe. Zoroaster sought to understand divine power—not just for the sake of his own people, but for the sake of humanity in general. This makes his religion more than just another set of divine beings to be worshipped, but a new way of understanding the connection between divine and earthly reality.

Like the God of the Jews, the Zoroastrian God, Ahura Mazda, cares about everyone and, ultimately, will reward good people and punish evil-doers. Unlike the Israelite God, Yahweh, however, Ahura Mazda (also known as Ohrmazd), which means "Wise Lord," is not all-powerful. Instead, the Zoroastrian god shares power with his evil twin, Angra Mainyu.

Jews, Christians, and Muslims have some explaining to do to account for why evil exists in a world created by an all-powerful, benevolent God. This is the 64,000-dollar question of monotheism. In some ways, this question gives monotheism its meaning, enabling different believers to come up with their own answers. It remains a logical problem, however, and makes God really hard to figure out.

Zoroastrianism doesn't have this problem. The benevolent god, Ahura Mazda, hates evil even more than people do. He's doing all he can to eradicate it from the universe. In fact, Zoroastrians believe that he and his angels will defeat evil—eventually. In the meantime, Ahura Mazda can use the help of human beings.

Wing Tip

Zoroaster, or Zarathustra as he is also known, supplied inspiration for the famous work by German philosopher Friedrich Nietzsche, *Thus Spake Zarathustra*. This work isn't actually about Zoroastrianism, but presents Nietzsche's ideas in a prophetic style.

Giving God a Hand

Existence is a constant struggle between good and evil. Enlisted in battle on each side are spiritual beings, who are currently deadlocked, but who will eventually engage in the final, decisive battle. Zoroaster says the smart money is on the side of good, who will destroy evil by flooding the world with molten metal in the final days. Meanwhile, good people get to go to paradise after they die.

The prophet and his followers therefore choose the way of goodness. He says all people must choose for themselves, which side to be on. By choosing good, human beings can aid Ahura Mazda in his cosmic struggle with evil. Thus, because Ahura Mazda is not an all-powerful god, Zoroastrians think of themselves as helping him gain the upper hand against his enemy.

Wing Tip

Zoroastrianism suggests the best way to defeat evil is not to seek it out and expose it, but simply to avoid it altogether. That way, evil doesn't have anything to work with.

Revelations

Just how big an influence Zoroaster exerted on the world is difficult to say, but some believe aspects of his thinking spread west to Greece where they were taken up and modified by Plato, perhaps the most influential philosopher of all time. In particular, some scholars have claimed that "Platonic ideas" such as courage and justice—which, according to Plato, are not mere abstractions, but really exist—derive from Zoroastrian "Fravashis," spiritual embodiments of all things, including abstract concepts.

Chain of Command

Ahura Mazda's chief assistants in the battle against evil are the Amesha Spentas, the "Holy Immortals." These are the other six archangels of Zoroastrianism (Ahura Mazda is the seventh archangel of Zoroastrianism). While they have separate roles, they reinforce one another and have overlapping duties as well. Here are their names, together with their chief duties. Notice that each has a special connection to a particular aspect of worldly existence:

➤ *Ahura Mazda, "Wise Lord."* Creator of all that is good in the universe and leader in the battle against evil. He has a special connection to human beings.

➤ *Vohu Manah, "Good Mind."* The first-created of the spiritual powers, he imparts enlightenment to humanity. He resides in heaven where he rises from a golden throne to greet the souls of the righteous as they arrive in the next world after death. He is also the spirit in charge of cattle and other animals.

➤ *Asha, "Righteousness."* The keeper of the immutable divine law who confers spiritual wealth to humanity and aids in healing of diseases. He is the spirit of fire.

➤ *Khshathra Vairya, "Wished-for Kingdom."* The promoter of Ahura Mazda's divine kingdom on Earth. He confers material wealth and is in charge of metal.

➤ *Spenta Armaiti, "Holy Devotion."* The only female archangel of Zoroastrianism, she fosters human love and reverence for the powers and the way of goodness. She is the spirit of Earth.

➤ *Haurvatat* and *Ameretat, "Perfection"* and *"Immortality."* Typically invoked as a pair, these archangels promote strength on Earth and immortality in the next life. They have charge of water and plants, respectively.

Holy Orders

Zoroastrianism places great importance on wisdom. This makes it as much a philosophy as it is a religion. The Middle East has a rich philosophical tradition that stems from Zoroaster, the first of many sages known as *magi*. A magus is a Zoroastrian wise man and priest. The magi on Earth correspond to Ahura Mazda in heaven, having the same relationship with the rest of the people as Ahura Mazda has to the rest of the Amesha Spentas.

Winged Words

Magi (singular magus) are Zoroastrian priests and sages. Christian tradition holds that the three wise men who followed a star to Bethlehem bearing gifts for the baby Jesus were Zoroastrian magi.

Lofty Concepts

The emphasis Zoroastrianism places on wisdom is clear from the names of the most important celestial beings, Ahura Mazda, "Wise Lord," and Vohu Manah, "Good Mind." The other archangels have conceptual, abstract names, too, suggesting they stand for ideals as much as for embodied, human-like beings. In fact, although the hymns of Zoroaster say the prophet longs for visions of the Amesha Spentas, they are said to be invisible.

Scholars say that when reading Zoroastrian scripture, it's often hard to tell the difference between human ideals such as righteousness, devotion, perfection, and the archangels named "Righteousness," "Devotion," and so on. There are few stories about the escapades and personalities of these figures among the philosophical accounts of their natures, which are more divine than human. Still, they are prayed to and even sacrificed to, so, like people, they can be pleased or displeased by the way you treat them.

A Lotta Yazatas

In addition to the seven chief Amesha Spentas, there are numerous other angelic figures known as Yazatas, "Adorable Ones." These beings are in charge of the natural and spiritual world and respond to the prayers and sacrifices of human beings. Their roles include governance of everything from truth and victory to the sun, moon, and the wind. There's even a Yazata for a sacred hallucinogenic plant! In addition, Zoroaster himself is sometimes referred to as a Yazata.

Although Yazatas often work independently of one another, they also work together. They cooperate, for example, to gather the rays of the sun and direct them onto the earth. They also unite in serving and worshipping Ahura Mazda.

Many of the names of the Yazatas predate the beginnings of Zoroastrianism, suggesting that they were once gods who later became incorporated into Persian belief as angels. Other Yazatas were imported from neighboring religions, including Hinduism. Some Yazatas later became central deities of their own sects and cults.

The most important of these was Mithras, who became the center of a cult that spread both east into India and west into Europe as far as Britain since the foundation of Zoroastrianism. The Mithras cult was strictly a guy thing, involving the sacrifice of bulls. Some Mithraic cults combined the figure of Mithras with that of Christ, who redeems his followers and defeats evil in the final days.

The special prominence of Mithras suggests that various groups of Zoroastrians had favorite Yazatas. Evidently, their popularity rose and fell, depending on public feeling at the time. As with other kinds of monotheism, Zoroastrian angels cluster around the fuzzy lines that separate mainstream religion from paganism.

Wing Tip

Don't be confused by the name changes that have seeped into Zoroastrianism over the years. Many names and terms have acquired shorter equivalents. Ahura Mazda is sometimes called "Ohrmazd"; the angel Vohu Manah is also known as "Vohuman"; the archangels known as Amesha Spentas are also called "Amarhaspands"; and the angelic Yazatas are sometimes shortened to the "Izads."

An Angel for Everything

The Zoroastrian cosmos is chock-full of benevolent divine beings. In addition to the Amesha Spentas and the Yazatas are still another class of immortals called Fravashis. The Fravashis are everywhere and in everything, on Earth as well as in the realm of the afterlife.

The Fravashis are the conscious, living essences of everything that exists. Their home is in the spiritual realm, but they volunteer to inhabit Earth in

The Devil Makes You Do It

Better avoid evil behavior, or your Fravashi will give a bad report of you to the divine immortals.

order to guide material reality and do battle with evil. Each thing has a Fravashi, including each individual person and animal. You might say that a Fravashi is akin to a guardian angel.

Humans have Fravashi in addition to their souls. Your Fravashi is your guide and friend, but it's not to blame if you choose the path of wickedness. After death, you may be condemned to eternal punishment, but your Fravashi will return to the world of the divine immortals, where it will think back on you and say, "What a turkey!"

The Bad with the Good

With all these do-gooding spirits to keep the world moving in a positive direction, you wouldn't think that the forces of evil would stand much of a chance. The problem is, though, that there is an equal number of evil demons, known as daevas, doing their best to gum up the works. As a result there is a standoff on Earth as the forces of good and evil counterbalance one another.

Revelations

Daevas, or devas, are demons—at least to Zoroastrians. The term actually originated in India, where it meant "shining ones" and was used to refer to gods and god-like beings that were not demonic at all. In fact, the word is related to the Latin word for god, *deus*. For some reason, as the term was imported into Persia, it acquired a negative meaning. In addition, at least three Indian gods moved to Iran and became evil spirits somewhere along the way. These are Indra, Sharva (who became the evil Saurva), and Nasatya (who became Naonghaithya). The term "deva" has been revised in a positive sense by some New Agers to refer to angelic beings with an exotic Eastern flavor.

In other words, there are battles going on all over the place—in the elements, in living things, in your lunch—between good and evil. Good and evil don't just measure morality, they are also physical characteristics. In fact, Zoroastrians are especially concerned with cleanliness. Impurity—whether moral or physical—enables evil spirits to get a toe-hold on the environment.

Most Wanted

Chief among the daevas are the seven evil spirits created by Angra Mainyu. Each of these is the particular enemy of a corresponding Amesha Spenta, as you can see from this list:

➤ *Angra Mainyu, "Evil Spirit,"* also known as *Ahriman.* Ahura Mazda's evil twin, the creator of death and all evil beings.

➤ *Aka Manah, "Evil Mind."* Opponent of the good Vohu Manah and originator of the bad attitude.

➤ *Druj, "Deceit"* or *"Wickedness."* Female nemesis of the righteous Asha. Although there is only one chief demon named Druj, later Zoroastrian tradition recognizes an entire class of evil female spirits known as drujes.

➤ *Saurva.* Originally an Indian god named Sharva, he became incorporated into Zoroastrianism as the adversary of the good Khshathra Vairya.

➤ *Taromaiti, "Heresy."* This female enemy of Spenta Armaiti runs screaming when she hears people pray.

➤ *Taurvi* and *Zairicha, "Fever"* and *"Thirst."* The archenemies of the good Haurvatat and Ameretat.

Full-Time Fight

Evil spirits are defeated not only by the good spirits, but by devout human beings. Any constructive or devout human activity deals a blow to the daevas, including ordinary productive work such as farming. Similarly, human enjoyment of the good things life has to offer makes the daevas unhappy.

Between the two sides there are no shades of gray. Those who are not faithful to Ahura Mazda and his angels are considered daeva worshippers, whether or not they actually are. Thus those who do not assist the forces of good are helping the evil spirits.

Wing Tip

If you feel beset by demons and evil spirits, try enjoying a nice meal or cleaning out the garage. That'll show 'em!

Persian Purity

Zoroastrianism doesn't make a sharp distinction between physical and spiritual reality. The Amesha Spentas govern the material world as well as the moral actions of human beings. The two are closely tied together. An important concept Zoroastrians use to make this connection is purity. Being good means being pure—morally, physically, and spiritually.

Clean Living

When something is impure, it is infected with evil spirits. Zoroastrians believe the demons can be removed through incantations and purification rituals and by summoning the appropriate Amesha Spentas and Yazatas. In addition, impurity can be prevented through a careful, clean lifestyle.

The Devil Makes You Do It

Before you decide to convert to Zoroastrianism, remember that notions of purity can vary from culture to culture. Many purification rituals in this religion involve the drinking of consecrated bull's urine!

Because of these beliefs, devout Zoroastrians are serious neatniks, being careful to clean up after whatever they do to avoid spreading evil spirits around. Priests even wear cloth masks resembling surgical masks to keep from breathing on consecrated objects during rituals. These objects represent the seven aspects of the material world sacred to the Amesha Spentas: fire, water, plants, metal, earth, animals, and human beings.

Hung Out to Dry

These material things, including people, are naturally pure. They become polluted by death. When a person dies, the body may become filled with evil spirits. The corpse, however, isn't buried, since this would pollute the earth. It isn't cremated either, since this would pollute fire. Instead, Zoroastrians traditionally lay their dead to rest on top of high towers. This practice has increasingly come into conflict with non-Zoroastrian laws, and is gradually disappearing.

Interestingly, the body of a virtuous person who has died is more likely to become seriously polluted by demons than the body of a sinful person. Zoroastrians believe that demons are responsible for killing people. It takes the demons an unusually great effort to kill a virtuous person, since such a person is best able to resist their power. As a result, the demons will rush in to fill the void left by a soul who has departed for paradise in the next world.

In contrast, a sinful person already shares his body with demons even before death, so the departure of his soul doesn't make much difference. Many Zoroastrians will not enter a house where someone has died for nine days after the death in order to avoid demons. Virtuous Zoroastrians also avoid sinful ones as hazardous to their spiritual health!

Revelations

Zoroastrianism became almost entirely supplanted in the Middle East by the spread of Islam. Even so, modern-day Zoroastrians still practice their faith in Iran and India. In fact, some of the information in this chapter comes from *Purity and Pollution in Zoroastrianism* (University of Texas Press), a book written in 1989 by Jamsheed K. Choksy, a Zoroastrian scholar who studied at Columbia and Harvard.

Chips Off the Block

Zoroastrianism has given rise to splinter groups—related sects and cults based on the prophet's teachings that differ from the mainstream. The most widespread of these is Zurvanism. Zurvan is thought to be the father of the twin beings, Ahura Mazda and Angra Mainyu. He is also the god of time, encompassing both good and bad, light and darkness, representing a unity that Zoroastrians do not accept.

Another offshoot of Zoroastrianism, considered heretical by the mainstream, is Manicheanism, named after the prophet known as Mani of the 3rd century C.E. The Manicheans believe in a duality between matter and spirit, seeing matter as a source of evil, in contrast to the Zoroastrians who see matter as essentially good. According to Mani, humanity was originally spiritual but has been dragged down into an evil material existence by demons.

Only through rigorous self-denial—fasting, poverty, and celibacy—can the individual be reunited with God. These *ascetic*—self-denying—practices are contrary to Zoroastrian teaching that encourages the enjoyment of life. Where Mani taught retreat and abstention from things of the world, Zoroaster teaches activity and enterprise.

Manicheanism became the most widespread sect of the religious philosophy known as Gnosticism (see Chapter 14), extending into Europe and as far east as China. Mani identified God flexibly as both the God of the Christians and Zoroaster's Ahura Mazda. To complete the religious mix, the Manichean emphasis on self-denial stems from Buddhism. Mainstream Zoroastrians attacked Mani and labeled him a Druj—an evil female spirit.

Still another Zoroastrian offshoot are the Parsees. This group migrated to India starting around 600 C.E. to avoid Muslim persecution. Here they picked up the name "Parsee" or "Parsi" from the locals who used it as their way of saying "Persians." The Parsees are commonly associated with fire worship.

Winged Words

Asceticism is the practice of self-denial through practices such as fasting and other voluntary hardships such as celibacy and poverty. Many major religions include ascetic subgroups.

The Least You Need to Know

➤ Zoroaster is the Persian prophet who taught his people about the god Ahura Mazda and his evil twin, Angra Mainyu.

➤ Zoroastrianism recognizes three classes of divine beings: the Amesha Spentas (Holy Immortals), the Yazatas (Adorable Ones), and the Fravashis.

➤ Everything in the universe, according to Zoroaster, is either good or evil. The two sides are completely opposed.

➤ Because they do not consider their god all-powerful, Zoroastrians feel they are helping him in his fight against evil.

➤ Zoroastrianism emphasizes moral, spiritual, and physical purity.

➤ Zoroastrian offshoots include the Zurvanists, Manicheans, and the Parsees.

Arabian Angels

Christians say that angels carry God's message wherever they go. This theory is amply supported by the example of Islam, the monotheistic religion founded by Muhammad with the help of the angels. When the angels moved to Persia, they brought word of a universal God who cares for everyone, regardless of their nationality.

Unfortunately, they also brought religious strife as their message clashed with the old beliefs. The new monotheism in old Persia shook up the traditional paganism of the tribesmen who lived there. Some of their gods and jinns (spirits that can be either evil or good) were incorporated into the new religion, but others were left behind in the wake of a bloody religious battle.

Despite the fighting—and because of it—Muhammad's message spread far and wide, giving rise to rich and various angelic traditions. At the same time, because Islam developed comparatively recently, many of its faithful adherents from the beginning have been skeptical about the existence of angels.

Incoming Angel

Islam is one of the three great monotheistic religions of the world and, like the other two, Judaism and Christianity, it recognizes angels. In fact, you could say that it was an angel who got the Islamic ball rolling by appearing to Muhammad, the prophet of Islam, with the word of Allah. The angel's name was Djibril, which is the Arab name for Gabriel, the same angel that told the Virgin Mary about Jesus.

The Big Mo'

Muhammad was born in the Turkish city of Mecca around 570 C.E. He became an orphan at an early age and was raised by an uncle. Muhammad worked for years as a caravan driver, businessman, and agent for a prosperous woman named Khadija, who was about 15 years older than he was. He eventually married her, making her the first of several wives. While young, he became a recluse, going off by himself on religious retreats. According to Muslim (Islamic) tradition, Muhammad was sleeping alone in a cave in the mountains outside Mecca when Djibril appeared to him and revealed to him the words of the Koran, holy book of Islam. The Koran contains the fundamental teachings of Islamic belief.

The Muslims share much of their religious history and belief, including angels, with Jews and Christians. Muhammad was deeply influenced by Jews and Christians he had met, so that aspects of these older religions became part of Islam. In addition to angels, Muslims recognize the Jewish and Christian prophets, including Moses and Jesus.

Although Muslims do not consider the written revelations of these other prophets on par with the Koran, they still recognize Judaism and Christianity as religions of the one true God, known to Muslims as Allah. The Koran even says that Jesus told his followers of a prophet that was to come named "Ahmad" (short for Muhammad). Muslims refer to Muhammad as "the seal of the prophets," meaning that he is the last prophet who will ever receive the Word of God.

In Your Face

The angel Djibril first appeared to Muhammad on what is called "the night of power." Djibril had a book in his hand and commanded Muhammad to recite from the book. Muhammad, however, wasn't too keen on the idea, so Djibril repeated the command. It was still no go, so Djibril started to smother Muhammad with the book.

Some say the "book" was actually cloth brocade with writing embroidered on it. Others say the smothering was a mystic experience and the book and the angel were present in Muhammad's heart. In any case, the angel didn't stop until Muhammad was close to death. This gave the future prophet the clue that the angel meant business, so he started reciting as soon as he could breathe again!

Making Sura of the Truth

He recited what later became part of the Koran, the holy book of Islam. It was Sura 96 about how Allah created man out of a blood clot. (A *sura* is a section of the Koran.) Muhammad woke up, but he hadn't seen the last of Djibril. When he left the cave, he looked to the horizon and saw the angel, high as the clouds, sitting cross-legged on the earth. The angel said that he would become the prophet of Allah, the God of all humanity. Muhammad looked away, but saw Djibril again in a new spot on the horizon. No matter where on the horizon Muhammad looked, Djibril was there.

Winged Words

A **sura** is a section of the Koran, the holy book of Islam. The Koran contains 114 suras, arranged roughly from the longest (number 2 is well over fifty pages long) to the shortest (the final suras are each only a few lines long).

A sura from the Koran.

Night Ride

One famous appearance of Djibril was more than a recitation session. This was the legendary Night Journey, in which Djibril took Muhammad on a mystic pilgrimage. In some versions of this story, Muhammad rode a winged horse. The first stop was Jerusalem, the holy city of the Jews and Christians. This visit was a way of connecting Islam to its monotheistic roots, since, even before becoming a prophet, Muhammad was influenced by Jews and Christians he had met in his travels.

Next on the itinerary was a tour of the seven heavens. Here he met the prophets of monotheism who had come before him, including Moses and Jesus Christ. Finally, at the high point of his journey, Muhammad entered the presence of Allah and his attendant angels.

Unnecessary Angels

The Koran itself doesn't specify that the angel who taught Muhammad the Koran was Djibril, or Gabriel. In fact, it's not perfectly clear from scripture that the spirit who imparted the Word of God to the prophet was even an angel, and Muslims disagree as to this spirit's identity. It seems that the more common, traditional view is that the angel Djibril appeared to Muhammad. Some disagree, however, and argue from evidence in the Koran itself, that Muhammad was inspired to write the Koran not by an angel, but by the holy spirit.

Wing Tip

If the angel Djibril appears to take you on a tour of the seven heavens, there's no need to cancel your appointments. The whole thing takes only an instant of Earth time. As proof, in the commotion of rushing off on his night journey with Djibril, Muhammad tipped over a jar filled with water. When he returned, water was still rushing out of the jar! (A similar temporal discrepancy took place in Carl Sagan's novel, *Contact*, in which a 12-hour trip to outer space and back took about two seconds.)

No-Show

Those who say an angel was not involved point to passages of the Koran in which unbelievers express doubts about Muhammad's claim to be a prophet of Allah. These doubters are home-boys from Muhammad's tribe, the Quraysh, from Mecca. They tell Muhammad, "We see you all the time getting hermit supplies at the sporting goods store and picking up turbans and shirts from the dry cleaners like everybody else. If you were really Allah's prophet, you wouldn't be such a regular guy. Instead, you'd seem more miraculous and God would have sent an angel along with you to convey his messages."

From this, some readers of the Koran conclude that it was not the angel Djibril who appeared to Muhammad. Their point is that miracles shouldn't be necessary to convince unbelievers. The important thing, anyway, is the monotheistic message contained in the Koran. If you don't have faith in that, you don't deserve to be a Muslim and go to heaven.

Revelations

In terms of numbers of members, Islam is one of the biggest religions of the world. Part of its success stems from the spread of the Persian empire during the Middle Ages. In recent decades, many African Americans have converted to Islam, notably boxing champion Muhammad Ali (born Cassius Clay), basketball star Kareem Abdul Jabbar (born Lou Alcindor), and the late political activist Malcolm X.

Three Against One

Additional angel-related confusion led to an even more serious disagreement involving the Quraysh. The Quraysh, by the way, were pagans. Among the gods they worshipped were three goddesses, al-Lat, al-Uzza, and Manat. They didn't have a serious problem with the idea of worshipping Allah, who, according to Muhammad, is the only true God. At the same time, however, they wanted to worship their three goddesses. This ran counter to the spirit of Muhammad's monotheistic message.

The disagreement caused problems for Muhammad, since he was a born member of the Quraysh himself and wanted to see eye to eye with his old group. Allah, however, had other plans. He didn't want his prophet fraternizing with goddess-worshipping pagans. According to legend, Satan got wind of the situation and came up with a plan to introduce paganism into Islam. This plan involved the notorious "Satanic Verses."

The Devil Makes You Do It

Be careful what you say about the Satanic Verses of the Koran. Novelist Salmon Rushdie wrote a book about them that elicited death threats from fundamentalist Muslims!

A Slip of the Tongue

Here's how the legend goes: One day, the angel Djibril came to Muhammad to dictate some more verses of the Koran, just as usual. He dictated Sura 53, which happens to be aimed at the Quraysh and their goddesses. The sura says that these goddesses are not the daughters of Allah, even though some people may wish they were. The sura goes on to say, "A lot of you out there are calling on angels and giving them female names, but it doesn't mean they have any authority or power. All the power and authority comes from Allah."

The point of the sura is that you're not supposed to worship the goddesses, so don't try that old trick of calling them angels in order to sneak polytheistic beliefs into a mono-theistic religion. Allah won't be fooled by that stuff. Now, as the prophet of Allah, Muhammad was duty-bound to report exactly what he heard from Djibril. As a member of the Quraysh tribe, however, he wasn't pleased about the contents of Sura 53. He knew it would cause trouble with the folks back home.

Satan, who happened to be on hand, took advantage of Muhammad's desires and made him insert some phony verses into the sura that Djibril was dictating. Right after the sura mentioned the three goddesses, Satan added verses that said, "They [the goddesses] are like beautiful cranes flying in the sky. People should hope for their intercession." When the Quraysh heard the Satanic Verses, they were overjoyed. Now it seemed they could embrace Muhammad's new religion and still pray to their goddesses.

Wing Tip

Problems are often easier to fix if you don't worry about inflicting punishment for wrongdoing. The fewer enemies you make, the fewer you have, enabling things to go more smoothly. This seems to have been the angel Djibril's attitude in correcting the Satanic Verses of the Koran.

Muhammad and his followers were happy too. It looked as though relations with the Quraysh would be less strained. And Satan, of course, was really happy. His whole purpose was to cause trouble for people and to turn them away from Allah. It looked like he had succeeded.

The story doesn't say how Allah felt about the whole thing. It merely suggests that Allah—or Djibril—figured out that something funny had happened to Sura 53. The problem was handled discreetly—no thunder and lightning, no threats of plagues or banishment to hell. Djibril simply showed up again and went over Sura 53 one more time in order to get it right. As a result, the Koran that Muhammad brought to the Muslims is the same as the Koran in heaven. The Satanic Verses were cut and the Quraysh and their goddesses were out of luck.

From Bad to Badr

Although Muslims can be cautious about their belief in angels, they do not ascribe all angelic belief to the influence of Satan. In fact, the Koran tells of angels who came to the assistance of Muhammad and his followers in a decisive battle against the Quraysh. It says that Allah inspired the angels to join in the fighting.

Relations between Muhammad's new followers and his old tribe deteriorated beyond repair. The Muslims were persecuted in and around Mecca—beaten, imprisoned, and excluded from commerce. So they migrated to the city of Medina, some 250 miles north of Mecca. From then on, the Quraysh and the Muslims launched raids on one another, until they finally clashed in full force to fight out their differences at a place called Badr Wells.

According to Muslim tradition, Muhammad and his forces were outmatched, but fought anyway. Allah turned the tide of the battle by sending down 1,000 angels to fight at their side. The battle was a turning point in Muslim history. After that, the faith of Islam began to take hold and spread throughout the Arab world. In fact, the Arab world itself began to spread. With the rise of the Persian empire, Islam was carried far into Europe, Africa, India, and Asia.

Revelations

After the Islamic empire took control of the holy city of Jerusalem, it triggered the holy wars known to Christians as the Crusades, which means "cross bearing." The Crusades took place during the 11th, 12th, and 13th centuries as Christian forces went to Jerusalem in the attempt to win the city for Christianity. The battles went back and forth. At various times, Christian leaders emerged victorious and made themselves kings of Jerusalem. Each time, however, the Islamic empire regained control eventually. Muhammad's own policy toward Jews and Christians was one of tolerance. Though he exacted taxes from Christians and Jews living in Muslim lands, he respected their religious beliefs.

Evil Ways

Like Christianity and Judaism, Islam recognizes fallen angels who disobeyed Allah and were cast from heaven. Their fall didn't result from a war in heaven, as Christians would have it, but from other episodes triggered by pride and lust. Since the time Allah kicked them out, these fallen angels have roamed the earth as enemies to humans, tempting them to do evil and playing tricks just for the hell of it.

What's in a Name?

The Muslims say Allah created the angels out of fire, or, alternatively, out of gemstones. Their job, like that of Jewish and Christian angels, is to worship Allah. Allah created Adam, the first man, out of clay and told the angels to submit to him too. Most of the angels went along with the idea, especially the angel Mikhail, the Islamic equivalent of Michael.

Many angels, however, refused to praise Adam, regarding him as inferior. So Allah put the matter to the test. He invited the angels to name things—plants, animals, rocks, and so on. They couldn't do it—they lacked the creativity.

Then Allah told Adam to name things. Names came out as though Adam were a living label-maker. The angels saw that Adam possessed a measure of Allah's creativity that they themselves lacked and so they submitted. All of them, that is, except an angel named Iblis, whose name means "despair." Iblis was cast out of heaven and remained the enemy of humankind.

Me and My Jinn

Some say when Iblis left heaven, he was transformed from an angel into a *jinn*. Jinn are spirits that can be either evil or good. They were believed to exist long before Muhammad came along and, unlike the goddesses al-Lat, al-Uzza, and Manat, they were successfully incorporated into Muslim belief.

Finding Out the Hard Way

Iblis is not the only fallen angel. Two others are Harut and Marut, who fell under completely different circumstances. It seems this once-angelic pair was hanging around in heaven, looking down on humanity, when Harut said to Marut, "These human beings are pathetic. Just look at 'em, sinning and being evil and forsaking the ways of Allah. What a bunch of losers!"

To which Marut replied, "You got that right. They're just a bunch of lying, fornicating, murderous infidels. It's a wonder Allah doesn't just exterminate them all like the vermin they are."

Harut responded, "Yeah, if you ask me, Allah's going way overboard in the mercy department. If I were Allah, I'd deep-fry all sinners to a crackly crunch the moment they strayed from the straight and narrow path of righteousness."

In the Flesh

Now, it just so happened that Allah was there and heard Harut and Marut talking. (Maybe this is not such a coincidence when you consider that Allah is everywhere and hears everything.) Anyway, he was benevolent and good-humored about the whole thing, despite the fact that he didn't like hearing his creations bad-mouthed by anyone, much less by a couple of high-flying feather-dusters who didn't have any idea what it's like being a flesh-and-blood human being. So Allah asked them, "You think you two could do better if I set you down on Earth inside human bodies?"

"You gotta be kiddin' us, Allah!" said Harut. "We're angels. We wouldn't sin even if you put us inside the bodies of a couple of high-school kids on prom night." "Yeah," said Marut. "We are unswerving in holiness as befits the celestial natures we were endowed with by our glorious creator. We're not like human beings who take to sin like sand to the desert."

"Well," said Allah, "let's just see about that." No sooner had he spoken than it was so. Harut and Marut found themselves on Earth inside human bodies.

The Devil Makes You Do It

It often happens that when you criticize people who are different from you that you end up making yourself look bad.

Sin City

As it happened, Harut and Marut found themselves in male bodies. And, as it also happened, there was another human body not far off—not a male body. This body was female—extremely female, and it belonged to a woman named Zorba—Zorba, as in ex-Zorba-dent! That is to say, she was too much for the new humans to deal with, and Harut and Marut were smitten with burning lust for this creature who, a moment before, when they were angelic non-bodies, would have seemed like a funny-looking sack full of unappealing glands and stuff.

Now, Harut and Marut didn't really understand what had happened to them and were in denial about their lustful condition. They imagined they were in complete control of the situation and were only there to reprove feckless mortals for their evil ways. They stared long and hard at Zorba until Harut finally said, "Sin much?"

Revelations

Muslims regard adultery as a sin, but that doesn't mean they think sex is bad. In fact, the Koran promises that there will be "young women with swelling breasts" in heaven as a reward for men who fear God during their lifetime. These maidens are known as houri. According to legend, they inhabit beautiful gardens where they sing and play music and practice other pleasure-giving arts. Some also add eating, drinking wine, and smoking to the list of pleasures to be enjoyed with the houri. Some legends speak as well of smooth-skinned youths as rewards for the righteous in paradise!

237

"Well," answered Zorba, "there's only one way to find out—if you *really* want to know." "Oh, yeah," said Marut. "We want to know. Show us everything."

So Zorba showed them everything—particularly the ropes of promiscuous sex. When show time was finally over, who should walk in but Zorba's husband? "You wicked adulterers!" he cried. "I will denounce your sin to Allah, and surely he will hear my prayers and punish you for your crime!"

Deserted Deserts

As angels familiar with the ways of Allah, what the man said seemed like a distinct possibility—a possibility Harut and Marut had only just begun to consider. Sadly, they panicked. In their shame and fear, and out of a vain hope to keep their activities secret, they bonked Zorba's husband over the head with a water jar. He fell down dead at their feet.

Zorba screamed and ran out to get help. Harut and Marut ran out too, to get away. They found themselves alone in the desert where Allah came to them. He told them, "You're busted for adultery and murder. Would you like your punishment here on Earth with your fellow sinners or up in heaven with me and my righteous angels?"

"You gotta be kiddin' us, Allah," said Harut. "We may be morons, but we're not stupid. Nothing could be worse than to be punished in heaven with you and your righteous angels around. Just fry me right here." "Me too," said Marut.

"I have other plans," said the Almighty One. "To teach you a lesson in mercy, I will not fry you. Instead, you shall be confined down in the bottom of a well as a sign of the depths of human depravity." No sooner had he spoken than it was so. The two sinful angels remained in the well, where you may be unlucky enough to find them yourself. In any case, it's certain the well hasn't dried up yet!

Wing Tip

Islamic angels often seem to work in pairs. One legendary angelic duo is Munkar and Nakir. These angels administer the final exam to human souls who have left their bodies. Like Christians, Muslims say that virtuous people who believe in God go to heaven, while evil unbelievers go to hell. Munkar and Nakir help sort out the good from the bad by asking the newly deceased a question: "Who is Muhammad?" Better study hard, it's pass/fail with no make-ups!

Hang on, Sufi

Islam may be the most recent of the major monotheistic religions, but it's already given rise to diverse traditions of angelic belief. One of these is the mystic sect known as Sufism. Sufis believe they can have a direct experience of God and the angels by means of meditation and ascetic discipline. (Asceticism involves fasting and renouncing worldly pleasures. In fact, the first rule of Sufism is to renounce the world. The second rule of Sufism is to renounce the pleasure of having renounced the world!)

One goal of Sufi meditation is to recreate the mystic experiences of Muhammad—being visited by angels and, in turn, visiting heaven. This experience may take years of training, practice, and self-denial, but the spiritual rewards, they say, are worth it. Many Sufis equate the presence of God and angels with a feeling of love.

A very different approach to angels within Islam is the tradition of Aristotelian thinking developed by Muslim philosophers of the Middle Ages. Muslim philosophers rediscovered many important writings left behind after Aristotle died, and combined them with religious ideas in order to develop an elaborate view of the cosmos as a complex machine kept in gear by angels. You can read more about this in Chapter 20.

Wing Tip

If you want to learn more about Sufism, you can consult the work of noted present-day Sufi scholar Annemarie Schimmel.

The Least You Need to Know

➤ The words of the Koran were brought to Muhammad by the angel Djibril.

➤ The Satanic Verses, deleted from the Koran, say that the pagan goddesses, al-Lat, al-Uzza, and Manat, are okay to worship.

➤ Iblis was kicked out of heaven for refusing to pay reverence to Adam.

➤ Jinns are spirits with free will who may be good Muslims or non-believers.

➤ Harut and Marut adopted human form and committed adultery and murder.

Chapter 19

Equatorial Angels

In This Chapter

➤ The orishas of Santería

➤ Santería sacrifice, initiation, and divination

➤ Possession by orishas

➤ Orishas and Catholic saints

➤ Legends of the orishas

Most people from Europe and North America don't ordinarily think of angels as beings who require blood sacrifices or speak through cowry shells or take possession of the bodies of their followers. To millions of people in Africa and Latin America, however, this angelic profile is not a bit surprising. Angels originating in Africa, specifically Nigeria, do all these things.

For these people, living with angels is part of everyday reality and many structure their lives around trying to make the angels happy through their actions and involvement with others. Whole social networks are formed around those who know the most about the angels and are best able to contact them and draw on their powers. And what dance party would be complete without at least some of the dancers getting possessed by their angels?

The angels are known as orishas and they form the basis of several closely related, highly organized religions practiced in Nigeria and in Latin American communities. No, the orishas don't want the blood of your children, but they are fond of chicken and goat's blood. And some of them even go for an occasional hamster! The rituals aren't just about death, however, but about building the bonds of society.

Out of Africa

Santería (known to its members as "the Religion") is originally based on the gods of the Yoruba tribe of Nigeria. Many of the Yoruba were brought to the new world as slaves where, in Central and South America, Yoruba gods gradually became identified with Catholic saints. Santería is thus strongly influenced both by Yoruba religion and Catholicism. It is practiced widely in Latin America and has spread to many North American cities as well.

The Devil Makes You Do It

It's not a good excuse for imperialism, but it often happens when one group of people dominates another that many features of the culture of the dominated group get picked up by those in control. The "classic" example is ancient Rome, which borrowed extensively from the conquered Greeks. A similar tendency can be seen in the spread of Santería throughout the new world.

Winged Words

Orishas are gods (either male or female) worshipped by the Yoruba tribe of Nigeria and brought to the new world by Yoruba slaves where they merged with Catholic saints. Orishas serve many of the same functions as angels.

Joining the Tribe

The gods of the Yoruba are known as *orishas*. This term has been carried over into Santería where the orishas are sometimes described as angels. Santería recognizes some 20 to 25 orishas, each with a different set of powers and characteristics, and each associated with numerous saints. The orishas resemble angels in that they are thought to serve as guardians over human beings and in that they are divine beings who are subordinate to the high god, known to the Yoruba as Olofi.

Orishas are central to the belief and ritual of Santería. According to Santería, each person has a guardian orisha, whether they believe in Santería or not. There is a special bond between human beings and their orishas, who guide and protect those who belong to them. The bond is thought to be determined by the orishas themselves who indicate a liking for particular people through oracles.

The orishas are sources of supernatural power, so those who know which of the many orishas they belong to can use their knowledge to maximize the help and protection the orisha has to offer. In addition, members of Santería can call upon other orishas for help under a variety of circumstances. Orishas can be contacted and influenced through magic and ritual, including sacrificial ceremonies, possession, divination, and amulets.

Bag of Tricks

Santería is highly ritualistic and secretive. Members go through numerous initiation ceremonies as they rise in the religious hierarchy and learn more and more of

Santería's secrets. These secrets include the proper uses of numerous ritual objects associated with the orishas.

Some ritual objects represent the orishas themselves. Others are used for communicating with them in order to see into the future. Still others are intended to influence them to provide help or protection in some way. Here's a list of some of the more important objects found in the Santería tool kit:

➤ *Elekes (necklaces)*. These five necklaces are made of different colored beads and correspond to five important orishas who are thought to protect the person wearing them. "The necklaces" is also the name of an initiation ritual in which new members get the necklaces.

➤ *Otánes (stones)*. The term "otánes" is a Spanish-ized version of the Yoruba word *otá*, meaning "stones." The otánes represent the orishas and contain their power. They are kept in covered bowls and receive sacrifices.

➤ *Diloggún (cowry shells)*. Twenty-one cowry shells used for divination (fortune-telling) are kept in the same bowl that contains the otánes. These are shells that look like mouths and are filed flat so they can fall with the "mouth" up or down. The number of mouth-side-up shells indicates the voice of the orisha.

➤ *Obi (coconut shells)*. Four pieces of coconut shell are thrown on the ground to see if an orisha answers yes or no to a question. Obi are especially useful for finding out if an orisha is pleased with an offering.

➤ *Opelé (divining chain)*. A chain with eight medallions on it is thrown to yield one of 256 possible combinations, depending on which side of each medallion lands face up. Each combination corresponds to a different bit of advice. This method of divination is reserved for the *babalawas*, or high priests of Santería.

➤ *Ewe (magic herbs)*. Plants associated with the orishas used in healing, purification, and magic.

➤ *Omiero (elixir)*. Water prepared from the ewe herbs and the blood of sacrificial animals used in rituals.

In addition, there are many other symbolic and ritual objects associated with particular orishas. Often these objects are carried around or kept in the home for good luck. For example, a mousetrap symbolizes the orisha known as Elegguá. A double-bladed ax (with the blades often carved out of wood) represents Changó.

Winged Words

A **babalawa** is a high priest of Santería. Traditionally, only men can become babalawas.

Turn to Stone

Of chief importance among the many ritual objects of Santería are the otánes. They are thought to contain the power of a santero's (note: a santero is a priest or priestess of santeria) orisha. The santero keeps the otánes in a large covered bowl inside his or her house. Offerings of fruit, candy, money, rum, coffee, or cigars may be placed on top of the otánes. On important occasions, the blood of sacrificial animals such as goats, hamsters, or chickens may be poured on the otánes.

Presenting ritual offerings to the otánes is known as "feeding the orishas." Different orishas are partial to different sorts of offerings, having different kinds of food that are set aside for them. Often, as the "child" of a particular orisha, a santero will abstain from eating the foods associated with his or her guardian being.

Orishas may be fed on a variety of occasions, especially on their "birthdays." An orisha's birthday is the feast day of a Catholic saint to which the orisha corresponds. Sacrificial feedings may take place on other occasions as well, including initiations. There are many different initiation ceremonies in Santería, at least one for each level of the religious hierarchy.

The Devil Makes You Do It

If you join Santería and participate in the ritual sacrifice of animals in the United States, watch out for the SPCA (Society for the Prevention of Cruelty to Animals), which has repeatedly made legal trouble for Santería members since it is illegal to sacrifice animals in the United States.

Revelations

The otánes representing a santero's orisha are sacred objects, normally kept hidden from view. Typically they are small, smooth, rounded stones which the santero finds outside. The santero is thought to be guided by his orisha in finding the particular stones that represent it.

Working your way up through the levels of Santería is a big part of life for many people. Each time a member moves up the religious ladder, he or she goes through another initiation. For some, the process begins before birth, since it's possible to be initiated into the first stages of the religion in the womb.

Human Rites

One of the most important of the many ceremonies of Santería is called "making the saint," in which a lay member (ayelo) becomes a priest or priestess (santero or santera) of Santería. On becoming a santero, an initiate is thought to be reborn as the child of his or her orisha and to receive special protection, power, and wisdom. In addition, he or she can perform certain rituals for lay members such as "the necklaces," which determines which orisha is the guardian of the initiate.

Just as new members must by initiated by santeros, new santeros must be initiated into the priesthood by high priests called babalawas. Traditionally, babalawas are only men. (Santero is one of many religions in which the upper priesthood has traditionally been closed to women.) The santero learns the mysteries of Santería from his or her babalawa, including how to use the otánes and diloggún.

Wing Tip

Thank your orisha if you break your eleke, or ritual necklace. Since it is thought that the orisha has transferred your future accident to your necklace, then it means he has just saved you from a serious accident!

The santero thus becomes qualified to hold consultation sessions with lay members. Members seeking help or advice visit the santero who, through the various divination techniques, consults the orishas and interprets their answers. Santeros provide medicine and magic as well as the advice of the orishas. For certain problems, the orishas may recommend some form of ceremony or ritual involving other members of the Santería community. Thus, members of Santería have an experienced team of priests and angels working for them!

There for You

Unlike other angels, orishas generally do not appear to human beings except in the form of the ritual objects that represent them. As a result, the usual way of communicating with an orisha is through divination. Some divination techniques require great skill and knowledge and can only be performed by experienced babalawas. Others are easier to learn and can be practiced by any santero.

Revelations

Santería made it into the movies with *The Believers* (1987), starring Martin Sheen and Helen Shaver, about a psychologist investigating Santería-style ritual human sacrifices. The film isn't bad, despite the fact that it misleadingly suggests that human sacrifice is a standard feature of Santería ritual, intended to confer an extended life span on those demonic enough to offer human blood to the orishas. Keep in mind real santeros say the orishas want to help people, not drink their blood!

Divination, however, is not the only form of contact between members of Santería and the orishas. On special occasions such as parties and dances held in their honor, the orishas enter and take possession of the bodies of their "children." This is seen as a good thing—a direct sign of the orisha's presence and care.

Possessed santeros may writhe on the ground or yell or dance wildly before becoming fully overtaken with the personality of their orishas. After that, however, the orisha in human form behaves in keeping with his distinctive personality. They may greet and bless members or talk and joke with one another. An orisha in human form may even drink the blood of a sacrificial animal, an act an ordinary human being is forbidden to do.

Gotta Love 'Em

Each orisha has a distinctive set of powers and a distinctive personality. Though they are beneficial forces, they can be temperamental and quarrelsome, especially if you don't know how to get on their good side. Learning how to propitiate the orishas may take years of study and practice, but the groundwork has already been laid by Santería tradition.

Orisha List

Here are profiles of some of the important orishas:

➤ *Elegguá*. The orisha of justice, he controls fate. He's often playful and unpredictable, but always fair. He likes rum, cigars, roosters, smoked fish, and candy—also toys for his childish side. He is associated with Saint Anthony.

➤ *Orúnmila*. The orisha of wisdom, he's known for gentleness and creativity. He controls the many techniques of Santería divination. He likes nuts, yams, and chickens. He is associated with Saint Francis of Assisi.

➤ *Babalú*. The orisha of disease and healing is unselfish, but dignified. He is lame and is said to walk on crutches. He likes beans, corn, and pigeons. He is associated with the Biblical beggar named Lazarus.

➤ *Changó*. The orisha of power is impetuous, macho, proud, and passionate. He is associated with thunder and lightning. He likes bananas, apples, and rams. He is associated with Saint Barbara, the patron saint of powder magazines and arsenals.

➤ *Obatalá*. The orisha of peace is benevolent, generous, and idealistic. He's in charge of

Wing Tip

Listen for the song "Babalú" sung by Desi Arnaz as Ricki Riccardo when you watch syndicated reruns of the TV sit-com *I Love Lucy.* It's about the orisha.

fatherhood. He likes everything white, especially doves, cotton, and coconut. He is associated with the Virgin Mary.

➤ *Oggún*. The orisha of work and warfare is straightforward, honest, and loyal, but unforgiving. He is in charge of weapons and metal. He likes rum, cigars, plantains, and pigeons. He is associated with Saint Peter.

➤ *Yemayá*. The orisha of women and motherhood covers all the feminine stereotypes and is associated with the ocean. She likes ducks, hens, sugar, and watermelon. She is associated with the Virgin Mary.

➤ *Oshún*. The orisha of wealth and love is loving, seductive, ambitious, and insatiable. She likes white wine, jewelry, cake, honey, and pumpkins. She too is associated with the Virgin Mary.

The Face Is Familiar

Orishas can be venerated in many forms. Not only are there particular sacrifices associated with each one, but specific plants, colors, and symbols as well. In addition, each one has a number of "paths" (aspects or manifestations) by which he or she can be recognized. The paths are represented by additional personalities associated with the orisha. Male orishas may have female or hermaphroditic paths. In fact, Changó, the most macho of all the orishas, has Saint Barbara as one of his paths.

The "paths" of the orishas include many Catholic saints. In fact, each orisha has numerous paths representing saints. Elegguá, for example, has Saint Anthony, Saint Martin, and Saint Benito as three of his twenty-one paths.

Orishas may have become associated with Catholic saints in Central and South America by African slaves who wanted to practice their Yoruba religion while keeping it secret from Catholic slave owners. Referring to the orishas by the names of saints may have helped them disguise their religion. This helps explain the secrecy that is part of Santería tradition.

Today, however, many members of Santería practice their religion openly (despite the fact that many of the rituals are secret in order to keep the priestly hierarchy intact) and practice mainstream Catholicism at the same time. Different representatives of the Catholic Church have expressed conflicting opinions about Santería. Some Catholic priests see Santería as "superstitious." Others note the positive effect Santería can have on the community and approve of the popularity of the religion.

The Devil Makes You Do It

Don't assume all santeros are Latin Americans by birth. Converts to Santería include North American Protestants, Catholics, and Jews.

Revelations

Santería is practiced widely in Cuba, where it originated. Not only has it been tolerated by the communist regime of Fidel Castro, but members say that Castro himself is a skilled santero, as are all the great Cuban leaders throughout history. They say the orishas helped Castro overthrow President Batista. In turn, Batista was able to survive and escape the country with a lot of money only because he was aided by his orisha!

All the Gossip

Members of Santería tell many anecdotes about the orishas to explain what they are like and what the world is like as well. Many of these stories originated in Africa and were passed along together with the ritual practices of the religion. Here are a few of the many stories told about the orishas.

Angels in Africa go way back. Here's a picture of archangel Michael from Africa done in the 17th century.

Feeling Daddy's Lava

Among the most colorful of the orishas is Changó, the orisha of power and passion. They say that he is the child of Yemmu, who is a female embodiment of Obatalá, and Aganyú, who is the orisha of volcanoes. In the story, Aganyú had the job of ferrying people across a river. Yemmu wanted to cross the river, but didn't have any money, so Aganyú agreed to have sex with her in exchange for passage to the other side.

Yemmu became pregnant with Changó as a result of this meeting. As Changó was growing up, Yemmu tried to keep the identity of his father secret from him. He kept pestering her to tell him, however, so she finally told him it was Aganyú. So Changó went off in search of his father, and finally found him on top of a mountain.

When Changó told Aganyú he was his son, Aganyú denied it. Changó was insistent, however, and kept pestering Aganyú. Eventually Aganyú, the volcano, blew his top! The explosion blew Changó all the way to Ilé-olofi, the house of God. Olofi, or God, sorted things out by putting young Changó under the care of Yemayá, who raised him. Since then, Changó and Aganyú became reconciled, and are often propitiated together.

A Fiery Relationship

Changó is a warrior and often fights battles. He is also a famous lover and has had affairs with many of the female orishas. He is often matched with Oyá, the orisha of the dead who rules over the cemetery. Oyá, like Changó, is known for her fiery personality.

In fact, one day Changó prepared a potion for war that would enable him to spit fire in battle. After he had gone off to battle, Oyá found what was left of the potion and drank it. Changó returned from battle in a bad mood, and looked for an excuse to taker his anger out on Oyá. When he couldn't find the rest of his potion, he accused Oyá of taking it.

Oyá denied the accusation vehemently, and resented Changó for suspecting her of stealing the potion. As she yelled at Changó, fire blew out of her mouth! Ever since then, Oyá and Changó have been the typically quarreling couple, always spitting fire at one another.

Wing Tip

If you're a woman, the proper way to supplicate Changó is to kneel and lift your breasts with your hands. They say Changó likes that!

The Devil Makes You Do It

Hold on to your cigars during Santería dances in which Changó possesses the bodies of his followers. He loves fire and has been known to grab people's lit cigars and eat them!

Stormy Weather

Changó is good at magic, and hot-tempered—a combination that can lead to catastrophic results. They say he went through an incarnation as a Nigerian king who destroyed his house and family by summoning a thunderstorm. Horrified at what he had done, he renounced his kingship and hanged himself.

He had been a tyrannical king and made many enemies during his lifetime. These enemies were overjoyed by his downfall and ridiculed his memory after his death. As a result, the kingdom was plagued by thunderstorms for years afterwards, until the people built a shrine to Changó and made sacrifices to propitiate him. After that, the thunderstorms diminished and the kingdom prospered.

Changó continues to be thought responsible for thunder and lightning. Santeros often go out after a storm to collect thunderstones. They say these stones have magical properties and are formed when lightning strikes the earth.

Drinking to Life

As you can tell from these stories about Changó, the orishas, despite their power, have human failings and weaknesses. Sometimes these failings account for things that go wrong in earthly life. For example, the story of Olofi (God) and Obatalá, the orisha of peace and fatherhood, explains why life on Earth is so far from perfect.

Olofi enlisted Obatalá to help him in the creation of living creatures. He showed Obatalá how to make their bodies out of clay and said that when they were dry, he would come back and breathe life into them. So Obatalá set to work, and before long had a good number of first-rate clay figures set out to dry.

After a while he grew hot and thirsty and decided to take a break and have some palm wine. It was a hot day, and the wine really seemed to hit the spot, so Obatalá had many gourds full of wine before returning to work. Obatalá resumed his task recklessly and many of the clay forms he made were blemished, or twisted, or missing features, or had extra features, but the orisha was too inebriated to know or care about the problems. He set these figures to dry next to the ones he had made previously.

When Olofi returned that evening, all the figures were dry. He looked carefully at the first figures Obatalá had made and saw they were perfect and breathed life into them. Olofi was so impressed with the quality of Obatalá's work that he assumed the orisha had mastered the art of creation and brought all the rest of the figures to life without checking them. As a result, many living things are filled with imperfections.

On His Metal

Obatalá felt bad about botching up his job and, as a result, is extremely patient with human shortcomings. This is not the case with Oggún, however, who is the orisha of work. He is a consummate craftsman, and gets irritated when others are unable to live up to his standards. In fact, they say he permits the occurrence of all accidents that result from human failure. He is also the orisha of war, so he clearly has destructive tendencies.

Oggún is in charge of metalwork and everything made of metal, especially tools. They say, however, that he became so disgusted by human ineptitude that he took all his tools away and went off by himself to live in the forest. Without Oggún and his tools, work came to a grinding halt.

All the orishas were worried about Oggún, especially since they all had to do without his handiwork. In fact, they say that as the orisha in charge of knives, Oggún is always the first to eat during a blood sacrifice since the blood of the sacrificial animal touches the knife before it touches the otánes of any of the other orishas. Without Oggún and his metal blades, the other orishas had to go around hungry.

Each of the orishas tried to persuade Oggún to return, but none of them were successful. Finally Oshún, the orisha of love and wealth, went into the forest to entice Oggún back to the world. Oshún is one of the sexiest of the female orishas, and she went into the forest wearing nothing but some handkerchiefs that she had tied together.

When she found Oggún, she pretended she didn't know he was there and began singing, dancing, and taking off the handkerchiefs. Oggún was spell-bound by the performance and came out of hiding to watch. As you might imagine, he watched with his mouth open and his tongue hanging out, and when Oshún swirled in front of him, she dipped her hand into a honey pot that she always carries and smeared honey into Oggún's mouth.

From then on, Oggún was under her power. She tied the handkerchiefs around his waist and led him back to society where he resumed working.

The Devil Makes You Do It

You never need to despair if you fall out of favor with an orisha. If one doesn't like you, there are others who will.

Revelations

Because of its secretive nature, you may have difficulty finding stories about the orishas without actually going to a santero. A few tales are told in Migene Gonzales-Wippler's book, *Santería, the Religion: A Legacy of Faith, Rites, and Magic* (Llewellyn Publications, 1994). If you want more of a taste of Nigerian-flavored supernatural doings, look for the novels of Yoruban writer Amos Tutuola, including *The Palm Wine Drinkard* (Greenwood Publishing Corp, 1970) and *My Life in the Bush of Ghosts* (Grove Press, 1994).

Mondo Orisha

Santería originates in Cuba and has spread from there to many countries. It is not the only Yoruba-based religion. These other versions of the Yoruba religion are practiced in Latin America as well:

➤ *Candomblé*—The national religion of Brazil, where orishas appear on postage stamps.

➤ *Macumba*—Another version of Santería practiced in Brazil, involving spiritualist practices such as seances.

➤ *Lucumí*—Version of Santería practiced in Cuba. The term means "friendship."

➤ *Shango*—A style of Santería native to Trinidad. Shango is another name for the popular orisha, Changó.

➤ *Voodoo*—The well-known Yoruba-influenced magic religion of Haiti.

Revelations

The orishas originally come from Nigeria. They are not the only angels who form the basis of Nigerian religion. The Cherubim and Seraphim Society, founded in Nigeria in 1925, models its worship of God and its church hierarchy on angels. The church was founded by Christianah Abiodun Akinsowon, who reported having numerous visions of angels before starting the church. Members believe they worship God in the same manner as the angels do, emphasizing singing as a chief religious activity. Members also have titles that correspond to the groups of angels mentioned in the Bible.

The Least You Need to Know

➤ Santería is based on the orishas, gods of the religion of the Yoruba tribe from Nigeria that became associated with Catholic saints.

➤ Orishas are thought to offer protection and knowledge of the future in exchange for sacrifice.

➤ Priests of Santería are called santeros. They perform sacrifices, conduct initiation rites, offer advice through divination, and become possessed by their orishas.

➤ Santería is secretive and ritualistic with initiation rites for each of several levels of priesthood.

➤ The many different orishas each have distinct personalities and preferences.

Part 5
Angels in Mind (Angelology)

Angels and philosophers have had lots to say to each other since people first started reading the Bible and the works of Plato and Aristotle at the same time. Angels seem to have a way of firing people's imaginations, including a number of creative and original thinkers. As a result, many fascinating and important ideas about the workings of the cosmos and the destiny of humanity have been inspired by angels.

In the following chapters, you'll see discussions of angels from the mouths of philosophers, and how those thoughts affected global ideas of angels and their actions.

Chapter 20

Angels Go Greek

In This Chapter

➤ Medieval angelology

➤ Greek philosophy applied to angels

➤ Pseudo-Dionysius and his angelic hierarchy

➤ Angels as Aristotelian intelligences

➤ Thomas Aquinas, "The Angelic Doctor"

Hallelujah University has always had a solid reputation as one of the most desirable places to learn the ultimate truths. A benevolent administration, enlightened faculty, pleasant surroundings, the popular "honor system," and the world-famous angelic choirs are just some of the areas of distinction that have set Hallelujah U. above all other institutions of higher learning.

As a result of a drastic shift in admissions policies, however, there's a whole new philosophy on campus, and more and more angels are going Greek. The traditional H.U. high spirits are still around, but they've been refocused by that old Greek idealism, and now it seems like the angels are running the world. They've got their own ideas about knowledge and they keep the rest of us guessing.

The new attitude has angels bunching together in groups. Rigid hierarchies have set in as angels seek, and find, a clearer sense of identity in fraternal associations—Alpha Omega and the others. In keeping with the group spirit, angels are trying out all kinds of stunts and initiation rites. All you ever hear about is how many of them can fit onto the point of a pin!

A New Paradigm for Paradise

But seriously, folks, the ancient Greek philosophers exerted a big influence on the Middle Ages and changed the way people thought about angels. Angels figure into lots of writing done in ancient times mainly because of their religious significance. This significance certainly doesn't go away in the Middle Ages, but at this time angels acquire a new, additional importance: They become key ideas in philosophy. Medieval philosophers used angels to help explain how the universe works.

Revelations

The early authorities in the Christian Church saw a lot in ancient Greek philosophy that reminded them of their own Christian beliefs. To explain the similarities, they reasoned that these philosophical truths must have been brought to the Greeks by an angel, specifically an ethnarch, or guardian angel of Greece.

A Heavenly Merger

Medieval philosophy in general tends to be religious. One of its goals was to square religious thinking with notions inherited and developed from the Greek philosophers—mainly Plato and Aristotle. Medieval philosophers developed elaborate theoretical systems that used Greek philosophy to talk about, and analyze, God and the angels.

Even though Greek philosophy and Judeo-Christian religion emerged as separate traditions, medieval philosophers and theologians found many ways of bringing them together. Aristotle and Plato both believed in higher truths that are not immediately apparent to the eye. They attempted to account for the natural world and human behavior in terms of these higher truths. Medieval philosophers extended this project by incorporating the higher truths of Plato and Aristotle into Jewish, Christian, and later Islamic religious thinking.

Winged Words

Platonic **forms** are aspects of ideal reality that give shape to material things and enable people to understand them. They are perfect and unchanging and influence human morality as well as the natural world.

256

Albrecht Durer's engraving, "Melancholia I," representing philosophical angels.

Big Ideas

Plato said that material reality was only an inferior version of an ideal, perfect reality. This perfect reality includes *forms* that give material things their shape, and gives the human mind the power to understand them. In contrast to ideal reality, material things are only temporary. After a while they fall apart. Their ideal forms, however, are perfect and permanent.

Phony Dioney

Many seized on Plato's ideas as philosophical confirmation of their religious views, including their ideas about angels. One of the first sustained efforts to use Plato's ideas to understand angels was a work by a writer known as Pseudo-Dionysius (that's "Fake Dennis" in English—or you could call him "Phony Dioney"). The *real* Dionysius is mentioned in the Acts of the Apostles as an Athenian converted to Christianity by Paul during the 1st century. Pseudo-Dionysius is an unknown writer who lived some 500 years later. No one knows exactly when he lived or where he is from.

The Devil Makes You Do It

Plato certainly had a point in suggesting that material reality is imperfect. Even so, if you reject material reality, you could be making a big mistake, since material reality is where human beings live!

Going with the Flow

Pseudo-Dionysius believed that all things come from God. This means not only that God created the world to begin with, but also that power keeps flowing from God to the world. This power has to flow through channels to get all the way from heaven to Earth, and this is where the angels come in. God spreads his power to the angels, who in turn pass it along to the rest of creation.

Wing Tip

If you want people to notice your work, try making it pseudepigraphical—that is, try saying it was done by someone famous. It sure worked for me when I said my play, *Hamlet*, was written by William Shakespeare!

Phony Dioney sees this as a pretty good arrangement for all concerned. Everyone gets free power just for being alive. Even God likes it because some of the power gets back to him in the form of the praise and worship of his creations. The power, however, is only perfect and pure at the source—God himself. As it gets passed along, it becomes gradually weaker and clotted up. As a result, the further you are from God, the less directly you experience the power.

Getting with the Spirit of Things

Being close or far from God doesn't just refer to spatial distance but to spiritual importance. The angels are closer to God spiritually than human beings, who are closer to God spiritually than animals, who are closer than plants, and so on down the line. All of creation figures into a hierarchical structure centered on God.

Revelations

The fact that there are nine groups of angels in the Pseudo-Dionysian scheme is significant because of the neo-Platonic significance of the number three that comprised a complete grouping including two extremes and the middle. As a grouping of three threes, the nine groups of angels represent completion. In addition, the medieval angelologist Pope Gregory interprets a parable told in Luke 15 as representing nine groups of angels. According to the parable, a woman who has ten pieces of silver loses one, and is willing to search all over for it. According to Pope Gregory, the lost piece of silver represents humanity, because we're in danger of being lost to sin. The other nine pieces that aren't lost represent the angels.

Angels are necessary within this structure. Without them there would be a huge power gap in the continuum of creation. In fact, the gap between God and humanity is so large, it takes many groups of angels to fill it. These groups pass God's power down along to one another before it gets to people. As a result, not all angels are created equal.

This is the thinking behind Phony Dioney's famous angelic hierarchy, a schematized grouping of angels that is based on groups named in the Bible, especially Paul's letter to the Colossians, but organized according to a power structure that was added later. As you can see from the following list, the hierarchy consists of three groups of three. Here you can see how these names were used in the Bible compared to how they are interpreted by Fake Dennis.

The Devil Makes You Do It

Don't expect to find a single official grouping of all the angelic hierarchies. There are too many different traditions that organize angels in different ways. Pseudo-Dionysius's scheme is perhaps the most influential and widely accepted.

Filling the Order

The first tier of angels, Seraphim, Cherubim, and Thrones, are closest to God and are the most pure, perfect, and wise of the angels.

➤ *Seraphim.* These are described in the Book of Isaiah as having six wings each and surrounding the throne of God. The word "seraph" means "fiery ones." Pseudo-Dionysius interprets this to mean that they are the closest to God and carry his power in its most concentrated form.

➤ *Cherubim.* These are mentioned in various places in the Bible, often serving as guards of a sacred place such as the Garden of Eden and the Ark of the Covenant. The word "cherub" means "full of wisdom," and Pseudo-Dionysius says this shows they have an especially direct understanding of God.

➤ *Thrones.* These are mentioned in the letter by the Apostle Paul to the Colossians, along with "dominions, authorities, principalities, and powers" as invisible beings created by God. "Thrones" also designates the ophanim and galgallim mentioned in the Books of Enoch. These are angels that resemble fiery wheels covered with eyes that serve as living accessories to God's chariot-throne. According to Pseudo-Dionysius, they most perfectly uphold the divine will because they carry God.

The second tier of angels, Dominions, Authorities, and Powers, have names that indicate how they imitate God and exhibit his characteristics to those below them.

➤ *Dominions.* These are mentioned in Paul's letter to the Colossians. Pseudo-Dionysius associates them with freedom, suggesting they influence earthly government to uphold God.

Wing Tip

It's usually a good idea to try to work problems out with your immediate superiors before complaining to the higher–ups. This is part of the idea behind angelic hierarchy.

The Devil Makes You Do It

However talented he may have been as a philosopher, Pseudo-Dionysius was no Hebrew scholar. He seems not to have realized that the "-im" suffix in Hebrew indicates the plural form of a word, as in elohim, seraphim, and cherubim. Thus, he refers incorrectly to "a seraphim," rather than to "a seraph."

➤ *Authorities.* Also mentioned in Colossians, these angels demonstrate the meaning of divine authority. They are commonly known as Virtues.

➤ *Powers.* Still another group of invisible beings mentioned by Paul in his letter to Colossians. Pseudo-Dionysius associates them with the courage to face God.

The lowest tier of angels are those closest to human beings, especially the ordinary angels.

➤ *Principalities.* The last group of invisible beings mentioned in Colossians, these angels are "Princes" who serve as guardian angels to the cities and nations on Earth.

➤ *Archangels.* These are mentioned in the Book of Revelation as seven angels around the throne of God. Despite the prefix "Arch," which means "ruling," Pseudo-Dionysius places them quite low on his angelometer.

➤ *Angels.* Mentioned throughout the Bible, these are the ordinary angels who appear to human beings. Even so, all the celestial beings, aside from God, get their name from this lowest group. Hence the seraphim are the highest group of angels, as opposed to the lowest group of angels called "angels."

Loose Ends

Phony Dioney, like many philosophers of his day, saw the world as a carefully ordered and well-organized state of affairs. Everything has its own set place in keeping with its nature, including the angels. In order to see things this way, Pseudo-D had to disregard, or explain away, a lot of the contradictory things that had been said about angels over the years.

For example, Michael, who is generally referred to as an archangel, is also said to be the chief of all the angels. Pseudo-D doesn't go into this problem. He does, however, tackle another difficulty, which is that, according to the system, only the lowest order of angels made contact with human beings. Higher angels would be too dazzling and powerful for people to deal with. In the Bible, however, angels from higher groups sometimes make contact with humans.

For example, Isaiah says that he was purified by a seraph who touched his lips with a hot coal. According to Pseudo-D, "a seraphim" wouldn't fly down so low as to purify a mortal human being. According to him, it wasn't really a seraph, but a regular angel who received the power to purify from higher up. The story doesn't say it was a regular angel to show that the power to purify came from a fiery seraph, in keeping with its nature. Also, the angel was being modest in keeping himself out of the story.

By analogy, if your postal carrier brought you a paycheck, you wouldn't say he or she paid you for the work you did, you'd say your company paid you. This may seem kind of pointless and nit-picky, but it actually ties in with Pseudo-D's whole way of seeing things. In his view, you can't take appearances at face value.

Revelations

According to Pseudo-Dionysius, even the most intelligent things people can say are at best imperfect approximations of the truth. This holds true even of sacred scripture and his own philosophical statements about angels. These things can only point our minds in the right direction. Beyond that, we have to live within the limits of human knowledge and rely on faith.

Signs Pointing Up

According to Phony Dioney, living on a plane of existence several rungs down the celestial ladder means we can't see the divine truth very clearly. It's not just that our knowledge is inaccurate or that we don't happen to know religious mysteries; the point is we *can't* know. We don't have the right mental equipment. Our spiritual souls are too bogged down in flesh and blood to be able to comprehend God and the angels truthfully, the way they know themselves.

Instead, we have to make do with rough approximations. These approximations are the best we can get from the physical reality we live in. Stories, descriptions, and pictures that represent God and the angels can't be true or accurate. Even so, they can get our minds headed in the right direction, toward the upper reaches of reality, especially if they don't really seem to make sense.

The Devil Makes You Do It

Many systems of spiritual and religious belief are set up so that you can't understand them unless you're willing to believe in them at the outset. For Pseudo-Dionysius, this was true of Christianity. While mysterious symbolism elevates the believer toward God, it poses a barrier to the understanding of the non-believer.

As an example, Pseudo-D talks about the cherubim as they're described by Ezekiel. Ezekiel says they have four faces, one like a lion, one like an eagle, one like a horse, and one like a man. In reality, says Pseudo-D, they don't look this way. In fact, they don't appear to visual perception at all. They're invisible. The visual description only suggests spiritual truths about their unknowable nature.

Moving in Intelligent Spheres

Plato was a dominant influence on the philosophy of the early Middle Ages. Starting around the 9th century, however, Islamic philosophers discovered some unknown works by Aristotle and began to share the ideas they found with the rest of the world. Included in the newly discovered philosophy of Aristotle was an explanation of the motions of the stars and planets.

Aristotle was impressed by what seemed to him to be a plan or purpose behind the movements of these heavenly bodies. He reasoned that they couldn't just move themselves, so something must be moving them—something intelligent that knew how to make the sky work. In fact, he posited a different intelligence for each planet and an additional one for the stars.

The Islamic philosophers (or *falasafahs,* as they called themselves) connected Aristotle's intelligences with the angels of religious scripture. In so doing, they promoted the idea that angels are necessary to keep the material world working. This notion reappeared later in the thinking of the philosopher and theologian St. Thomas Aquinas.

The Substance of the Argument

Aquinas was way into angels—so much so, in fact, that he is known as "the Angelic Doctor." He drew on Aristotelian and Platonic thinking in his attempts to prove the existence of angels in philosophical terms. His proofs depended on his idea of what angels are made of: spiritual substance that exists independently of matter. This idea is known as *the doctrine of separate substance.* (Notice that, according to Aquinas, a substance is not necessarily physical stuff. Instead, it can be immaterial.)

Immaterial substance can think and can move material substance. We can tell this because we can see that material substance doesn't move itself (rocks, for example, don't move themselves), and creatures that can move themselves are evidently capable of at least rudimentary thinking. Even bugs seem to make reasonable choices in deciding where to move. Bugs, then, like people, are made of a combination of material and spiritual (thinking) substance. We call our spiritual substances our souls.

Winged Words

The doctrine of separate substance is Aquinas's idea that spiritual (immaterial) substance can exist independently from matter. Spiritual substance is pure intellect and what angels are made of.

Evidently, material substance can exist independently of spiritual substance (again, rocks don't seem to have an spiritual substance in them, and they exist just fine). The question is, can spiritual substance exist separately from material substance? If so, we've got the raw materials for angels. Aquinas set out to prove that angels exist by proving that separate spiritual substance exists. If you like brain-teasers, go ahead and set yourself to work on these Aquinas-esque arguments:

➤ It only makes sense that spiritual substance ought to be able to exist without matter, since spiritual substance is more perfect. Just as people (made of a mixture of spirit and matter) are more perfect than rocks (made only of matter), there must be creatures made only of spirit that are more perfect than people.

➤ We know spiritual substance is more perfect than material substance because there appear to be degrees of perfection in the world, and the most perfect material creature (that's the human body) has the most spiritual substance in it. The next step up after people must be a creature that is completely spiritual—that would be an angel.

The Devil Makes You Do It

Metaphysical speculation (thought about things that can't be observed) has been a favorite philosophical pastime for centuries. Most academic philosophers of the 20th century, however, point out that it's impossible to draw reliable conclusions about the nature of metaphysical reality.

➤ God's creation mirrors his nature in various ways. It seems God wants to express himself in his creation. It only makes sense that he would want to express his power and wisdom by making purely spiritual beings. If he's going to make cockroaches, you'd think he'd make angels, too!

➤ For all we know (if we're medieval philosophers), angels could exist. We also know that angels are more perfect than material creatures. They couldn't be more perfect, however, if their existence was only potential, or possible, instead of actual, since (according to Aristotle) actual existence is more perfect than potential or possible existence. The idea of a perfect creature existing only in potential is a logical paradox. Therefore angels must exist.

➤ We need spiritual substance to keep the stars and planets moving. Aquinas acknowledges that the stars and planets could have their own souls that move them, but they don't appear to be living things, so it must be either God or the angels that does it. It probably isn't God, because it looks like kind of boring work, so God probably delegated the responsibility to angels.

➤ Without angels, there'd be a big gap in the chain of being leading from God through humanity down to mud.

Pinpointing Angels

Does this seem like a bunch of useless wool-gathering to you? You're not alone. Starting in the Renaissance, people began regarding angelology as unimportant and just about the biggest waste of time imaginable. That's why the famous question about how many angels can fit on the point of a pin got asked. The angelological answer depends on whether immaterial substance takes up space. If it doesn't, then angels have no physical size, so infinite numbers could be in the same place.

Revelations

Apparently, the first writer known to raise the subject of the number of angels that can fit on the point of pin was Johannes "Meister" Eckhart, a German mystic philosopher of the late 13th and early 14th centuries. Eckhart claimed, "The masters say, a thousand souls in heaven sit on the point of a pin." His *point* was that the "masters," or scholastic philosophers, spent their time thinking about ridiculous and useless questions and developing inconsequential theories. Eckhart set a trend of "master" bashing that reached a peak in the 17th century with the materialist philosophers like Francis Bacon and Thomas Hobbes, who despised the medieval Aristotelians.

Wing Tip

Much writing about angels suggests that their nature cannot be adequately understood in terms of a human scale of size. Jewish legends of the Middle Ages say that angels can be hundreds or even thousands of miles tall.

A more common response, however, is, "Who the heck cares?"

If your curiosity about the burning question of how many angels fit onto the point of a pin is still not satisfied, you can take your pick from any of these answers:

➤ Not as many as before the new fire codes prohibited seating in the aisles.

➤ At least one. Beyond that I can't tell, since the angel I stuck with the pin told me he'd nuke me into the pits of hell if I ever tried it again.

➤ Tough question. Even an angel would get stuck on that one.

The Least You Need to Know

➤ Medieval angelology uses ancient Greek philosophy to make sense of angels.

➤ Pseudo-Dionysius came up with a famous hierarchical grouping of angels.

➤ According to Pseudo-Dionysius, the human intellect can have only an imperfect understanding of angels.

➤ Islamic philosophers combined scriptural angels with Aristotelian astronomy.

➤ Thomas Aquinas argued that angels are made of an immaterial substance of pure intellect.

➤ Any number of angels may or may not be able to fit on the point of a pin!

Chapter 21

Against the Grain

In This Chapter

➤ Swedenborg and Blake

➤ Communicating with angels

➤ Angelic societies and the three heavens

➤ Angels as restrictive conventional thinking

➤ The Four Zoas

Angels had been part of people's belief systems for years and few seriously questioned their existence until around the 17th century, when a whole new way of thinking developed. This way of thinking is called science. Thanks to scientific thinking, many came to look at angels as mere creatures of the imagination.

Not all scientific thinkers abandoned angels, however. In fact, a Swedish scientist named Emanuel Swedenborg rose to their defense, attempting to explain how science and angels can coexist peacefully in the same universe. In doing so, he identified problems with conventional religion and attracted many followers.

One of those whom Swedenborg influenced was the English poet and printer, William Blake. Blake wasn't too big on science or conventional religion, but incorporated angels into his surprising and powerful artistic visions. Swedenborg and Blake both bucked the current trends of their day, fashioning their own angelic views of reality and making their mark on Western art and philosophy.

A Great Communicator

Emanuel Swedenborg (1688–1772) spent years studying math, science, and philosophy before turning his attention to the spiritual work for which he became famous. He eventually moved away from science, saying that what we can see, hear, and touch with our physical senses is only a small part of the story. The ordinary senses can tell us only so much about reality. To see and know more we need to use our spiritual minds, as he claimed he was able to do.

Thanks to his spiritual awareness, Swedenborg says he has been able to visit heaven and see angels in their shining raiment and celestial dwelling places. He says he even talks to them to find out what they're like and how they live. He wrote about his experiences and published numerous books, hoping to influence people to revise their ideas about God and heaven.

Revelations

Swedenborg was known to have fainting spells, leading some psychiatrists after his death to question his sanity during life. Some suggest that his experiences with angels are the result of hallucinations. Others have told unconfirmed stories that he behaved in public in a bizarre and uncontrollable manner. His defenders assert that he was widely respected and competent throughout his lifetime. They also point to an incident in which he is said to have gone out for a walk and returned with the news that a fire had broken out in the faraway city of Stockholm. This happened, of course, before the days of electronic communication. News arrived by mail the following day confirming Swedenborg's announcement!

Although angels are spiritual, rather than physical beings, their physical nature corresponds to physical reality in every respect. They have spiritual bodies that are just like human physical bodies, with arms, legs, fingernails, and the whole caboodle (no wings, though). Angels can even have sex. They have to be married, however, and marriages in heaven are really close, loving relationships. It sometimes happens that people who were married on Earth get to heaven and realize they weren't cut out to be together, so they split up, and possibly find their perfect partner.

The Real Deal

Swedenborg says he is one of the lucky few who is able to speak directly with the angels in this lifetime. He believed, however, that everyone can learn about angels and heaven by adopting his method for interpreting reality. He says that the natural world can give us clues about celestial reality if we know how to look at it. Things in the physical world correspond to higher, spiritual truths, but we need to be able to see through them to understand their meaning. This includes natural things like plants and animals, the physical laws of time and space, and the writings left by ancient people, including the Biblical prophets.

Swedenborg complained that people tend to interpret these things in their physical, rather than their spiritual, sense. He believed an excessive concern with physical things prevents you from understanding spiritual truths. Missing the spiritual truth that lies behind physical reality cuts us off from God, who wants us to get close to him by opening ourselves up to his love and wisdom. Because knowledge involves an emotional connection with God and truth, you need to be open to it in order to perceive it. Otherwise, you remain in the dark.

Class Status

Surprisingly, human beings aren't the only ones who can be ignorant and closed off from God; angels can, too. All angels, like all humans, differ in their knowledge and love, which comes from God. In fact, Swedenborg believed that there are three different heavens, and every angel and every human being occupies one of the three. Which heaven you live in depends on how close you are to God.

The first heaven is the ultimate heaven, the heaven of nature, which is furthest from God. (It is "ultimate," not in the sense of being the best, but in being the furthest away.) The angels and people who belong to this heaven are basically ignorant of God and love only themselves. The middle heaven, which Swedenborg calls the spiritual heaven, is made up of people who love their neighbors. This is a good thing, since it gets people past selfish desires into an appreciation for others and for society.

The Devil Makes You Do It

The problem with spiritual truths is that there is no hard evidence for them. That's one of things that makes them spiritual.

Revelations

Swedenborg was not only a respected scientist and philosopher, he was also a member of the House of Peers in Sweden (an Aristocratic legislative body). He later abandoned most of the worldly interests and ambitions of his younger days in order to write about angels and spirituality. It is for these writings of the later period of his life for which he is best known.

The best heaven and the one closest to God is the celestial heaven, also called the internal heaven. This is for people and angels who love God. Beings in this heaven are happiest and wisest, receiving knowledge directly from God.

In addition to these three heavens is hell. This is made up of people and angels who are evil and want to harm one another. Ironically, hell includes many people who claim to be religious, but are hypocritical and use religion as an opportunity to dominate others.

Wing Tip

You'll want to set aside some time to study theology before you die, so you'll have something to talk about when you get to Swedenborg's heaven!

Soul Mates

According to Swedenborg, although God is the source of love and wisdom, he did not create the angels. Instead, they evolve from the souls of deceased human beings who attempt to return to God. After death, they wind up in one of the heavens in any of various angel societies where they lead busy, active afterlives discussing intellectual and theological issues and guiding living human beings.

Group Thinking

Angel societies are formed as angels with similar ways of understanding things get together. Unlike humans, angels can tell immediately what other angels are like. Angels that like each other sense an immediate common bond; they know right away that they share an understanding of how things are and what's important.

The Devil Makes You Do It

Watch out for sneering, snarling, teeth-gnashing angels in Swedenborg's heaven. They're the bad ones!

In fact, the same sort of love and understanding that determines how close the angels are to God also determines how they organize themselves into societies. This is one reason it's important to adopt and maintain the right religious beliefs and attitude; otherwise, you'll wind up running around with the wrong crowd! The wisest and kindest angels are the happiest and best-connected.

Losing Face

Swedenborg says he has known of hypocritical angels who tried to fool the good ones, imitating their kind, affectionate way of talking in order to join their society. They were unable to keep up the ruse for very long. In a little while, their hypocrisy became evident in their facial expressions and they started gnashing their teeth and snarling! Good angels find that sort of behavior extremely unpleasant and shun the society of such inferior angels.

Conversely, bad angels have a hard time dealing with the conversation of the good ones. Again, Swedenborg claims to speak from personal experience in saying that he has seen a conversation between a good and bad angel. After a few minutes, the bad angel became upset by the kind and loving words of the good one and dissolved into tears.

Keeping in Touch

The amount of love and understanding the angels have shows not only in their faces, but in other ways, including their clothes and their houses in heaven. The wiser and more loving the angel, the more resplendent are its garments and the nicer its living arrangements. These are provided by God! According to Swedenborg, it's possible to improve your situation at any time, either as a human being or an angel. This can be difficult to do, however, since selfishness and ignorance die hard, even in heaven.

It often happens that angels temporarily slip down a notch in the celestial scale and become less wise, kind, and happy as they drift farther from God. Swedenborg calls this experience *vastation*, and says that it happens to human beings, too. Vastation occurs, says Swedenborg, through self-love. Angels feel great sadness when this happens, since they sense they are moving away from God, but in the long run, this isn't such a bad thing—as long as you return to God.

Changing conditions provide variety in the existence of angels that allows them to appreciate the good times. If you were constantly in a perfect state, the blissful feeling would wear off and you'd stop enjoying it. Taking a step back from God helps you see what you're missing and makes you all the happier when you return.

Winged Words

Vastation is the experience of slipping farther away from God as a result of self-love. It happens to angels as well as human beings and results in a feeling of sadness.

Dim Recollections

Although there are many degrees and levels of existence in Swedenborg's theology, the distinction between life and death isn't especially important. In fact, Swedenborg says that you can be dead for a while before you even realize it! This is because angels come to be with you in order to help you make the transition from life to death smoothly. As a result, you can get used to heaven gradually.

Not only do they help people adjust to the afterlife, angels influence people in this life. Swedenborg says everyone has both good and bad angels influencing their thoughts, feelings, and behavior, whether they realize it or not. By and large, says Swedenborg, angelic influence goes unrecognized by living human beings. This is because the love and kindness that is important in heaven often seems useless on Earth.

This is true of all spiritual communication that takes place between beings in different heavens. Some of the love and kindness gets lost as the message travels from one place to another. Swedenborg says he has experienced this problem in trying to relay angel messages to human beings.

Even though angels communicate spiritually, they still use words and language. Swedenborg says that when his spirit leaves his body and he visits the angels, he can understand them perfectly. In fact, they can communicate much more efficiently—not only more directly, but in much less time than it takes people on Earth to convey their ideas.

Sadly, however, it often happens that when Swedenborg returns to his body, he can't remember what the angels told him. Other times he remembers what was said, but it seems much less important than it seemed at the time. As you might imagine, this greatly increases the challenge of convincing people of the existence of the angels!

In spite of the difficulties, however, Swedenborg managed to influence many people through his writings. Many of his followers even formed a separate denomination of Protestant Christianity called the New Church. He also influenced a number of literary figures, including Baudelaire and Emerson. Among famous people most deeply influenced by Swedenborg is the poet and printer William Blake (1757–1827).

Wing Tip

You may have had dreams in which you came up with brilliant ideas, only to forget what they were after waking. This is similar to many of Swedenborg's experiences in the realms of the angels. So think twice before assuming that these experiences don't mean anything!

Winged Words

Illumination is the medieval art of decorating book manuscripts with colorful pictures and designs. The art was revived by William Blake, who illuminated his own poetry in print form.

Prints of Peace

Blake was an English poet who often incorporated angels and angelic beings into his poetry. He was also a visual artist and was unusual for *illuminating* and printing his own poetry. (Illumination originally refers to the medieval practice of making colorful illustrations to decorate the pages of written manuscripts.) Blake illuminated his poetry with his own illustrations, so that his poetry and his visual art were closely connected. As you probably noticed, Blake did many of the illustrations used in this book.

Angel Fluff

Blake picked up on a number of Swedenborg's ideas. He could relate especially to the notion that conventional religious thinking is often hypocritical and stands in the way of true religious experience. He also liked the idea that people are in heaven already and have angels all around them, only most of us don't realize it.

At the same time, Blake felt Swedenborg didn't go far enough in rethinking the age-old problem of good and evil. He didn't feel Swedenborg gave evil enough credit as a necessary and vital aspect of reality. By focusing only on good, Swedenborg was placing harmful restrictions on religious experience.

Blake criticizes Swedenborg in his illuminated poetic work, *The Marriage of Heaven and Hell*, in which he treats "good" as a constraining social convention. In this work, angels represent shallow, orthodox belief. Devils, in contrast, display original, revolutionary thinking. Yet Blake does not simply reverse good and evil. Instead, he suggests that you need to appreciate both to get the whole picture.

Monkey Business

As an example, Blake told a story in which an angel came to him and criticized him for being evil. The angel adopted a conventional religious attitude and threatened him with eternal torment in a "hot, burning dungeon" unless he changed his ways. Blake wasn't scared. He said, "Show me this dungeon and we'll see whose eternal lot is better, yours or mine."

So the angel led him down through a church vault and through a mill until they came to a vast abyss, filled with smoke and fire and spiders who were devils and thunder and blood. Suddenly, out of the abyss, the beast Leviathan came toward them, foaming at the mouth. When this happened, the angel flew off back into the mill, leaving Blake to face the beast alone.

The Devil Makes You Do It

Don't believe everything an angel tells you. It may be one of William Blake's angels of conventional morality!

The Leviathan from Blake's illuminated poetic work, The Marriage of Heaven and Hell.

As soon as the angel disappeared, however, the Leviathan and the abyss disappeared. Blake found himself on a pleasant riverbank in the moonlight, listening to a man singing and playing the harp. The words of the song went, "The man who never alters his opinion is like standing water and breeds reptiles of the mind." When Blake returned to the mill and found the angel, he told him that the vision of the abyss resulted from the angel's mistaken metaphysical views.

Fighting Ever After

Then Blake said, "Let's see how you'll be spending eternity!" The angel just laughed. But then, suddenly, Blake grabbed the angel and took off with him. They went right into the sun where Blake changed into white garments. He also grabbed a set of Swedenborg's volumes! Then they flew past Saturn and leapt into a void.

"This is where you'll be spending eternity!" said Blake to the angel. Then they saw the church again and went inside and found a Bible. They opened the Bible and found a big pit inside the book. Blake dove down into the pit, pushing the angel in ahead of him.

Down in the pit they found seven brick houses and went into one of them. Inside was a roomful of monkeys and baboons with chains around their waists. Sometimes the strong monkeys were able to catch hold of the weaker ones. When this happened, things got pretty sick. The strong monkeys had sex with the weak ones and then ate them, kissing and caressing them even as they ate!

Revelations

Although Charles Darwin didn't come up with his theory of evolution until decades after the death of Blake, English and European intellectuals had long been fascinated by the similarities and differences they observed between people and animals. In fact, the tradition of telling stories about animals that behave like humans goes back to the 6th century B.C.E. and the beast fables of Aesop. A vogue for beast fables was revived in the 17th and 18th centuries. Blake's anecdote about the cannibalistic monkeys can be understood as an unusually bizarre example of a beast fable.

As you might think, the room smelled really awful, so Blake and the angel went back out to the mill. There the angel said, "Thy fantasy has imposed upon me and thou oughtest to be ashamed." Blake answered, "We impose upon one another." So much for the glorious power of angels!

From all this, you might think that Blake and the angel were enemies. In fact, the story ends with a motto that says "Opposition is true friendship." Neither Blake nor the angel were simply either right or wrong; instead, they both had different ways of seeing things. Blake saw the disagreement as a creative and constructive process.

Elsewhere, he calls this process "mental fight." This is impassioned, creative argument that is a beneficial enterprise.

An image of mental fight from Blake's epic work, Milton.

Revelations

Blake uses the phrase "mental fight" in a famous poem that was set to music and sung as a hymn. This hymn has been especially popular in England and was sung in the hit movie, *Chariots of Fire* (1981), which won Oscars for best picture, screenplay, costumes, and musical score. The film's title comes from Blake's poem. Here are the last two verses:

Bring me my bow of burning gold:
Bring me my arrows of desire:
Bring me my spear: O clouds unfold!
Bring me my chariot of fire!

I will not cease from mental fight,
Nor shall my sword sleep in my hand
Till we have built Jerusalem
In England's green and pleasant land.

Long Lasting

For Blake, mental fight is the best way to understand and experience Eternity. Eternity is the fruit of imagination. It is liberation from all restrictive ideas. Unfortunately, ideas have a way of restricting people. It is up to artists and prophets to cut through the restrictions and get people back in touch with Eternity.

Zoas' Forever

Blake invented a whole imaginative world to show how we get separated from Eternity. The key characters in this world are angelic beings known as the Four Zoas ("four beasts") who live in Eternity but get separated. The Four Zoas are based on the four living creatures surrounding the throne of God in the vision of the prophet Ezekiel. Ezekiel described them as fiery wheels covered with eyes.

Blake's Zoas represent four basic aspects of humanity: body, reason, imagination, and emotions. Originally, these aspects were integrated into the ancient Eternal Man, who Blake names Albion. Albion, however, falls asleep, and the Four Zoas become separated. What's more, they become further divided into emanations and specters that bring restrictive realities into being.

Blake's Four Zoas are named Tharmas, Urthona, Luvah, and Urizen. They have feminine aspects called emanations, which were originally integral parts of them, but which separated from them and became antagonistic. These are Enion, Enitharmon, Vala, and Ahania. Separated from their emanations, the Zoas become specters. In order to contain the specters and emanations and limit the destruction they threaten to wreak, Divine Mercy lets them descend into the space and time of the created world. Meanwhile, Albion is still snoozing in the world of Eternity! Blake calls this eternal world Eden.

The Four Zoas correspond to four states of existence. These are called Eden (humanity), Beulah (Emanation), Ulro (Specter), and Shadow (generation). They also correspond to the four continents, Europe, America, Asia, and Africa. These beings have numerous children and lower manifestations, including Orc, Rintrah, Palamabron, Theotormon, Leutha, and Oothoon. Each of them are associated with different characteristics. Theotormon, for example, is Desire. His emanation, Oothoon, is Free Love.

Wing Tip

Notice that Blake's poetic conceptions, like Swedenborg's philosophy, have much in common with Gnosticism in suggesting that what most people think of as good is actually evil. In addition, Blake's "emanations" seem indebted to Gnostic thinking as well.

The Devil Makes You Do It

Blake's narrative poems can be extremely difficult to follow. Although they often follow a broad, basic outline, they include many digressions and sudden shifts among his various cosmic worlds. Don't let this keep you from enjoying his language and illustrations.

Standing behind Rintrah are two of Enitharmon's daughters, the angels of France and England.

Split Personalities

Here's a little sample of Blake's writing; an episode from his unfinished masterpiece, *Vala, or The Four Zoas*, in which Los, a manifestation of Urthona (Imagination), is separated from Enitharmon (Spiritual Beauty), his emanation, by the jealous Tharmas (Senses).

> *What sovereign architect, said Tharmas, dare my will control?*
> *For I will urge these waters. If I will they sleep*
> *In peace beneath my awful frown. My will shall be my law.*
>
> *So saying, in a wave he rap't bright Enitharmon far*
> *Apart from Los, but covered her with softest brooding care*
> *On a broad wave in the warm west, balming her bleeding wound.*
>
> *O how Los howld at the rending asunder—all the fibers rent*
> *Where Enitharmon joined to his left side—in grinding pain,*
> *He falling on the rocks behind his dolor till the blood staunched, then*
> *In ululation waild his woes upon the wind.*
>
> *And Tharmas called to the dark specter who upon the shores*
> *With dislocated limbs had fallen. The specter rose in pain,*
> *A shadow blue obscure and dismal, like a statue of lead*
> *Bent by its fall from a high tower, the dolorous shadow rose.*

You get the flavor, anyway. It goes on like this for a couple hundred pages!

Mind Over Matter

Like Swedenborg, Blake is interested in an ideal communion, which he describes in spiritual, psychological, and poetic terms as a reunion of divided aspects of humanity. He suggests that human beings are made up of the principles represented by his angelic figures. Happiness can be achieved when these figures are reintegrated in the imagination of the individual. This happens only as a result of imaginative struggle.

Blake often presents this struggle in theological terms. Built into his conception of the human predicament are the ideas of the fall of humanity, divine judgment, and redemption. In fact, Jesus appears as a character in several of Blake's poems. The concept of Biblical history, however, pretty much disappears. The concept of time loses its meaning.

Wing Tip

Try thinking of different approaches to understanding things—including poetic, theological, philosophical, psychological, and scientific—not as completely separate fields, but as alternative ways of seeing reality.

As for Swedenborg, earthly time for Blake is unimportant, since time doesn't exist in Eternity. This means the fall, judgment, and redemption can happen in the individual at any time. As a result, these religious concepts become psychologically important and stand for phases of individual experience.

This doesn't mean that, for Blake, his imaginary world was merely psychological. In fact, psychology as we know it today hadn't been invented yet! Neither Blake nor Swedenborg saw the "real world" as something that existed apart from their psychological worlds. In fact, Swedenborg would say that his heavens are, if anything, more "real" than the world we can perceive with our senses. Blake would say the same thing about his Eternity.

The Least You Need to Know

➤ Emanuel Swedenborg studied science and philosophy before turning his attention to angels.

➤ For Swedenborg, things in spiritual reality correspond to things in physical reality.

➤ Swedenborg's ideas led to the forming of the New Church and inspired numerous writers, including William Blake.

➤ Blake's work supports the idea that heaven and hell are necessary complements of one another.

➤ "Mental fight" is Blake's term for creative struggle, including criticism of conventional ideas.

Chapter 22

Evolving Angels

In This Chapter

➤ The angelic beings of theosophy

➤ Madame Blavatsky and occult wisdom

➤ Karma, consciousness, and angelic evolution

➤ Masters and adepts

➤ Theosophical splinter groups

Many believe angels were not simply created by God in their present form, but evolved gradually over periods of thousands and thousands of years. This is an exciting idea that has had angel archaeologists taking off on expeditions into the clouds to search for evidence. Any day now, stratocumulus deposits could yield the fossil remains of missing angelic links!

The leading group of angel evolutionists are known as theosophists. Many of these doughty explorers of the celestial regions are widely read in esoteric and occult writings and are interpreting them in a surprising way in order to draw their conclusions about the evolution of angels and the heavenly destiny of human beings. They have brought together huge amounts of lore from all kinds of sources and say it all adds up to a heavenly game plan to raise spiritual consciousness on Earth.

Even more astonishing is the claim made by many theosophists to have direct contact with angelic beings who have evolved from humans. With their controversial hot lines to other worlds, they've been acquiring disciples and spreading their message internationally. In the process, they've also elicited a lot of criticism—not only from outsiders but from within their own ranks as well.

Something Old, Something New

Much of the thinking behind what's commonly known as the "New Age" is actually not all that new. Not only is it based on esoteric knowledge that supposedly goes back thousands of years, it also became systematized and applied as a spiritual movement back in 1875. This movement is called theosophy, and it brings together ideas from Judaism, Christianity, Gnosticism, Hinduism, Buddhism, Cabala, rosicrucianism, spiritualism (a practice that was popular in the 19th century involving mediums who contacted the spirits of the dead through séances) and even science. This kitchen-sink approach to religion paved the way for the New Age a full century ahead of time.

Hidden Truth

The leading figure in the beginning of the theosophy movement was Helena Blavatsky. Blavatsky was an insatiable reader of ancient lore, and claimed that the ancients possessed secret knowledge of the truths of divine creation and human destiny. She helped form the Theosophical Society to study these truths.

Revelations

Blavatsky was especially interested in the religious philosophy and spiritual discipline associated with the Orient. She claimed to have spent seven years traveling by herself in Tibet learning ancient secrets from monks and spiritual adepts. Theosophists put her in good company, since they say that Jesus Christ passed through a similar apprenticeship in Tibet. Some even say that the body of Christ is buried in Japan! Scholars, however, have found no historical evidence that either Jesus or Blavatsky spent time in Tibet.

Blavatsky developed her own way of putting together various religious ideas. She saw Gnosticism, Cabala, and ancient Hinduism as originally all part of the same ancient occult tradition. (Most scholars today would disagree. Gnosticism developed much later than ancient Hinduism and Cabala developed later still.) In addition, she drew on ideas she found in the occult novels of a now-obscure English writer named Edward Bulwer Lytton (1803–1873).

According to Blavatsky, mainstream orthodox religions, most notably Judaism and Christianity, are inferior approximations of the "secret doctrine" possessed by the ancient "oriental Gnostic Cabalists," as she called them. In fact, the whole reason the doctrine is secret is so that people who aren't ready for it will leave it alone. It takes lots of training to understand its teaching. Aspects of other religions are similar to parts of the secret doctrine, but they oversimplify things.

Even though the supposedly more recent religions are inferior to the secret doctrine, they can still be useful in teaching people about the original ancient truths. Blavatsky wrote some popular and influential books explaining how orthodox religious ideas stem from the original "secret doctrine" of the ancients. She suggests that if you know how to decode scripture in the right way, you can see how it points to this doctrine.

Mix 'n' Match

Theosophy manages to combine so many different philosophical and religious ideas by finding correspondences among diverse traditions. For example, figures from the Bible correspond in theosophy to gods from Hindu mythology, archons and aeons from Gnosticism, and sefirot from the Cabala. Theosophists suggest that different religions have different ways of saying the same thing. And they go even further in claiming that the secret lore of the ancients often reveals knowledge of the natural world only recently rediscovered by modern science!

As you may remember from Chapter 4 and elsewhere in this book, angels have supplied an extremely useful connection between different religions. For example, by associating pagan gods with monotheistic angels, Greeks, Romans, Egyptians, and others have been able to adjust gradually to the spread of Christianity. Rather than abandoning their old gods, people could look at them as angels and carry on their traditions within the framework of the new religion.

Theosophy revives this age-old use of angels by associating them with divine figures from various ancient religions. Theosophists recognize a variety of angelic beings that stem from different traditions, including Hindu devas, Gnostic aeons, and Judeo-Christian angels. You might think that this would lead to confusion and, to a degree, it does. Theosophical writings—especially Blavatsky's—can be dense and hard to follow, drawing on all kinds of religious ideas most people know little about.

The Devil Makes You Do It

Theosophist Helena Blavatsky's famous books, *Isis Unveiled* (1877) and *The Secret Doctrine* (1888) make for challenging reading, especially if you're not already familiar with ancient Hindu mythology! It's also impossible to see from reading how she knows what she says about the truckload of ancient lore she discusses. Her followers say they have traced references in her work to rare books located in the British museum which Blavatsky "read" psychically, without seeing the actual books!

Wing Tip

Common ground is a good place to start in any religious discussion. Angelic beings can often be found wherever distinct religious traditions intersect.

Eastern Potentates

Many arcane beings out of ancient Hindu belief—and there are a lot of them—get lumped together with angels in theosophical thinking. Bet you find at least one grouping in this list you've never heard of:

➤ *Devas.* A generic Hindu term for "gods," which theosophists associate with angels.

➤ *Dhyan Chohans.* The highest order of angelic being corresponding to archangels, credited with creating the universe.

➤ *Lipika.* Also known as the "lords of karma," these are angelic intelligences who record actions in the physical world and enforce the resulting dictates of karma.

➤ *Sons of Wisdom.* These are angelic emanations who are in the process of taking on physical bodies for the first time.

➤ *Ghandarvas.* Nature spirits from Hindu scripture.

➤ *Avatars.* Manifestations of divine beings on Earth. According to theosophists, the Hindu idea of avatars contains secrets of human and angelic evolution.

➤ *Mahatmas.* Also known as "masters" and "the white brotherhood," these are highly evolved intelligences who choose to remain on Earth in physical form in order to teach and assist humanity.

In addition, there are many other beings, including rishi-prajapati, manus, ah-hi, pitris, suras, daityas, adityas, and danavas. You'd need to have the key to ancient occult wisdom just to know what all these beings are! Like the entities in the previous list, however, they are frequently lumped together under the category of devas or angels.

The Devil Makes You Do It

Bringing separate religious traditions together by suggesting they are all somehow connected and all mean the same thing obscures real and important differences between them. If you insist on thinking all religions are the same, you either have to ignore these differences or write them off as mistakes or fallacies.

Not only that, theosophists sometimes associate these ancient occult angels with scientific principles. For example, Blavatsky says that in their manifestations as physical elements, some of the dhyan chohans constitute "missing links of chemistry." She describes them as natural forces, as gasses, and as atomic substances, and even talks about their electrical polarity. Science, then, like mainstream religion, contains some rough approximations of theosophical truth if you know how to read it correctly!

But wait, there's more! Angelic beings also get tied to the lost city of Atlantis and to the inhabitants of other planets. In short, theosophists are prepared to work with just about any sort of idea that comes along. Practically everything turns out to be either an ancient secret or a falsehood intended to conceal the ancient truth.

Can You Handle It?

Of course, the esoteric, hard-to-understand quality of theosophy is all part of its occult appeal. Many theosophists say that you have to be especially wise and insightful to fully appreciate theosophical teachings. They say these secret teachings have been around for centuries and, whenever they become known to the general public, they become criticized and the teachers become persecuted.

In fact, some theosophists say Jesus Christ was really a teacher of the secret doctrine. He was crucified not for spreading radical new ideas, but for teaching ancient occult wisdom! You can see this, of course, only if you interpret the Bible properly in light of ancient Eastern teachings.

In spite of the radical cosmic truths theosophy is supposed to contain, many theosophists say the day will soon come when large numbers of people will become ready to deal with the ancient secrets. This, they say, will represent a turning point in the evolution of the human race. Whether or not this turns out to be the case, it is true that theosophy has attracted significant numbers of followers over the years. Meanwhile, the movement has been beset with numerous problems, including internal disagreement, accusations of fraud, and sexual scandals.

Wing Tip

When people ridicule you for your nutty ideas, just point out that the world's great spiritual leaders have always been persecuted for daring to speak the shocking truth!

Revelations

Madame Blavatsky is said to have staged "miraculous events"; for example, by preparing notes with "secret" messages on them that supposedly came from spiritual beings. Other leaders within the theosophy movement have also encountered problems by claiming to have direct access to spiritual wisdom through supernatural sources. Some have even been accused of lying by other members of the movement.

In the Know

Despite the large quantity of esoteric lore that it deals with, theosophy manages to stay coherent by suggesting that all religions have the same universal function: to promote spiritual consciousness. In fact, theosophy has a unique way of understanding what spiritual consciousness is, why it's important, and how it develops; this sets it apart from other religions, including those that it draws on.

Getting Physical

Theosophists say physical reality exists as a stage in the evolution of spiritual consciousness. This stage is only one of three major stages. The other two are emotional reality and mental reality. Living beings inhabit all three realities. These worlds aren't completely separate, but form a continuum. The emotional world surrounds the physical world and also exists inside it, diffused among material existence. Similarly, the mental world surrounds the emotional and physical worlds and also exists inside them.

Wing Tip

No need to feel self-conscious when you're in the presence of theosophical adepts who can see your aura. Even if you think yours is filled with ugly black streaks, it's not your fault. Your spiritual degradation is the result of mistakes made by angels eons ago when the physical world was still coming into being. Adepts know this and won't hold you responsible!

The emotional world is made of finer material than the physical world—so fine you can't detect it with your physical senses, although many people are supposedly able to sense it. Some say that if you could break down the finest particles of physical matter, it would dissolve into the coarsest particles of emotional reality.

The emotional world is also known as the astral plane. It is inhabited by various creatures who have astral bodies. Astral bodies are living bodies made up of the emotional substance that also forms the emotional world.

Theosophists say human beings have astral bodies as well as physical bodies. Some theosophical adepts can supposedly see these bodies and even move around in them, independently of their physical bodies. When they appear as layers of variously colored light surrounding people's physical bodies they are known as auras. Auras are in constant motion; their movements and colors change with people's moods.

The Devil Makes You Do It

It's best not to travel around without your physical and astral bodies until you know you're ready. You might have a tough time making your way around the world of disembodied intellect!

Surrounding and permeating both the emotional and physical worlds is the intellectual world. This world is made up of finer material than the emotional world. This third world can be further divided into higher and lower levels. The lower, less subtle level consists of concrete, imagistic ideas. The higher intellectual level is more abstract. Only the wisest, most fully evolved angelic beings can live in the intellectual world without astral or physical bodies.

Making the Bed and Lying in It

These worlds, and the beings who live in them, are manifestations of divine energy that emanate from God. They took eons to develop and are still in the process of becoming fully realized. First, the intellectual world and its beings emanated from

God. These intellectual beings go by many names, but they are most commonly known in the West as angels. From them emanate the emotional and physical worlds.

According to theosophy, God is not the one who creates the world. God, in theosophy, is an unknowable source of divine energy. God is so unknowable, in fact, that theosophy attributes to angels functions other religions reserve for God. For example, angels, not God, create and maintain the universe.

After the angelic beings create emotional and physical reality, they don't just sit back and watch, but they enter it, becoming emotional and physical creatures themselves, including animals and human beings! In doing so, they don't lose their angelic nature or divine, spiritual intelligence, although they may forget it.

Learning from Experience

People, in other words, are angels who have partly forgotten what it's like to be purely intellectual. Our job is to remember how—to regain our intellectual purity. Doing so will enable us to live as angels again, without our physical bodies. Until we do, we'll remain stubborn, ignorant, and beset with vain desires that can never be satisfied.

You're probably wondering, if we're all really angels trapped in physical bodies, why did we decide to enter these bodies in the first place? Why not stay out of trouble and keep flitting around in the intellectual world? The answer is that even though we lose our intellectual purity in our physical bodies, our physical existence gives us valuable experience—experience we need in order to reascend to God.

Once we gain experience from physical reality, we can become angels again, and we'll be even wiser than we were before we entered physical existence. Yet, we'll be as pure as we ever were. We'll have the best of both worlds. In short, we will have evolved into a higher nature.

Revelations

Theosophical views of evolution react against Darwinian evolution. Theosophists say that humanity evolved in a latent form from angelic beings before other animals evolved. (Darwinists, in contrast, say human beings descend from animals.) Later, say the theosophists, we evolved into our current, physical form. In support of this idea, they point to the myth of pre-Adamic races (humans thought to exist before God made Adam). Of course, not all theosophists agree about angelic and human evolution. Some say angels and humans evolved along separate lines, with angels giving rise not to humans, but to elemental spirits and fairies!

Angels Late for Work

Of course, some of the experiences we get in the physical world are better than others. Some theosophists say that whole process of emanation and evolution hasn't exactly come off without a hitch. Mistakes were made. A number of angelic beings wouldn't stick with the program, but decided to improvise when they shouldn't have. As a result, the physical world is full of evil and injustice.

Wing Tip

Notice that much theosophical thinking draws on Gnosticism. For example, the theosophical idea that slip-ups took place in the evolution of spiritual beings at the stage of their physical embodiment stems from the Gnostic idea that the creation of the physical world disrupted the spiritual integrity of the universe.

What happened was that the physical world emanated gradually, in stages. During the early stages, certain physical bodies were prepared for certain angelic beings (never mind who!) who chickened out at the last minute. They didn't feel ready to cope with physical reality yet, especially not in the bodies they were supposed to get. So they said, "Gross! Let's wait 'til some better bodies come along." Which they did.

One result was a lot of vacant bodies running around. They did things they shouldn't have, like beget horrible, ugly monsters, which had to be destroyed. For another thing, when the reluctant angels eventually did take bodies, they got stuck in them longer than they should have, which slowed down the whole evolutionary process. In general, the intelligence didn't get distributed through the physical world according to plan. Theosophists say we're still dealing with the problems caused by this age-old angelic mistake.

High Hopes

Theosophists say there are many groups of intelligent beings, ranging from humans up to the highest archangels, or dhyan chohans. It is the purpose and destiny of all of them to evolve back up into greater intelligence. All human beings should eventually evolve into angels.

Not Again!

It may take a while—lifetimes, in fact—for this to happen. That's okay, though, because you can have as many lifetimes as it takes. Theosophists believe in reincarnation. When a human being dies, he or she will be born again—probably as another human being—unless he or she has evolved the spiritual wisdom necessary for becoming an angel. Once you become an angel, you will no longer be born into physical existence, but will continue to live as an intellectual entity.

Not only that, you will merge with other intellectual entities of your kind. Some theosophists say that angelic beings don't exist as individuals, but as pools made up of a number of formerly human souls. Individual identity, they say, is an illusion that disappears once you get outside of physical reality.

Karma Kings

Whether or not you are ready to move on to the next level of existence depends on your karma. Karma is the Hindu idea that what happens to you in the future results from your actions in the past. People's actions show how spiritually wise or foolish they are and influence their karma—their destiny in their next life. Hopefully, after a few lifetimes, you will achieve the experience necessary to behave wisely, giving yourself the karma you need to be released from the cycle of physical existence and become an angel.

Theosophists say the workings of karma are controlled by angelic beings called lipika. The term comes from a Hindu word meaning "scribe." Lipika are thought to record or "write down" all the significant actions taken by people on Earth and use these records to determine how people will spend their next lifetime.

Revelations

Lipika are theosophical angels of karma who are said to keep track of all the significant events of existence, including the experiences of individual people. Through their efforts, good and bad acts will receive the appropriate reward or punishment through the process of karma. Although the lipika stem from Hindu mythology, theosophists relate them to the Judeo-Christian tradition that says angels keep track of human deeds by recording them in the Book of Life.

Presence of Mind

Even though, in general, it's a good thing to graduate from physical existence, theosophists say that some especially wise spirits choose to inhabit a physical body in order to communicate more easily with the rest of us who are stuck in physical reality. This makes it easier to teach a select few the secrets of the universe. These angels in the flesh are called "mahatmas" or masters. Some say that the masters are able to move around outside their physical bodies at will and exert psychic control over physical objects.

Wing Tip

If a theosophist tells you that you lived your previous life as a pig or an insect, don't get defensive. You can say you appeared in a lowly physical body as a favor to the animals to help them make progress on their spiritual path!

The Devil Makes You Do It

Religious organizations have traditionally functioned as agents of charity, collecting money and goods from contributors and redistributing them to the needy. And, of course, they use some of the money for their own expenses, including evangelical activities. Unfortunately, it's often hard to say whether a particular organization is really a "good cause."

There have been many mahatmas who have appeared at various times and places on Earth. In fact, theosophists identify a number of famous religious and philosophical figures as mahatmas, including the Buddha, Confucius, Lao Tzu, Moses, Abraham, Solomon, Jesus Christ, Plato, and Sir Francis Bacon! (Theosophists say that before appearing on Earth as Jesus, Christ sometimes manifested himself as the archangel Michael.) Helena Blavatsky claimed to be in spiritual communication with several mahatmas who, she says, directed her to start the Theosophical Society.

Flaking Off

Blavatsky inaugurated a precedent among leaders of the theosophy movement who have claimed to have special access to spiritual secrets. This became a problem, since different theosophists claimed to receive conflicting messages from their masters. These conflicts have led to disagreements, which have led, in turn, to dissent within the Theosophical Society and the formation of numerous splinter groups.

The leaders of the various theosophical splinter groups often claim either to be "masters" or to receive direct communication from them. Here's a list of just some of the many chips off the theosophical block. Many of these groups have international followings:

➤ *Anthroposophy.* Founded by Rudolf Steiner in 1924. An early offshoot founded by Rudolf Steiner that has kept in step with the New Age by emphasizing ecology.

➤ *The Saint Germaine Foundation.* Founded by Guy Ballard after a run-in in 1930 with the "ascended master" Saint Germaine.

➤ *The Church of Aetherius.* Founded in 1956 by a prominent occultist who was visited by Cosmic Master Aetherius from the planet Venus.

➤ *Universal White Brotherhood.* Group in England devoted to cosmic harmony and love through yoga and spiritualism, founded by Omraam Mikhael Aivanhov.

➤ *The Summit Lighthouse, later the Church Universal and Triumphant.* Founded in Washington, D.C., in the mid-20th century by angel-seer Reverend Mark Prophet and taken over by his widow, the charismatic Elizabeth Clare Prophet, the church advocates simple living for its members, from whom it makes a tidy profit!

➤ *Eternal Flame.* A group in London that, for a small fee, offers members immortality.

Sects Appeal

Despite conflicts and scandals, theosophy and its offshoots have been tremendously influential from its beginnings down to today. Its appeal has a lot to do with its ability to incorporate a huge range of ideas and beliefs. Few of these ideas are absolutely essential to theosophy in and of themselves, so different theosophists can develop different beliefs and specialties. As a result, there's room for disagreement.

Perhaps still more appealing is the hope theosophy holds out for the spiritual improvement of the universe. It sees everyone as being closely tied with a grand cosmic process in which there is no sin; only temporary setbacks on the road to physical, emotional, and spiritual enlightenment. Finally, however kooky many theosophical ideas may seem, they're often fascinating in their own right. Thus theosophy opens up exciting new possibilities for religious belief while integrating this belief with other aspects of modern existence. These are things that traditional, mainstream religion often fails to do!

The Least You Need to Know

➤ Theosophy draws on a huge range of ideas, especially Hinduism, Gnosticism, and Cabala, but also Judaism, Christianity, and science.

➤ Theosophists say humans evolve from angels and will ascend to angels again.

➤ According to theosophy, divine and cosmic revelations come from "masters" who are angelic beings inhabiting human bodies.

➤ Despite continual internal disagreement and numerous scandals, theosophy has been and remains influential, giving rise to numerous splinter groups.

New Age Angels

During the 1990s, huge numbers of people have come forward and claimed they have been touched by an angel. Although many have written these angel seers off as being touched in the head, reports of angel encounters are common. Not only do angels seem to abound, so do readers who want to learn what they're doing here on Earth.

Angels have become such a familiar presence that many writers advocate techniques for meeting them, communicating with them, and learning about them. The idea is not simply to dabble in spiritualism, but to help transform the spiritual consciousness of the entire planet—and to become healthy, wealthy, and wise in the process. In fact, angels seem to fit in well with just about anything that's good and good for you.

That's the New Age for you—pulling out all the stops with every conceivable approach to spiritual happiness. Of course, traditional religious authorities are crying foul, complaining that God is getting lost in the shuffle. For many people, however, angels form the perfect compromise between traditional religion and the New Age.

Flying High

A tremendous amount of excitement over angels has been fueled by New Age thinking. New Agers see angels as heavenly helpers in improving personal well-being and cosmic harmony. In fact, a key (and controversial) idea in New Age thinking is that promoting personal well-being will lead to cosmic harmony. They say that as increasing numbers of people become happier, healthier, wealthier, and more spiritually aware, the better things will be for the universe itself. Many New Agers see angels as key players in this cosmic plan.

Bottom Line

Angels are only a small part of the New Age movement, but this movement is so large and all-encompassing that no single spiritual belief stands out as crucial. New Age combines metaphysical ideas from all over the world and all periods of history. It is a general trend rather than an organized movement, although there are numerous organizations within it. New Age is thus a blanket term that accounts for all kinds of loosely organized and independent spiritual activities.

Wing Tip

"New Age" is a label not all New Agers accept. Some call themselves "metaphysicians." Others resist any sort of label for their thinking. Even so, "New Age" continues to be a useful name for the eclectic, independent popular spiritualism of our day.

These activities often combine elements borrowed from Eastern philosophy and mysticism, Third World and tribal practices, experimental health and relaxation technology, and mainstream religions. The movement depends not on a single rigidly defined set of beliefs, but on a variety of teachers, gurus, and self-help specialists, who have set themselves up as independent authorities on spiritual well-being. Though all of these independent authorities have slightly different philosophies, all New Agers tend to believe that personal spiritual consciousness-raising will lead to global improvements.

Revelations

The angel trend is such a success, there's even an organization out there designed to help get people started in the angel retail business! It's called HALOS, which stands for Helping Angel Lovers Own Stores. HALOS was founded in 1993 by Denny Dahlmann, the owner of Angel Treasures Boutique in Ann Arbor, Michigan.

Bless This Mall

Although there are New Age cult groups that have formed their own churches, New Age's biggest impact has been made in secular settings—in seminars and workshops, in private get-togethers, and especially in stores. New Age does well outside of church because it has a practical focus and holistic approach. Many New Agers look to spiritual improvement as a way to economic, interpersonal, and psychological success. In fact, New Age is not only a spiritual philosophy, it's big business, accounting for billions of dollars worth of products and services over the years.

The angel business is no small part of the New Age's commercial appeal. Of course, angel products have always been popular retail items since the early days of the department store. A new and recent phenomenon, however, is the emergence of specialty stores open year-round and devoted entirely to angel merchandise. Angel stores proliferate in cities and on the Internet. Angel art, clothes, jewelry, books, and cards are among the most popular products, but keep on the lookout for angel air freshener!

> **The Devil Makes You Do It**
>
> Don't think that just because they have angel stores these days means that angels are for sale. Most retailers will tell you angels can only be bought with kindness!

Best of Both Worlds

The popularity of angel merchandise is an indication, obviously, of a rising popular interest in angels. One explanation for this interest may lie in the fact that New Agers and mainstream Christians alike can relate to them. In fact, their broad appeal is in keeping with a centuries-old social function angels have served. In situations where different sets of religious ideas rub up against each other, angels have repeatedly supplied common ground.

Angels often tend to occupy a theological gray area, obscuring the difference between mainstream monotheism and less orthodox beliefs, including paganism, *pantheism*, and magic. You can look at them as messengers of God or as divine forces in their own right. As a result, angels appeal to people with a variety of religious orientations, including all kinds of New Agers and all kinds of monotheists.

Christian hard-liners, however, tend to be leery of New Age. Some argue that New Age is really a big narcissistic fantasy that exposes people to all kinds of social, moral, and spiritual evils. They say New Agers don't give God Almighty enough credit. In turn, many New Agers say mainstream religion is puritanical and oppressive—too concerned with following the rules and not concerned enough with how people feel.

> **Winged Words**
>
> **Pantheism** is the belief, embraced by many New Agers, that God is everything, including people and the natural world.

Angels in the Middle

There are a number of sticking points between New Age and traditional Christianity. One is the question of a heavenly afterlife versus reincarnation. Another is whether it's better to pray or to meditate. Still another is unselfish concern for others versus self-actualization and personal fulfillment. Another big one is the question of whether the church should be the center of the community or somewhere else—like the local bookstore or yoga class.

Angels are caught in the middle of this argument. They are part of accepted monotheistic theology and they also figure into some of the wackiest beliefs this side of Looney Toons. Despite (or because of!) the hard-liners of established religion and the way-out beliefs of the more eccentric New Agers, many people seem happy occupying the middle ground with the angels.

For these middle-of-the-heavenly-roaders, angels provide an important expression of spirituality without forcing them to take a stand on the tough theological questions raised by the tensions between New Age and established religion. Many people seem to think it's cooler to go around saying they're into angels than saying they're into Christianity or New Age. And, of course, it's possible to be into all three.

Psyching Up

Different New Agers have different beliefs, but one common New Age angel idea is that the angels are closely linked to an individual's mind, body, and spirit. According to this view, whether an angel comes to pay you a visit depends on your emotional, psychological, and physical state. The idea is that angels are always helpful, but they can't help us unless we prime our own spiritual pumps in order to encourage them.

Revelations

Some New Age teachers say that Eastern meditation techniques can help attract angels. The Eastern practice of chanting a mantra (a special word that facilitates meditation) can be used as a technique for summoning your guardian angel. Once you have named your personal angel, you can use the name as your mantra.

Angels Within

Many New Agers say the best way to meet angels is to look inside yourself. According to some, the angels are already there inside you waiting to be discovered. According to others, they're all around, but they won't come to say hello unless you first make the inner you a nice place to visit. Either way, the thing to do is to ditch your ugly, negative feelings so that the healthy, positive you and your angels can have your inner space all to themselves.

This internal housekeeping can be done through mental and spiritual techniques including thinking good thoughts, meditation, and yoga. Mental-spiritual aids such as crystals and soothing music may help too, and, of course there's always herbal tea. Most New Agers say to leave the drugs alone, however, since they're giving off bad vibes these days. Angel dust is strictly a misnomer! In fact, any sort of addictive behavior is bad and keeps the angels away.

When you meditate and free yourself of negative feelings, you can feel all sorts of good things start to happen. You may be able to visualize angels more clearly, or get angels to help you visualize your self, your life, and your relationships. Angels can act as guides on journeys of inner discovery, provided you're willing and able to let go of your negative attitudes—especially negative attitudes toward yourself. If you don't like yourself, your angels won't like you either!

Wing Tip

If angel meditation is not satisfying enough for you, there's always angel channeling. Channeling is the practice of acting as the human mouthpiece for a spirit of some sort. Channelers may channel for angels as well as historical figures, people from previous lives, or beings from outer space or even from other dimensions.

Wings Around the World

You might think the benefits of heightened, angel-assisted, personal well-being would be good enough in their own right, but New Agers say there's much more to be gained. For example, angels can be instrumental in maintaining and improving your physical health. New Agers stress the connection of mind, body, and spirit, and say that angels are good at healing sicknesses in all three.

What's more, they say that it's not just you, but millions of other angel lovers are cleaning up their psycho-spiritual acts. With all this heightened consciousness and spiritual love overflowing all over the place, things are bound to get better for everyone in all possible ways. Angelic improvement starts out as personal, but as more people get into it, the results are global.

In fact, the idea of global transformation is one reason why they call it New Age. People started to use the term way back in the 1970s to refer to the idea that human history was entering into a whole new *paradigm*. This means that human consciousness and understanding are supposedly entering a new level for everyone on Earth.

Winged Words

A **paradigm** is the way a group of people thinks about a particular subject. More broadly, it refers to the way all human beings think at a particular stage in history. According to New Age thinking, an old paradigm is currently shifting to a new one characterized by greater spiritual awareness.

The Devil Makes You Do It

Your angels may love you, but it doesn't necessarily follow that the ecosystem will automatically take care of itself. As a case in point, the Church Universal and Triumphant, led by angel-seer Elizabeth Clare Prophet, perpetrated a minor ecological disaster on their retreat in Montana when one of their oil tanks leaked into the Yellowstone River.

The idea of the New Age is an important 20th-century take on the idea of the millennium. In Christian terms, the millennium refers to the claim in the Book of Revelation that Christ will soon return to Earth to rule for a thousand years. Since Biblical times, the millennium is usually understood as any sort of drastic change in human history. Many people expected a big millennial change around the year 1000 C.E. (it didn't happen). Similarly (but often in a distinctively New Age fashion), many people these days expect a big change to take place around the year 2000. In fact, some say this change is a paradigm shift that is already taking place.

This big shift will globalize the personal benefits people receive from heightened spirituality. This improvement will have far-reaching effects. For example, some say the environment will improve. New Agers claim that spiritually in-tune individuals are cosmically incapable of harming the ecosystem. As angels recycle their heavenly energy through spiritually receptive human individuals, those individuals will be recycling their empty massage-oil bottles!

Getting in touch with angels also gets people more spiritually in tune with the natural world, including plants, animals (wild and domestic) and rocks. Better still, some say that angel love has proven instrumental in averting nuclear catastrophe. Angels prefer melted hearts to nuclear melt-downs any day of the week!

New Agers say that angel love also pays political peace dividends. Angels are exerting greater influence on political leaders to do right by the citizens of the world. According to the popular book *Ask Your Angels* by Alma Daniel, Timothy Wyllie, and Andrew Ramer (Ballantine Books, 1992), the United Nations has its own guardian angel named Eularia who is making angelic presence felt in the global political arena.

Angels on the Shelf

New Age, and, in particular, New Age angels, are promising all sorts of good things for everyone who is willing to improve their spiritual awareness. Advice on how to do this is not hard to find. In fact, there are dozens of New Age angel books to choose from. Some may seem pretty kooky, linking angels to all sorts of esoteric practices, including astrology, aromatherapy, tarot, and astral travel. Others stick pretty close to traditional Christian teachings. Here are just some of the many angel titles out there:

➤ *Ask Your Angels* by Alma Daniel, Timothy Wyllie, and Andrew Ramer (Ballantine Books, 1992). How to cooperate with your angels to improve everything about you using Eastern-influenced meditation techniques.

➤ *Touched By Angels* by Eileen Elias Freeman (Warner Books, 1993). A classic bestseller of New Age/Christian angel watching.

➤ *A Book of Angels: Reflections on Angels Past and Present and True Stories of How They Touch Our Lives* by Sophy Burnham (Ballantine Books, 1990). Another classic bestseller, including encounter stories and angel lore.

➤ *Angels: God's Secret Agents* by Billy Graham (Word Books, 1994). A Christian bestseller by the famous televangelist.

➤ *Angel Wisdom: 365 Meditations and Insights Centering Around the Theme of Angels* by Terry Lynn Taylor and Mary Beth Crain (Harper San Francisco, 1994). Day-by-day meditations.

➤ *A Message for the Millennium* by K. Martin-Kuri)Ballantine Books, 1996). How to make the tough choice between greed, hatred, and jealousy on one side, and angels on the other.

➤ *Angels Within Us* by John Randolf Price (Fawcett Books, 1993). Twenty-two angels in charge of each of our lives correspond to pagan deities, astrology signs, and tarot cards.

➤ *Guardians of Hope* by Terry Lynn Taylor (H J Kramer, 1993). How to nurture your "inner angel child."

➤ *Angels of Mercy* by Rosemary Ellen Guiley (out of print). Includes information about Gnostic and theosophical angels, incarnated angels, and channeling.

➤ *Angelspeake: How to Talk With Your Angels* by Barbara Mark and Trudy Griswold (Simon and Schuster, 1995). Discussion on the rewards of speaking to your angels.

➤ *Divine Guidance: How to Have Conversations with God and Your Guardian Angels* by Doreen Virtue, Ph.D. (Audio Renaissance, 1998). Discussions on how to access divine guidance to answer everyday life questions by tapping into what everyone calls either the conscience, that "little voice," a guardian angel, or the voice of God.

➤ *100 Ways to Attract Angels* by Sally Sharp (Trust Pub., 1994). Inspiring yet practical steps to connect with angels.

➤ *The Angel Book* by Karen Goldman (Simon & Schuster, 1993). A handbook for people who want to become angels!

➤ *Angel Cats* by Bonnie Altenhein (Wings Press, 1995). A whimsical and delightful celebration of the charms of both cats and angels for cat and angel lovers alike. (Maybe, but I doubt if the mice see it this way!)

Revelations

New Agers have taken a lot of flack for their beliefs, which some say can be intellectually flaky and socially dangerous. Theology professor Duane Garrett complains that New Age angel lovers are self-absorbed and naïve. Literary critic Harold Bloom complains that New Age writing about angels is vapid and lacks insight into the human condition. It's no surprise that the harshest criticism of New Age should come from academics and theologians, since disenchantment with the academy and conventional religion is a big cause of the popularity of New Age in the first place. The very fact that New Age is popular suggests it has something going for it that churches and schools don't!

Inside, Outside

Angel lovers tend to go for two kinds of angel books. The first is the New Age "get in touch with angels" book. The other is the more traditional "rescued by an angel" encounter story. Some of the most popular angel writers have combined these two approaches in their bestsellers.

Splitting the Difference

New Age angel watchers often emphasize the need for having the right inner attitude in order to benefit from the help angels have to offer. Many suggest that it's possible to enhance your awareness of angels, as well as the help they supply, through mental, physical, and spiritual techniques, regardless of whatever may be going on in your life. This attitude suggests that angels are always there if we can just figure out how to get in touch with them.

Others take a more traditional attitude, insisting that angels come to Earth and appear to people only for important, specific reasons at crucial moments. They are not simply on tap whenever we want to get in touch with them. Instead, it's all in the timing. They appear to ward off disasters or in the wake of a disaster for damage control, rather than simply to keep people company.

Some of the most famous angel writers have managed to combine these two popular approaches, recounting nick-of-time angel appearances that have changed their lives at crucial moments, and talking also about how the right attitude can bring people closer to angels all the time. A case in point is noted angel writer Eileen Elias Freeman, one of the most prominent popular writers on angels. Freeman's writing career traces a gradual shift from the "angel to the rescue" approach to the "enhance your angel consciousness" attitude.

Night Light

Freeman made a splash in 1992 with her first book, *Touched By Angels* (Warner Books, 1993). The book tells of two notable encounters between Freeman and her guardian angel, whom she named Enniss. Enniss appeared to fulfill specific purposes. The first encounter took place when Freeman was a little girl, soon after the death of her grandmother. She loved her grandmother very much, but the death made an unusually painful impression on her, bringing not only grief, but terror.

The fear became so intense that little Eileen couldn't sleep at night. Finally one night she saw a light at the foot of her bed. The light started growing and eventually took human form. The human night light looked at the little girl and told her not to be afraid, because her grandmother was happy in heaven. From then on, little Eileen felt better, evidently having been saved from a serious case of nervous depression in her formative years.

Enniss appeared to her again in later life when she was in college in the form of a hand on her shoulder that stopped her in her tracks. (This is evidently where the famous title of her book comes from.) Then she heard a voice that told her not to enter a building. Fortunately for her, she obeyed the voice and avoided a run-in with a murderer who did his dirty work on someone else.

In *Touched By Angels*, Freeman stressed the view that angels appear only in times of need. In a later book, *Angelic Healing: Working With Angels to Heal Your Life* (Warner Books, 1995), she went through a prolonged time of need during which she felt the need of angelic company. This was when she was diagnosed with cancer.

The Devil Makes You Do It

Special things, including angels, can be cheapened through too much familiarity. If your angels hang around all the time, you may find yourself getting tired of them!

Wing Tip

Many of those who suffered from cancer—including some who have had surprising recoveries—have said that medical science can't always predict the outcome of the illness. A lot can depend on intangibles like the state of mind (or spirit) of the patient.

An Angel's Work Is Never Done

Angelic Healing talks about how important it is to rid yourself of fear and guilt. Sometimes angels can help you do this; at other times you need to do it on your own. It's a toss-up, in other words, whether angels help you cope with your mental difficulties, or whether coping with difficulties helps put you in touch with angels. Either way, Freeman survived and recovered from her illness with the help not only of Enniss, but of a second angel she identifies as Raphael, "the healer of God."

Prior to cancer surgery, the angels answered her prayer to alleviate a bad reaction to antibiotics. Immediately after surgery, she met with Raphael in an out-of-body experience above the operating table and learned that she was going to be okay. Finally, an angel prompted her to stay away from the hospital food, which contained too much sugar and salt. She was able to heal more quickly after making a special request for salt-free, sugar-free foods!

The book talks about many other instances of angelic healing as well, including environmental healing, emotional healing, and relationship healing. The stories Freeman tells combine the traditional "angel rescue" theme with the New Age "how to communicate with angels" motif. Thus she succeeds in walking the fine line between traditional angel-inspired Christianity and New Age angel channeling.

Freeman's interest in angels incited her to start AngelWatch, a non-profit foundation intended to monitor and report angelic activity on Earth. This group has published the *AngelWatch Journal*, a newsletter that reports on angelic doings.

The Devil Makes You Do It

Notice that not all angels give the same advice. Raphael, the "healing angel," told Eileen Freeman to stay away from sugar. In contrast, the angel Michael in the 1996 movie *Michael* starring John Travolta, says, "You can never have too much sugar!"

Coming Soon

By now you should know more than enough to write your own New Age angel self-help book. Here's a list of titles you can use, but hurry; they're going fast!

➤ *Chicken Soup for Your Angel's Soul*

➤ *When Bad Things Happen to Good Angels*

➤ *Angel Etiquette: What to Say When You Belch in Front of Your Heavenly Host*

➤ *Wings of Steel: Angel Workout Routines for the Nineties*

➤ *Angel Dating: How to Say "Halo" to the Perfect Angel Stranger*

➤ *Why Angels Fear to Tread: Helping Your Angel Find the Courage to Walk on Two Feet*

➤ *A Field Guide to Angels: How to Spot 'Em in the Wild*

➤ *Angel Management Musts: How to Handle the Awesome Power of Angelic Coworkers*

See you on the talk-show circuit!

The Least You Need to Know

➤ Many New Agers incorporate angel lore into their holistic, pragmatic spirituality.

➤ Tensions between New Age and traditional religion include meditation vs. prayer, self-fulfillment vs. concern for others, and the heavenly afterlife vs. reincarnation.

➤ Angels tend to form an area of compromise between New Agers and traditional religion.

➤ Eileen Elias Freeman combines the popular "angel rescue" story with the equally popular "how to work with angels" advice book.

Part 6
Angels in the Arts

Much of the best angel lore is not the work of priests, prophets, theologians, and philosophers, but of writers, painters, storytellers, and film-makers. After all, angels don't have to be real or even holy to be important, entertaining, inspiring, and uplifting. In fact, angels and the arts work especially well together, since both have a lot to do with the imaginary possibilities of human existence.

In this part, you'll see that angels indeed are everywhere, from epic poetry to the Sistine chapel. Artists through the ages have been enraptured by these celestial beings. After reading these chapters, take a closer look at the books, artwork, films, and television shows around us today...you may find that there are more angels in your life than you once thought!

Chapter 24

Lookin' Good

> **In This Chapter**

> ➤ Angels in medieval and Renaissance art

> ➤ Winged Victories and cupids

> ➤ Icons and iconoclasts

> ➤ The Acts of the Angels

It may seem that angels appear only to a lucky few, but the fact is you don't have to be a prophet or a mystic to experience angel visions. All you have to do is visit the "angel wing" of your local art museum. After all, seeing an angel painted by an artistic genius is at least the next best thing to seeing one in person.

Some see angels as idealized versions of human beings, just as the world of art is an idealized version of reality. It makes sense, then, that art and angels should go together. And they do. Angels have appeared in all periods of Western art since the early Middle Ages.

Angels in art have been giving people a lift for centuries. As works of art, angels are not only aesthetically beautiful, but instructive and spiritually potent. What's more, they must really like posing for their portraits, since artists have painted so many!

Clear Pictures

Angel art is not limited to the European Middle Ages and Renaissance, of course, but has popped up all over, in many times and places. Yet religious painting in Europe from the 4th to the 17th century has had an especially powerful influence on the way people imagine angels. The angel stories in the Bible and other religious writings tend to describe angels as surprising, unearthly creatures or as ordinary people. The familiar humanoid with wings that most people think of when they hear the word "angel" comes not so much from the Bible as from religious art.

They Said It Would Never Fly

Angels didn't always have wings—at least, not according to stories in the Bible and the earliest depictions of angels in Christian sculpture and painting. Instead, they looked pretty much like everybody else. In several angel paintings done during the 1st and 2nd centuries, you can recognize the angels only if you know the story the picture is telling. For example, if you know the story of Jacob's Ladder, you can figure out that the guys going up and down the ladder are angels. Otherwise, for all you know, they could be house painters or cat burglars!

During these early days of Christianity, very little Christian art existed at all. This is because the Jesus-thing was still something of an underground movement. Christians were often persecuted by the Roman Empire, so they conducted their activities in secret. They did so much sneaking around that they didn't have much time to create angelic artwork. Of the small amount of Christian art that did exist, much of it was underground too—literally.

The Devil Makes You Do It

Be careful not to perpetuate angel stereotypes. They come in all shapes, sizes, and colors, and, of course, don't necessarily have wings.

Buried Angels

When Christians died, they were often buried in secret underground passages called *catacombs*. The catacombs contained little rooms that may have been used as chapels, including altars for the popes and martyrs buried there. These were sometimes decorated with artwork. In fact, the first known Christian religious paintings were recovered from catacombs, including scenes from the Bible representing angels.

Other depictions of angels dating from this time have been recovered from houses used for religious meetings. Like the paintings in the catacombs, paintings from inside early Christian houses include depictions of wingless figures who can be identified as angels from the stories the pictures represent. It wasn't until after Christianity became a widely accepted religion that angels in art began to sprout wings.

Winged Words

Catacombs are underground passages used for burial of the dead. Catacombus was originally the name of a place in Rome, but the term became used more generally for tunnels found not only in Rome, but in a number of cities in southern Italy and North Africa including Naples, Malta, Syracuse, and Alexandria. The catacombs in Rome are the most extensive, winding along for 350 miles beneath the city.

Getting Their Wings

Celestial beings with wings go way back in the history of the world's art. Although you probably won't find winged bison or antelope in most prehistoric cave paintings, winged creatures loom large in the religious art of many cultures. Strictly speaking, of course, not all of these high-flying figures are angels, especially if you limit your definition of angel to include only those celestial beings who are subordinate to a monotheistic God.

Yet art historians have found that angels of monotheism and pagan winged gods are often separated only by a fine and blurry line. Where angels flock together in works of art, you can sometimes see a few pagan gods nearby, spreading their wings right along with the angels. The two kinds are easily confused if you're not careful.

When in Rome

This is especially true during the early days of Christianity when the new religion was just beginning to spread into the Greek and Roman worlds. Greek and Roman art already included representations of winged beings even before Christianity came along. Chief among these were sculptures used in temple decorations and funeral monuments depicting the Greek gods Eros (or Cupid, as he was known by Romans) and Nike (also known as Victory).

Eros is the ancient Greek god of love. He was pictured as a young man or boy with wings and was often thought to be the companion of Psyche, the soul. Because of Eros's link to the soul, he was sometimes thought to guide the soul to the afterlife after the death of the body. For this reason, Eros is pictured on stone coffins called *sarcophagi*, to suggest that the soul of the person whose body lay in the sarcophagus had gone safely to the next world.

The god Eros was so popular that he became a class of celestial being. More than one Eros were called erotes, and a single sculpture or painting might depict several erotes together. On Greek sarcophagi it was customary to have two winged erotes hovering in the sky, but facing each other like bookends. This artistic tradition continued even after the Hellenistic (Greek-influenced) world converted to Christianity. Often, the erotes were depicted with a cross between them to show that the dead person was a Christian.

Winged Words

A **sarcophagus** (plural, sarcophagi) is a stone coffin. Sarcophagi were often beautiful works of art covered with elaborate carvings. These would be placed in a crypt or mausoleum rather than buried.

A Shared Victory

The erotes weren't the only winged beings to be converted from Greek mythology into Christian angels. Another popular Greek deity was the goddess Nike, or Victory. Victory was often depicted with wings in Greek art, hovering above a famous warrior or athlete. The ancient Greeks, of course, were fond of competition, especially when they won! In fact, as everyone knows, they invented the Olympic games. So, even though Greek athletes didn't wear shoes, Nike was still important to them!

Revelations

The ancient Greeks left behind some magnificent statues representing Nike. Perhaps the most famous of these is the Winged Victory of Samothrace, created around 190 B.C.E. The statue is about eight feet high with windswept, flowing robes and a magnificent set of wings spread out behind. It was found in 1813, broken into bits, but originally stood in a pool of water on a pedestal made to look like the prow of a ship to commemorate a navel battle. It now stands in the grand staircase of the Louvre Museum in Paris, where it is the second-most popular attraction in the whole place. (The first is the Mona Lisa.) The Winged Victory is an impressive sight—despite the fact that it's missing its head.

Victory was a popular goddess in Rome as well as Greece. Rome was a militaristic society and Romans had a special reverence for the goddess. This reverence continued when Rome became a Christian city. As a result, the idea of the winged victory was incorporated into Christian religious art around the 4th century during the time of Emperor Constantine.

Wing Tip

While not all angels have wings, not all winged human figures are angels—at least, not according to the strict definition that says angels are features of monotheistic religion. Winged figures can sometimes be found outside monotheism; for example, in art from China or Africa.

Victory by Design

Like Eros, who gave rise in art to numerous erotes, the goddess Nike inspired artists to paint and sculpt numerous victories. This is one reason why, when we picture angels, we think of human beings with wings. Stone carvers already knew how to make winged people when the religion got started. I guess it's a good thing that Eros and Nike had wings and not elephants' trunks or lobster claws. Angels just wouldn't be the same!

The view of angels as winged beings isn't obvious from the Bible. In fact, only a very few of the many angels mentioned in scripture are actually said to have wings or fly, as in Revelation 14:6. In contrast, winged gods of Greece and Rome were conventional figures in art that clearly predate Christianity. Hovering victories appeared on triumphal arches and in temples.

Roman Christians adopted the winged victory as a symbol that fused many ideas. Constantine believed that Christ helped him win decisive battles for the struggling Roman Empire, and the winged victory stood in part for the military triumph over pagan foes. The winged figure also stood for the triumph of Christ over evil. Finally, the winged victory symbolized the triumph of life over death.

Like the erotes, victories appeared on sarcophagi, sometimes with the victor holding the image of the cross. Other times, victories were shown holding a palm branch. Palms were a symbol of victory for pagans as well as Christians. Much as Jesus' followers carried palm branches on Palm Sunday, victorious gladiators were presented with palms.

See You in Church

Gradually, the Christian Church got more organized and started sending clearer signals about which ideas were consistent with Christianity and which weren't. Similarly, the Christian Bible had finally taken shape, and copies were made for churches and monasteries. Artists who painted and sculpted for the churches drew on Biblical stories in their work and increasingly left out pagan influences.

The Devil Makes You Do It

Angel artists who based their work on scriptural stories have not always been faithful to the written word. At least one painting representing Tobias with the angel Raphael includes the angel Michael, who is not mentioned in the story.

Seeing the Story

Christian artists made scenes depicting Biblical stories as Church decorations. Decoration, however, wasn't the only purpose behind religious art. Paintings, frescoes, and murals helped people understand and remember figures and events from the Bible. Most people during the Middle Ages couldn't read, so looking at pictures helped them learn about religion.

Angels, of course, are among the popular religious themes in these paintings. Often, angels were more or less just part of the scenery, added by the painter to make the painting look good and to lend an aura of holiness to the work. Many paintings, however, feature angels in specific roles, performing feats made famous in the Bible. These events are known conventionally as the eleven Acts of the Angels.

Famous Feats

The Acts of the Angels are the most memorable angelic moments from the Bible. Today, these live-action stills would make great bubble-gum cards for angel fans. Back before bubble gum was invented, they made them into paintings. Churches could collect 'em all and trade 'em with friends. Remember these famous scenes?:

➤ *The fall of Lucifer.* The story of the angel known in heaven as Lucifer, but whose name was changed to Satan when he rebelled from God, is alluded to in Revelation 12:3–4, but not explicitly told. Instead, he is allegorically described as a dragon who falls to Earth. As he falls, his tail sweeps one-third of the stars out of the sky. This is taken to mean that a third of the angels rebelled with Lucifer and were thrown out of heaven.

➤ *The expulsion of Adam and Eve from the Garden of Eden.* Genesis 3:23–24 speaks of cherubim with a flaming sword who escort the sinful couple out of paradise and block their way back in.

➤ *The three angels appear to Abraham.* Genesis 18 tells the story of the angelic trio who visit everyone's favorite Biblical patriarch.

➤ *The angel of the Lord prevents Abraham's sacrifice of Isaac.* Genesis 22:11–12 tells of this angel of last-minute mercy, who is popularly believed to be Michael.

Etching by Rembrandt of the Sacrifice of Isaac.

➤ *Jacob wrestles with the angel.* The big-time bout is described in Genesis 32:25.

➤ *Jacob's Ladder.* The high-steppin' angels appear in Genesis 28:12.

➤ *Shadrach, Meshach, and Abednego are saved from the fiery furnace.* The heat-resistant angel saves the day in Genesis 3:23–28.

➤ *An angel slays the army of Sennacherib.* The angel of death does away with 85,000 Assyrians who made the mistake of messing with God's chosen people in 2 Kings 19:35–36.

➤ *Raphael guides Tobias.* The boy, his dog, and his angel are on their way to Ecbatana with a dead fish to fix Tobias up with a wife and vanquish the demon Asmodeus in the Book of Tobit.

➤ *The punishment of Heliodorus.* The second Book of Maccabees 3:25–26 tells of a ghostly horseman clad in golden armor and a couple of sharply dressed angel tough-guys who beat the daylights out of a bureaucrat who tried to take money intended for the poor from the Temple in Jerusalem.

Wing Tip

If you live in a cool climate, chances are you have been an angel artist yourself at some point in your life. Remember those angels you used to make by lying on your back in the snow and moving your arms and legs back and forth?

Dore's punishment of Heliodorus.

➤ *The Annunciation.* The most popular of all the angelic themes is based on Luke 1:26–38, which tells of the first person ever to say a "hail Mary." This is the angel who brought Mary the news that she would give birth to Christ. Traditionally, the angel is Gabriel, but he is not named in the Biblical account.

Angels Say Halo

In addition to paintings that could be hung in chapels, cathedrals of the Byzantine empire typically contained frescoes and murals depicting saints, martyrs, and angels lining their high domes. You might think they were posing for a group photo! Relief sculptures of religious figures, including angels, were often carved into panels and columns as well.

Artists developed religious symbolism to make their subjects easier to identify. You can always tell the saints, angels, and other holy folks by their halos. Angel wings and halos were often painted with shiny gold paint to reflect the light and really stand out from the flat background of other colors. The shiny gold helped produce the effect of angelic radiance.

Picture Power

In addition to their decorative and educational purposes, Byzantine art served a spiritual purpose. Many Christians attributed spiritual power to religious works of art. This was especially true of the paintings known as *icons*. Icons are sacred paintings— usually representations of saints, but often of angels—used in the Byzantine Church.

Not all Christians venerated the icons. Many felt that the idea that an image had sacred power was idolatrous and distracted people from worshipping God. These were the iconoclasts or "image-breakers" of the 8th century. True to their name, the iconoclasts expressed their views by going around smashing icons.

Fortunately for art lovers of today and for icon lovers of the Middle Ages, the Council of Nicea ruled in 843 that icons were not heretical or idolatrous and could be revered by Christians in church or at home. The iconoclasts put away their hammers, but the word "iconoclast" caught on, and has been used ever since to describe those who speak out, or act out, against conventional ideas.

Icons have a stark quality that probably results from the fact that they are more important as sacred objects than works of art. They generally aren't supposed to be lifelike or realistic. The point isn't for the artist to demonstrate his skill as a painter. In fact, icon painters

Winged Words

Icons are sacred paintings of the Byzantine Church and later, of the Eastern Orthodox Church that split off from the Roman Catholic Church. The word comes from the Greek word *eikon*, which means "image." Icons were thought to have spiritual power and were venerated by many Christians.

are almost totally unknown. Instead, the value of an icon depended on whether it contained the spiritual power of the figure it represented. Today, however, icons are often regarded as beautiful works of art as well as valuable cultural artifacts.

Revelations

Historically, Christians have been the least strict of the big three monotheisms in prohibiting visual representations of divine beings. This may be partly because Christians have had the most money to spend on art. Muslim paintings frequently depict angels and the revered prophet Muhammad, but show the face of the prophet covered with a veil. This is not because he wore a veil in life, but because he is too holy to be represented in painting. Jews tend to be even stricter. Many Jews interpret the commandment, "Thou shalt not worship graven images," as a prohibition not only of idols but of all visual depictions of divine beings. A notable exception was Marc Chagall, a Jewish modernist painter who deals with religious themes, including angels, in his work.

Lightening Up

In general, judging from modern standards, figures in medieval painting tend to look stiff and inexpressive. Medieval painters didn't try to make their paintings look realistic, since the important thing was to get the spiritual message across. Late in the Middle Ages, however, a change gradually became noticeable in religious painting. It started to become more expressive and realistic.

People started to exhibit more interest in art for art's sake. Individual artists became known and appreciated for their talent. Paintings became important not only because of what they meant, but because of how they made people feel. Angels looked less like shiny gold puppets and more like breathing, feeling people who could spread their wings and fly to heaven—and maybe take you with them.

This gradual change that came over the Western world of art is known as the Renaissance. It occurred all over Europe, but the heart of it all was in Italy, where a powerful family known as the Medicis became famous patrons of the arts. Now, with a

The Devil Makes You Do It

Aesthetic pleasure and spirituality in art can be hard—if not impossible—to distinguish. In Renaissance art especially, the two are typically intermingled. Protestant sectarians known as puritans sometimes reacted against the celebration of physical beauty in Renaissance religious art, saying true spirituality is best expressed in plain and simple fashion.

little initiative and determination, an aspiring young painter could make a name for himself not just in a monastery as before, but in an artists' guild, or even at court, painting for the nobility.

The idea, though, was not just that there was suddenly money to be made in painting. The spirit of the Renaissance also had to do with the idea that heaven and Earth weren't so far apart as people used to think. It began to occur to people that the best way to get close to heaven was through a healthy appreciation of things on Earth.

Putti in Their Hands

This made a big difference in the way artists painted angels. In general, Renaissance angels had more personality. What's more, they were often represented as women or children, whereas angels of the Middle Ages were almost always men, or so nondescript that you couldn't really tell their age or sex. This helped Renaissance angels seem less like government officials sent from God and more like neighbors or even members of the family.

Winged Words

Putti are the naked babies with wings that appear frequently in Renaissance paintings. They may represent angels or cupids. The word comes from an Italian word for "children."

As angels became more human, they also became less strictly Christian. The old classical practice of combining the image of angels with the images of pagan gods and goddesses was revived by many Renaissance painters. "Cherubs" appeared in paintings of secular as well as religious subjects and were virtually indistinguishable from cupids. These Renaissance cupid-angels are known as *putti*.

It's highly appropriate that "putti" rhymes with "cutie," since their whole purpose in paintings was to be cute. Look closely at many Renaissance paintings and you can see them peeking out from behind a cloud or frolicking in the sky. Typically they're laughing or looking with big-eyed wonder at whatever holy or mythic event is taking place.

Revelations

Renaissance painters sometimes used their angelic art to make political statements. Raphael, for example, painted the Biblical scene *The Expulsion of Heliodorus from the Temple,* in which an angelic horseman prevents a government official from taking treasures out of the Temple in Jerusalem. Scholars have suggested that this painting represents Astorre Baglione of the city of Perugia, who did battle on horseback in the public square of the city with a band of enemies.

Putti by Albrecht Durer.

The Angelic Touch

While Renaissance artists turned increasingly to classical and secular subjects, angels remained high on the list of favorite things to paint. It's safe to say that most Renaissance painters painted at least some angels. A few, however, seem to have had a particular affinity for the winged ones, as you can see from this list:

➤ *Giotto (1267–1337).* A church painter who went on to become a member of an artist's guild and to paint for court nobility, Giotto is often said to have occupied the turning point between medieval and Renaissance painting. His many expressive angel paintings include *Birth of the Madonna* and *Mourning the Dead Christ*.

➤ *Fra Angelico (1387–1455).* A monk whose real name was Giovanni da Fiesole, he picked up the nickname Fra Angelico ("Angelic Brother") from his fellow monks. He was one of the first to paint angels as women. Some of his more famous works are his *Angel of the Annunciation*, *The Last Judgement*, *St. Michael*, and *The Coronation of the Virgin*.

➤ *Raphael (1483–1520).* He worked his way up from apprentice to one of Rome's top painters. Raphael epitomizes the high Renaissance style, characterized by innocent sensuality. He is appropriately named for an angel, since he painted so many, including those in the *Deliverance of Saint Peter* and *Virgin and Child with St. Raphael and St. Michael*.

315

Wing Tip

Don't expect to see wings on all of Michelangelo's angels. Although his cherubs have wings, his adult angels tend not to. He may have wanted to suggest a close resemblance between angels and human beings.

➤ *Michelangelo (1474–1564).* Yet another Italian Renaissance angel painter to be named for an angel, his most famous angelic work is the ceiling of the Sistine Chapel, which depicts numerous religious figures and scenes, most notably the *Creation of Adam* and the *Last Judgement.* Pope Paul IV condemned the nudity of these figures and compared the painting to a brothel! In fact, many of the nude figures had clothes and draperies painted over them, although these have since been removed.

➤ *Rembrandt (1606–1669).* Dutch master whose angelic paintings include *The Angel Departing from the Family of Tobias* and *Jacob Wrestling with the Angel.*

The Least You Need to Know

➤ Angels go wingless in the earliest-known Christian paintings.

➤ The convention of depicting angels with wings evidently comes from statues and paintings of pagan deities, especially Eros (Cupid) and Nike (Victory).

➤ Religious paintings of the Middle Ages were intended to be decorative and educational. Icons were considered sacred relics in their own right.

➤ The Acts of the Angels were conventional subjects for paintings taken from events in the Bible.

➤ Angels acquired lots of personality during the Renaissance as female and juvenile angels replaced males.

Chapter 25

Jewish Angel Tales

In This Chapter

➤ Angels in Jewish legends

➤ Michael and the death of Abraham

➤ Abraham and the gates of Judgment

➤ Moses debates the angels over the Torah

Traditionally, Jews have been great storytellers. Of the countless Jewish folk tales that have been told over the years, many are probably lost. Many others have been written down, and others, no doubt, continue to be passed along through the generations by word of mouth.

Many of these stories expand on people and events described in the Bible. They are part of the tradition of Biblical commentary practiced in Jewish schools and synagogues. At the same time, they are the kinds of yarns people spin around the fire before going to bed. They are not only entertaining, but help keep Jewish traditions alive, even though Jews are scattered all over the world.

Some are funny, some are sad, and most contain kernels of wisdom and morality that help you see what God is like and how people should think and act in God's world. Angels come and go throughout many of these tales, and a few, of course, feature angels more prominently. Here are a couple of these angel tales, adapted for contemporary readers.

Bearer of Bad News: Michael and Abraham

The first and most important Jewish patriarch is Abraham. The Bible tells what a good host Abraham was when three angels came to see him, and how he interceded on behalf of thousands who had sinned, and how obedient to God he was when he almost sacrificed his own son before an angel told him to stop. In addition, there are a number of stories about Abraham that aren't in the Bible. Here's the story of how the archangel Michael appeared to Abraham bearing bad news.

Revelations

These and hundreds of other Jewish legends are collected in Louis Ginzburg's remarkable seven-volume set, *Legends of the Jews*, translated by Henrietta Szold (see Appendix A for more information). Most are based on the Bible, supplying background for the lives of the important Biblical people and events. Unfortunately your local public library is unlikely to have a set, unless it happens to be a big research library.

Just Passing Through

Abraham was 175 years old when God realized it was about time for him to die. The patriarch had accomplished a lot over the years, and God knew it, so he didn't want to hit Abraham with death out of the blue like he does most people. Instead, he sent the archangel Michael down to warn him of what was in store.

Michael appeared on Earth as an ordinary mortal so as not to arouse unnecessary attention. He found Abraham sitting with his oxen after a day of plowing in the fields. When Abraham saw Michael, he thought the angel was just an ordinary traveler and treated him the way he always treated ordinary travelers: He invited him to sit down and rest and have a cool drink.

Wing Tip

Next time you have guests, try washing their feet like they used to do back in Biblical times. Maybe you'll get a reputation for hospitality like Abraham had!

Michael thought it would be more discreet to give Abraham the bad news inside his house, so he suggested they go in. Abraham said okay, and in they went. Once inside, Abraham called for a basin of water, in keeping with the Biblical custom of washing the feet of guests. His son Isaac filled a basin and brought it to Abraham.

As Abraham looked into the basin of water, a strange premonition came over him, and he said, "Something tells me this is the last pair of feet I'll ever wash." As he spoke he had a doleful, tragic expression on his face. Isaac, who was a sensitive lad, took all this in and began to cry.

Abraham started crying, too. He had washed a lot of feet over the years, and sometimes things like that kind of get to you. Even Michael started to cry. Angels aren't made of stone, you know. Angels' tears, however, are made of more than salt and water, because when Michael's tears fell into the basin of water, they turned into precious gems.

Return to Sender

As you can tell, Michael was having a tough time with his assignment. He couldn't bring himself to relay the message he was sent to deliver, and it didn't help a bit that Abraham had already sort of figured out what it was. Michael excused himself, pretending he needed to use the outhouse out back. He knew this was a lame excuse and that Abraham wouldn't be fooled, but he needed to buy some time.

Once outside, he shot back up to heaven in a heartbeat and appeared before the throne of the Almighty. "I can't go through with it, God!" he said. "Heck, you saw him there with Isaac, thinking about all the feet they've washed. Couldn't you just leave him a note?" As he spoke he brushed aside a tear with his wing. God took pity.

"Tell you what, Michael," said God. "Go on back down to Earth and stay at Abraham's overnight. I'll send a mystic dream down to Isaac and when he tells Abraham the dream, you can use your angelic insight and interpret it for them. That way Abe'll get the message and it won't seem like you only came down to spoil his day."

Michael had his usual excuse all ready: "Lord, you know I can't eat Middle Eastern food. What happens when they ask me to dinner?" "Don't worry about that," said God. "I'll send down a hungry spirit who'll eat anything. The spirit can hide in your mouth and take care of whatever Abraham wants to dish out—the spicier the better."

The Devil Makes You Do It

Angel tears may be made of precious stones, but that's not a good reason to make them cry.

Die Hard

So Michael returned to Earth, not happy, but ready to get his mission over with. He tried to keep up appearances during dinner, doing his best to laugh at Isaac's silly angel jokes. "How do angels curl their hair?" Isaac asked. Michael pretended not to know. "Holy rollers!" said Isaac.

After dinner, they all said their prayers and went to bed. Michael and Abraham slept in the same room and Isaac slept in his own room. In the middle of the night, however, Isaac gave a yell and came running to Abraham. "I had a bad dream!" he said, and he burst into tears. Michael and Abraham hadn't been sleeping too well either. Abraham started crying and Michael joined in too. Abraham's wife Sarah finally heard them from her room and came in to find out what was wrong. Michael tried to get a grip. "Isaac had a bad dream, that's all. Right, Isaac?"

Now Sarah is one of these people who never forgets a face, and she recognized Michael from years ago when he appeared to them along with two other angels on their way to destroy the city of Sodom. She pulled Abraham aside and said "Abe, do you know who that is? That's the archangel Michael!" Abraham replied, "I thought I'd washed those feet once before!"

Revelations

The archangel Michael appears in numerous Jewish legends. He is said to have appeared to Moses in the burning bush, to have restrained Abraham from sacrificing Isaac, to have destroyed Sennacherib's army, and to have taught Adam the art of farming. He is also said to have debated with Satan over the body of Moses. Perhaps Michael's most glamorous role, however, is in the New Testament Book of Revelation, in which he led the army of heaven against the army of Satan in the final battle.

Meanwhile, Michael was collecting his powers of angelic insight in order to interpret Isaac's mystic dream. "I wonder what symbolism God will use this time," he thought to himself. "Maybe the sun will set in the east, or a mighty eagle will plummet into the sea." He looked steadily at Isaac and said, "Tell us your dream, son."

Isaac burst out, "I dreamt that Dad is going to die!" Michael nodded and said, "That seems pretty clear." Abraham and Sarah looked at Michael. "Is it true?" they asked.

Michael was staring at his feet, noticing for the first time how clean they were. Then he looked up and smiled to show that Abraham had nothing to fear. "Sorry Abraham, it's all over," he said. "You've lived a good life and we're all proud of you. But now it's time to go. I've come for you."

Wing Tip

Not only was Michael specially selected by God to tell Abraham of his coming death, he's also the angel whose job it is to guide departed souls to the next world.

Michael's wings materialized, spread above his shoulders. He smiled more brightly and his face became radiant. His eyes became filled with the depths of heaven. "This is it," he said, and his voice sounded like faraway music. He reached out to embrace Abraham and carry him off, when suddenly...

"I'm not going!" said Abraham.

"Wha?" Michael stammered.

"Zap me with a thunderbolt if that's what you've gotta do, but I'm not moving from this spot!"

As you might imagine, this took the wind out of Michael's sails. It never occurred to him that the first patriarch would put up a fight about going to heaven. "Darn it!" he said, and marched out of the house into the dusty road and then streaked like a beam of light back to heaven to report to God.

Bon Voyage

God laughed when Michael told him Abraham didn't want to go. "Offer him a trip around the world first," said God. "Tell him he can pretend he's me. Whatever he wants to happen, make happen." God was all smiles. He liked this idea. Then his face became serious. "And that's my final offer," he said.

So Michael returned to Earth and found Abraham sitting with his oxen again, as if he had just plowed all his fields. "You know," said Michael, "it would be better if you'd come quietly."

"I don't want to," Abraham said.

Michael looked down at his dusty feet and waited. Abraham stared straight ahead, trying not to look at anything, but there it all was. He could hear the soft slap of the tails of his oxen behind him, swatting flies. After about a minute, Michael made the pitch. "God says I can fly you around the world. On the way, whatever you want to happen will happen."

Abraham thought for a moment. "I'd like that," he said, and instantly, a flaming chariot descended, drawn by four four-faced cherubim and attended by sixty angels. It had all the latest features, including dual airbags, A/C, and solid-gold cup holders. Best of all, the flaming wheels had eyes, so when you sat in the chariot, you could see everything. "I've always wanted to fly one of these," said Abraham.

Wing Tip

This flaming chariot, or one just like it, would be used years later to take the prophet Elijah to heaven. Elijah, unlike Abraham, did not die, but went to paradise as a living, embodied soul.

Torched by an Angel

Michael let Abraham take the reins and off they went. What they saw is too much to describe, because they saw everything. "This is great!" said Abraham, who had never seen everything before. Everything fit together and made sense and looked really good—the whole world. After a while, however, they saw something that kind of spoiled things. There were two adulterous lovers, going at it where they thought no one could see them.

Abraham was livid. "They can't do that! Don't they realize they'll ruin everything?" Michael just looked at his feet again and shook his head, which only made Abraham even madder. "We'll show them!" he yelled. "Incinerate them!" At that moment the lovers were engulfed in flames and quickly consumed to ashes. "Serves 'em right," said Abraham. "Whose world did they think this is?"

Not long afterward, they came upon three thieves who had broken into a house and were stealing the computer, TV, and stereo. Abraham didn't even bat an eyelid this time. He just gritted his teeth and said "Let them be torn to pieces by wild beasts." Suddenly a lion, a tiger, and a grizzly bear jumped out of the broom closet and devoured the thieves.

A little later they came upon someone who was about to commit murder. "Let the earth open up and swallow him," said Abraham. Immediately the earth obeyed and closed back over as if nothing had happened. Just then, the cell phone rang, which Michael answered. It was God calling, and he was mad. When Michael hung up the phone, he said, "We have to turn around, God wants the chariot back." Abraham didn't complain, even though they hadn't yet gone halfway around the world.

Happy Landings

Soon Abraham and Michael arrived at the gate of paradise. God had originally planned to let Abraham in through the side entrance right away, but because he was mad, he made him wait in line with everyone else. Abraham didn't care, though. He felt bad about the sinners he had smitten. Michael waited in line with him.

Right next to the gate of paradise was a gate leading down to hell. One by one, the angel of Judgment directed the departed souls through one of the gates. The soul who stood right in front of Abraham turned out to be a tough case. He had to stand there in front of the gates while the angel of Judgment shuffled through the Talmud, shaking his head.

"Oy, veh," said the angel. "What am I going to do with you? You're a little too much bad for paradise, but a little too much good for hell. Can you think of anything what for you should not be suffering eternal torment?" The soul just shrugged. "What do I know from eternal torment?"

Just then Abraham recognized the soul standing in front of the gates. It was the thief who had just been eaten by the grizzly bear that had jumped out of the broom closet. Abraham turned to Michael. "Quick," he said, "let me use the cell phone!" "Too late," said Michael, "it's in the chariot back in the garage." "Can you take a message to God for me right away?" Abraham asked. Michael checked his watch. "Impossible," he said. "The boss is in an important meeting with the Principalities."

The angel of Judgment had made a decision. "Okay, right this way, please. Watch your step going down."

The Devil Makes You Do It

It's not worth compounding sin upon sin just to speed up the sorting process outside the gates of Judgment. Good souls don't mind waiting for the angel to make a tough call, and bad souls don't mind waiting for any reason!

"Wait!" shouted Abraham. He looked around and slowly dropped to his knees, folded his hands, bowed his head, and prayed unselfishly that the thief be allowed to enter paradise.

Revelations

According to Jewish legend, prayers are conveyed by angels to the angel Sandalfon, who weaves them into a crown for God. Once the crown is made, Sandalfon charms it, so that it floats in the air and goes to wherever God may be sitting. As the crown rises, all the angels in heaven can feel it and tremble in awe and adoration. When the crown reaches God and lowers itself on his head, the wheels of the throne start to move, heaven shakes, and all the angels start singing.

After a while, as he prayed, Abraham smelled a sweet fragrance and saw a beautiful light and then saw a glorious and beautiful form approach him. It was the most beautiful human form he had ever seen, so that all he could do was stare. "Don't think I appear this way to everyone, Abraham," said the form, and it held out a crown and put it on Abraham's head.

"You're Death, aren't you?" Abraham asked. "Let me see how you appear to sinners." As he looked, the flesh on Death's beautiful face was consumed by maggots, and a horned serpent wound itself in and out of the empty eye sockets and thrust its face at Abraham and flashed out its tongue, which was a long, sharp sword. All the while, a disgusting stench wafted out.

"Okay, I get the idea!" Abraham said, and Death resumed its lovely appearance. "Your prayer has been answered," said Death. "The thief is now in paradise. In fact, any time you want to intercede for sinners from now on, go right ahead." Abraham thought about that. He could think of quite a few sinners already who would be in need of interceding.

"Okay, so what happens now?" Abraham asked, but there was no answer. He could see Death and his body below him and sinking further away. His soul was in Michael's hands, together with myriad angels, all flying into paradise.

Required Reading: Moses and the Torah

The most important thing to the Jews as a people is the Torah, the book of teaching that God gave to Moses on Mount Sinai. It's important as a symbol, of course, because it represents the covenant between God and his chosen people. Just having this covenant in book form isn't enough, though. Jews also want to figure out what it means. In fact, the whole tradition of rabbinical Judaism is chiefly devoted to this task.

Revelations

The tradition of commentary and interpretation of the Torah is divided into two categories, called the halakah and the haggadah. The halakah is more formal and technical and has to do with legal matters. The haggadah is informal and often takes the form of stories such as the ones in this chapter. Some say that if you want to know God, you should study the haggadah.

The work isn't easy, though. After all, the Torah is written by God himself. The greatest Jewish scholars in history have devoted their lives to unwrapping its mysteries and have produced mountains of interpretation and commentary. It has appeared to many that to understand the Torah properly is beyond the reach of ordinary mortals, but instead requires the understanding of the angels. That's how deep and dark the Torah's secrets can be. The most important secret of all, however, is revealed in the story of how Moses ascended to heaven from Mount Sinai to receive the Torah from God.

Feet of Clay

Moses was terrified. Not only was he going to have to go all the way to heaven to receive the Torah—past all those menacing angels—but while he was there—if he even got that far—he would have to study it and figure out what it meant. When he answered the classified ad for "leader of God's chosen people" he had no idea this was part of the job description. And to think he could have been an Egyptian prince!

By rights his brother Aaron ought to be doing this. Aaron was the smart one with books. He should be, he's a priest! Moses, in contrast, had the charm and good looks of the two. Charm and good looks wouldn't help him in heaven, though, where holy wisdom is all that counts.

The cloud-nine elevator let Moses off at the top floor. Slowly, taking short little steps, he walked into a lobby where an angry and impatient-looking angel sat behind a big desk, talking on the phone in *glossolalia*, an angel

Winged Words

Glossolalia is the language of the angels when they're not speaking Hebrew. It's also the gibberish people speak when they're possessed by the holy spirit and start "speaking in tongues."

language Moses didn't understand. The nameplate on the desk said "Kemuel." There was no place to sit down, so Moses just stood and waited.

After what seemed like a long time, the angel finally looked up, still holding the phone, and said, "What in heaven's name do you think you're doing here, Earth creature?"

"I came for the T-Torah," said Moses, who suddenly seemed to have acquired his brother Aaron's stutter. "You came for the Torah?" the angel responded in disbelief. "The divine and holy book of wisdom written by God himself? In your dreams, mud puppy! Go take a flying leap." The angel motioned to the door with the phone. Moses tried again. "But G-God said—"

"I'm telling you," the angel interrupted. "No Torah for earthworm. Go away." Moses was close to tears. He'd never felt so angry and ashamed at the same time. He looked around and saw a door on the other side of the big desk. The name on the door was "Hadarniel." Moses decided Hadarniel couldn't be much worse than Kemuel, so he broke for the door.

Inside was a huge angel, sixty myriads of *parasangs* tall. "What are you doing here?" he roared, and twelve thousand bolts of lightning shot off from his mouth when he spoke. "I'll make scorched Earth out of you for barging in here like this!" Moses had fallen backwards into the corner. He put his arm over his face and cried "No!"

Winged Words

A **parasang** is a unit of measurement used in ancient Persia, roughly equal to three and a half miles long.

The Path to Knowledge

Just then God's voice came in over the intercom. "Is Moses here yet? The Torah's ready." Hadarniel glared at Moses. "Yes, he's here." "Send him up," said God. "Follow me," said Hadarniel with a sneer, and walked through another door, down a long hall, and into a huge reception room, crowded with myriad angels of Terror who appeared to be arguing with God.

When Moses entered, they fell silent and stared at him in anger. In the center of the room was God's throne, hidden behind a curtain. In front of the curtain was a coffee table with a book on it. Moses took a step toward the book and the angels began yelling: "Why are you wasting the Torah on this dust clod? Leave it here in heaven with us!"

From behind the curtain came the sound of God clearing his throat. The angels fell silent. "There's the Torah, Moses," said God. "Take it." Moses ran forward, quivering. As he ran, the angels began yelling again; this time at Moses. "Why should you get the Torah and not us? You are not wise or holy like we are! You do not deserve this precious book!"

Hard to Grasp

Moses grabbed the Torah, but his hands were trembling. He tried to clasp it to his body, but it slipped and dropped out of his hands onto the floor. The pages fell open in front of him. "Why should you get the Torah?" the angels yelled again.

Moses stooped down to pick up the book and saw it written, "I have led thee out of the land of Egypt and out of the house of bondage." He kept the book open as he picked it up and read the words out loud. Then he read, "Thou shalt have no other Gods." Then he read, "Thou shalt not steal." Then he read, "Honor thy father and thy mother."

He looked around the room to see if any angels looked like they had spent time in Egypt, or worshipped idols, or stole things, or had fathers and mothers. It didn't appear that they had. As he looked, the angels of Terror didn't look so terrifying. In fact, they were smiling and laughing at him.

Wing Tip

As you may know already, the Torah Moses brought to the Jews was carved in stone. According to legend, however, it was carved in magic stone that could be rolled up like a scroll or folded into pages like a book.

"It's for people!" Moses shouted. "Angels don't need the Torah!" Everyone cheered. Hadarniel slapped Moses on the back. The holy animals started singing paeans to God, and the seraphim burst into flame and chanted the trisagion: "Holy, Holy, Holy is the Lord of hosts; the whole Earth is full of his glory."

Moses remained with God and the angels for forty days and nights, studying the Torah before returning with it to his people.

Revelations

The story told here is only one of several legends concerning Moses' trip to heaven to get the Torah. Another story pokes fun at a rabbi who pretended to know too much. In this story, Moses finds God adding little tiny knobs as decorations for the letters of the Torah. God tells Moses that the rabbi will write a mountain of scholarship on each little knob! Moses says he would like to see this rabbi and God reveals him in a vision, saying words which make no sense to Moses. A student asks the rabbi how he knew what he had just said, and the rabbi answers, "It was revealed to Moses on Mount Sinai!" The story is told in ironic fashion, as the bemused Moses fails to understand why God chose him rather than the "erudite" rabbi to receive the Torah.

Dore's view of Moses returning from Mount Sinai with the Torah.

The Least You Need to Know

➤ Jewish folk tales help keep Jewish traditions alive, serve as entertainment, and contain moral teachings.

➤ Abraham, the first patriarch, is known for being a good host to angels and interceding with God on behalf of sinners.

➤ The archangel Michael is known for guiding departed souls to paradise.

➤ Moses, who led the Jews out of the Wilderness, spent forty days and nights receiving the Torah from God.

➤ The Torah is God's covenant with the Jews and was written for people, not angels.

327

Epic Proportions

During the Renaissance, back before pulp fiction dominated the bookstores, people turned to recreational reading not only for a good read, but for historical and cultural background, inspiration, and moral instruction, too. They found works of great literature to supply all these things at once. Among the favorites were books that brought together familiar and important ideas out of classical and Biblical traditions and made sense of them both together.

Making moral and intellectual sense out of all of Western history and culture—and, in the process, telling a good story—is no easy task. It takes profound insight into the human condition. You also need to be a venerable scholar, a gifted poet, and a seasoned moralist. It also helps to have lots of angels around.

Angels can help make sense of even the messiest of situations, such as the human condition and the vicissitudes of history. This is what the great poets Dante and Milton found when they tried to tell the story of human existence. These writers suggested that, in order to understand how things are for us, we need to have at least a little bit of insight into how it is for the angels.

Poetry in Motion

During the Middle Ages, the pagan ideals of Greece and Rome were largely rejected as monotheism spread throughout Europe. People of the European Renaissance, however, developed a new-found appreciation for their classical (ancient Greek and Roman) heritage. Greek and Latin poetry were held in particularly high esteem by growing numbers of readers. (The printing press was invented just prior to the Renaissance, so books were easier to get. As a result, more people learned to read, fueling the demand for more books.)

Winged Words

Epic poetry is narrative poetry concerned with lofty, important themes. The classical models of epic poetry were written by the Greek poet Homer and the Latin poet Virgil.

Wing Tip

If you're looking for the movie version of Homer's *Odyssey*, it's called *Ulysses*, which is the Latin name for Odysseus. It was made in 1954 and stars Kirk Douglas and Anthony Quinn. Sure, it's a little corny in spots, but it has some cool 1950s special effects!

We Can Be Heroes

The Bible remained at the top of just about everyone's required reading list, but now the so-called heathen authors were in vogue, too. These classical writers wrote all kinds of what you might call recreational reading, including songs, poems, plays, and stories. Of these, the works that had the reputation for being the most noble and inspiring were the *epic* poems of the Greek poet Homer and the Latin poet Virgil. Epic poetry tells an important story, often of national significance.

Usually there's an epic hero who is a human being descended from one of the gods. In fact, the word "hero" comes from epic poetry and originally meant someone with one human and one divine parent. The hero fights many battles and has supernatural adventures, and, with a little divine assistance, makes the world a safe place for his countrymen to live. Today, the best-known epic is Homer's *Odyssey*, about a hero named Odysseus who has all kinds of adventures on his way home from the Trojan War, only to find his house full of guys who want to marry his wife Penelope.

A New Convert

Although traditionally epic poetry was considered a non-Christian literary form, Christians writers of the Renaissance had such high respect for it that they wanted to write it themselves. They wrote epics on all kinds of subjects. The usual approach was to combine the idea of the classical epic with the Christian "romance" theme of knights in shining armor. There have been some good epic romances about knights and dragons and so forth, but many critics today think these stories are pretty corny compared with the best epics.

It should come as no surprise to angel fans that far and away the greatest epics of the Renaissance have a heck of a lot to do with angels. Instead of the knight-in-shining-armor approach, the best epic masterpieces take on Biblical themes. These are Dante Alighieri's *Divine Comedy* (written c. 1300; published 1472) and John Milton's *Paradise Lost* (1667).

These epics borrow many features and conventions of the classical epic and adapt them to a Christian world view. They show angels instead of gods favoring and assisting the human heroes. They make numerous allusions to classical figures and myths. Both poems include versions of the epic convention of the hero's journey to the underworld, changed from the classical Hades into the Christian hell. When all is said and done, however, there's a major difference between the Christian and classical epic. The point of the Christian epic isn't to show the value of worldly human prowess and cunning, but spiritual virtue.

Revelations

Milton not only modeled his epic after classical epics, but modeled himself after classical epic poets. One striking feature shared by Milton and the Greek poet Homer was blindness. Many believe blindness enhances creative insight and contributed to Homer's and Milton's greatness as poets. Milton, like Homer, calls attention to himself as an epic poet by invoking the muse at the beginning of his poem. Muses are goddesses of classical mythology who inspire human artists to be creative. In his variation on the tradition, Milton invokes the angel who brought the Ten Commandments to Moses, saying this angel is also Urania, the classical muse of astronomy.

No Laughing Matter

Actually, the *Divine Comedy* isn't funny. In fact, it's pretty serious. Dante called his epic poem "Comedia," or comedy, because for him comedy was anything that has a happy ending. At the risk of spoiling it for you, it ends when Dante, who is the main character in his own poem, gets to see heaven, swarming with angels. Best of all, his old girlfriend Beatrice forgives him for chasing after earthly pleasures (such as other women) after she is dead. In fact, she changes his life from beyond the grave to help him repent, renounce sin, and become worthy of salvation.

Out of the Woods

The Devil Makes You Do It

Don't think you can get away with a slap on the wrist for committing white-collar crimes in Dante's Inferno. You are guilty of corruption, and the punishment is to be boiled in a trench filled with stinking ooze. If you try to come out to cool off, you'll be punctured or flayed by a demon with a pitchfork!

The story begins with Dante lost in the wilderness. As if that wasn't bad enough, he's chased by wild beasts. This is where Beatrice first starts helping him out. She pulls strings up in heaven to arrange for a guide who will lead Dante out of the woods. This guide is none other than Virgil, the famous epic poet of ancient Rome. Virgil wrote the *Aeneid*, which Dante and his friends thought was just about the greatest thing ever written by a heathen poet.

Virgil shows Dante a secret tunnel that leads out of the wilderness, straight to the center of the earth. The problem is, this turns out to be an even worse place, namely hell, or "Inferno" in Italian. Fortunately for Dante, he and Virgil are just visiting, so none of the torments prepared for the eternally damned are inflicted on the two travelers. Even so, hell is not exactly a nice place to visit. In fact, no one there is a happy camper.

This is what happens to you if you're corrupt in Dante's hell, from Dore's illustrations for the Divine Comedy.

Just Desserts

You may be aware that some prisons in America are involved with so-called "scared straight" programs for kids. The kids visit the prison and see first-hand the kind of stuff that goes on there. They talk to inmates who say things like, "Prison really stinks; I wish I had never done whatever it was that got me sent here!" This is supposed to help kids decide to stay out of trouble in later life. That's sort of the idea behind Dante's trip to hell. He meets lost and tortured souls who show him that it's worth being good on Earth in order to avoid an eternity of horrible suffering.

The scary thing is, you don't even have to be all that bad to end up in Dante's Inferno. In fact, there are nine levels of hell; which level you go to depends on how bad you are. Each punishment is symbolically suited to the crime. For example, if you committed violent crimes on Earth, you are condemned to be boiled in blood in hell. Flatterers are drowned in sewage. Blasphemers get rained on by droplets of fire.

The deepest pit, where Satan lives, is where traitors go. That's the worst place you can be in Dante's Inferno. Satan sits in the bottom of the pit with Judas Iscariot, the betrayer of Christ, in his mouth, chewing eternally. Satan is pictured as a beast with three mouths. The other two are used for gnawing on Brutus and Cassius, Roman conspirators responsible for the assassination of Julius Caesar.

Other crimes aren't so bad, but still receive eternal punishment. You can even go to Dante's hell for doing nothing. This means you're guilty of sloth. Angels have to look sharp too, or they'll be punished. The outer level just outside of hell itself is the final abode of the angels who remained neutral in the war in heaven. When Satan and his crew rebelled and the righteous angels cast them out of heaven, a number of angels chose not to get involved. That evidently ticked God off, because, according to Dante, they've been condemned to chase after a waving banner for the rest of eternity.

The Devil Makes You Do It

Don't let it show that you're reading about Dante's hell because of the sadistic pleasure you get out of the diabolical punishments prepared for sinners. Pretend that you're absorbing moral lessons that will help you avoid sin!

Wing Tip

If you're writing a religious epic in which part of the action takes place in hell, go ahead and include interviews with real people you used to know but never liked. Dante did, and found it to be a great way to let the world know how he felt!

Working Things Out

Fortunately for Dante, the tunnel that led all the way down to hell leads back out to the other side of the earth. He and Virgil take the tunnel back to the surface and find themselves on an island with a single mountain on it. This is Purgatorio, where all righteous or repentant human beings go temporarily in order to be purified for heaven.

Ordinarily, souls don't take the subway to purgatory as Dante and Virgil did. Instead, they sail there in a ship propelled by an angel who uses his wings as sails. His wings are so perfect, the feathers don't even ruffle in the wind. Dante calls him a "bird of God."

Purgatorio has seven levels, which lead up the mountain to heaven instead of down into a pit. An angel stands at the gate outside to let Dante and Virgil in. This angel is kind of like a tattoo artist, except he uses a sword instead of a needle and ink. He takes the sword and carves seven Ps on Dante's forehead. P stands for "peccatum," or sin. The seven Ps stand for the seven deadly sins Dante is guilty of and must repent.

The mountain of purgatory is bustling with activity. There are assertiveness training seminars for those who lack courage, sensitivity training to help people deal with their anger, and self-control workshops for obsessive types. In fact, whatever your problem is, you can deal with it in purgatory. It's like a retreat and awareness program that adjusts your attitude and gets you ready for heaven.

Even though Dante isn't dead yet, he benefits vicariously from his experience in purgatory, having visions that bring out remorse for his earthly sins. When this happens, an angel appears and brushes his forehead with its wing. Each time, another one of the Ps becomes healed until finally Dante's forehead is clear again. After that, Dante and Virgil come to a wall of flame that purifies Dante completely, so that he's ready to see Beatrice.

Eyes on the Prize

At this point, Virgil can go no further. He may be the greatest poet that ever lived, but he's still a heathen. Dante goes on to the top of the mountain by himself, which turns out to be the earthly paradise (which for Dante was the same thing as the Garden of Eden), where he sees angelic visions before meeting up with Beatrice.

Revelations

Christian theologians who respected the virtues exhibited by ancient Greeks and Romans struggled with the problem of what happened to pagans (non-monotheists) after death. Hard-liners said that anyone who isn't Christian goes to hell and that's that. Many pagans, however, such as Socrates and Plato, were admired for their moral goodness, so it didn't seem right that they should have to go to hell just because they weren't Christian. Some Christians speculated that they must have gone to purgatory where they wouldn't have to suffer. This is the fate of the pagan poet Virgil in Dante's epic.

Beatrice is even better-looking than Dante remembered. He's really glad to see her, even though she tells him he could have been a really swell guy, but instead became a jerk after she died. Dante gets all choked up and admits she's right. After that she forgives him and takes him on a tour of the nine spheres of heaven.

In heaven, Dante gets to meet all his heroes, like St. Thomas Aquinas and Adam, the first man. Near the end of the trip, Dante gets a vision of the nine choirs of angels and finds out about what they do. Finally, he gets to see God with all the angels and the blessed souls surrounding him. The whole thing looks like a white rose. Dante compares the angels to bees swarming in and out of the petals of the flower.

Dore's interpretation of Dante's heaven.

Higher Truths

Dante's story is grand for its own sake. After all, you get to find out all about what eternal punishments are in store for all kinds of sin, and how repentant sinners can get over their problems and move up to be closer to God. The poem is chock-full of interviews with souls in heaven, hell, and purgatory who share their deepest secrets and provide valuable tips on how to succeed in the afterlife. You find out how the entire cosmos is laid out and how divine justice works, and you get to meet a lot of angels along the way.

Winged Words

An **allegory** is a story that can be read on a literal level and a symbolic level at the same time. Dante's *Divine Comedy* is an allegory of personal salvation.

Wing Tip

There's nothing necessarily wrong with idealizing women, but most women today will settle for respect and appreciation.

More Meanings

You'd think this would be enough, but there's more. The whole poem is an *allegory*, which means there's a whole extra layer of meaning built in. The long journey is not just a journey; it also symbolizes the process of sin, repentance, redemption, and blessing that human beings go through starting in this life and continuing in the next.

Remember at the beginning when Dante is lost in the wilderness and chased by wild beasts? The wilderness symbolizes spiritual darkness and confusion. The beasts represent sinful desires that pursue people who haven't figured out the right way to behave. These people need a guide like Dante had. On the literal level, this guide is Virgil, but Virgil also represents human reason, the God-given ability to think things through and think about where we're headed.

But reason, in Dante's world, can only take you so far. After that you need to have faith in higher truths that you can't figure out for yourself. You can find out about these higher truths only if you have a spiritual girlfriend like Beatrice to teach you. Beatrice stands for divine revelation. Dante's love for Beatrice is a spiritual thing, because she helps him come closer to God.

All Mapped Out

These allegorical meanings are woven into the poem, despite the fact that the literal details are thoroughly worked out. Dante has a very clear picture in mind of just where hell, heaven, purgatory, and the rest of the world are in relation to one another. Dante's keen sense of cosmic order is very much in keeping with late medieval–early Renaissance philosophy.

This conception of order involves the belief that angels are very different from, and superior to, human beings. They help fill the big gulf of spiritual space between God and humanity. As a result, they appear in Dante's poem as beautiful, mysterious visions whose touch is magical. Even though they are filled with divine love, ordinary human souls are incapable of understanding them fully.

Angels Like Us

The angels in John Milton's *Paradise Lost* are very different from Dante's. Human beings can talk to them and find out what they're like—and, as a matter of fact, they're not all that much different from us. Or, at any rate, they aren't that much different from the way we would have been if Adam and Eve hadn't disobeyed God and got themselves kicked out of paradise.

Revelations

Milton was attracted to the theme of rebellion, since he was a revolutionary himself. He sided with the Puritans and Parliamentarians who overthrew the British monarchy in 1649. The revolt culminated in the beheading of the English King Charles I. Since this took place before the separation of Church and state, many saw this as a shocking act of sacrilege as well as disloyalty. In fact, some readers claim to sense an affinity between Milton and his rebel angel Satan, identifying the fallen angel as the real hero of *Paradise Lost*. Others associate Satan with tyrannical kingship. Milton advocated political and religious freedom throughout his life.

Angels in Action

In fact, *Paradise Lost* tells the story of how the first humans fell from grace. This story had already been told in the Book of Genesis, but Milton fills in lots of extra details not mentioned in the Bible. For example, he tells of a war in heaven between the righteous and rebellious angels before the earth was even created. In epic fashion, the angels get all done up for battle as Greek warriors, with plumed helmets, round shields, and chariots.

The story of the battle is told as a flashback. First we hear about the plot of Satan and the fallen angels in hell to get Adam and Eve to eat the forbidden fruit of the Tree of Knowledge. The point is simply to cause trouble and bother God. Satan comes off as a politician in hell, making a long speech to the rest of the fallen angels about how you can't keep a bad angel down. They all cheer him and put him in charge of Operation Original Sin.

Then the angel Raphael goes to Eden to warn Adam and Eve not to disobey God. Raphael and Adam have a nice long conversation in which they trade stories about Earth and heaven. This is when we hear about the war in heaven. In addition, before and during the war, there's a lot of trash-talking between good and bad angels, only they go after one another with big, fancy words.

Finally, after Adam and Eve eat the forbidden fruit, the angel Michael comes down and makes them leave paradise. Before they go, however, he shows Adam everything he needs to know about the

The Devil Makes You Do It

Don't think justifying the ways of God to man is easy. It took Milton a decade of study and practice before he wrote his epic poem.

future of humanity. Milton's whole story, in fact, is designed to tell you what you need to know as a God-fearing Christian. The point, in his words, is to "justify the ways of God to man."

High Style

One great thing about Milton's story is the way he tells it. He uses language that makes the actions and ideas sound important and exciting. If you've ever read superhero comic books, you probably know what I'm talking about. They say things like, "The Caped Crusader strained his mighty sinews" because it's a cool way of saying "Batman flexed his big muscles." Milton does this sort of comic-book talk throughout his whole poem, only he does it even better than they do in the comics!

For example, here's how he describes Satan getting kicked out of heaven:

> *Him the Almighty power*
> *Hurled headlong flaming from the ethereal sky*
> *With hideous ruin and combustion down*
> *To bottomless perdition, there to dwell*
> *In adamantine chains and penal fire,*
> *Who durst defy the omnipotent to arms. (I, 44–49)*

Makes you feel kind of tingly all over, huh? They call this way of talking "heroic diction," or "Miltonic diction." This is the way epics are supposed to sound, and pretty much everyone agrees Milton wrote the best epic in the English language.

The bad angels get the old 'heave ho' in Dore's illustration for Paradise Lost.

Heavenly Bodies

This lofty, dignified style is appropriate to Milton's lofty subject—God, angels, and the first human beings. The language has to be lofty, because angels are the main characters. They perform most of the action and do most of the talking. In fact, the only human characters in the whole thing are Adam and Eve.

Revelations

Milton's contemporaries were familiar with superhuman characters from classical poetry and drama who appeared briefly to alter the course of the action before vanishing in the clouds. These godly figures were known as "machines" after the Latin phrase "deus ex machina," which means "a god out of a machine." The phrase refers to the device, used in ancient Greek plays, of a god who is lowered onto the stage from above by a crane to clear up messy situations. In Milton's time, the conventional view was that writers should use "machines" only sparingly, if at all. Milton surprised his readers by filling his epic with "machines" in the form of angels.

Having angels as his main characters was a pretty daring move on Milton's part, especially since he says things about them that contradict the standard view of what angels are like. For example, he says that angels are material beings, although they are formed of an especially rarified substance. As a result they can feel pain and even bleed, but their wounds close up again right away.

Here's how Milton describes what happened when Michael wounded Satan with his sword:

> *Then Satan first knew pain,*
> *And writhed him to and fro convolved; so sore*
> *The grinding sword with discontinuous wound*
> *Passed through him, but the ethereal substance closed*
> *Not long divisible, and from the gash*
> *A stream of nectareous humor issuing flowed*
> *Sanguine, such as celestial spirits may bleed.*
> *(VI, 327–333)*

Not only do Milton's angels bleed, they do other things. We hear about some of them when Raphael pays Adam and Eve a visit in the Garden of Eden. Eve makes everyone some fruit compote and Raphael has some, and says that angels eat all the time. He explains that the food they eat becomes rarified and more spiritual in their angelic digestive systems!

Satan gets taken out with the trash in Dore's illustration for Paradise Lost.

The Devil Makes You Do It

Don't get carried away with the traditional interpretation of the forbidden fruit as a symbol for sex. In fact, Milton was not the only reader of Genesis who did not equate the eating of the fruit with sex. Some Biblical commentators not only believed that Adam and Eve had sex before the fall, but that sexual arousal and orgasm was completely subject to their will, just like moving their arms and legs!

Guy Talk

Raphael and Adam have a long talk about life in heaven compared to life in the Garden of Eden. Both agree that life is pretty good in both places. Adam is especially happy because, unlike in other versions of the story of Adam and Eve, sex is not "original sin" in Milton's version. The first couple get to have all the sex they want as far as God is concerned, just so long as they leave the forbidden fruit of the Tree of Knowledge alone!

Anyway, Eve goes off by herself so Adam and Raphael can talk about guy stuff: the recent battle in heaven, whether the sun orbits the earth or the earth orbits the sun, whether there's life in outer space, etc. Finally, Adam can't help mentioning that Eve makes him flip his fig leaf! He wants to know if Raphael knows what he means and whether angels have sex.

This makes Raphael blush "with a smile that glowed/ Celestial rosy red." Not only do angels have sex, they do it by totally mingling their spiritual substance:

We enjoy
In eminence, and obstacle find none
Of membrane, joint, or limb, exclusive bars.
Easier than air with air, if spirits embrace,
Total they mix, union of pure with pure
Desiring. (VIII, 623–628)

The Party's Over

As you can see, Adam and Raphael get pretty chummy in Eden. Before he goes, Raphael reminds Adam to watch out for Satan and stay away from the forbidden fruit. Unfortunately for the human race, the warning went unheeded. Satan disguised himself as a snake and told Eve that eating the forbidden fruit enabled him to speak. He went on to play on her vanity by telling her that since the fruit made him think and talk like a human being, it would make her think and talk like a goddess. Sure enough, as everybody knows, she bit.

She persuaded herself that the fruit was as great as Satan said it was and persuaded Adam to try some, too. They turned the occasion into a party. They had a great time, talking about how much knowledge they were going to get as a result of eating the fruit. Finally they fell asleep, only to wake up with the spiritual equivalent of a really bad hangover.

Why They Invented Bootstraps

That morning they realized they were in big trouble and bickered about it for a while and blamed each other. Then they talked about what to do next. Eventually, they decided that the best thing was to pray to God for forgiveness, which turned out to be a good idea, since it made God decide not to zap them with a lightning bolt. (Actually, God knew they would pray for forgiveness and be spared. He knows everything.)

God sent archangel Michael down to lay down the new law and let Adam and Eve know what to expect in the cruel world. Michael appears in Eden to kick the fallen couple out, but first he shows Adam a vision of Biblical history leading all the way to the coming of Christ. The thought that everyone would be able to become Christian makes Adam feel better about things as he and Eve walk off into the world, hand in hand.

So Milton's epic ends on a hopeful note. The good news is, despite the fact there's a lot of suffering that people have to go through as mortals, like getting sick, paying taxes, and dying, we get to

Wing Tip

Try to see the original sin and expulsion from paradise as being all for the best. That's Milton's attitude. He regarded the event as a "felix culpa," or a "happy fall."

participate in our own salvation. If we still lived in paradise, we wouldn't get to take any of the credit for God's love for us. As fallen beings, though, we have a chance to work our way back up into God's good graces. We are free to work hard to get to be good and righteous, or we can go to hell.

The Least You Need to Know

➤ Dante and Milton wrote epics combining classical and Christian themes.

➤ Dante is guided through hell and purgatory by the great Roman epic poet, Virgil.

➤ The *Divine Comedy* is an allegory of personal salvation. Dante's guide, Virgil, stands for human reason. His spiritual girlfriend, Beatrice, stands for divine revelation.

➤ Milton surprised his readers by including numerous angels as main characters in *Paradise Lost.*

➤ *Paradise Lost* accounts for the fall of humanity in positive terms as creating the opportunity for people to exercise free will.

Chapter 27

Angel Pages

In This Chapter

➤ Angels in fiction

➤ 19th-century angel tales

➤ Angel novels and short stories

➤ Action angels in popular novels and comics

Angels have been in stories for many thousands of years, infusing elements of wonder and surprise and presenting earthly battles, love relationships, intrigues, and accidents in a whole new light. Even if you don't believe in angels, stories about them can affect you in most of the ways actual angels are supposed to. They can make you feel happy to be alive, sorry to have done bad things, and wiser and more thoughtful about things in general.

Of course, the same can be said for any good story, but angel stories have a way of coming at things from a fresh perspective. After all, angels are good at showing that there's more to life than people ordinarily imagine. And, since angel stories are just stories, you don't have to worry about things like truth and reality, which have a way of dampening the wings of angels that are actually supposed to exist.

It's the job of theologians to tell us what God, heaven, and the angels are like and how we should behave in this world if we want to make it to the next. It's the job of writers of fiction to take these ideas and run with them—modifying them, popularizing them, taking them to extremes, and thinking up strange things that could happen if what the theologians say is really true. Angel fiction may not help you get into heaven, but it can help you be prepared for just about anything if you actually get there!

Hard to Put Down

Ever since John Milton's *Paradise Lost*, angels have been the subject of popular reading. Of course, Milton's epic isn't *Reader's Digest* material. Even so, he showed how entertaining angel stories could be, and started a precedent for stories that put angels in realistic earthly situations. The angel-powered presses have been rolling ever since. Of course, the angel trend has spiked and declined at various intervals, but it doesn't ever seem to go away entirely.

Racy Romances

Quite a few book-length narrative poems written in England early in the 19th century retell the Biblical story of Enoch and the angels from the perspective of popular romance. Enoch's rise to heaven is associated in the Bible with the fall of the "watchers," lustful angels who come to Earth to have sex with human beings. This subject is treated in *The World Before the Flood* (1813) by James Montgomery; *The Angel of the World* (1820) by George Croly; *Irad and Adah, a Tale of the Flood* (1821) by Thomas Dale; *The Loves of the Angels* (1822) by Thomas Moore; and Lord Byron's *Heaven and Earth* (1823).

The racy subject matter had a popular appeal, but the fact that the stories were based on a Biblical story made them morally acceptable, too. The theme of good versus evil, tied to the themes of exotic love and the boundaries between the human and divine realms, fit right in with the preoccupations of the time, known as the Romantic period. Few people read these poems today, but they were hot stuff at the time.

Women's Ward

Another group of books to treat angelic themes became hugely popular toward the end of the 19th century. These were the novels of Elizabeth Stuart Phelps Ward, an American who wanted to make heaven seem more real to her readers than the Bible and established religion were doing. She said church theology was too cold, dry, and hard for her taste.

In fact, thousands of Ward's contemporaries felt the same way. America had just suffered through the Civil War, and many were mourning the loss of friends and relations and questioning the purpose of existence. Some of the most serious questioning was coming from women. After all, women suffered through the war, too

The Devil Makes You Do It

Don't be fooled by the Biblical subject matter and literary treatment of the early 19th-century angel tales by Byron and the others. In her book *England's Amorous Angels* (Atlanta-Maryland University Press of America, 1990), scholar Gayle Shadduck claims that this literature represents the first "pulp fiction" written in English!

Wing Tip

Many of the best and most influential religious ideas have been inspired by the desire for comfort in bad times.

and endured the loss of loved ones, but had very little say in the course of events that led to the loss and destruction.

Ward believed that women, in particular, stood to gain from a new, warmer, and more personal sense of heaven than the sterile, icy place that religious authorities often made it out to be. So she wrote a novel called *The Gates Ajar* (1869), in which a wise woman who lost her husband helps other grieving women by telling them about the comforts of heaven in terms they can appreciate. This heaven is a very human place, with nice houses and good food, and society is set up so that people get special respect, not as a result of their accomplishments, but because of how nice they are. As a result, women who went through life simply and meekly, being nice to others, got the recognition Ward felt they deserved!

Revelations

In Ward's day, it was commonly believed that a woman's proper sphere of activity was the home, and that women should stay out of worldly affairs, but be caring, supportive, and sympathetic without having strong opinions of their own. In a famous speech called "Professions for Women" (published in "The Death of The Moth and Other Essays," Harcourt and Brace, 1942) read before the Women's Service League, author Virginia Woolf personified this belief as "the Angel in the House." She said she had to do battle with and finally kill this angel in order to write.

Ward's book became a huge hit, not only with women in America, but in England, too. It was soon translated into French, Italian, German, and Dutch. The book's popularity prompted Ward to write follow-ups, including *Beyond the Gates* (1883), *The Gates Between* (1887), and *Within the Gates* (1901). *Beyond the Gates* tells of the out-of-body experiences of a woman who is seriously ill from fever. While she's on her sickbed, her soul visits heaven and meets the soul of her father who had died long before.

An Amusing Twain of Thought

Since Ward's books came out, many noted writers have taken on the job of fleshing out heaven, both imagining what it might be like, and making fun of conventional ideas about it. One of these is Mark Twain, who, after writing *Tom Sawyer* and *Huckleberry Finn*, wrote *Captain Stormfield's Visit to Heaven* (1909), about a poorly educated but widely experienced sea captain who goes to the next world. Twain uses the crusty, worldly-wise captain to poke fun, among other things, at the traditional notion of angels.

345

In Twain's book, people get to do whatever they want in heaven. On first arriving, what everyone *thinks* they want is to dress up in flowing white robes and halos, wave palm branches, and play golden harps in the clouds. The story tells of millions of new arrivals, eagerly equipping themselves with harps and halos and setting off joyously for the nearest cloud bank. After a few hours of playing harps in the clouds, however, they start to realize that this idea of heaven is actually a ridiculous waste of time, so they ditch their harps and halos and set off in search of more productive things to do.

Revelations

Many artists and intellectuals have suggested that conventional ideas of heaven are boring and insipid. Poet Wallace Stevens asks,

Is there no change of death in paradise?
Does ripe fruit never fall? Or do the boughs
Hang always heavy in that perfect sky,
Unchanging, yet so like our perishing earth
With rivers like our own that seek for seas
They never find...?

Similarly, songwriter David Byrne says, "Heaven is a place where nothing ever happens."

More in Heaven and Earth

Since Twain's tale, a number of short stories have suggested changes in traditional notions of heaven. One of these is "Mr. Andrews" by E.M. Forster, published in his book *The Eternal Moment and Other Stories* (Harcourt, Brace and World, 1928). (Forster is famous for several books that were made into popular screen costume-dramas, including *A Passage to India*, *A Room With a View*, and *Howard's End*.)

In the story, Mr. Andrews is an Englishman who has just died and, on the way to heaven, meets up with the soul of a devout Muslim. On the way, they become friends, but each is saddened to think that the other, as an "unbeliever," is unlikely to get into heaven! They are delighted when it turns out that they both are allowed in.

Another revisionary take on the hereafter is presented in "Aerial Football: The New Game," by the famous English playwright G.B. Shaw, reprinted by the society of authors. The story tells of the soul of a stodgy English bishop who arrives in heaven expecting to be treated with dignity and respect, but is offended to find that the saints and angels treat him casually, the same way they treat everyone else. So he stalks out of the gates of heaven in a huff!

He comes back soon after, however, compelled by an unexplainable urge. Giving a yell, he takes off his bishop's apron, puts it inside his bishop's hat, and kicks it into the sky. The saints and angels yell too, and they all take off after the hat to play a rousing game of aerial football (that's soccer to us Yanks)! Heaven turns out to be a lot of fun after all!

Revelations

One famous angel tale figures into the history of widely reported angel sightings in 1914. Many English soldiers at the battle of Mons in Belgium against German troops (World War I) claimed that angels came to their aid at a crucial moment in the fighting, turning the tide of battle. English author Arthur Machen claimed he hadn't heard any such reports when, the same year, he wrote his short story, "The Bowmen," which tells of how Saint George and an army of angelic bowmen came to the aid of doomed English soldiers by routing a host of German troops. Machen claims his story gave rise to the "angels of Mons" frenzy.

Gabriel's Angel

In addition to stories that provide fresh conceptions of heaven are a number of tales that portray angels on Earth in an unusual manner. Often, what's unusual is not how unearthly the angels are, but how much they resemble ordinary people. A haunting story by Gabriel Garcia Marquez, "A Very Old Man With Enormous Wings," published in his book *Leaf Storm and Other Stories* (Harper and Rowe, 1971), is one example. It presents a surprising view of what might happen if a disabled angel were to become stranded in a small Latin American town.

The angel in the story is sick and elderly and gets caught in the rain and is unable to fly. He has lost a lot of feathers and his wings have parasites in them. Instead of showing concern for the angel, however, the people of Earth are chiefly worried about whether he can do them any harm and interested in what miracles he can perform for them. He is kept in a chicken coop and fed eggplant mush as people are charged an admission fee to come and see him. Many pluck out the few remaining feathers he has in hopes of obtaining miracles.

The Devil Makes You Do It

Beware of unscrupulous people out to make money by dealing in "miracles." This happened in an episode of the cartoon series *The Simpsons*, when a mysterious angel turned out to be a publicity stunt.

Fortunately for the angel, people eventually lose interest in him, enabling him to recover and fly away. The story shows how short-sighted, selfish, and suspicious people can be, and how these human feelings can prevent us from appreciating the wonders around us. It is told in a dry, matter-of-fact manner, however, and is not the least bit preachy or sentimental.

They Don't Look Jewish

A very different story with a similar theme is Bernard Malamud's "The Angel Levine," published in his book *The Magic Barrel* (Farrar, Strauss and Giroux pub, 1955) about a Jewish tailor in New York City whose guardian angel is black. (The tale was made into a movie in 1970 starring Zero Mostel and Harry Belafonte.) The tailor has a hard time accepting his angel—believing that his is an angel and accepting his help. Eventually, however, his problems pile up, so he sets his prejudice aside so his angel can help him.

In contrast to the very human angels in Marquez' and Malamud's stories is an angel in a story by Edgar Allen Poe called "The Angel of the Odd." The angel is made of liquor containers—a punch bowl for a body, beer kegs for legs, liquor bottles for arms, a canteen for a head, and a funnel for a hat! This angel is responsible for all the bizarre accidents that happen on Earth.

The main character refuses to believe in the angel, despite the fact that it appears to him and talks to him. In revenge, the angel inflicts a sequence of freak accidents on the man. Finally, the man agrees to believe in the angel out of self-defense!

Feeling Our Pain

Even stories with fairly conventional-looking angels manage to seem memorable and unusual. One example is a tale by Howard Fast called "The General Zapped an Angel," (William and Morrow, 1978). The angel in the title role is a larger-than-life Christmas card, twenty feet tall with snow-white skin, blue eyes, and golden hair. Unfortunately, the angel is hit by artillery in the Vietnam war by an American general.

The Devil Makes You Do It

Theologian and critic Duane Garrett expresses the concern that readers of popular angel-adventure novels will confuse the fictional representations of angels they contain for spiritual truths. Garrett prefers novels that advance orthodox Christian theology.

The angel's body is taken to a hangar as military chaplains argue about where it should be stored. A Catholic priest wants it taken to the Vatican. A Jewish rabbi thinks it should go to Jerusalem. Everybody has different ideas about what the angel means. Meanwhile, the press are beating down the doors for the story. Fortunately, the angel was only hurt and recovers. The angel is not resentful and does not punish anyone, but is patient about everything. He only shakes his head as if to say, "These human beings are a piece of work!"

Another injured angel tale is "It Had Wings" by Allan Gurganus (published in his book *White People*, Alfred Knopf pub, 1991), about a lonely, elderly widow who finds a hurt angel in her back yard. The story describes the delightful manner in which the angel is nursed back to health: He becomes healed by soaking up the woman's infirmities! She buries her arthritic hands in his sprained wings and the result is that her arthritis goes away as his wings become sound again. The angel is further nurtured by taking on the woman's emotional woes and worries. By the time the angel is ready to fly again, the woman feels terrific!

Angel Adventure

Angel stories of recent years have taken the form of swashbuckling, good-against-evil adventure novels. Fueling the rise of angel popularity over the past two decades have been novels that portray angels as adventure heroes and spiritual warriors. These popular warrior angels really know how to give demons hell!

Dark Doings

By now a minor classic among contemporary conservative Christians is the novel *This Present Darkness* (1986) by Frank Peretti. The novel pits handsome, muscular angels against ugly, smelly demons in swashbuckling holy warfare. Corresponding to, and involved in, the supernatural action are events that take place in the small college town of Ashton, where decent, God-fearing Christians squabble with demonic New Agers and diabolical teachers and administrators over the souls of the community!

The bad news is, there's a whole infernal crew of demons, possessing half the town's inhabitants. The good news is, once the demons get exorcised, everyone turns out to be Christian underneath it all, so their troubles go away. After all, there are angels like Tal and Guilo on the scene, who carry angelic swords, capable of slashing the demons back to the abyss. What's more, human beings can help the angels win their battles through prayer.

In fact, when the chips are down in a climactic battle between Tal and the evil demon, Rafar, it is human prayer that gives the angel the strength he needs to overcome his adversary. Critics have hailed Peretti as a conservative Christian Stephen King, on account of his flair for supernatural suspense. *This Present Darkness* was followed by *Piercing the Darkness* in 1989.

Garden Guardian

Another popular angel page-turner is *Stedfast: Guardian Angel* (1992) by Roger Elwood. The title character tells his own story, and he's got a lot to tell. He got started in the guardian angel racket way back in the Garden of Eden where Adam was his first assignment. As he tells of his adventures, he sheds a garish white Christian light on all sorts of perplexing historical and theological issues. For example, according to Stedfast (who is a fan of confederate Civil War general Robert E. Lee), most slaves were happy with their lives on Southern plantations!

Stedfast also gets involved in the debate over abortion, weighing in heavily with the right-to-lifers. He says that an angel is present in the womb with every human fetus as it develops. If the fetus is aborted, the angel carries the unborn soul to heaven, where it can mature to spiritual adulthood. (Evidently, heaven isn't a bad place to grow up, especially since dogs go to heaven, too.) Stedfast says heaven is full of the souls of aborted babies who would have been presidents and great scientists!

Stedfast does battle for human souls with ugly demons, one of which is Satan. Another demon is called Observer. It's finally up to God where human souls end up, and not the angels or demons. The Stedfast book is the first of a trilogy, including *Angelwalk* and *Fallen Angel*.

Wing Tip

Don't be surprised to find people using angels to support bizarre notions of history and politics. After all, there are angels for just about everything!

See You in the Funny Papers

For those of you who yearn for graphic angel action, you'll be glad to know that angels have made their appearance in comic books! Most notably, Image Comics and Maximum Press have come out with "Avengelyne," a sexy fallen angel doing time on Earth for her celestial sins. Although she lives as a mortal, she is super-strong and, as a former *warrior* of God, knows how to handle a sword.

In fact, Avengelyne combines the theological concept of an angelic warrior with the comic book concept of a superhero warrior. Once an angel warrior, she becomes an earthly comic book warrior in order to continue the battle against the forces of evil. (Ordinarily, comic books don't draw on theology. For example, the "X-man" warrior known as "Angel" never had divine powers, but is a mutant human with wings.)

Winged Words

The term **warrior** has a particular meaning in the world of angels as well as in the world of comics. In comics, the term is applied to any superhero who battles the forces of evil. Among angels, "warriors" are sometimes considered a distinct class of angels. (Milton uses the term this way, for example, in *Paradise Lost*.)

Avengelyne teams up with a Ninja warrior named Cybrid and a Catholic priest named Preacher John to battle cyborg Ninjas and demons who look like lizard men on steroids. In one episode, she is visited from heaven by her younger angel sister, Divinity, who is not a "warrior," but a "messenger." She turns out to be an impish troublemaker who has the hots for Preacher John! She uses her angel powers to make herself look like Avengelyne in order to seduce him, but before she gets a chance, she's kidnapped by demons who think she's Avengelyne! (They wrap her up in a demonic tapestry that neutralizes angelic powers and take her to the underworld.) Now it's up to Avengelyne and Preacher John to find and rescue her.

The Avengelyne series went through twelve issues in the mid-1990s. Many are still available in stores that sell comic books.

Angels on Stage

An especially topical and controversial angelic work is Tony Kushner's Pulitzer Prize-winning play, *Angels in America: A Gay Fantasia on National Themes*. Among other things, the play is about a gay man named Prior Walter who has AIDS, who is visited by an angel and called to be a prophet. The angel appears numerous times and reveals to him the location of a large book, a flaming Hebrew letter aleph, and other visions. At one point, Prior and the angel wrestle. At other times, they both become sexually aroused!

Prior is reluctant to assume the mantle of prophecy, despite his numerous visions. His health is bad and getting worse. To add to his troubles, his lover has left him in his time of need. As a result, he doesn't feel like spreading divine messages to the world.

As it turns out, the angels in heaven know what it's like to have someone walk out on them. It seems that God walked out on the angels decades ago and hadn't been heard from since! According to the play, he left heaven on April 18, 1906, the day a major earthquake devastated San Francisco.

The angels have decided that the human and divine problems everyone is faced with stem from too much moving around and they want it stopped. This is the message they want Prior Walter to deliver to the world. Even though he can relate to this message, having been abandoned himself, he decides he can't do it, so he makes a trip to heaven to return the book.

When he arrives, heaven is a mess. In fact, it looks just like San Francisco after the earthquake! The angels have been having a tough time without God. Instead of resorting to prophecy, Prior recommends the angels "sue the bastard for walking out."

Angels in America caused a sensation in the years following its debut in 1991. Although many have found it disturbing, theater-goers and critics have been impressed with its political wisdom, poetic depth, and humor. Many regard it as the most important theater production in decades. Literary critic Harold Bloom went so far as to include it in his book, *The Western Canon* (1994) as one of the most important literary works ever written in the West.

A concluding scene from *Angels in America* takes place near Bethesda fountain in Central Park in New York City. In this scene, we learn that the fountain was named for a fountain in Jerusalem

Wing Tip

You can think of angel appearances as divine special effects. Prior Walter, the angel seer in Tony Kushner's play, *Angels in America*, describes his angelic visions as being "very Steven Spielberg!"

mentioned in the Bible as having healing powers. According to legend, this fountain sprang up in ancient times at the spot where an angel set foot in Jerusalem. It ran dry, however, when the Temple was destroyed. They say its healing waters will flow again when the millennium comes.

The Least You Need to Know

➤ Narrative poems about angels falling in love with human women were popular in England in the early 19th century.

➤ American writer Elizabeth Stuart Phelps Ward became hugely popular in the late 19th century for portraying heaven as a warm, livable community.

➤ Many angel stories of the 20th century challenge traditional theological notions about angels and heaven.

➤ Frank Peretti and Roger Elwood have written popular adventure novels about angels in recent years.

➤ Comic book angel Avengelyne is a former heavenly warrior fallen to earth.

Reel Angels

Heaven knows, anything as irresistible as angels has got to wind up in feature films and TV shows. After all, there are so many ways to go with the heavenly visitor theme. They're just the ticket for pulling off a picture-perfect happy ending at the last minute, or for injecting an element of mystery and romance into ordinary life. And for light humor, it's hard to get any lighter than jokes about heaven.

In fact, angels on screen tend to be pretty lightweight. I guess something heavy like *Paradise Lost* wouldn't make much of a film—too much dialogue, and the price of special effects would be out of this world for the battle scenes alone. Even so, despite the limitations imposed by the medium, angels have made myriad appearances on film.

There are all kinds of angel shows: mostly romantic comedies and melodramas, but also mysteries and thrillers. It's true that most of these fall short of blockbuster status, but there is one bona fide all-time great classic angel movie: *It's a Wonderful Life*. And many of the others are well worth checking out.

Us and Them

In general, when angels appear in movies, there are two things going on: Usually, a human being (or a group of human beings) has a problem and the angel is going to solve it. And usually, the angel has a life (so to speak) and a personality of its own, which influence the way the problem gets worked out. Some movies focus more on the human-problem side of it, going for that touching, sentimental effect. Others emphasize the angel's situation in order to inject a little heavenly humor. Both aspects almost always come into play at least to some extent.

A Good Fight

Among the first, and best, angel films to come out of Hollywood is *Here Comes Mr. Jordan* (1941) about a cocky prizefighter named Joe who dreams of becoming cham-

pion. He's ambitious and self-confident, so he wouldn't ordinarily need angelic assistance, except that he gets caught up in the complexities of heavenly bureaucracy. The result is a sequence of out-of-body run-arounds that make for some good celestial situation comedy.

In addition to boxing, Joe is fond of playing his lucky saxophone and flying his own one-man plane. Unfortunately, while flying himself to a fight, his plane takes a nose-dive, and it looks like it's all over for Joe and his dreams. Even his guardian angel thought he'd bought a last one-way ticket to heaven.

It turns out, though, that Joe's guardian angel makes a big mistake in assuming Joe was KO'd for good. Of course, he had the best intentions. He didn't want Joe to have to suffer an agonizing death, so he slipped in just before the plane crashed and carried his soul off to heaven.

The Devil Makes You Do It

Here Comes Mr. Jordan (1941) was remade in 1978 as *Heaven Can Wait*. Neither of these should be confused with another movie called *Heaven Can Wait*, made in 1943, which concerns the life of a married playboy who has died and must go either to heaven or hell. As it turns out, adultery is okay after all, so he gets to go to heaven!

Revelations

There is a rich tradition of angels filling the role of soul-carriers of the dead, or "psycho-pomps" as they are sometimes called. Often, the angel is said to carry the dead soul to heaven where the acts of the soul during its stay on Earth are read from the book of life. At the point, an angel of Judgment or God himself determines the final destination of the soul. The movie *Here Comes Mr. Jordan* is premised on an angelic error in carrying out this process.

When Joe's soul gets to heaven, it turns out that they weren't expecting him. The angel in charge (Mr. Jordan, played by Claude Rains) informs him and his bumbling guardian that he wasn't scheduled to die for another 50 years! In the meantime, he still had a rich, full life in store.

Restless Spirit

Joe's guardian angel, who is new at the business, made a rookie mistake that would have to be fixed. He and Joe went back to the scene of the accident so Joe's soul could re-enter his body. Unfortunately, the body had already been taken away and cremated! As you may imagine, Joe's soul was livid. He wanted a new body and insisted that it be as strong and fit as the old one. This wouldn't be easy, since he used to be in such good shape.

So Joe, his guardian, and Mr. Jordan scour the earth for a new body. During the search, Joe's soul witnesses the troubles of a beautiful woman whose father has been falsely convicted and put into jail for stock fraud. He agrees to take over the body of the wealthy and crooked financier who is about to be murdered by his wife and personal secretary, in hopes of helping the woman and of getting together with her.

Joe succeeds in setting things straight in his new body and he and his dream girl fall in love. Meanwhile he starts training for the ring again. (It seems he was destined in heaven to win a championship fight.) At this point, however, Joe's soul goes back to square one again, when the wife and secretary of his new self succeed in killing him.

The mess finally resolves when Joe enters the body of a murdered boxer just in time to avoid a knockout and come back to win the championship fight! Mr. Jordan seals Joe's fate by making him forget his previous identities. Despite this angel-induced amnesia, the new man gets back together both with his old manager (who had given him his lucky saxophone back when he was Joe) and, you guessed it, with the woman of his dreams. (They each felt there was something about the other that they couldn't explain!)

Here Comes Mr. Jordan inspired numerous imitations, most notably the popular remake, *Heaven Can Wait* (1978) starring Warren Beatty as a disembodied pro football player. Unfortunately, most angel movies (and there have been dozens) are not as imaginative as these two. Still, there are a few other shining lights that do justice to their angelic premises.

The Devil Makes You Do It

Never discourage the one you love from falling in love again after you're dead. The new lover may turn out to be you in a different body!

Reel *Life*

Undoubtedly the best angel movie ever made is Frank Capra's *It's a Wonderful Life* (1946), starring Jimmy Stewart as the struggling George Bailey, who has sacrificed his personal ambitions for the sake of his small-town community of Bedford Falls. This movie makes classic use of the guardian angel motif. George's angel appears at a crucial moment to help give him a new perspective on his life. The great thing about the film is the way the angel (kindly and unprepossessing Clarence Oddbody) gets George to change his attitude.

Revelations

As an A–S2 (angel second class), Clarence from *It's a Wonderful Life* is limited in sight and power. At the start of the film, he has to rely on the powers of a superior angel named Joseph to understand the situation on Earth into which his assignment will take him. On completing this assignment, he will not only "get his wings," but acquire the ability to see things more clearly.

Taking the Plunge

As you probably know from watching the movie many times already, George reaches an especially tough and frustrating point in a tough and frustrating life. It seems that years of hard work and sacrifice for the sake of his community have come to nothing. The Building and Loan company he runs, which has helped low-income working people build houses so they could move out of the slums, is on the verge of collapse, thanks to the absent-minded Uncle Billy, who accidentally dumped an envelope containing $8,000 into the lap of the mean and miserly Mr. Potter. George faces arrest on account of the missing funds, and on top of that, knows deep down that the town of Bedford Falls will go to the dogs once the Building and Loan is gone and the gouging Mr. Potter takes over.

Filled with shame, despair, and disgust, he finds himself on a bridge and prepares to leap to his death into the icy waters below. (As it turns out, the waters aren't that icy or that far below.) Fortunately, the angel Clarence

Wing Tip

Notice how the attempted suicide scene contrasts with the earlier scene at Harry's high school prom in which everyone falls or jumps into the pool. Getting wet is all part of being human.

prevents the suicide by jumping in first, so that George, instead of killing himself, dives in to save Clarence. As the two dry out afterwards in a nearby shack, Clarence hits on a plan to help George put his life in perspective.

It Might Have Been

Clarence gets his bright idea when George mutters that he wishes he had never been born. Realizing what a difference that would make, Clarence grants the wish in order to show George how important his life has been. It soon becomes clear that, without George, the town of Bedford Falls (re-named "Pottersville") is a lousy place to live.

Actually, George remains alive, but loses his identity. None of his former friends know who he is, so instead of the friendship and kindness he is used to, he is treated with suspicion by everyone he meets. The suspicion results not simply because George is a stranger, but because everyone's quality of life has plummeted. Without George the Building and Loan closes, so working people have a hard time. They act mean and frightened and want to be left alone.

And those are the lucky ones! George's brother Harry is dead, Uncle Billy is in an insane asylum, his former employer at the drugstore is a broken-down alcoholic, and Violet, a girl he grew up with, is a showgirl whose home gets raided by the police. His wife Mary is a timid librarian and his mother is a haggard boarding-house keeper. Both are terrified of strangers and refuse to talk to him.

The film provides a bleak but believable picture of a society bogged down in fear and selfishness. Suddenly, the light situation comedy has changed into *film noire*. The grim flavor of life in Pottersville is made especially vivid by the presence of the stranger who we know is George Bailey, horrified to find his hometown has no place for him now that his connections to people have been severed. It is these human connections, the movie suggests, that determine the quality of people's lives.

Pursued by a policeman (who used to be his friend), George finds himself back on the bridge where, earlier that evening, he had contemplated suicide. This time, he prays to get his old life back. The prayer is answered, of course. When the policeman catches up to him, he doesn't want to shake down an addled stranger but help out an old friend.

Few movies have happy endings as ecstatic as *It's a Wonderful Life*. It's hard to keep from smiling when George comes home to find his friends have come over on Christmas Eve with bucketfuls of cash to replace the lost money. Clarence, too, gets a happy ending, since he finally gets his wings for a job well done.

Wing Tip

Clarence Oddbody says, "No one is a failure as long as he's got friends."

High–Fly Films

A couple of popular films with heavenly humor are the two versions of *Angels in the Outfield* (1951 and 1994), about a major league baseball team that turns around a losing season with the help of a team of angels. (After all, there are plenty of good ballplayers who have been called up to the big leagues in the sky!) In the earlier version, the Pittsburgh Pirates find themselves in the bottom of the standings, despite their many talented players. The team's troubles can be traced to the crusty manager, played by Paul Douglas, whose foul mouth and bad temper bring bad luck for everyone.

Fortunately for the team and their fans, a little orphan girl named Bridget prays for the manager. As a result, he receives a visit from the angel Gabriel who tells him that if he cleans up his language, the Heavenly Choir Nine baseball team from beyond the blue will make sure the Pirates win games. Sure enough, the manager stops cussing and the team starts making miracle plays.

As it turns out, Bridget is the only one who can see the angels when they appear on the field. The story gets out that she and the manager believe that angels are helping the team win games, so the Pirates leader must appear before the baseball commissioner to answer questions. Fortunately, an interdenominational panel of theologians shows up in time to say that it's A-OK to believe in angels!

Right before the championship game, the manager loses control of his temper and loses his heavenly back-up players, but the underdog Pirates pull off a miracle win anyway. As if that wasn't enough good news, the Pirates manager decides to adopt little Bridget, along with a gorgeous household-hints columnist-turned sports writer named Jennifer Paige, and everyone decides he isn't such a bad guy after all.

Revelations

Baseball in America is often thought of in religious terms. Other movies that deal with America's reverence for baseball are *The Natural* (1984), which presents the game as magical and mythological; and *Field of Dreams* (1989), in which a farmer receives a prophetic message to build a baseball field in order to host a game played by the ghosts of famous ballplayers.

Angel Makes Three

Many angel movies are love stories in which angels help people straighten out their relationships. Of course, match-making and marriage-counseling angels can't just zap people and change their personalities; changes have to take place slowly in response to miracles that teach people something. In fact, angels in love stories sometimes have to explain that their powers are limited. The real work of falling in love always rests with the human beings involved.

Domestic Bliss

A classic angel-assisted love story is *The Bishop's Wife* (1947), starring Cary Grant as the charming and genial angel Dudley, who answers a bishop's prayer for help. Bishop Braugham, played by David Niven, is struggling to raise funds for a new cathedral, and is in the midst of stalled negotiations with an arrogant patroness who wants to make the cathedral into a monument to her dead husband.

Looking back after fifty years, *The Bishop's Wife* seems a little dated. The bishop has a maid, a cook, a secretary, a rich benefactor, and a devoted wife, so it's kind of hard to see why he really needs a guardian angel, too. His problem, as it turns out, is that he doesn't take the time to enjoy what he has. In fact, the bishop expects the angel to help him with his work, but Dudley focuses instead on teaching him to relax.

It seems that the bishop has been working so hard on fund-raising that he doesn't have time to spend time with his wife Julia and their young daughter. The cathedral is a good cause, of course, but it's interfering with the marriage. When the bishop is forced to break a lunch date with Julia, Dudley steps in to take his place.

Of course, Dudley and Julia have a swell time. Meanwhile, things just keep getting worse for the bishop. He finally decides to knuckle under to the demands of the rich widow who wants to glorify her late husband. As if that weren't bad enough, he starts to suspect that Julia is falling in love with Dudley.

At the last minute, Dudley goes to see the rich widow and charms her into changing her mind about using the cathedral to memorialize her husband. It seemed she never really loved him anyway. The bishop, however, is not all that appreciative of Dudley's efforts. Instead, he starts to panic because he thinks he's lost his wife's affection.

He gets some timely advice from a human friend, however, and manfully claims his wife as his own. A good thing, too, because, as it turns out, Dudley actually has developed a crush on Julia. Even though she likes to have a good time, Julia remains as pure as the driven snow, and never gives up on the bishop. When Dudley leaves, he casts an angelic spell so that no one remembers him, gratified by the knowledge that he averted some minor unpleasantness in the life of a man who didn't have much reason to complain to begin with.

The Devil Makes You Do It

Be careful about praying for angelic assistance when you're having difficulties in a love relationship. An angel might show up and try to steal your lover!

Revelations

Because they're comedies, angel films like *The Bishop's Wife* often deal with problems that really aren't all that serious, including work-related difficulties and mix-ups in love. The weightier problems of good and evil and life and death tend to get left aside. A notable exception to this rule, of course, is *It's a Wonderful Life*, in which the main character is driven to the brink of suicide.

Angel Fluff

Dudley is a fairly sophisticated angel. He's a great figure skater, speaks fluent French, plays the harp, and dresses well. He appears to have no human failings, except maybe for his susceptibility to Julia's charms, which can be seen as a good thing, since the point of the movie is that it's good to enjoy people and things. These traits make him very different from a match-making angel in the 1996 movie, *Michael*, starring John Travolta in the title role.

Unlike Cary Grant's Dudley, Michael is gross. He has a beer gut, smokes a lot, is a messy eater, and scratches his private parts in public. Like Dudley, however, Michael really appreciates earthly pleasures—especially having sex with women, but also fighting and doing campy things like going to see the world's biggest ball of yarn. Despite his quirks, though, he has a great attitude about life, which rubs off on the pair of reluctant lovers he has come to help, played by William Hurt and Andie McDowell.

Michael's great attitude has to do with the fact that he's in the same boat we are (us humans, that is). It seems angels only get to perform a certain number of miracles before they have to hang up their wings for good, and Michael has just about reached the bottom of his bag of tricks. He is wistful about the prospect of leaving Earth and he wants to have a good time while he's got the chance.

Wing Tip

It's probably best to hold off asking for a miracle unless you really need one. Otherwise, there may not be enough to go around.

For a while there, it looks like he's left with one miracle too few, since he's unexpectedly called upon to bring back to life a very important dog that was hit by a truck. (The dog is a gimmick used by the tabloid journalist played by William Hurt. He has come to do a story on Michael for his paper.) In fact, Michael runs out of celestial steam before Hurt is ready to commit to

McDowell. In the last reel, he sheds all his feathers, collapses, and finally disappears, leaving the human beings to muddle through their problems on their own.

And muddle they do—so much so that it comes as a complete surprise when, in a moment of desperation, William asks Andie to marry him, despite the fact that neither one has shown much in the way of sense or commitment skills. The uplifting message of the movie is that it's great to fall in love, even if you have a long history of romantic failures and no good reason to believe that this time will be any different!

Down to Earth

A different kind of angel love story focuses on romance between angels and human beings. This kind of story provides a twist on the "men are from Mars, women are from Venus" idea in suggesting that men are from heaven, women are from Earth. Of course, as most people realize, men aren't actually from heaven. To many, though, it can seem that they have to be in order to be viable prospects for a relationship!

Revelations

A number of movies deal with the theme of romantic attraction between angels and humans. Most notable of these are *I Married an Angel* (1942), in which an angel enters the love life of a playboy; *Date With an Angel* (1987), which tells an angelic tale of young love; *Always* (1989), in which a recently disembodied soul is assigned to serve as guardian angel to the lover of his former girlfriend; and *Faraway, So Close* (1993), which is the sequel to *Wings of Desire*.

This is a subtle suggestion of Wim Wenders' artsy *Wings of Desire* (1988), about an angel who falls in love with an Earth girl and decides to trade in his wings for a chance at human-style romance. Of course, he doesn't really know what he's getting into, either by falling in love or falling to Earth. He can't resist finding out, though, so after an eternity of providing spiritual comfort to a sea of vulnerable humanity, he tries mortality on for size.

The film is quite poetic and philosophical, portraying life as a complex experience driven by mysterious but ultimately good desires, despite its many hardships. It's fun to watch the angels, who are invisible to the movie's mortals, but not to the viewers, as they watch and listen to people and comfort them just by coming near. They hang out at the Berlin Library (the film is mostly in German, with English subtitles) but range throughout the city, keeping track of unusual human moments for reasons that never become entirely clear.

Wings of Desire was remade as the Hollywood film *City of Angels* (1998), with Nicolas Cage as the angel, Seth, who falls in love with Maggie, a surgeon played by Meg Ryan. In the Wenders film, the female love interest is a trapeze artist who wears angel wings as part of her act. She's the struggling-artist type. In contrast, Meg Ryan's Maggie is a hardworking, scientific sort. Still, she has her sensitive side, as we see from her reaction to losing a patient.

Seth falls for Maggie when he sees how devoted she is to her patients and he wants to help her out as a human being instead of as an angel. It is Maggie, though, who faces the biggest challenge in coming to terms with the relationship. This aspect of the plot of *City of Angels* makes it different from *Wings of Desire*.

The Devil Makes You Do It

As *Wings of Desire* suggests, things that seem unimportant to you may not be unimportant to others—including God and the angels.

Even so, the two films are quite similar in the mood they set and in emphasizing the mood over plot. In both films, you get a lot of footage of the big city (Berlin or Los Angeles; the latter of course is Spanish for "city of angels"). The urban setting emphasizes the bigness and complexity of the human predicament and the challenges of being human. That's one reason for the appeal of watching an angelic being struggle with the decision to become one of the human crowd.

Networking

Wings of Desire and *City of Angels* are somewhat unusual among angel films, which have tended to be comedies rather than serious dramas. In contrast, angels on TV have tended to be dramas. A forgettable exception is *Good Heavens,* a show airing in 1976 about an angel in a pinstripe suit who grants people wishes. A 1982 pilot, *The Kid With a Broken Halo,* never got off the ground.

Wing Tip

Watch for religious symbolism incorporated into episodes of *Touched by an Angel.* Situations in the show often suggest scriptural and legendary things and events.

Getting Serious

Television dramas have been more successful. Angels made occasional appearances on episodes of *The Twilight Zone* in the 1960s. Updating the supernatural slant of *The Twilight Zone* for the 1990s is *The X-Files*, which has featured angels in at least one episode.

Highway to Heaven, starring Michael Landon as the earthbound angel Jonathan Smith, was popular in the 1980s. Posing as a traveling odd-jobber, Jonathan wandered around on miscellaneous rescue missions, helping those in need while helping viewers to plenty of warmth and sentiment. The show was one of Landon's last roles before he died of cancer. He was best known as *Bonanza*'s Little Joe.

Television angels get righteous in the 1990s on *Touched by an Angel*, starring gospel singer Della Reese, Roma Downey, and John Dye as angels Tess, Monica, and Andrew, respectively. These angels aren't afraid to throw a little holy weight around in order to promote human rights. They have been known to say things like "We're angels of God, and you'd better do the right thing!" Even so, their high moral tone doesn't prevent them from sympathizing with good folks in need.

The Least You Need to Know

➤ Angel features tend to be romantic comedies or melodramas.

➤ *Here Comes Mr. Jordan* presents heaven as a mysterious bureaucracy.

➤ *It's a Wonderful Life* is a comedy interrupted by a brilliant *film noire* segment.

➤ Good angel–human love stories are *Wings of Desire* and the remake, *City of Angels*.

➤ Popular TV angel melodramas are *Highway to Heaven* and *Touched by an Angel*.

Unaccountable Encounters

In This Chapter

➤ First-hand angel reports

➤ Disillusionment with science and technology

➤ Evaluating (and *not* evaluating) angel encounters

➤ Accounts from Sophy Burnham, *Time* magazine, and Billy Graham

There hasn't been anything in history quite like the recent interest in angelic appearances that seems to have taken hold of growing numbers of people these days. That's why this last chapter goes best by itself. It won't tell you whether angels really exist or not, but help you decide for yourself. At any rate, perhaps you'll see why so many people are getting high on angels.

Not so long ago, when most people still had faith in "progress," anyone who went around saying they saw angels would be considered a prime candidate for the insane asylum. The idea was that people could take care of themselves without the aid of supernatural assistance. Why worry about angels when modern science can supply you with every necessity and convenience?

These days, however, lots of people are claiming to have seen or experienced angels. Instead of being thought loopy, angel seers are often heard with respectful attention, interest, and belief. Scientific rules for testing reality—and scientific solutions for human problems—seem far less interesting and appealing to growing numbers of angel watchers.

This is not to say that angel appearances prove that the scientists have been wrong about reality all this time—they don't. It does seem, though, that the social and spiritual climate is right for increased angel migrations to Earth. Of course, many rationalists complain that it isn't the weather that's turned balmy, but the people who claim to have seen angels. Increasingly, however, rationalist grousing is ignored as more and more people listen instead for the flutter of angel wings.

Wing Tip

It's usually not a good idea to spend too much energy trying to disprove reported sightings of angels. Few people will appreciate your efforts!

Divine Demographics

According to a poll conducted by *Time* magazine in 1993, nearly a third of Americans have sensed an angelic presence. Angel reports indicate that celestial visitors have a variety of ways of making themselves known. An angel may appear as a light, a touch, an inward sense, an ordinary-looking person, or an unearthly being. Some say that a single angel can manifest itself in different forms to different people at the same time. Whether, and how, such reports can be verified often seems beside the point.

We're Number One

People who claim to have experienced angels identify a variety of purposes for angelic visits. Angels rescue those in trouble, warn those about to get into trouble, heal the sick, provide comfort and encouragement to the sad and discouraged, proclaim or signify the power of God, and assign selected human beings special tasks. All these purposes have the result of making those who experience angels feel especially significant. After all, if some form of divine power singles you out for recognition, you must be pretty important. In fact, by making people feel important, angels are doing what religious ideas have always done.

Virtually all religious and mythological thinking from prehistoric times points to the idea that people have central importance in the universe. Reality itself is all about us. The importance of human beings is woven into the material of the universe. People have cosmic significance and, conversely, the significance of the cosmos boils down to people.

Religion says we are made in the image of God, who cares about us deeply. It says the world is a testing ground for our immortal souls, which will go on to reap reward or punishment for our actions and beliefs. This means God understands us perfectly and that we matter to God as individuals, as groups, and as a species.

Religions Are Us

For centuries, traditional wisdom has supported this idea. When lightning strikes, the reason has something to do with human beings. Floods and droughts are divine responses to human behavior. Unexplainable events are somehow meant to be mysterious, so that people can keep thinking about what it is these events have to do with them.

It may not be so surprising that myth and religion are centered on human beings, since we are the ones who invented them. Wherever you go, people seem to need to think they are important. As a result, we act as if things that exist and things that happen are somehow designed with us in mind. In fact, religious beliefs have helped keep society organized by giving people ideas about how they fit into a larger scheme of things. For example, religion often tells those who have little political and economic power within society that they are important, too. It also tells those in charge of things not to be too heavy-handed and controlling.

In fact, the pervasiveness of people-centered thinking tends to encourage us to think it's true—people are, somehow, at the center of the universe. However important people may be in a cosmic sense, we are vitally important to one another, and religious ideas—including angels—provide us with expressions of this importance and with guidelines for interacting with one another.

The Devil Makes You Do It

If you keep acting as if you're at the center of the universe long enough, you're likely to find yourself left out entirely!

Science Takes Over

The gradual development of scientific thinking has led many people to doubt our cosmic importance as a species and as individuals. Science tells us that the universe is far older and much bigger than we had imagined. It turns out that people occupy only a tiny portion of the seemingly endless stretches of time and space that make up reality. Our existence can be accounted for as an endless series of evolutionary accidents. Even our most profound religious ideas make sense as mere wishful thinking and self-serving *propaganda*. (In fact, the word "propaganda" comes from the name of a group within the Catholic Church in charge of spreading Catholic beliefs.)

Winged Words

Propaganda is the effort to spread a particular set of ideas and beliefs. Today, the word usually refers to political ideas, but originally it comes from the name of a group within the Catholic Church organized to spread or "propagate" Catholicism.

Science, however, does not completely refute the notion that people are important. In fact, the idea is so hard to get away from that pretty much everyone, including scientists, tend to think they are especially important in some way. For centuries now, the importance of science has had a lot to do with the hope that it will improve the quality of human life. Scientists, and all those who believe in science, have always liked to think that their efforts and ideas are improving the world.

In many respects, science has made good on this promise, enabling world-changing technological advances in virtually every area of human existence: medicine, agriculture, transportation, and recreation. Science and technology have been so successful

367

that, for many people around the world, the ideal of "progress" has provided an alternative to traditional religious beliefs. Like religion, this ideal offers hope and assurance—not in God, but in the ability of humanity to take care of itself.

Angelic Answers

These days, although many continue to have faith in the ideal of progress, growing numbers of people have serious doubts about the potential of science and technology to continue improving human life. Although in theory science can provide unlimited benefits, in practice it is often misapplied. As a result, despite centuries of scientific "progress," we are faced with serious problems—problems that science and technology may be unable to solve in and of themselves.

Many believe that, instead of making our lives easier, technology makes us work harder in order to pay for the growing supply of technological products we need to function in an increasingly complex world. Many believe that too much reliance on science and technology has severed important human connections—the kind fostered by religion. What's more, many feel that the sci-tech idea that we can control the world has led to the serious environmental problems we face. As a result, many have been looking for solutions to personal and global problems outside of scientific thinking.

Enter the angels. Angels seem to be increasingly popular these days in part because of growing disillusionment with science and technology. In fact, part of the appeal of angels is that you don't have to be an astrophysicist or a computer genius to appreciate them. All you need is a little faith, and the solutions to your biggest problems may swoop down on you.

Revelations

Recent medical studies have shown that people who pray and have faith in God are more likely to live longer and recover from serious illnesses than those who don't. The studies do not conclude that God rewards those who pray and have faith, but that faith and prayer are psychologically effective and can result in physical as well as mental well-being. Those who lack religious faith tend to feel less of a sense of purpose and importance for their lives. Evidently, this attitude has a harmful effect on people's health over time.

Seeing Through the Angels

Of course, angelic appearances are not consistent with ordinary scientific thinking. Instead, those who think rationally and empirically about angels tend to explain them away. As a result, skeptics tend to remain skeptical despite the growing piles of angelic testimony from so-called eyewitnesses.

Reasonable Doubts

Critics offer a number of responses to those who claim to have seen angels:

➤ *Angel seers may be lying in order to gain prestige, make themselves seem important, or just for fun.* A religious leader or teacher who claims to have seen an angel can obviously claim special authority. Ordinary people can get recognition and attention. And, since lots of people like "strange but true" stories, claiming to have seen an angel can add excitement to everyone's lives.

➤ *Angel seers may be mistaking people for angels.* Often, "angels" appear in human form and help out in ways that would not exceed the abilities of a human being. The angelic aspects of helpful humans may reside in their timely appearances and sudden disappearances. These may seem miraculous, especially to someone who needs help, but may be mere coincidence.

➤ *Angel seers may be hallucinating under stress.* Many accounts of angel appearances come from people who are traumatized or disoriented—for example, in the hospital on medication, after an accident or close call, or during a time of intense emotional or psychological pressure.

➤ *Angel seers may be creating false memories of their experiences.* Memories can be embellished during the process of recollection without people noticing. Details from various experiences may be combined into one event to make people think things happened a certain way, regardless of the facts.

Wing Tip

Stories about mysterious strangers who appear in the nick of time to perform generous acts of rescue and assistance, and then suddenly disappear without waiting to be thanked, are perennially popular. Two examples are the classic TV shows *The Fugitive* and *The Lone Ranger*. We can think of many angel appearances as examples of this type of story.

Fine-Tuned Angelvision

Angel watchers in turn often claim that you need to have an open mind in order to see angels. Angels only appear to those with the right mental and spiritual qualifications, such as faith, purity, innocence, and simplicity. This, they say, is why skeptics who are always trying to poke holes in everything never see angels.

Every once in a while someone tries to use scientific technology to verify a supernatural event or occurrence. Tabloids, for example, sometimes claim to have obtained photographs of heaven or of an angel. More sensible accounts of angels, however, tend not to be overly concerned with proving the experience. Typically, an angelic experience is subjective and its importance is personal.

Angel Earmarks

Of course, even among those who believe in angels, there are different criteria for figuring out whether you've actually seen one. After all, angels don't usually wear signs or "I'm an angel" T-shirts, so whatever it was you experienced may have been something else—a demon, an elf, a ghost, or an extraterrestrial, for example. Different sets of criteria have been put forth by New Agers and Christians.

Wing Tip

It's a good idea to ask what an angel experience means before asking whether or not it really happened.

New Agers say that an angel encounter should leave you feeling good. This goodness may take the form of a sense of love and well-being, including emotional, spiritual, and physical health. This is in keeping with the New Age belief that angels are good for you. This attitude suggests that good feelings do not come from evil sources. Bad spirits make you feel bad; angels make you feel good.

Revelations

Sometimes people claim encounters not only with their own guardian angels, but with the guardian angels of other people. A famous example is the Roman Catholic priest Padre Pio, who claimed to be able to communicate with Jesus, the Virgin Mary, saints, and angels. He achieved great popularity and many came to him for spiritual advice. In order to help larger numbers of people, Padre Pio suggested that people send their guardian to him so that he could advise people through their angels. He claimed to have stayed awake at night consulting with people's angels. When he died in the late 1960s, close to a hundred thousand people came to his funeral.

Christians say that a visit from an angel should leave you feeling clear-headed, despite any sense of wonder you may have. In other words, the angel didn't show up just to give you an emotional high, so a sense of euphoria doesn't mean you've seen an angel.

You may feel encouraged, however, so that you will be better able to serve God. Some mainstream Christians also stress that an angel's appearance must be consistent with scripture. If a supernatural being tells you that you can redeem your soul by taking a breath mint after every meal, it's not an angel. Christian angels advocate salvation through Christ.

In the real world of angel watching, however, there are no rules. Angels are in the eyes of the beholder.

Evidence on the Rise

First-hand accounts of angelic experiences can be found all over—in magazines, in books, and on the Internet. The popularity of these accounts has remained sky-high throughout the 1990s, although many of them predate the last decade of the millennium. A breakthrough best-selling book including many angel-encounter stories is Sophy Burnham's *A Book of Angels* (Ballantine, 1990). Burnham tells of numerous angel appearances, including some she experienced, some she read about, some experienced by friends, and others by people who wrote to her of their encounters.

Divine Coincidence

Many of the experiences Burnham describes are fairly subtle. Many of the people she talks about have sensed angelic assistance in their lives but do not insist that angels are the only explanation for their experiences. Instead, many simply talk about things that happened and how they felt, suggesting angels only as a possibility.

An example is the story of a woman named Susan, who had barely any familiarity with yachting when she became trapped in a storm on a shipwrecked yacht. She said she somehow knew that she would be able to save herself. So she took one of the yacht's life rings and made for shore, despite the enormous waves that were churned up by the storm.

As the huge waves engulfed her, she simply held her breath, waiting for them to pass over. Between each wave she took a breath and kept swimming until she made it to shore. Through the ordeal she felt perfect confidence that she would survive. A more experienced sailor remained on board the yacht after she abandoned ship and was later found dead.

Susan can't explain how she knew what to do or how she knew she would survive, but attributes her knowledge to divine assistance. She didn't hear a voice or see an angelic vision. The only unusual circumstance related to the story, aside from the woman's sense of security, was the fact that prior to the wreck, the yachting party had lost a special wrench—a 5/8-inch spanner—which was needed to

Wing Tip

Keeping calm in an emergency may not always keep you out of danger, but panicking almost never will.

repair the ship's motor. The lack of the wrench was a contributing factor in the ship-wreck. At an inquest into the wreck, Susan noticed the same kind of wrench sitting on a desk in the government office. She interprets this coincidence as evidence that she received divine guidance during the shipwreck.

Revelations

Psychoanalyst Sigmund Freud explained the "uncanny" sense people get when faced with coincidental repetitions of experiences as the result of a repressed instinctual "compulsion to repeat." As infants, said Freud, we find it pleasurable to repeat experiences over and over again. As we grow to adulthood, we repress this desire to repeat experiences in order to carry on with adult life. If certain experiences are repeated by accident, we often attach special significance to them (saying they are uncanny or supernatural) due to the strange feeling we get as a result of being reminded of a compulsion we have repressed.

Uplifting Experiences

In addition to many subtle accounts like Susan's, in which personal feelings and strange coincidences are the only clues to angelic presence, Burnham's book includes a number of stories that are more obviously supernatural. She repeats, for example, the story of a theology professor who claims that he and his wife saw angels while out on a walk. There were a half dozen of them who appeared as women in flowing robes who floated overhead. They appeared to be radiant, wise, and good, and were speaking a language the couple couldn't understand. Both of them witnessed the apparition. As you can imagine, it made them feel pretty special.

A more dramatic angel experience described in Burnham's book is reported by a woman named Sarah, who was vacationing in Greece. She was returning to her hotel on foot after dark on a road that passed through a graveyard. She was already feeling apprehensive about being out by herself at night and when she reached the graveyard she became especially frightened. Then she heard a blood-curdling cry she couldn't identify and became petrified. She was so frightened she couldn't move.

She believed she was in serious danger and spoke the words, "In the name of Christ, save me." She repeated these words over and over again as she stood in her tracks, unable to move. Later, she was unable to say how long she stood by the graveyard asking to be rescued.

Eventually, Sarah felt herself being lifted up by someone or something she couldn't see. She only felt herself being lifted off the ground from under her arms. Whoever or whatever it was came from above, lifted her, and carried her past the graveyard and over a footbridge before setting her down. Throughout the trip, she was carried about six inches above the ground.

As soon as she felt him (she refers to the presence as "he"), she felt comforted and at peace. She even said thank you as she was being carried! She says the experience was not surprising or shocking, but seemed appropriate somehow. She believes her guardian came to rescue her when she was in trouble. When she arrived back at her hotel, she was told that, as she approached, she was surrounded by a bright light.

Since the experience in the graveyard, Sarah felt herself in need of her guardian angel at other times during her life as well, most notably, she says, when she was tied up and raped at knifepoint! She was not saved, however, from this hellish experience, despite expecting her guardian angel to come to her rescue again. She can't explain why she was rescued in the graveyard, but not rescued from being raped. Still, she believes that both events took place for reasons she doesn't understand.

The Devil Makes You Do It

It may be dangerous to draw conclusions about what an angelic appearance means for your future. If an angel appears to you, it doesn't necessarily mean that your troubles will be over for the rest of your life. Many who claim to have been helped by their guardian angels also say that they have since suffered through terrible experiences without angelic assistance. Similarly, an angelic appearance doesn't necessarily mean you are good, virtuous, or blessed. An angel appeared to Balaam, the bad magician in the Bible, and to the disobedient Laman in the Book of Mormon, both of whom later suffered punishment for their deeds.

Appearing in *Time*

A December 1993 issue of *Time* magazine ran a cover story on angels that included an encounter related by a woman named Ann Cannady who had been suffering from uterine cancer. As you can imagine, the illness was extremely stressful and worrisome for her and for her husband Gary. Gary was even more disturbed than he would have been otherwise because he had been married previously and lost his former wife to the same disease.

Ann prayed frequently, either to be cured of her illness, or to be taken quickly so as to spare her husband a long and agonizing ordeal of losing a second wife to uterine cancer. One day her prayer was answered in an astonishing manner. She heard a knock at the door and found an angel.

The angel was tall—about 6'5"—and completely black except for piercing blue eyes. He introduced himself as Thomas and explained that he had been sent by God. When she heard this, she collapsed on the floor. While she lay on the floor, he stood over her and stretched out his hand. He didn't touch her, but she could feel it. Tremendous heat emanated from the hand and passed through her body.

The angel slowly waved his hand over her, starting at her feet and moving up to her head. He then announced that she could stop worrying and that her cancer had been cured, and quoted a passage from the Bible: "...and with his stripes, we are healed," Isaiah 55:5. Soon afterwards, when Thomas the angel had departed, Ann was certain that her cancer was gone and called her doctor to cancel her upcoming surgery. The doctor insisted on running tests and was amazed when the tests came up negative. He called her recovery miraculous.

Wing Tip

If you look for Graham's book, *Angels: God's Secret Agents*, be aware that recent editions are entitled simply *Angels*. The title may have been changed in order to tone down any suggestion of flaky theology. In fact, the book does not portray heaven as an intelligence agency!

The Devil Makes You Do It

If you want others to trust you, it's better to say something that really happened is just a story than it is to take a story and say it really happened.

Angel Tales Retold

Some angel apparition stories are so good, they get told over and over again. One such oft-told angel tale appears, among other places, in Billy Graham's book *Angels: God's Secret Agents* (Doubleday, 1975).

Graham's story, repeated as true, tells of a well-known neurologist from Philadelphia named S.W. Mitchell who, in recent years, was awakened from sleep late at night by a knock at his door. He answered the door and found a little girl outside. She was poorly dressed in shabby winter clothes on a cold, snowy and windy night. She was upset and told Dr. Mitchell that her mother was very sick and asked him to follow her.

Dr. Mitchell followed the little girl out into the snow. She led him back to her house where he found her mother. It turns out the mother had a terrible case of pneumonia and would have died if he had not come in time to take care of her. When the danger had passed, Dr. Mitchell told the woman what her little daughter had done.

Imagine the doctor's surprise when the woman replied that her daughter had died the previous month! She also mentioned that she still had her coat and shoes in the closet. In case you're wondering whether the coat and shoes were the same as those the little girl was wearing, the answer is yes. Graham goes on to speculate that the little girl was really an angel who had been sent by God to rescue the sick woman.

This story was repeated in Joan Wester Anderson's book of angel encounters, *Where Angels Walk: True Stories of Heavenly Visitors* (Ballantine, 1993). Billy Graham said he found the story in *Reader's Digest*. A critic of paranormal phenomena, Joe Nickell, claims the story can be found in a book by Margaret Ronan called *Strange, Unsolved Mysteries* (Scholastic Book Services, 1974). Here, the tale is told not as a recent angel apparition, but as a ghost story set in 1880!

In the Wings

Well, that's a wrap for unaccountable encounters with angels, and for the chapters of this book. If, now that you've read about the origins of angels, their roles around the world, and the different ways they have appeared to humans you still feel up in the air about the heavenly host, you might want to consult the appendices. Appendix A lists further angelic reading; Appendix B is a filmography of angels on screen; Appendix C is a compendium of the best-known angel names, with brief explanations of what made them famous; and finally, Appendix D is a glossary of the terms used in this book.

The Least You Need to Know

➤ Angel encounters are on the rise in recent years, judging from the number of best-selling books, magazine articles, and Web sites.

➤ Disillusionment with technology has fostered a climate conducive to angel sightings.

➤ Rationalists say those who see angels may be hallucinating, remembering falsely, or deliberately distorting the truth.

➤ Angel accounts range from the subtle and unusual to the bizarrely supernatural.

➤ Some angel tales are repeated and reprinted in different forms.

Good Books

Altenheim, Bonnie. *Angel Cats*. Wings Press, 1995.

Anderson, Joan Wester. *Where Angels Walk*. New York: Ballantine, 1993.

Blavatsky, Helena. *Isis Unveiled*. Los Angeles: The Theosophy Company, 1975.

Bloom, Harold. *Omens of Millennium: The Gnosis of Angels, Dreams, and Resurrection*. New York: Riverhead Books, 1996.

Bunson, Matthew. *Angels A to Z: A Who's Who of the Heavenly Host*. New York: Crown, 1996.

Burnham, Sophy. *A Book of Angels: Reflections on Angels Past and Present and True Stories of How They Touch Our Lives*. New York: Ballantine, 1990.

Charlesworth, James H. *The Old Testament Pseudepigrapha*. Two volumes. New York: Doubleday, 1983.

Chessman, Harriot Scott. *Literary Angels*. New York: Fawcett Columbine, 1994.

Choksy, Jamsheed K. *Purity and Pollution in Zoroastrianism: Triumph Over Evil*. Austin: University of Texas Press, 1989.

Cohen, A. *Every Man's Talmud*. New York: Dutton, 1949.

Daniel, Alma, Timothy Wyllie, and Andrew Ramer. *Ask Your Angels*. New York: Ballantine, 1992.

Danielou, Jean. *The Angels and Their Mission According to the Fathers of the Church*. David Heimann, trans. Westminster, MD: Newman Press, 1993.

Eliade, Mircea. *A History of Religious Ideas*. Three volumes. Chicago: University of Chicago Press, 1982.

Freeman, Eileen. *Angelic Healing: Working With Angels To Heal Your Life*. Warner Books, 1995.

———. *Touched By Angels*. New York: Warner Books, 1993.

Garret, Duane A. *Angels and the New Spirituality*. Nashville: Broadman and Holman, 1995.

Ginzberg, Louis. *Legends of the Jews*. Henrietta Szold, trans. Seven volumes. Philadelphia: Jewish Publication Society, 1938.

Godwin, Malcolm. *Angels: An Endangered Species*. New York: Simon & Schuster, 1990.

Gonzales-Wippler, Migene. *Santeria, the Religion: A Legacy of Faith, Rites, and Magic*. New York: Harmony Books, 1989.

Graham, Billy. *Angels: God's Secret Agents*. New York: Doubleday, 1975.

Grey, Cameron, ed. *Angels and Awakenings: Stories of the Miraculous by Great Modern Writers*. Rockland, MA: Wheeler Publishing, 1980.

Guiley, Rosemary Ellen. *Angels Of Mercy*. Out of print.

Lewis, James R. and Evelyn Dorothy Oliver. *Angels A to Z*. Detroit: Visible Ink Press, 1996.

MacGregor, Geddes. *Angels: Ministers of Grace*. New York: Paragon, 1988.

Margolies, Morris B. *A Gathering of Angels: Angels in Jewish Life and Literature*. New York: Ballantine, 1994.

Mark, Barbara, with Trudy Griswold. *Angelspeake*. New York: Simon and Schuster, 1995.

Martin-Kuri, K. *A Message For The Millennium*. New York: Ballantine Books, 1996.

Melton, J. Gordon. *Encyclopedic Handbook of Cults in America*. New York: Garland Publishing, 1986.

Pagels, Elaine. *The Origin of Satan*. New York: Random House, 1995.

———. *The Gnostic Gospels*. New York: Random House, 1979.

Price, Jonathan Randolph. *Angels Within Us*. Fawcett Books, 1993.

Ronan, Margaret. *Strange, Unsolved Mysteries*. Scholastic Book Service, 1974.

Rosenberg, David, with Harold Bloom. *The Book of J*. New York: Grove Weidenfeld, 1990.

Shadduck, Gayle. *England's Amorous Angels*. Atlanta-Maryland University Press of America, 1990.

Sharp, Sally. *100 Ways To Attract Angels*. Trust Pub., 1994.

Taylor, Terry Lynn. *Guardians Of Hope*. H.J. Kramer, 1993.

Taylor, Terry Lynn, with Mary Beth Crain. *Angel Wisdom*. Harper San Francisco, 1994.

Trachtenberg, Joshua. *Jewish Magic and Superstition: A Study in Folk Religion*. New York: Atheneum, 1979.

Tutola, Amos. *My Life in the Bush of Ghosts*. Grove Press, 1994.

———. *The Palm Wine Drinkard*. Greenwood Publishing Corp., 1970.

Virtue, Doreen. *Divine Guidance: How to have Conversations With God and Your Guardian Angels*. Audio Rennaissance, 1998.

Washington, Peter. *Madame Blavatsky's Baboon: A History of the Mystics, Mediums, and Misfits Who Brought Spiritualism to America*. New York: Schocken Books, 1995.

Angels on Screen

Always (1989), Richard Dreyfuss, John Goodman, Audrey Hepburn, and Holly Hunter.

The Angel Levine (1970), Zero Mostel and Harry Belafonte.

The Angel Who Pawned Her Harp (1954), Diane Cilento, Felix Aylmer.

Angels in the Outfield (1951), Paul Douglas, Janet Leigh.

Angels in the Outfield (remake) (1994), Danny Glover, Christopher Lloyd.

The Bishop's Wife (1947), Cary Grant, Loretta Young, David Niven.

Cabin in the Sky (1943), Eddie Anderson, Ethel Waters.

Charley and the Angel (1973), Fred MacMurray, Cloris Leachman, Harry Morgan, Kurt Russell.

City of Angels (1998), Nicolas Cage, Meg Ryan.

Clarence (1991), Robert Carradine, Kate Trotter.

Date with an Angel (1987), Emmanuelle Beart, Michael Knight.

Faraway, So Close (1993), Otto Sander, Peter Falk.

For Heaven's Sake (1950), Clifton Webb, Joan Bennett.

Forever Darling (1956), Lucille Ball, Desi Arnaz, James Mason.

Green Pastures (1936), Rex Ingram, Eddie Anderson.

A Guy Named Joe (1944), Spencer Tracy, Irene Dunne.

Heaven Can Wait (1978), Warren Beatty, Jack Warden, Dyan Cannon.

Heaven Only Knows (1947), Robert Cummings, Brian Donlevy.

Heavenly Kid (1985), Lewis Smith, Jason Gedrick.

Here Comes Mr. Jordan (1941), Robert Montgomery, Claude Rains, Evelyn Keyes.

The Horn Blows at Midnight (1945), Jack Benny, Alexis Smith.

Human Feelings (1978), Billy Crystal, Nancy Walker.

I Married an Angel (1942), Jeanette MacDonald, Nelson Eddy.

It's a Wonderful Life (1946), Jimmy Stewart, Donna Reed.

The Kid with the Broken Halo (1982), Gary Coleman, Robert Guillaume.

Michael (1996), John Travolta, William Hurt.

Mr. Destiny (1990), James Belushi, Linda Hamilton.

Prophecy (1997), Christopher Walken.

The Seventh Sign (1988), Demi Moore, Michael Biehn, Jürgen Prochnow.

Two of a Kind (1983), John Travolta, Olivia Newton-John.

Waiting for the Light (1990), Shirley MacLaine, Teri Garr.

Wings of Desire (1988), Bruno Ganz, Peter Falk.

Who's Who in Heaven

This list of names includes angels from all over—from the Bible to popular culture. We'll help you pinpoint that angel here.

Abigrail New-Age angel from the self-help book *Ask Your Angels* by Alma Daniel, Timothy Wyllie, and Andrew Raymer. (Also spelled Abigrael)

Abraxas Angel of Cabala whose name forms the basis of the magic word, "abracadabra."

Adoneus In Gnosticism, a dragon-faced archon.

Aetherius Theosophical Cosmic Master said to reside on the planet Venus.

Ahriman See *Angra Mainyu*.

Ahura Mazda, "Wise Lord," also known as Ormazd Zoroastrian creator of all that is good in the universe and leader in the battle against evil. He has a special connection to human beings.

Aka Manah, "Evil Mind" A Zoroastrian daeva, the opponent of the good Vohu Manah and originator of the bad attitude.

al-Lat, al-Uzza, and **Manat** So-called "daughters of Allah" said by some to be angels and by others, pagan goddesses. They are mentioned in the infamous "Satanic Verses" of the Koran.

al-Uzza See *al-Lat, al-Uzza, and Manat*.

Amasras Angel from the Book of Enoch who taught humans horticulture and magic spells.

Ameretat Zoroastrian Amesha Spenta of "Immortality," typically invoked with Haurvatat, Amesha Spenta of "Perfection," these archangels promote strength on Earth and immortality in the next life. They have charge of plants and water, respectively.

Andrew   Angel from TV's *Touched by an Angel*, played by John Dye.

Angra Mainyu, "Evil Spirit," also known as Ahriman   In Zoroastrianism, Ahura Mazda's evil twin, the creator of death and all evil beings.

Angel of the Lord   Said to be either a manifestation or a representation of God, mentioned frequently in the Bible.

Angel of the Odd   Angel from the short story by Edgar Allan Poe in charge of freak accidents. His body is made out of drinking vessels.

Anu   Sumerian sky god enshrined at Uruk, who was supplanted by Enlil when Uruk was overthrown by the city of Nippur.

Anubis   Jackal-headed god of ancient Egypt assigned the angelic function of weighing the souls of the dead.

Asderel   Fallen watcher from the Book of Enoch who taught humans astrology.

Asha, "Righteousness"   Zoroastrian Amesha Spenta who keeps the immutable divine law, confers spiritual wealth to humanity, and aids in healing of diseases. He is the spirit of fire.

Asherah   Female consort of the ancient God El, of Israel. She became demonized as the consort of Baal when El became absorbed into Yahweh.

Astaphaeus   Gnostic archon with the face of a hyena.

Avengelyne   Comic book warrior angel who is doing time on Earth.

Azazel   Fallen angel in the Book of Enoch who taught men to make weapons and taught women to use cosmetics. He appears in the Old Testament Book of Leviticus as a desert spirit who receives scapegoats—goats ritually infected with the sins of the Jews.

Azrael   In Islamic tradition, the angel of death.

Babalú   The orisha of disease and healing. Unselfish but dignified, he is lame and is said to walk on crutches. He likes beans, corn, and pigeons. He is associated with the Biblical beggar named Lazarus.

Baradiel   The ruler of Sehaqim, the third heaven in the 3rd book of Enoch.

Baraqiel   The ruler of Raqia, the second heaven in the 3rd book of Enoch.

Beatrice   The angelic beloved of Dante in the *Divine Comedy*. She arranges in heaven for him to travel through Hell, Purgatory, and Paradise to see her.

Beelzebub, Lord of the Flies, also known as Baal   Originally a heathen god of the Canaanites who was later demonized by the Jews as the Prince of Devils.

Behemoth   See *Leviathan, Behemoth, and Rehab*.

Cassiel   Angel popular with occultists. Also the angel sidekick of Seth in the film, *City of Angels*. Cassiel is played by Andre Braugher.

Changó   The orisha of power, said to be impetuous, macho, proud, and passionate. He is associated with thunder and lightning. He likes bananas, apples, and rams. He is associated, believe it or not, with Saint Barbara.

Cupid   See *Eros*.

Dagon   Babylonian god in competition with Yahweh, God of the Hebrews. Dagon is sometimes seen as a fallen angel, as in *Paradise Lost*.

Djibril   The Islamic Gabriel, he appeared to the prophet Muhammad with the holy Koran.

Druj, "Deceit" or "Wickedness"   An evil Zoroastrian daeva, the female nemesis of the righteous Asha. Although there is only one chief demon named Druj, later Zoroastrian tradition recognizes an entire class of evil female spirits known as drujes.

Dubbiel   Said by the ancient Jews to be the guardian angel of Persia, sometimes considered a fallen angel.

Dudley   Amiable angel from the movie *The Bishop's Wife,* played by Cary Grant.

El   Ancient high God of the Hebrews who was absorbed into Yahweh.

Eleggua   The orisha of justice who controls fate. He's often playful and unpredictable, but always fair. He likes rum, cigars, roosters, smoked fish, and candy—also toys for his childish side. He is associated with Saint Anthony.

Elijah   Hebrew prophet who was taken alive up to heaven where he was transformed into the angel Sandalphon.

Eloeus   In Gnosticism, an archon with the face of a donkey.

Elohim   The plural form of eloha, a word for "god," it can refer to angels, to pagan gods, to spirits, or simply to God himself.

Enlil   Ancient Sumerian god worshipped at Nippur and Uruk.

Enniss   Guardian angel of famous angel watcher Eileen Elias Freeman.

Enoch   Hebrew patriarch who ascended alive up to heaven where he was tranformed into the angel Metatron.

Eros   Greek god of love, known in Latin as Cupid. Artistic representations of Eros influenced the Christian visual conception of the winged angel.

Four horsemen of the apocalypse   Angels from the Book of Revelation: The first, on a white horse, is usually said to be Christ. The next, on a red horse, represents war; the black horse is famine, and the pale horse is death.

Four Zoas   Literary creations of William Blake; they are named Tharmas, Urthona, Luvah, and Urizen. They have feminine aspects called emanations, which were originally integral parts of them, but separated from them and became antagonistic. These are Enion, Enitharmon, Vala, and Ahania.

Gabriel   One of only three angels mentioned by name in the Bible, his name means "God is my strength." Gabriel is credited with announcing the coming of Christ to the Virgin Mary and with blowing the trumpet call to wake the dead on Judgment Day. Compare *Israfel*.

Hadarniel   In Jewish legend, the fearsome keeper of the gates of heaven. When he speaks, lightning bolts flash from his mouth.

Harut and Marut   In Islamic tradition, angels who succumb to the temptation to sin while visiting Earth. They are said to have taught human beings the art of sorcery.

Haurvatat   Zoroastrian Amesha Spenta of "Perfection," typically invoked with Ameretat, the Amesha Spenta of "Immortality," these archangels promote strength on Earth and immortality in the next life. They have charge of water and plants, respectively.

Ialdabaoth   The chief Gnostic archon and demiurge who created the world. He has the head of a lion and, for that reason, is also called Ariel, "lion of God."

Iao   In Gnosticism, a serpent-faced archon with seven heads.

Iblis   Chief of the fallen angels of Islam who rebelled out of envy of humankind.

Isis   Egyptian fertility goddess sometimes represented with wings.

Israfel   In Islamic tradition, the angel who will sound the trumpet call to wake the dead on Judgment Day.

Jehovah   English name for Yahweh, the God of the Hebrews.

Jordan (Mr.)   Angel bureaucrat in the film *Here Comes Mr. Jordan* (1941), played by Claude Rains.

Kemuel   In Jewish legend, an angel in charge of the angels of terror.

Khshathra Vairya, "Wished-for Kingdom"   Zoroastrian Amesha Spenta who promotes Ahura Mazda's divine kingdom on Earth. He confers material wealth and is in charge of metal.

Leviathan, Behemoth, and Rehab   Giant sea beasts associated in Jewish prophecy with the evils of non-Jewish nations.

Lilith   In Jewish legend, she was Adam's first wife. She wasn't happy in her subordinate position in Paradise, so she left and became an evil spirit.

Lucifer   The name used in heaven for the fallen angel Satan.

Manat   See *al-Lat, al-Uzza, and Manat*.

Marut   See *Harut and Marut*.

Mephistopheles   The demon who appears to serve Dr. Faustus in the legend of the magician who sold his soul to the Devil.

Metatron   The most important angel of Jewish legend and Merkabah mysticism. He is sometimes called "the lesser Yahweh." He was once the Biblical patriarch, Enoch, who ascended to heaven in bodily form before becoming transfigured into Metatron.

Michael   Chief of the angels, angelic prince of Israel, and Catholic saint, one of the three angels mentioned in the Bible. A warrior, Michael is credited with defeating the dragon (Satan) and casting him into hell.

Mithras   Persian god sometimes assimilated to monotheism as a fallen angel.

Moloch   Ammonite God said to require child sacrifice, he is identified as a fallen angel in *Paradise Lost*.

Monica   Angel from TV's *Touched by an Angel*, played by Roma Downey.

Moroni   Angel of Mormonism who appeared to Joseph Smith with Mormon scripture.

Munkar and Nakir   Islamic angels who help sort out the good from the bad human souls by asking the newly deceased a question: "Who is Muhammad?"

Nakir   See *Munkar and Nakir*.

Nike   Greek goddess of victory, often represented with wings. Representations of Nike dovetailed into early Christian conceptions of angels.

Obatalá   The orisha of peace, known to be benevolent, generous, and idealistic. He's in charge of fatherhood. He likes everything white, especially doves, cotton, and coconut. He is associated with the Virgin Mary.

Oggún   The orisha of work and warfare, said to be straightforward, honest, and loyal, but unforgiving. He is in charge of weapons and metal. He likes rum, cigars, plantains, and pigeons. He is associated with Saint Peter.

Oreus   From Gnosticism, an ape-faced archon.

Ormazd   See *Ahura Mazda*.

Orúnmila   The orisha of wisdom, known for gentleness and creativity. He controls the many techniques of Santería divination. He likes nuts, yams, and chickens. He is associated with Saint Francis of Assisi.

Oshun   The orisha of wealth and love, said to be seductive, ambitious, and insatiable as well as affectionate. She likes white wine, jewelry, cake, honey, and pumpkins. She is associated with the Virgin Mary.

Pistis Sophia   Gnostic angel of faith and wisdom who gave birth to the demiurge, Ialdabaoth.

Raguel   Angel of vengeance from the book of Enoch.

Raphael   One of three angels mentioned in the Bible (if you count the Apocrypha), he is an angel of healing and science, with a reputation for friendliness garnered from the Book of Tobit and *Paradise Lost*.

Raziel   Angel of magic, said to have given the Book of Raziel (a book of spells) to the first man, Adam.

Rehab   See *Leviathan*.

Remiel   Angel of those who rise, from the Book of Enoch.

Sabaoth   In Gnosticism, an archon with a face made of flame.

Sahaqiel   The ruler of Zebul, the fourth heaven in the 3rd book of Enoch.

Samael   Fallen angel of Jewish legend and consort of the demon Lilith.

Sandalphon   Important angel of Jewish legend who weaves crowns for God out of human prayers. He started out as the prophet Elijah. Elijah ascended into heaven without dying and was transfigured into Sandalphon.

Sansanvi   See *Sanvi, Sansanvi, and Semangalaf*.

Sanvi, Sansanvi, and Semangalaf   Angels of Jewish magic and Cabala said to provide protection against evil. In particular, they guard against the demon Lilith.

Saraqael   Angel in charge of sinners from the Book of Enoch.

Satan   The adversary, originally an angel who did God's bidding in opposing misguided humans, but later the fallen angel Satan, the Prince of Darkness, chief of all the fallen angels and enemy of God and humanity.

Satqiel   The ruler of Maon, the fifth heaven in the 3rd book of Enoch.

Saurva   Originally an Indian god named Sharva, he became incorporated into Zoroastrianism as the adversary of the good Amesha Spenta, Khshathra Vairya.

Semangalaf   See *Sanvi, Sansanvi, and Semangalaf*.

Semyaza (or Semihaza)   Leader of the fallen angels in the Books of Enoch who mated with mortal women.

Seth   Angel main character in the film *City of Angels*, played by Nicolas Cage.

Shepherd of Hermas   Angel who appears as a good shepherd in the early Christian moral allegory by Hermas. The Shepherd of Hermas provides hope of salvation for repentant sinners.

Sidriel   The ruler of Wilon, the first heaven in the 3rd book of Enoch.

Smith, Jonathan   Angel from TV's *Highway to Heaven*, played by Michael Landon.

Sophia   See *Pistis Sophia*.

Spenta Armaiti   "Holy Devotion," the only female archangel of Zoroastrianism, she fosters human love and reverence for the powers and the way of Goodness. She is the spirit of Earth.

Stedfast   Angel hero of Roger Elwood's novel, *Stedfast: Guardian Angel*.

Stormfield (Captain)   Deceased sea captain turned angel in Mark Twain's novel, *Captain Stormfield's Visit to Heaven.*

Tal   Heroic warrior angel from Frank Peretti's novel, *This Present Darkness.*

Tamiel   Fallen watcher from the Book of Enoch who taught humans astrology.

Taromaiti, "Heresy"   An evil Zoroastrian daeva, the female enemy of Spenta Armaiti who runs screaming when she hears people pray.

Taurvi and Zairicha, "Fever" and "Thirst"   Evil Zorastrian daevas, the arch enemies of the good Haurvatat and Ameretat.

Tess   Angel from TV's *Touched by an Angel,* played by gospel singer Della Reese.

Uriel   Often thought to be the fourth most important angel (after Michael, Gabriel, and Raphael). In Jewish legend, he warns Noah of the coming flood.

Victoricus   The guardian angel of St. Patrick, who brought Christianity to Ireland.

Victory   See *Nike.*

Vohu Manah, "Good Mind"   The first-created of the Zorastrian spiritual powers known as Amesha Spentas, he imparts enlightenment to humanity. He resides in heaven where he rises from a golden throne to greet the souls of the righteous as they arrive in the next world after death. He is also the spirit in charge of cattle and other animals.

Yahweh   The God of the Hebrews.

Yemayá   The orisha of women and motherhood. She covers all the feminine stereotypes and is associated with the ocean. She likes ducks, hens, sugar, and watermelon. She is associated with the Virgin Mary.

Zadkiel   Credited in Jewish legend with preventing Abraham from sacrificing his son, Isaac.

Zairicha   See *Taurvi and Zairicha.*

Speaking in Tongues

allegory   A story that can be read on a literal level and a symbolic level at the same time. Dante's *Divine Comedy* is an allegory of personal salvation.

androgyny   The combination of female and male characteristics into one. Androgyny was an important aspect of Gnostic belief, since many Gnostics associated the separation of the two sexes with the fall of humanity.

angelolatry   The worship of angels, declared idolatrous by the Christian Church in the year 343.

angelophany   The appearance of an angel. The term derives from the Greek words *angelos*, meaning "messenger," and *phainein*, meaning "to show." Someone to whom an angel appears is an angelophant.

Annunciation   The appearance of the angel Gabriel to Mary when he told her she would give birth to Christ.

apocalypse   Both an event that transforms the world as we know it and a prophetic writing that says how this event is going to happen. The most famous apocalyptic text is the Apocalypse of John, better known as the Book of Revelation. The word comes from the Greek word for revelation.

Apocrypha and Pseudepigrapha   Scripture named for terms meaning "outside writings" and "falsely attributed writings." Written from 200 B.C.E. to 100 C.E., they were excluded from the official Bible by rabbinical decree.

apostle   One of the twelve followers of Jesus appointed by him to convey his teachings. Like "angel," "apostle" comes from a Greek word meaning "messenger."

archangels   Sometimes considered the highest order of angels. In the system of Pseudo-Dionysius they are messenger angels, delivering God's decrees to people on Earth.

archetype   A term coined by psychologist Carl Jung for a manifestation of the shared aspects of the human subconscious. Archetypes provide an explanation for resemblances among separate cultures.

Ascension   The rising of the resurrected Christ into heaven.

asceticism   The practice of self-denial through fasting and other voluntary hardships such as celibacy and poverty. Many major religions include ascetic subgroups.

Assumption   A non-Biblical legend in which the Virgin Mary ascends into heaven.

Avatars   Manifestations of divine beings on Earth. According to theosophists, the Hindu idea of avatars contains secrets of human and angelic evolution.

babalawa   High priest of Santeria. Traditionally, only men can become babalawas.

canon   The body of writings that have been officially accepted as part of the Bible.

catacombs   Underground passages used for burial of the dead. Catacombus was originally the name of a place in Rome, but the term became used more generally for tunnels found not only in Rome, but in a number of cities in southern Italy and North Africa including Naples, Malta, Syracuse, and Alexandria. The catacombs in Rome are the most extensive, winding along for 350 miles beneath the city.

chain of being   The medieval idea that everything in the universe is connected to everything else in a specified, hierarchical order. God is at the top of the chain, angels come next, then humans, then animals, and then inanimate objects.

Cherubim   The order of angels often said to guard sacred places, including the throne of God. Representations of cherubim, or cherubs, range from bizarre winged animals to chubby little winged children.

choirs   Groups of the angel hierarchy, often said to range through nine orders from Seraphim to Cherubim down to archangels and angels.

Dead Sea Scrolls   Discovered in 1947, the scrolls include copies of known writings including the oldest known copies of many texts from the Bible, as well as newly discovered works resembling the Apocrypha and Pseudepigrapha.

demiurge   A minor deity who creates the world. The Gnostics attribute the creation of the world to a demiurge, although the idea was set forward centuries earlier in the philosophy of Plato.

devas   A generic Hindu term for "gods," which theosophists associate with angels.

dhyan chohans   The highest order of angelic being corresponding to archangels, credited with creating the universe.

doctrine of separate substance   Aquinas's idea that spiritual (immaterial) substance can exist independently from matter. Spiritual substance is pure intellect and what angels are made of.

Dominions, or Dominations   Often said to be the oldest group of angels, in the system of Pseudo-Dionysius they have the job of supervising the angels below them (the ones above need no supervision).

elohim   The plural form of eloha, a word for "god," elohim can refer to angels, pagan gods, spirits, or simply God himself.

epic   Narrative poetry concerned with lofty, important themes. The classical models of epic poetry were written by the Greek poet Homer and the Latin poet Virgil.

ethnarch   The guardian angel of an entire country. In a recent book, theologian and literary critic Herald Bloom named the angel Metatron as the ethnarch of the United States.

forms   In Platonic philosophy, aspects of ideal reality that give shape to material things and enable people to understand them. They are perfect and unchanging and influence human morality as well as the natural world.

galgallim   Angels in the shape of wheels made out of fire with eyes in them. They stem from Ezekiel's vision of the chariot-throne of God and correspond to the group known as Thrones in the hierarchy proposed by Pseudo-Dionysius.

ghandarvas   Nature spirits from Hindu scripture associated with angels in theosophy.

glossolalia   The language of the angels when they're not speaking Hebrew. It's also the gibberish people speak when they're possessed by the holy spirit and start "speaking in tongues."

golem   Hebrew for "unformed," a golem is an artificial human being made of earth by a magician, either for experimental purposes or for use as a servant.

Hadith   In Islam, the scriptural Traditions of the Prophet, which supplies background and commentary on Muhammad and the Koran.

halo   Also called a nimbus, it denotes glory, holiness, and wisdom. The circular shape also represents perfection and completeness. Saints as well as angels are often represented with halos.

heretics   Christians who hold beliefs that are condemned by the established church. The Gnostic Christians were generally considered heretics during the early days of Christianity.

hierarchy   "Sacred rule," the pecking order applied to the organization of angels as well as to the structure of the early church.

icons   Sacred paintings of the Byzantine Church and, later, of the Eastern Orthodox Church which split off from the Roman Catholic Church. The word comes from the Greek word *eikon*, which means "image." Icons were thought to have spiritual power and were venerated by many Christians.

illumination   Medieval art of decorating book manuscripts with colorful pictures and designs. The art was revived by William Blake, who illuminated his own poetry in print form.

jinn   In Islamic tradition stemming from ancient Persia, spirits with free will that can be evil or good. They are familiar to Westerners as "genies" in many fantastic stories from Arabia, most notably the story of Aladdin and the magic lamp.

legend   A popular story that gets told from generation to generation and the story of the life of a saint. Typically, these stories are filled with angels, miracles, and martyrdoms.

lipika   Also known as the "lords of karma," these are angelic intelligences who record actions in the physical world and enforce the resulting dictates of karma.

liturgy   A plan for group worship. The term is usually used in the context of Christian worship services, but also applies to worship practiced by angels, as in the group of psalms called the Angelic Liturgy.

logos   To the ancient Greeks, the natural process of the universe, which could be understood philosophically. To Christians, the word of God by which he created the world. The Gospel of John draws on both these senses of logos in saying that Christ is the word made flesh.

magi (singular, magus)   Zoroastrian priests and sages. Christian tradition holds that the three wise men who followed a star to Bethlehem bearing gifts for the baby Jesus were Zoroastrian magi.

mahatmas   Also known as "masters" and "the white brotherhood," highly evolved intelligences who choose to remain on Earth in physical form in order to teach and assist humanity.

Messiah   The King of the Jews whose coming is predicted in Biblical prophecy. The word means "anointed one" and refers to the ancient practice of pouring ointment on the heads of kings. Devout Jews still expect the Messiah to come and usher in the Kingdom of Heaven on Earth. Christians, of course, regard Jesus Christ as the Messiah.

Midrash   The tradition of Jewish Biblical commentary and interpretation passed down from generation to generation.

millennium   A 1,000-year period. *The* millennium is the 1,000-year period during which Christ will supposedly rule the earth. Millenarians are groups that believe that this millennium is imminent.

monotheism   The belief in a single all-powerful God. The three big monotheistic religions are Judaism, Christianity, and Islam. All three of these religions stem in part from the ancient dualistic religion known as Zoroastrianism.

myriad   Technically, "ten thousand," from the Greek word for "uncountable." Angels are often visualized by the myriad, as in the Book of Revelation.

nimbus   See *halo*.

Ophanim   See *galgallim.*

orishas   Gods worshipped by the Yoruba tribe of Nigeria and brought to the new world by Yoruba slaves where they merged with catholic saints. Orishas serve many of the functions of angels.

Pandemonium   The capital city of Hell in John Milton's *Paradise Lost.* The word is Latinized Greek for "place of all demons."

pantheism   The belief, embraced by many New-Agers, that God is everything, including people and the natural world.

paradigm   The way human beings think at a particular stage in history. According to New-Age thinking, an old paradigm is currently shifting to a new one characterized by greater spiritual awareness.

parasang   A unit of measurement used in ancient Persia, roughly equal to three and a half miles long.

patriarch   A father who is the ruler of a clan. The term is used specifically to refer to Abraham, Isaac, Jacob, and Jacob's sons, who were absolute rulers of their families. This was before Israel recognized priests or kings, so the patriarchs filled these roles. Paternal authority in the Bible tends to enforce rules aimed at maintaining the physical, spiritual, and cultural purity of the Jews. In short, patriarchal rules say not to worship strange gods, eat strange foods, or sleep with strange women.

Pentateuch   Another term for the Torah, meaning "five scrolls."

pleroma   Divine realm of light recognized by Gnostic Christians as existing above and beyond the reality created by God. Gnostics see themselves as sparks that have been separated from this light and hope to be reunited with it once more after the death of their bodies.

polytheism   The belief in more than one god.

Powers   Angelic order in the system of Pseudo-Dionysius. If the Virtues are the "good cops" who take care of people, Powers are the "bad cops" who come down on evil. The main role is to keep demons, devils, and evil spirits at bay.

Principalities   In Pseudo-Dionysius, these angels protect cities and nations as well as the leaders of religious faiths on Earth.

psychopomps   Spirits (pagan gods or angels in monotheism), who conduct souls of the dead to their abode in the afterlife.

putti   Naked babies with wings that appear frequently in Renaissance painting. They may represent angels or cupids. The word comes from an Italian word for "children."

sarcophagus (plural, sarcophagi)   A stone coffin. Sarcophagi were often beautiful works of art covered with elaborate carvings. These would be placed in a crypt or mausoleum rather than buried.

sefirot   The ten levels of reality which, according to Cabalism, emanate from God.

Septuagint The Greek version of the Hebrew Bible, which includes other sacred scriptures. These other sacred scriptures are not included in Jewish canon.

seraphim Angels mentioned in the book of Isaiah having six wings each, said by Pseudo-Dionysius to be the angels closest to God. They continually sing God's praises. They are "fiery ones," whose name is derived from the word for "serpent."

Seven Heavens In Jewish legend, from one to seven, they are Wilon, Raqia, Sehaqim, Zebul, Maon, Makon, and Arabot, as listed in the third Book of Enoch. Each heaven is a palace, one inside the other, with the throne of God in the center, the seventh heaven. This layout involves an unexplainable paradox, however, since the heavens are also concentric spheres with the seventh heaven as the outermost layer containing all the others. Each heaven has a gate guarded by angels to keep out the riff-raff—mystics from Earth who are not properly prepared to enter the supernal realms.

shofar A trumpet made of a ram's horn traditionally sounded as a call to repentance. They say the shofar will sound to announce the coming of the Messiah.

sura A section of the Koran, the holy book of Islam. The Koran contains 114 suras, arranged roughly from the longest (number 2 is well over fifty pages long) to the shortest (the final suras are each only a few lines long).

syncretism The merging of several different beliefs into a single religion. Many pagan gods have been turned into angels by becoming syncretized with Christianity.

Talmud Written from 200 to 500 C.E., the Talmud consists of commentary on the Bible as well as sermons and religious lore known as Midrash.

tetragrammaton From the Latin words "four letters," the Hebrew letters standing for the consonants in the name of God which correspond to the letters YHWH or JHVH. Christians have traditionally translated these letters as the name, "Jehovah." Theologians today recognize "Yahweh" as a more accurate translation.

Thrones The order of angels in the system of Pseudo-Dionysius based on the vision of Ezekiel. Thrones are often said to take the form of fiery wheels covered with open eyes.

Torah Named from a term meaning "the law" or "the teaching," this consists of the first five books of the Hebrew Bible.

transcendence Existence above and beyond material reality or above and beyond the human capacity of understanding.

Transfiguration Biblical moment in which Jesus appeared to shine like an angel.

urim and thummim Ancient symbols of the judgment of God and stones used to divine God's will. Joseph Smith used them as "seeing stones." He said he was able to look through them and see the writings on the plates of Nephi translated from "reformed Egyptian" into English.

vastation   In the writings of Swedenborg, the experience of slipping further away from God as a result of self-love. It happens to angels as well as human beings and results in a feeling of sadness.

Virtues, also known as Authorities   A group of angels in the system of Pseudo-Dionysius who work miracles on Earth and serve as guardian angels.

Vulgate   Latin translation of the Bible used by the Catholic Church. The work was done late in the 4th century and attributed to Saint Jerome.

warrior   Sometimes considered a distinct class of angels (Milton uses the term this way, for example, in *Paradise Lost*). In pulp fiction the term is also applied to any superhero who battles the forces of evil.

Zohar   Written during the 13th century, the most important of the medieval Jewish writings. This is a book of magic and mysticism central to the tradition known as Cabala.

Index

Other Best-Selling Titles in the
Complete Idiot's Guide® Series:

Business

The Complete Idiot's Guide to Assertiveness
ISBN: 0-02-861964-1
$16.95

The Complete Idiot's Guide to Business Management
ISBN: 0-02-861744-4
$16.95

The Complete Idiot's Guide to Dynamic Selling
ISBN: 0-02-861952-8
$16.95

The Complete Idiot's Guide to Getting Along with Difficult People
ISBN: 0-02-861597-2
$16.95

The Complete Idiot's Guide to Great Customer Service
ISBN: 0-02-861953-6
$16.95

The Complete Idiot's Guide to Leadership
ISBN: 0-02-861946-3
$16.95

The Complete Idiot's Guide to Managing People
ISBN: 0-02-861036-9
$18.95

The Complete Idiot's Guide to Managing Your Time
ISBN: 0-02-861039-3
$14.95

The Complete Idiot's Guide to Marketing Basics
ISBN: 0-02-861490-9
$16.95

The Complete Idiot's Guide to New Product Development
ISBN: 0-02-861952-8
$16.95

The Complete Idiot's Guide to Office Politics
ISBN: 0-02-862397-5
$16.95

The Complete Idiot's Guide to Project Management
ISBN: 0-02-861745-2
$16.95

The Complete Idiot's Guide to Speaking in Public With Confidence
ISBN: 0-02-861038-5
$16.95

The Complete Idiot's Guide to Starting a Home Based Business
ISBN: 0-02-861539-5
$16.95

The Complete Idiot's Guide to Starting Your Own Business
ISBN: 1-56761-529-5
$16.99

The Complete Idiot's Guide to Successful Business Presentations
ISBN: 0-02-861748-7
$16.95

The Complete Idiot's Guide to Terrific Business Writing
ISBN: 0-02-861097-0
$16.95

Personal Finance

The Complete Idiot's Guide to Buying Insurance and Annuities
ISBN: 0-02-861113-6
$16.95

The Complete Idiot's Guide to Managing Your Money
ISBN: 1-56761-530-9
$16.95

The Complete Idiot's Guide to Making Money with Mutual Funds
ISBN: 1-56761-637-2
$16.95

The Complete Idiot's Guide to Getting Rich
ISBN: 1-56761-509-0
$16.95

The Complete Idiot's Guide to Finance and Accounting
ISBN: 0-02-861752-5
$16.95

The Complete Idiot's Guide to Investing Like a Pro
ISBN:0-02-862044-5
$16.95

The Complete Idiot's Guide to Making Money After You Retire
ISBN:0-02-862410-6
$16.95

The Complete Idiot's Guide to Making Money on Wall Street
ISBN:0-02-861958-7
$16.95

The Complete Idiot's Guide to Personal Finance in Your 20s and 30s
ISBN:0-02-862415-7
$16.95

The Complete Idiot's Guide to Wills and Estates
ISBN: 0-02-861747-9
$16.95

The Complete Idiot's Guide to 401(k) Plans
ISBN: 0-02-861948-X
$16.95

Careers

The Complete Idiot's Guide to Changing Careers
ISBN: 0-02-861977-3
$17.95

The Complete Idiot's Guide to Freelancing
ISBN: 0-02-862119-0
$16.95

The Complete Idiot's Guide to Getting the Job You Want
ISBN: 1-56761-608-9
$24.95

The Complete Idiot's Guide to the Perfect Cover Letter
ISBN: 0-02-861960-9
$14.95

The Complete Idiot's Guide to the Perfect Interview
ISBN: 0-02-861945-5
$14.95

Education

The Complete Idiot's Guide to American History
ISBN: 0-02-861275-2
$16.95

The Complete Idiot's Guide to British Royalty
ISBN: 0-02-862346-0
$18.95

The Complete Idiot's Guide to Civil War
ISBN: 0-02-862122-0
$16.95

The Complete Idiot's Guide to Classical Mythology
ISBN: 0-02-862385-1
$16.95

The Complete Idiot's Guide to Creative Writing
ISBN: 0-02-861734-7
$16.95

The Complete Idiot's Guide to Dinosaurs
ISBN: 0-02-862390-8
$17.95

The Complete Idiot's Guide to Genealogy
ISBN: 0-02-861947-1
$16.95

The Complete Idiot's Guide to Geography
ISBN: 0-02-861955-2
$16.95

The Complete Idiot's Guide to Getting Published
ISBN: 0-02-862392-4
$16.95

The Complete Idiot's Guide to Grammar & Style
ISBN: 0-02-861956-0
$16.95

The Complete Idiot's Guide to an MBA
ISBN: 0-02-862164-4
$17.95

The Complete Idiot's Guide to Philosophy
ISBN:0-02-861981-1
$16.95

The Complete Idiot's Guide to Learning Spanish On Your Own
ISBN: 0-02-861040-7
$16.95

The Complete Idiot's Guide to Learning French on Your Own
ISBN: 0-02-861043-1
$16.95

The Complete Idiot's Guide to Learning German on Your Own
ISBN: 0-02-861962-5
$16.95

The Complete Idiot's Guide to Learning Italian on Your Own
ISBN: 0-02-862125-5
$16.95

The Complete Idiot's Guide to Learning Sign Language
ISBN: 0-02-862388-6
$16.95

Food/Beverage/Entertaining

The Complete Idiot's Guide to Baking
ISBN: 0-02-861954-4
$16.95

The Complete Idiot's Guide to Beer
ISBN: 0-02-861717-7
$16.95

The Complete Idiot's Guide to Cooking Basics
ISBN: 0-02-861974-9
$18.95

The Complete Idiot's Guide to Entertaining
ISBN: 0-02-861095-4
$16.95

The Complete Idiot's Guide to Etiquette
ISBN0-02-861094-6
$16.95

The Complete Idiot's Guide to Mixing Drinks
ISBN: 0-02-861941-2
$16.95

The Complete Idiot's Guide to Wine
ISBN: 0-02-861273-6
$16.95

Health and Fitness

The Complete Idiot's Guide to Beautiful Skin
ISBN: 0-02-862408-4
$16.95

The Complete Idiot's Guide to Breaking Bad Habits
ISBN: 0-02-862110-7
$16.95

The Complete Idiot's Guide to Eating Smart
ISBN: 0-02-861276-0
$16.95

The Complete Idiot's Guide to First Aid Basics
ISBN: 0-02-861099-7
$16.95

The Complete Idiot's Guide to Getting and Keeping Your Perfect Body
ISBN: 0-02-861276-0
$16.95

The Complete Idiot's Guide to Getting a Good Night's Sleep
ISBN: 0-02-862394-0
$16.95

The Complete Idiot's Guide to a Happy, Healthy Heart
ISBN: 0-02-862393-2
$16.95

The Complete Idiot's Guide to Healthy Stretching
ISBN: 0-02-862127-1
$16.95

The Complete Idiot's Guide to Jogging and Running
ISBN: 0-02-862386-X
$17.95

The Complete Idiot's Guide to Losing Weight
ISBN: 0-02-862113-1
$17.95

The Complete Idiot's Guide to Managed Health Care
ISBN: 0-02-862165-4
$17.95

The Complete Idiot's Guide to Stress
ISBN: 0-02-861086-5
$16.95

The Complete Idiot's Guide to Vitamins and Minerals
ISBN: 0-02-862116-6
$16.95

Home and Automotive

The Complete Idiot's Guide to Buying or Leasing a Car
ISBN: 0-02-861274-4
$16.95

The Complete Idiot's Guide to Buying and Selling a Home
ISBN: 0-02-861959-5
$16.95

The Complete Idiot's Guide to Decorating Your Home
ISBN: 0-02-861088-1
$16.95

The Complete Idiot's Guide to Gardening
ISBN: 0-02-861-096-2
$16.95

The Complete Idiot's Guide to Motorcycles
ISBN: 0-02-862416-5
$16.95

The Complete Idiot's Guide to Smart Moving
ISBN: 0-02-862126-3
$16.95

The Complete Idiot's Guide to Trouble-Free Car Care
ISBN: 0-02-861041-5
$16.95

The Complete Idiot's Guide to Trouble-Free Home Repair
ISBN: 0-02-861042-3
$16.95

Leisure/Hobbies

The Complete Idiot's Guide to Antiques and Collectibles
ISBN: 0-02-861595-6
$16.95

The Complete Idiot's Guide to Astrology
ISBN: 0-02-861951-X
$16.95

The Complete Idiot's Guide to the Beatles
ISBN: 0-02-862130-1
$18.95

The Complete Idiot's Guide to Boating and Sailing
ISBN: 0-02-862124-7
$18.95

The Complete Idiot's Guide to Bridge
ISBN: 0-02-861735-5
$16.95

The Complete Idiot's Guide to Chess
ISBN: 0-02-861736-3
$16.95

The Complete Idiot's Guide to Cigars
ISBN: 0-02-861975-7
$17.95

The Complete Idiot's Guide to Crafts with Kids
ISBN: 0-02-862406-8
$16.95

The Complete Idiot's Guide to Elvis
ISBN: 0-02-861873-4
$18.95

The Complete Idiot's Guide to Extra-Terrestrial Intelligence
ISBN: 0-02-862387-8
$16.95

The Complete Idiot's Guide to Fishing Basics
ISBN: 0-02-861598-0
$16.95

The Complete Idiot's Guide to Gambling Like a Pro
ISBN: 0-02-861102-0
$16.95

The Complete Idiot's Guide to a Great Retirement
ISBN: 0-02-861036-9
$16.95

The Complete Idiot's Guide to Hiking and Camping
ISBN: 0-02-861100-4
$16.95

The Complete Idiot's Guide to Needlecrafts
ISBN: 0-02-862123-9
$16.95

The Complete Idiot's Guide to Organizing Your Life
ISBN: 0-02-861090-3
$16.95

The Complete Idiot's Guide to Photography
ISBN: 0-02-861092-X
$16.95

The Complete Idiot's Guide to Reaching Your Goals
ISBN: 0-02-862114-X
$16.95

The Complete Idiot's Guide to the World's Religions
ISBN: 0-02-861730-4
$16.95

Music

The Complete Idiot's Guide to Classical Music
ISBN: 0-02-8611634-0
$16.95

The Complete Idiot's Guide to Playing the Guitar
0-02-864924-9
$17.95

The Complete Idiot's Guide to Playing the Piano and Electric Keyboards
0-02-864925-7
$17.95

Parenting

The Complete Idiot's Guide to Adoption
ISBN: 0-02-862108-5
$18.95

The Complete Idiot's Guide to Bringing Up Baby
ISBN: 0-02-861957-9
$16.95

The Complete Idiot's Guide to Grandparenting
ISBN: 0-02-861976-5
$16.95

The Complete Idiot's Guide to Parenting a Preschooler and Toddler
ISBN: 0-02-861733-9
$16.95

The Complete Idiot's Guide to Raising a Teenager
ISBN: 0-02-861277-9
$16.95

The Complete Idiot's Guide to Single Parenting
ISBN: 0-02-862409-2
$16.95

The Complete Idiot's Guide to Stepparenting
ISBN: 0-02-862407-6
$16.95

Pets

The Complete Idiot's Guide to Choosing, Training, and Raising a Dog
ISBN: 0-02-861098-9
$16.95

The Complete Idiot's Guide to Fun and Tricks with Your Dog
ISBN: 0-87605-083-6
$14.95

The Complete Idiot's Guide to Living with a Cat
ISBN: 0-02-861278-7
$16.95

The Complete Idiot's Guide to Turtles and Tortoises
ISBN: 0-87605-143-3
$16.95

Relationships

The Complete Idiot's Guide to Dating
ISBN: 0-02-861052-0
$14.95

The Complete Idiot's Guide to Dealing with In-Laws
ISBN: 0-02-862107-7
$16.95

The Complete Idiot's Guide to a Healthy Relationship
ISBN: 0-02-861087-3
$17.95

The Complete Idiot's Guide to a Perfect Marriage
ISBN: 0-02-861729-0
$16.95

The Complete Idiot's Guide to the Perfect Wedding
ISBN: 0-02-861963-3
$16.95

The Complete Idiot's Guide to Surviving Divorce
ISBN: 0-02-861101-3
$16.95